GOSSAMER WINGS . . . LITTLE GREEN SUITS . . .
FAIRY MUSIC . . . DANCES IN THE MIST . . .
FOR THESE WITNESSES, THE "LITTLE PEOPLE"
ARE VERY REAL—

In September 1979, four children in Wollaton Park, Nottingham, observed more than sixty tiny wizened men dressed in little jackets and tights, joyously playing.

In 1910, on the island of Muck off the Scottish coast, two boys, ages ten and seven, encountered two tiny boys dressed in green and a woman in a tiny boat who gave them a loaf of fairy bread and even conversed with them.

In the early 1960s, a botanist camping in Wales swore to a local farmer that he had seen "hordes of tiny people" playing at the spot where he was hunting for plants. When he showed the farmer the spot on a map, the farmer translated the Welsh name—"Fairies Bog."

"Little green men," often dancing along the road, appeared in Nome, Alaska, in 1988. More than a dozen people saw them on five separate nights. And the reporter who wrote the news account later traced similar sightings among the Eskimos of the region dating back 200 years!

DISCOVER THESE AND MORE
*REAL ENCOUNTERS WITH LITTLE PEOPLE*

## QUANTITY SALES

**Most Dell books are available at special quantity discounts** when purchased in bulk by corporations, organizations, or groups. Special imprints, messages, and excerpts can be produced to meet your needs. For more information, write to: Dell Publishing, 1540 Broadway, New York, NY 10036. Attention: Director, Special Markets.

## INDIVIDUAL SALES

**Are there any Dell books you want but cannot find in your local stores?** If so, you can order them directly from us. You can get any Dell book currently in print. For a complete up-to-date listing of our books and information on how to order, write to: Dell Readers Service, Box DR, 1540 Broadway, New York, NY 10036.

# FAIRIES

*Real Encounters with*
*Little People*

## Janet Bord

A Dell Book

Published by
Dell Publishing
a division of
Random House, Inc.
1540 Broadway
New York, New York 10036

ISBN: 0-440-22612-0

Reprinted by arrangement with Carroll & Graf Publishers, Inc.
Printed in the United States of America
Published simultaneously in Canada
September 1998

10   9   8   7   6   5   4   3
OPM

# Acknowledgements

I wish to thank the numerous friends and fellow researchers who have been so kind as to supply me with information: W. Ritchie Benedict, Lindsey Campbell, Mark Chorvinsky, David Cowan, Ron Drabble, Tristan Gray Hulse, Peter D. Jackson, Ulrich Magin, Michel Raynal, Bob Rickard, Doc Shiels, Dr Karl P.N. Shuker, Margaret Stutley, Ken Webster, Anthony Weir, and especially my husband Colin, whose comments and suggestions have proved invaluable. Also my thanks are due to those who have supplied illustrations: Fortean Picture Library; Ulster Folk and Transport Museum; Cambridge University Library; Warrington Museum and Art Gallery; Christopher Somerville; Leeds University Library; Mary Evans Picture Library; Bill Cox, *The Pyramid Guide*; Peter Hough; and the Museum of Antiquities of the University and Society of Antiquaries of Newcastle-upon-Tyne.

J.B.

# Contents

# Contents

# Foreword

Fairies are . . . Immediately I am at a loss for words, for fairies cannot easily be defined. They are different things to different people—tiny gossamer beings with wings or malicious creatures who play tricks on humans; the lost souls of the dead or fallen angels; our primitive ancestors or beings from another world—the interpretations are many and varied, and all with convincing supporting evidence. For years I have wondered what fairies really are: are they objectively real, semi-real (perhaps from other dimensions), or imaginary? To many people fairies exist only in fairy tales, but my research has shown me that many people today, at the end of the twentieth century, are still seeing fairies, and not only at the bottom of the garden—though "nature spirits" are still abundant, apparently not yet polluted out of existence. Anyone who thinks fairies are a joke will be very surprised to learn how many first-hand sighting reports are in existence, and it is on these accounts that I intend to concentrate in my search for the identity of the "Little People."

# FAIRIES

# 1

# ''TWAS ONLY A
# PACK OF FAIRIES'

## Fairy Lore in
## Great Britain and Ireland

As we prepare to leave the tumultuous and fast-changing events of the late twentieth century for the uncertainties of the twenty-first, we find ourselves in a very different world from that inhabited by our great-grandparents at the end of the nineteenth century. Industrial technology, space research, worldwide jet travel, computers, televisions were all undreamt of, and country people, especially those in the more remote areas of Britain and Ireland, were familiar with knowledge and beliefs which today have lost their importance. This loss has left us the poorer. I refer to their harmony with the environment and with the seasonal cycles of the natural world; their knowledge of herbal medicine; their instinctive awareness of the life-force present in all living things, which could manifest itself in strange ways. They knew that other levels of existence interacted with our own, and they had evolved rules for dealing with this interaction. They sometimes inadvertently encountered the denizens of these other worlds, but they were not alarmed and took such encounters almost for granted. One group of entities frequently seen was the fairies.

Such a statement may seem incredible today, most people believing that the fairies only ever existed in folklore and fairy tales, so far have we progressed into the brave new world of technology since the time when the reality of fairies was widely accepted. Yet the fact remains that only just over 100 years ago, the existence of fairies was very widely accepted in the rural areas of Britain and Ireland, and a rich lore based on this knowledge had evolved. Fortunately a large amount of fairy lore was recorded for posterity, just before the rural areas became urbanized during the twentieth century. Today the knowledge of and belief in fairies has all but died out among country people, who now are subjected to the same cultural influences from the media as are urban dwellers. However the changes that have occurred this century have not resulted in the complete extinction of the fairies: they have survived, because people still see them. Does this mean that, far from being the product of a bucolic imagination, they really exist?

In later chapters I will describe many first-hand encounters with fairies, the sheer quantity of these reports being persuasive of an objective reality behind a phenomenon which has almost been relegated to the children's bookshelf. I will also discuss the many theories put forward over the years to explain these encounters. Initially, however, I want to 'set the scene', to outline some aspects of fairy lore which relate directly to the country people's experience of fairies and their interaction with them, and I hope that by doing so it will then be easier to comprehend and make sense of the first-hand accounts which follow.

In the English-speaking world the name 'fairy' is the best

known, but the word 'fairy' is relatively recent, deriving from the earlier 'fay', which came from the old French *feie,* which itself came from the Latin *fata,* the fates. These were the supernatural beings who presided over human fortunes. 'Fairy' should, strictly speaking, be used only as an adjective, meaning 'enchanted' or 'illusory', but nowadays it is used as the name for the inhabitants of the enchanted land, fairyland. Chaucer and other writers of his time used 'faerie' to mean 'enchantment' or 'illusion'.[1] Another familiar name is the 'Little People', which is a descriptive term, as are many of the other lesser-known alternative names, like the wee folk, the good folk, the blessed folk, the good neighbours. In Ireland the *sidhe* (hill folk) is a familiar name; they are also known as the gentry. In Wales they are called *y tylwyth teg* (the fair family) or *bendith y mamau* (their mother's blessing). These descriptive names are used because it was thought to be unlucky to use more direct names: to know the name gave one power over the individual, and the fairies would take their revenge on anyone being so familiar as to refer to them directly.

There are also many names descriptive of specific types of fairy creature, like brownie, pixy, goblin, elf, and other less familiar ones like urisk, hob, farisee and derrick. These and many other names are given and explained in what must be the most comprehensive collection of fairy lore ever compiled, Katharine Briggs's invaluable book *A Dictionary of Fairies.* Anyone wishing to acquire a more detailed background knowledge of fairy lore than there is room for in this book should read Katharine Briggs's writings; two other important books of hers are *The Fairies in Tradition and Literature* and *The Vanishing People.*

The fairies were believed to live underground, or inside

A sixteenth-century illustration of fairies living inside a hill, trying to entice a knight to join them (Fortean Picture Library)

prehistoric earth mounds, cairns and forts. This belief led to many such sites being named for the fairies: Fairy Hill, Fairy Mount, Fairy Knowe (several Scottish cairns by this name), and in Scotland numerous sites called Sithean so-and-so (Sithean means fairy knowe).[2] One theory is that the fairies were associated in people's minds with prehistoric forts because these were the dwelling places, or at least the refuges in times of trouble, of the earlier races of people, while the cairns and tumuli were their burial places, and the fairies were memories of these ancestors.

Lewis Spence saw the fairies as 'the spirits of the departed', and explained in his book *British Fairy Origins* that this was why they were thought to haunt prehistoric monuments: the ghosts of the dead were believed to dwell in the standing stones which marked their burial places, and also in other burial sites like cairns, barrows and tumuli. Spence gave numerous examples of this association between the fairies and ancient stones, like the pillar with a Latin funerary inscription which once stood on a tumulus at Banwan Bryddin near Neath (Swansea, South Wales). An old man who had seen fairies dancing at the tumulus worked on the estate of Lady Mackworth, and he expressed concern when he heard that she was planning to remove the pillar to a grotto she was having built. Sure enough, soon after it was moved, a terrific thunderstorm struck the area, and next morning the grotto had disappeared, buried under the hill. The old man was not at all surprised, and said that he had heard the fairies laughing after the storm had died down.[3]

Both these theories as to why the fairies should be so strongly associated with prehistoric sites seem plausible, at least superficially, but for further discussion of these and other possibilities, see Chapter 6. The story of the fairies of Banwan Bryddin also illustrates another dominant theme: that they would retaliate whenever their sacred territory was interfered with. There are many instances of such behaviour documented in folklore, especially in connection with the Irish raths (forts), such as the following. A small rath only four yards in diameter was held sacred as a fairies' dancing ground and no one dared remove even a handful of earth. At night, music as if played by silver bagpipes could be heard floating round the hill, and a boy who lay down on the ground one evening to listen to it, at the same time idly picking up lumps of earth and throwing them about him (as boys are wont to do), was suddenly knocked back as if struck a violent blow. He was found lying unconscious, and it was a long time before he came to his senses and behaved normally again, the clear inference being that anyone who dares to desecrate the fairies' sacred ground will be punished by them.[4]

Such tales are not only part of the old Irish tradition: they have also been recorded in the present century. D.A. Mac-Manus writes of a farmer called O'Sullivan, who 'some fifty years ago' (c. 1910) was mowing the grass inside the 4-acre fort of Rathmore between Tralee and Killarney. The grass was lush, but it was always difficult to mow because the earth banks prevented his getting the mowing machine inside and it had to be scythed by hand. O'Sullivan determined to make things easier for himself by getting his two sons to remove one of the banks. So next day they brought a horse and cart and loaded up two or three cartloads of earth, dumping it in a hollow nearby. After a while they sat down to rest and smoke a pipe. It took them no more than thirty seconds to light up, turning away from the wind to do so, but when they turned back again they were amazed to see that the horse, who only seconds before had been standing harnessed into the cart close by them, was now quietly cropping the grass a distance away. Somehow, without a sound, it had been separated from its harness and from the cart, which was still close to them, its shafts on the ground. The men immediately realized that this was a sign to desist from interfering with the fort, and they returned home with horse and cart without further delay.[5]

This attitude of deference to the fairies still lingers on. In 1968 it was reported that the course of a new road in Donegal had been altered because workmen refused to cut down a tree which was believed to be frequented by the fairies. Even though he had just felled a wood, contractor Roy Green stopped work when he reached the gnarled tree standing alone in a field. 'I refused to cut it down, and I would not order any of my men to do the job. I have heard so much about these fairy trees that I would not risk it.' Another contractor was asked to do the work, but he also refused. 'There is something uncanny about it,' he said. 'The roots are not more than a couple of feet below ground—yet it defied a hurricane seven years ago.'[6]

The earth mounds and forts where the fairies lived were not necessarily large to look at, but once inside a different world was visible. One Irish man who was in fairyland for seven years told how he was taken to an area that looked just like 'hills and hollows', 'but when he was brought in, he saw what was like a gentleman's avenue, and it leading to a grand house.'[7] Another man told of 'the most splendid town that was ever seen' in the hill behind the abbey at Corcomroe in Ireland,[8] and the folklore descriptions of the fairyland hidden inside the hollow hill paint idyllic pictures of rich kingdoms where the Little People live in luxury.

The presence of fairies at a fort was sometimes signalled by a display of lights, and D.A. MacManus describes in his book *The Middle Kingdom* some instances of 'fairy lights' being seen in Ireland earlier this century. Two sisters who lived close to the fairy fort of Crillaun, for example, more than once saw lights on calm nights. One sister saw red, green, blue and yellow lights, the other saw white lights, and in the latter case she watched as they sailed in formation through the air to another fort on the far side of a small lough.[9] Another of MacManus's informants claimed actually to have seen fairies entering a rath. She was working as a maid when this happened, during the last century, and on her day off she was outside in the sunshine when she saw a party of eight riders, men and women, colourfully dressed and laughing. Thinking they were visitors ('quality', as she referred to them) coming to the big house, she started to hurry back, but as she did so, she saw them ride across a small field and into the side of a small fairy fort that was circled by thorn bushes. When her friends asked why she had not continued back to the house, she replied, 'Ah, 'twas no quality, at all. 'Twas only a pack of fairies going into the fort.'[10] This calm reaction clearly demonstrates that the fairies were accepted as everyday inhabitants of the environment by the rural people in Ireland only 100 years or so ago.

The way into their kingdom was not invariably through a hill or fort, however. On Anglesey, the island off north-west Wales, a woman was brought a weekly loaf of bread by a fairy in return for the loan of her baking grid. The fairy told her not to watch when she left the house, but one day she did, and saw the fairy go to the nearby lake, Llyn Rhosddu near Newborough, and plunge into the water.[11]

Heart Lake, south of Sligo in Ireland, is another body of water through which the fairies were believed to pass from their land to ours. W.B. Yeats noted that on one occasion, a group of men started to drain the lake, but one of them soon became aware that his house was on fire. Turning to look, the other men also saw their houses aflame and, leaving their task, they hurried home, where they found no trace of fire: it had been a trick played by the fairies to lure them from the lake.[12] Clearly there are many points of transition into fairyland; but it is unusual for humans to be able to follow the fairies through the entrance and also foolish to try, for not all of those who visited fairyland were able to return at will.

Not only should humans not interfere with fairy dwellings, they must also beware of harming fairy trees, and of obstructing fairy paths. Ireland has many fairy thorns (see page 3 of photograph section), which must not be touched, but also hazel, blackthorn, elder and several other species were special to the fairies. We saw earlier how even in recent years people have refused to cut down fairy trees: here is an example of what can happen if such a tree is felled. In Kiltimagh in Ireland around 1920 there were plans to build a new hospital, but two fairy thorns grew in the chosen field and the hospital could not be built without cutting one of them down. It was difficult to find someone prepared to do the deed, but at last a man came forward, and after completing his task some of the local lads jokingly shouted a warning to him. He called to them, 'I'll be back, never fear, and to hell with your bloody fairies!' That night he had a stroke; he survived in a crippled state for another year before he died and was brought back to the town, as he had predicted—but in a coffin. The hospital was built, but never opened.[13]

Buildings constructed across fairy paths also failed to prosper. The people living there suffered mystery illnesses, their animals died, noises plagued the offending cottages as if they were haunted; some even collapsed. The doors or windows along the line of the fairy path had to be kept open at night so that the fairies could pass through; or if only a corner of the cottage obstructed the path, all would be well again if that corner was removed. Ideally the fairies had to be consulted before building was started, and this was done by turning one sod and next day checking if it was untouched. If so, the fairies approved, but if it was turned back, a new site had to be found.[14]

So far I have spoken generally of 'the fairies' without giv-

A girl in Welsh costume accompanied by diminutive fairies, some winged, in a wide range of dress; a late nineteenth-century view of the Little People (Fortean Picture Library).

ing any indication of their appearance. Most people have their own fixed idea about this, being familiar since childhood with the fairies depicted in their picture books, but the reality is somewhat different, and the ephemeral, gauzy-

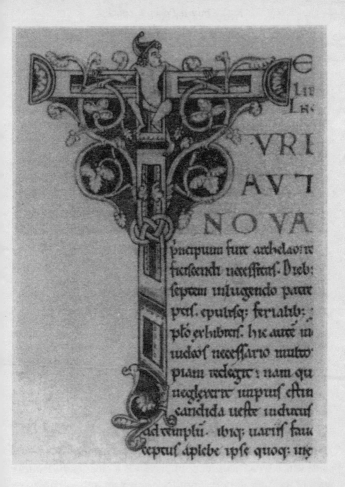

A twelfth-century manuscript illustration of a naked elf wearing a pointed hat with a bobble, which should be compared with the twentieth-century child's drawing of one of the little men seen in Wollaton Park (see page 74). This may be the earliest known fairy picture in Britain (St John's College MS A.8; Cambridge University Library).

winged creatures of fairy tales are definitely not the norm (see pages 6–8 of photograph section). A close study of the fairy lore of different areas of Britain and Ireland reveals that the appearance of the fairies differs from area to area, and from one type of creature to another. They vary in fact from the tall to the minute, and cover all sizes in between: yet the average seems to be that of a small human, around four feet tall. However, this question is complicated by the fairies' claimed ability to change their appearance. An Irish peasant living beneath Ben Bulben in County Sligo, a noted fairy location, told W.Y. Evans Wentz, who was collecting fairy lore, that one of the 'gentry' he had spoken to, who had seemed only four feet tall, had said: 'I am bigger than I appear to you now. We can make the old young, the big small, the small big.'[15]

I will return to this aspect of fairy power, known as glamour, in Chapter 7; it may be important in helping to shed light on the nature of the fairies. If they do often, or even always, influence the way they are seen by humans, then a detailed discussion of fairy appearance may be judged somewhat superfluous! In the following chapters where first-hand encounters with the Little People in modern times are described, variations in shape, size and dress will be noted but need not necessarily be evidence of anything other than the fairies exercising their powers to confuse; and certainly variations in appearance as described by witnesses cannot alone be used to judge an account to have come solely from the teller's imagination. Details of costume vary as much as physical appearance: green has apparently always been popular with the fairies, but they do favour other colours, and their costume ranges from drab to colourful. It is not outlandish, but echoes human dress of the

Hairy dwarfs dancing in a ring in a sixteenth-century drawing. These are perhaps the 'shaggy aboriginals' described on page 144, a primitive race of pygmies (Fortean Picture Library).

place and time. Some Scottish fairies, for example, wore plaids and kilts. Cloaks were often worn, and hats of various kinds: red pointed caps seem to have been popular.[16]

In addition to generally looking similar to humans, the fairies also behaved like humans in many respects. They married and had children, they enjoyed eating and drinking, dancing and having a good time. Although mortal, they lived longer than humans, and also differed from them in possessing magical powers, but their closeness to the human race is obvious, and their interaction with humans reinforces this. Folklore is rich in tales describing how fairies have either helped or hindered people. They could be very useful in a domestic situation, and the brownie in particular was known for his keenness to help with the daily chores.

He would not accept payment: indeed he could even be very offended by such offers. However he did like to take food left out for him. When humans did the fairies a good turn, it was generally rewarded. In an Anglesey home, for instance, the fairies used to come down the chimney at night, bringing their children, who they would wash in a basin of water using the soap and towel left out for them. Next day the family would find that the towel had been washed and ironed and that the basin had been emptied and was now half full of sovereigns.[17] Gifts of money from the fairies had to be kept secret, however, or they would stop. A man living near Corwen in North Wales used to regularly find silver coins lying on the ground by a certain gate. He kept his good fortune to himself, until his wife began to pester him to tell her where all his money came from, as he only worked in a tan-yard. He told her that he believed the fairies were responsible. Shortly afterwards he died, and no one ever found silver in that spot again.[18]

It might be as well for me to comment on the veracity of the tales in this chapter so far. Of course, not having been present, I am not in a position to verify any of them. Some are clearly folklore, and I hope these are distinguishable from the first-hand accounts, or those said to be based on reliable sources. It must always be remembered that the reliability of a tale becomes less so the further one is from the original source. The last case, of the silver, is a good example: the letter containing this tale appeared in a Welsh history journal in 1886, and the writer said that his informant was 'personally acquainted' with the subject's wife and children, and 'he has no doubt as to the truth thereof'. That may be so, but the circumstances bring to mind the modern tales which do the rounds today, those we hear from a friend who tells us that it all happened to 'a friend of a friend', but which students of folklore will realize are of very questionable authenticity. So throughout this book, any tale which is not clearly seen to be a first-hand account should be treated with caution.

Although they are often helpful to humans, the fairies can equally well be a nuisance, or even positively harmful, as related in several of the tales earlier in this chapter. Their antics seem often to have resulted from their malicious and spiteful nature, this being especially so on those occasions when people have been led astray, unable to find the correct path, and maybe lost for hours. In England, the victim is said to be pixy-led; in Ireland the term is 'the stray sod', which refers to a turf on which a fairy spell has been laid, so that the person who steps on it loses his or her way. A number of modern accounts exist, like that from the president of the Nettlecombe Women's Institute, Somerset, recorded in 1961. She described her journey to a Cornish house, following directions from a nearby farm that when she reached two gates she should be sure and take the white one. It was a misty winter's day and the atmosphere was 'creepy'. She came to a thick hawthorn hedge with only one gate, not white, so she worked her way along the hedge, but could find no trace of a white gate. Then a farm boy came along whistling; he pointed out the white gate, just beside the other one, and returned to the farm.[19]

Turning one's coat inside out was said to be the way to counter the fairy spell, but it did not always work. Other protections against fairy interference included a bunch of rowan berries, a staff of rowan wood, iron horseshoes fastened on the house and stable walls, holed stones hung over the cattle's food manger, and religious acts such as making the sign of the cross, sprinkling holy water, and ringing church bells.[20]

In his book *The Middle Kingdom* D.A. MacManus devotes a chapter to modern instances of 'the stray sod'. These include the rector who in 1916 got lost while walking on a path he knew well. A stile set in a thick thorn hedge had disappeared, as had the gate he had passed through a short while before. He walked the entire length of the hedge back to his starting point, but found neither stile nor gate. Suddenly, two hours later, the spell was lifted and both stile and gate were where they should have been.[21]

Even stranger was the story of the girl who, in 1935, lost herself on Lis Ard, a fairy fort in County Mayo. When she tried to leave the hill, she found herself unable to pass through the gap in the outer bank: some internal force prevented her, even turned her round so she was walking back into the fort again. Panic-stricken, she tried again and again to leave, but an invisible wall was stopping her. She also felt an atmosphere of hostility growing around her. Darkness came and soon she saw the lights of men searching for her, calling her name. She called back, from only twenty or thirty yards' distance, but they seemed unable to hear her, and went away. Later, she suddenly realized that the barrier had vanished, and she was able to leave the fort and return home.[22]

When people experience 'the stray sod' or are 'pixy-led', there is usually nothing to link the event to the fairies directly, other than the belief that they were responsible—although in a few instances the victims have heard laughter in the air around them, as if the fairies were amused at their misfortune. Likewise when 'fairy music' is heard, the witness's linking it with fairies is a result of the local existence of deeply ingrained fairy lore. Dr Thomas Wood, composer and author, heard fairy music on Dartmoor (Devon) when camping there with friends in 1922. He would go off alone to think, make notes for a book and write music. On one occasion, he heard a voice calling his name, but could see no one. Next day, visiting the same place again, he heard music in the air.

> It was overhead, faint as a breath. It died away, came back louder, over me, swaying like a censer that dips. It lasted 20 minutes. Portable wireless sets were unknown in 1922. My field glasses assured me no picnickers were in sight. It was not a gramophone nor was it an illusory noise in my ears. This music was essentially harmonic, not a melody nor an air. It sounded like the weaving together of tenuous fairy sounds. I listened with every faculty drawn out to an intensity . . . The music drifted into silence. No more came, then or since. I was reasonably certain that I had been deliberately encouraged to listen to the supernatural.[23]

Many other people have heard supernatural music, but it is not always attributed to the fairies. The psychic researcher D. Scott Rogo made a detailed study of 'music of the spheres' and he published two fascinating volumes of case studies and commentary relating the experience to other psychic happenings. He referred to the phenomenon as NAD, a Sanskrit word which refers to the 'audible life stream'.[24]

Ethereal music may often be associated with fairies, although they are invisible, because of the well-known love of the fairies for dancing. In addition to many folklore accounts of this pastime, there are also some modern accounts of people actually seeing this happening, a few being included in Chapter 2. Here is an older account given by seventeenth-century antiquarian John Aubrey.

In the year 1633–4, soone after I had entered into my grammar at the Latin Schoole at Yatton Keynel, (near Chippenham, Wiltshire), our curate Mr Hart, was annoy'd one night by these elves or fayries. Comming over the downes, it being neere darke, and approaching one of the faiery dances, as the common people call them in these parts, viz. the greene circles made by those sprites on the grasse, he all at once sawe an innumerable quantitie of pigmies or very small people, dancing rounde and rounde, and singing, and making all maner of small odd noyses. He, being very greatly amaz'd, and yet not being able, as he sayes, to run away from them, being, as he supposes, kept there in a kind of enchantment, they no sooner perceave him but they surround him on all sides, and what betwixt feare and amazement, he fell down scarcely knowing what he did; and thereupon these little creatures pinch'd him all over, and made a sorte of quick humming noyse all the time; but at length they left him, and when the sun rose, he found himself exactly in the midst of one of these faiery dances. This relation I had from him myselfe, a few days after he was so tormented; but when I and my bedfellow Stump wente soon afterwards, at night time to the dances on the downes, we saw none of the elves or fairies. But indeede it is saide they seldom appeare to any persons who go to seeke for them.[25]

People who inadvertently came across fairies dancing were sometimes taken into the circle, with disastrous consequences, a theme I will return to later. Mr Hart was lucky that he was not abducted by the fairies, but only pinched. They do not like being disturbed at their revels, as was made clear to a Welshman, Edward Jones, who lived at Llanidloes in Mid Wales. Returning home late one evening, 'Ned the Jockey', as he was known, came across a troop of fairies who were annoyed at his intrusion into their company.

> Requesting him to depart, they politely offered him the choice of three means of locomotion, viz., being carried off by a 'high wind, middle wind, or low wind'. The jockey soon made up his mind, and elected to make his trip through the air by the assistance of a high wind. No sooner had he given his decision, than he found himself whisked high up into the air and his senses completely bewildered by the rapidity of his flight; he did not recover himself till he came in contact with the earth, being suddenly dropped in the middle of a garden near Ty Gough, on the Bryndu road, many miles distant from the spot whence he started on his aerial journey.

Note that both the victim and his place of descent are named; the author of the account also claims acquaintance with him and adds that 'Ned, when relating this story, would vouch for its genuineness in the most solemn manner, and the person who narrated it to the writer brought forward as a proof of its truth, "that there was not the slightest trace of any person going into the garden while Ned was found in the middle of it".' But can we really believe that the events occurred as related? This story demonstrates very well the ever-present difficulty in distinguishing between events that actually occurred as described, events that have been altered and embellished in the telling, and events that are based on tradition rather than fact and have had familiar names and places added to give an aura of authenticity.[26]

Circles of withered or bright green grass were often claimed as fairy dancing grounds, but these are likely to have been caused by a fungus in the soil, similar to the visible circles of fungi sometimes seen in the grass. Although known by country people as fairy rings, their true cause is now undisputed. This cannot be said of the mysterious circles currently appearing every summer in the cornfields of Britain. Although these have not seriously been attributed to fairies, such an explanation might seem no more far-fetched than some of the theories aired. It seems worth mentioning this modern mystery in passing, because of the feeling of many people that supernatural forces may be at work, despite the insistence by the rationalists that natural forces and hoaxers can together account for the manifestations. In addition, at least one tantalizing mention of a direct link between fairies and a crop circle site has been published. Writing of crop circles in Leicestershire, medium Rita Goold said that she heard from the elderly lady who owned the land that as a child seventy years before, she was told to keep away from the field after dark, because fairies had been seen there and weird noises heard. Whether 'the fairies' were used as a convenient explanation for early twentieth-century crop circles, or whether actual sightings were made of fairies in the field, is not clear, but the association of the two is worth recording.[27]

Far from being safely relegated to children's fairy tales, or disregarded as merely creatures of folklore, the fairies have many points of contact with the twentieth century. Anyone who doubts this has only to read the succeeding chapters, where many intriguing first-hand accounts are recorded. Even among people who have not actually seen fairies, fairy lore is still alive in the background of their existence, as evidenced by the way in which strange happenings are sometimes attributed to the fairies. For example in 1907 the *Coleraine Chronicle* published an account of strange happenings in the house of John M'Laughlin, an elderly farmer living in County Londonderry, Northern Ireland. He cut down a holly bush with which to sweep his chimney, disregarding warnings from his neighbours that the bush was sacred to the fairies. He soon began to regret his folly, when the soot he had buried in the garden found its way mysteriously back into the kitchen. He reburied it; again it returned. Lumps of the soot were found in the kitchen utensils, and it had marked the white walls and broken the crockery. Stones also appeared from nowhere, breaking the windows and other glass indoors. In addition:

A piece of bathbrick in a closed cupboard was, several people maintain, seen by them to hurl itself across the kitchen and smash into seven or eight pieces against the window sash. A stone weighing two pounds, used as a griddle balance, was also observed to dash about. After negotiating two successive corners, it passed through the closed door into the parlour, where it smashed the window and tore a hole in the curtain . . . Stones were heard to crash through the roof of the house and wood-sheeted ceiling of the kitchen without making any perforations, and were found resting on the kitchen floor. Some of the stones were removed outside but returned inside, of their own volition . . . The milk vessels in the pantry were filled up with stones. Some persons say the threshing machine in the barn began to work of its own accord on Sunday.

Many independent witnesses saw the strange events for themselves. No one could control the phenomenon, and eventually the house had to be abandoned.[28]

Students of psychic research will quickly have noted that the happenings in the farmhouse would nowadays be attributed to a poltergeist; though using that term no more explains the mechanism behind the events than would attributing them to the fairies. The same kind of phenomenon (whatever it might be) may also have been responsible for some of the happenings once attributed to brownies, who were said to both help and hinder the housewife in her domestic chores. As reported in a French book published in the early seventeenth century:

. . . there are plenty of houses haunted by these spirits and goblins, which ceaselessly disturb the sleep of those who dwell in them; for now they will stir and overturn the utensils, vessels, tables, boards, dishes, bowls, and now they will draw the water from a well, or make the pulley squeak, the slates and tiles fall from the roof, throw stones, enter chambers, imitate now a cat, now a mouse, now other animals, lift up persons lying asleep in their beds, pull the curtains or coverlets, and perpetrate a thousand tricks. These Folets do not bring any other nuisance than disturbing them, oppressing them, or hindering their sleep; for the household vessels all of which they seem to have smashed and broken, are found the next morning to be intact.[29]

Colin Parsons reported a modern version of the brownie giving a helping hand in the house in his book *Encounters with the Unknown*[30] when he wrote of a couple who moved to a new house and were told by the former occupants that they had brownies at the bottom of the garden who did little jobs for them. The new occupants soon found out for themselves that this amazing assertion was true:

> Dishes would be washed while they were out at work, the washing-machine would be operated and the clothes transferred to the tumble-drier. At first Jenny Bolton was convinced that she must be doing these things herself and forgetting them, and she visited her doctor. He found her perfectly well and prescribed a course of mild tranquillizers. The odd events continued, however, and now began to involve Peter Bolton. He would find the garden shed tidied or his clothes put in the wash or hung up in the wardrobes.

However, there was a sudden change of attitude on the part of the brownie after Jenny lost her temper with their invisible helper. Thereafter chaos reigned. 'Soap powder had been tipped all over the vegetables, taps had been turned on and plugs put in, furniture had been knocked over and jam rubbed into her Persian carpet.' Things got so bad, with the house shrouded in malevolence, that the couple had to move out permanently.

This account does bear out the folklore accounts of brownies being helpful if they felt kindly disposed towards a house's occupants, but turning into the most unbelievable nuisance if crossed or annoyed in any way. Perhaps other events described in folk tales also carry a grain of truth in them, being based on real-life events. Stripping away the story-teller's added layers to reveal the kernel of fact at the heart of a folk tale, belief or superstition can be an intriguing pursuit, but it is one fraught with danger, especially if the person wielding the scalpel starts his or her task with a pet theory needing to be supported. Even the most cautious seeker-after-truth tends to have some biases, and these invariably colour one's attitudes towards the material being studied so that awkward facts which do not support one's preconceptions will be discarded. In fact, I would go so far as to suggest that no one is capable of studying any subject from a completely neutral standpoint; the conclusions reached are bound to reflect to some degree the beliefs and preoccupations of the mind from whence they came.

The following two tales seem straightforward enough. In both cases the events were attributed to the fairies, and who is to say that they were not responsible? If the witnesses are describing the facts truthfully, no logical explanation springs to mind in either case. In the early 1970s Charles Williams wrote in a letter to *The Countryman* magazine that his isolated Cornish cottage was supplied with water from a well that in summer became very low. He tried to find someone to deepen the well for him, but was advised by a local to enlist the help of the pixies. What he should do was put 'corners of pasty' all round the top of the well on the night of the new moon. It was stressed that it must be a genuine Cornish pasty, and Mr Williams followed the suggestion. At that time the water in the well was only nine inches deep, there had been no rain for quite a while, and it was a fine, dry night. He reported that 'When I went to the well next morning all the pasty had gone and there was 11 ft of water in the well.' So long as he continued to put out pasty, the water supply was reliable, but when he was away, the cottage caretakers failed to take pasties to the well, and it ran dry.[31]

The custom of leaving out something edible to placate the fairies is deeply enshrined in fairy lore. Among the items traditionally used were barley-meal cakes (left near wells on two hills in Aberdeen, to propitiate the banshee), cheese (near the Cheese Well on the summit of Minchmuir, Peebles),[32] and milk (newly-taken milk being poured on a fairy mound night and morning in the Hebrides to propitiate the 'good people').[33] If an offering were not left, the fairies were quite likely to take something anyway, as happened to Mr and Mrs Coleman, friends of author D.A. MacManus, who were holidaying in a caravan in Ireland in 1938. They stopped one evening beside a quiet country road in County Leitrim and got ready for the night. A country woman passing by spoke to them, and she advised them to 'leave something for the fairies', but they soon forgot her advice. Mrs Coleman decided to put their supply of butter outside to keep cool, so she placed the 2 or 3 pounds into a bowl, smoothed the top with a knife, put a plate on top and a heavy stone on the plate. She placed the butter under the caravan where it only just fitted as there was a mere twelve-inch ground clearance. Next morning she retrieved the butter. Both stone and plate were still in place, but when she removed them she was amazed to find two-thirds of the butter missing. 'All the butter had disappeared from one half of the bowl which was empty right to the bottom, as if someone had cut down through the butter with a knife. The top part of the other half was also gone, having clearly been scraped out in a rounded way by something soft and blunt—a large tongue or a small hand, perhaps.' There is no apparent way that either a human or an animal could have taken the butter. The Colemans had two dogs with them, who were on guard outside the van all night; they did not bark, nor did the couple hear any noises. In the end they had to accept the only possible explanation: that it was the fairies who took the butter.[34]

Although a belief in the existence of fairies was deeply ingrained in country folk over the centuries, objective proof of their existence has never been easy to obtain. This may explain why anything tiny has tended to be ascribed to them. If the item is an article of clothing, and especially if it seems well worn, there certainly does not appear to be any other explanation than that the wearer was a very small person. A good example is the 'fairy shoe' found on the Beara Peninsula in south-west Ireland in 1835 (see page 4 of photograph section). A labourer was following a remote mountain track when he saw the tiny shoe, which was 2⅞ inches long but only ⅞ inch wide, and in style like the shoe of an eighteenth-century gentleman. It was worn down at the heel. The finder was afraid to keep it, and so passed it on to others. When it was eventually examined under a microscope at Harvard University in the States, tiny hand-made stitches and eyelets could be seen. The shoe was thought to be made of mouseskin. Another 'fairy shoe' was found in a bog in County Donegal.[35]

Other tiny artefacts attributed to the fairies include a mirror, which consists of a brass plate on a moulded handle, and is currently in the Scottish Highland Folk Museum, and 'fairy pipes', small clay pipes with bowls scarcely large enough to admit the tip of the little finger. Found in various parts of England and Wales, they were known as *Cetyn y tylwyth teg*.[36] Fairy cups and saucers, basins and other utensils were found by children searching in the Fairy Glen or

Nameless Dean not far from Melrose in southern Scotland, after heavy rain had washed from the stream bank small stones in the shapes of these items. The children believed that to find one would bring them good luck.[37] Tiny flint arrowheads made in prehistoric times and widely found in Britain and elsewhere in the world were known as elf-shot. Isobel Gowdie, a Scottish witch who claimed to have visited fairyland, said she had seen elves shaping arrows under the Devil's direction.

Fairy food has also been found: a species of fungus called Tremella, yellow and gelatinous, and growing on furze and broom, was in East Anglia called 'fairy butter';[38] while in the same area of Britain a fossilized sea-urchin was described as a 'fairy loaf'. One seen in a cottage during the last century had been covered in black lead 'to give it a polish' and was kept on the mantelpiece, the finder believing that to have a fairy loaf in the house ensured that they would never want for bread.[39] In Wales, an oil found in limestone rock was called fairy butter. It had a pleasant smell, and was rubbed on the body by people suffering from rheumatism.[40]

What all the fairy artefacts have in common is their small size. Although some classes of fairy folk are diminutive, there are many who are not, and so there should logically be fairy artefacts which are closer in size to their human counterparts—but of course, who would then be able to distinguish them from ordinary human artefacts! Fairy artefacts are usually (not always, but usually) easily identifiable as some natural object or obvious fake, and the only physical evidence really worth having would be a corpse. No physical remains of fairies have ever been found, though fairs have occasionally advertised exhibits claiming to be fairies, such as 'a living FAIRY, supposed to be a hundred and fifty years old, his face being no bigger than a child's of a month: was found sixty years ago; looked as old then as he does now. His head being a great piece of curiosity, having no skull, with several imperfections worthy of your observation.'[41]

Photographs claiming to show fairies are in existence, some of them being described in Chapter 6 and reproduced in the plate section, but these too are open to suspicion, and some, such as the famous Cottingley photographs, are now confirmed hoaxes. If a few dubious photographs are the closest we can get to proving that fairies exist, are the doubters justified in stating that fairies live only in the imaginations of those who claim to have seen them? There is a huge number of reports of sightings, and only some of those which have come to my attention are quoted in the following chapters. But as with any mysterious creature— like the Loch Ness Monster or Bigfoot, which also have allegedly been seen by thousands of people—until physical remains are found which can be examined and identified, we are kept tantalizingly at arm's length from the creature itself. Whether or not positive proof of the fairies' objective existence is ever obtained, literally millions of people around the world have, in centuries past, been convinced of their existence, and those who in recent times have seen them with their own eyes will continue to believe.

# 2

# 'DANCING WITH GREAT BRISKNESS'

## Reports from Great Britain and Ireland Before the Twentieth Century

The previous chapter contained a mixture of folklore and fact: I hope that the majority of the material in the next six chapters is factual—but readers should still be critical, even of the first-hand accounts. None of this material is verifiable. It may well be that only those people who are psychically gifted are ever likely to see fairies, because the Little People are not physical in the way that human beings are.

Although most reports before 1900 consist of retold tales whose basis in fact is now impossible to determine, a few first- and second-hand accounts of a tolerable degree of reliability do survive. The earliest I have found is the seventeenth-century report by John Aubrey of Mr Hart being pinched by fairies after watching them dancing (see page 18).

Around the same time that Mr Hart had his uncomfortable encounter, Scottish witch Isobel Gowdie was getting to know the Little People, as she explained in 1662 in her confession to witchcraft. Here are relevant extracts, which I have rendered into current English, for ease of reading:

I was in the Downie-hills, and got meat there from the Queen of Faery, more than I could eat. The Queen of Faery is well clothed in white linens, and in white and brown clothes, etc.; and the King of Faery is a fine man, well favoured, and broad faced, etc. There were elf-bulls 'rowtting and skoylling' up and down there, which frightened me.

As for elf arrowheads, the Devil shapes them with his own hand and delivers them to elf-boys, who shape and trim them with a sharp thing like a needle, . . . the Devil gives them to us, each of us so many . . . We have no bow to shoot with, but jerk them from our thumb-nails. Sometimes we will miss, but if they touch, be it beast, or man, or woman, it will kill, even if they are wearing a coat of mail.[1]

John Beaumont, who published his *Treatise of Spirits* in 1705, wrote in some detail of his encounters with various spirits. Those I judge to have been fairies, he described as

being of a brown complexion, and about three foot in stature; they had both black, loose network gowns, tied with a black sash about their middles, and within the network appeared a gown of a golden colour, with somewhat of a light striking through it; their heads were not dressed with topknots, but they had white linen caps on, with lace on them . . . and over it they had a black loose network hood . . .

On one occasion he saw them 'dance in a ring in the garden, and sing, holding hands round, not facing each other, but their backs turned to the inner part of the circle'. He once asked them who they were, and they told him that 'they were an order of creatures superior to mankind, and could influence our thoughts, and that their habitation was in the air'.[2]

It is perhaps wise not to take the two previous reports too seriously. Alleged witches' confessions are notoriously unreliable, and John Beaumont, judging by a fuller reading of his description of the spirits who visited him, seems to have been living in something of a dream world, and perhaps was not too able to distinguish between reality and imagination. The next witness, however, was a well-respected eighteenth-century cleric, at one time Principal of the Independent Academy at Rotherham.

The Reverend Dr Edward Williams was born at Bodfari (Denbighshire, North Wales), and the events he describes took place there in 1757 when he was seven years old. In later life he said he was 'forced to class it among my *unknowables*'.

On a fine summer day (about midsummer) between the hours of 12 at noon and one, my eldest sister and myself, our next neighbour's children Barbara and Ann Evans, both older than myself, were in a field called Cae Caled near their house, all innocently engaged at play by a hedge under a tree, and not far from the stile next to that house, when one of us observed on the middle of the field a company of— what shall I call them?—*Beings*, neither men, women, nor children, dancing with great briskness. They were full in view less than a hundred yards from us, consisting of about seven or eight couples: we could not well reckon them, owing to the briskness of their motions and the consternation with which we were struck at a sight so unusual. They were all clothed in red, a dress not unlike a military uniform, without hats, but their heads tied with handkerchiefs of a reddish colour, sprigged or spotted with yellow, all uniform in this as in habit, all tied behind with the corners hanging down their backs, and white handkerchiefs in their hands held loose by the corners. They appeared of a size somewhat less than our own, but more like dwarfs than children. On the first discovery we began, with no small dread, to question one another as to what they could be, as there were no soldiers in the country, nor was it the time for May dancers, and as they differed much from all the human beings we had ever seen. Thus alarmed we dropped our play, left our station, and made for the stile. Still keeping our eyes upon them we observed one of their company starting from the rest and making towards us with a running pace. I being the youngest was the last at the stile, and, though struck with an inexpressible panic, saw the *grim elf* just at my heels, having a full and clear, though terrific view of him, with his ancient, swarthy, and grim complexion. I screamed out exceedingly; my sister also and our companions set up a roar, and the former dragged me with violence over the stile on which, at the instant I was disengaged from it, this warlike Lilliputian leaned and stretched himself after me, but came not over. With palpitating hearts and loud cries we ran towards the house, alarmed the family, and told them our trouble. The men instantly left their dinner, with whom still trembling we went to the place, and made the most solicitous and diligent enquiry in all the neighbourhood, both at that time and after, but never found the least vestige of any circumstance that could contribute to a solution of this remarkable phenomenon.[3]

If Dr Williams remembered the events accurately, and was not inadvertently blending details of fairy lore he had been told as a child with some other real but explicable frightening event in his childhood, then there seems no easy explanation—other than that the children were somehow for a short while able to glimpse what humans cannot normally see.

A similar vision, of strange cavorting figures in a field, was seen in the Isle of Man, some time in the eighteenth century, by a man who until that time did not believe in fairies. The experience is described by George Waldron, an Englishman on the island who was acting for the British government, watching and reporting on the import and export trade of the country between 1720 and 1730.

A gentleman, my near neighbour, who affirmed with the most solemn asseverations that, being entirely averse to the belief in fairies, or that any such beings were permitted to wander for the purposes related of them, had been at last convinced by the appearance of several little figures, playing and leaping over some stones in a field, whom, a few yards distant, he imagined were school boys, and intended, when he came near enough, to reprimand, for being absent from their exercises at that time of the day, it being then, he said, between three and four of the clock. But when he approached, as near he could guess, within twenty paces, they all immediately disappeared, though he had never taken his eye off them from the first moment he beheld them; nor was there any place where they could so suddenly retreat, it being an open field, without hedge or bush, and, as is said before, broad day.[4]

## 'Dancing with Great Briskness'

The host of fairies seen at Ilkley Wells (West Yorkshire) in 1815 by the man in charge of the healing baths were the smaller variety clad in green, rather than the much more common human-looking creatures. William Butterfield went to unlock the door to the baths early in the morning, but found that the key turned round and round in the lock. His story of what happened next was told to John Dobson, also from Ilkley, who reported it in these words:

Then he endeavoured to push the door open, and no sooner did he push it slightly ajar than it was as quickly pushed back again. At last, with one supreme effort, he forced it perfectly open, and back it flew with a great bang! Then whirr, whirr, whirr, such a noise and sight! all over the water and dipping into it was a lot of little creatures dressed in green from head to foot, none of them more than eighteen inches high, and making a chatter and a jabber thoroughly unintelligible. They seemed to be taking a bath, only they bathed with all their clothes on. Soon, however, one or two of them began to make off, bounding over the walls like squirrels. Finding they were all making ready for decamping, and wanting to have a word with them, he shouted at the top of his voice—indeed, he declared afterwards he couldn't find anything else to say or do—'Hallo there!' Then away the whole tribe went, helter skelter, toppling and tumbling, heads over heels, heels over heads, and all the while making a noise not unlike that of a disturbed nest of young partridges. The sight was so unusual, that he declared he either couldn't or daren't attempt to rush after them. . . . When the well had got quite clear of these strange beings he ran to the door and looked to see where they had fled, but nothing was to be seen. He ran back into the bath to see if they had left anything behind; but there was nothing: the water lay still and clear just as he had left it the previous night. He thought they might perhaps have left some of their clothing behind in their haste, but he could find none, and so he gave up looking, and commenced his usual routine of preparing the baths; not, however, without trotting to the door once or twice to see if they might be coming back; but he saw them no more.[5]

Very often, people who see fairies come across them suddenly and unexpectedly; certainly they are not thinking about them at the time of the encounter. It may be that a certain detachment of mind may be a prerequisite to having what is clearly some kind of psychic experience, and the lone traveller is well placed to be in a receptive condition. A Stowmarket (Suffolk) man walking home one moonlit night in 1842, suddenly came across a group of fairies:

There might be a dozen of them, the biggest about three feet high, and small ones like dolls. Their dresses sparkled as if with spangles, like the girls at shows at Stow fair. They were moving round hand in hand in a ring, no noise came from them. They seemed light and shadowy, not like solid bodies. I passed on saying, the Lord have mercy on me, but them must be the fairies, and being alone then on the path over the field could see them as plain as I do you. I looked after them when I got over the stile, and they were there, just the same moving round and round. I ran home and called three women to come back with me and see them. But when we got to the place they were all gone. I could not make out any particular things about their faces. I might be forty yards from them and I did not like to stop and stare at them. I was quite sober at the time.[6]

The next witness was similarly alone at the time of his experience, which took place around the mid-nineteenth century. The account is second-hand, but as the author was a relative of the witness, I am assuming it is reliable.

. . . a near relative of the writer, not more imbued with superstition than the majority, firmly believed that he once saw a real dwarf or fairy, without the use of any incantation. He had been amusing himself one summer evening on the top of Mellor Moor, near Blackburn, close to the remains of the Roman encampment, when his attention was arrested by the appearance of a dwarf-like man, attired in full hunting costume, with top-boots and spurs, a green jacket, red hairy cap, and a thick hunting whip in his hand. He ran briskly along the moor for a considerable distance, when, leaping over a low stone wall, he darted down a steep declivity, and was lost to sight. The popular opinion of the neighbourhood is, that an underground city exists at this place; that an earthquake swallowed up the encampment, and that on certain days in the year the hill folk may be heard ringing their bells, and indulging in various festivities. Considerable quantities of stone, which still remain around the ditches of this rectangular place, may have suggested the ideas of a city and an earthquake. On other occasions the fairies are supposed to exhibit themselves in military array on the mountain sides; their evolutions conforming in every respect to the movements of modern troops. Such appearances are believed to portend the approach of civil commotions, and are said to have been more than usually common about the time of the rebellion in 1745–6.[7]

W.Y. Evans Wentz, who was collecting fairy lore in Ireland early this century, was told by Neil Colton, then seventy-three years old, of a sighting he had had personally, close to the shores of Lough Derg in County Donegal. This probably took place around the middle of the nineteenth century.

One day, just before sunset in midsummer, and I a boy then, my brother and cousin and myself were gathering bilberries (whortleberries) up by the rocks at the back of here, when all at once we heard music. We hurried round the rocks, and there we were within a few hundred feet of six or eight of the *gentle folk,* and they dancing. When they saw us, a little woman dressed all in red came running out from them towards us, and she struck my cousin across the face with what seemed to be a green rush. We ran for home as hard as we could, and when my cousin reached the house she fell dead. Father saddled a horse and went for Father Ryan. When Father Ryan arrived, he put a stole about his neck and began praying over my cousin and reading psalms and striking her with the stole; and in that way brought her back. He said if she had not caught hold of my brother, she would have been *taken* for ever.[8]

Also around the mid-nineteenth century, a strange encounter with supposed fairy folk took place in Wales. Although a considerable quantity of fairy lore has been collected in Wales, first-hand accounts are in short supply.

This one reminds us that such encounters are often accompanied by a strange otherworldly atmosphere.

A very old man named John Jones, who lives at Llanddeiniol, about six miles from Aberystwyth, informed me that many years ago, when he was a young man, or a lad of 18, he was engaged as a servant at a farm called Perthrhys, in that neighbourhood. One evening after supper he went to the tailor who was making him a suit of clothes; but as the clothes were not quite ready he had to wait till a late hour before returning home, but it was a delightful moonlight night. As he proceeded along a lonely path across a certain moor known as Rhosrhydd, and happened to look back he was suddenly surprised by seeing two young men or boys as he thought, coming after him. At first he thought these were some boys trying to frighten him; but after they had followed him for a short distance till they came within about 30 or 40 yards of him, they turned out from the path, and began to jump and to dance, going round and round as if they followed a ring or a circle just as we hear of the fairies. They were perfectly white, and very nimble, and the old man informed me that there was something supernatural both in their appearance and movements; and that he is convinced to this day that they could not have been human beings. When he arrived home at the farm, and related his adventure, every one in the house was of the opinion that the strange beings he had seen were the Fairies.[9]

Unlike the previous encounter, the next one did not feel supernatural to the onlookers. They were surprised to see men (as they thought) behaving so strangely, but never considered there might be a supernatural explanation. How-

An old English chapbook illustration of fairies dancing. This drawing has several intriguing features. Note on the left the fairy hill, complete with door—clearly an entrance into fairyland. Note also the face in the tree foliage: the green man or vegetation spirit described on page 148. There is even a prominent 'magic mushroom', the mind-affecting qualities of which may have had a part to play in some encounters with Little People (see page 133) (Fortean Picture Library).

ever, the behaviour they described is familiar, echoing as it does that of the other dancing fairies already described. One (unanswerable) question that arises is: Why are the fairies so often seen 'dancing'?

In August, 1862, David Evans, and Evan Lewis, went from the Coast of Cardiganshire with their waggons all the way to

Brecon for some timber for ship-building, which was going on at New Quay. On their return journey, through Carmarthenshire, they stopped for a short time at a place called Cwmdwr on the road leading from Llanwrda to Lampeter. It was about 2 o'clock in the afternoon, and the two men and their horses and waggons were standing opposite a farm known as Maestwynog, where the reapers were busy at work in a wheat-field close by. As they were looking in the direction of a hillside not far off, David Evans saw about fifty small wheat stacks (sopynau bychain), as he at first thought. On second sight, however, he noticed that they were moving about, he took them for reapers. They were all dressed exactly alike, and walked fast one after another up the hillside footpath. David Evans now called the attention of his companion Evan Lewis, whom he asked who the men could have been; but before he had time to make any further remarks, the first of those who were climbing up along the winding footpath had reached a small level spot on the top of the hill. The others quickly followed him, and each one in coming to the top, gave a jump to dance, and they formed a circle. After dancing for a short time, one of the dancers turned in into the middle of the circle, followed by the others, one by one till they appeared like a gimblet [sic] screw. Then they disappeared into the ground. After a while one of them reappeared again, and looked about him in every direction as a rat, and the others followed him one by one and did the same. Then they danced for some time as before, and vanished into the ground as they had done the first time. The two men, David Evans and Evan Lewis, were watching them from a distance of about 400 yards and were more than astonished to see men, as they thought, acting in such a strange and curious manner on the hill. They continued looking for some time but the dancers did not appear again. At last the two men proceeded on their journey till they came to an old man working on the road whom they asked whether he knew anything about the men they had seen dancing in a circle on the hill behind Maestwynog. The old man replied that he had not the least idea, but had heard his grandfather say that the Tylwyth Teg (Fairies) used to dance in his time, at which explanation our two friends smiled.[10]

After two encounters with dancing fairies in west Wales, there follow two experiences involving Isle of Man fairies, all dressed in red. Around 1870, T.C. Kermode, a member of the Manx Parliament, saw them, as he later described.

There is much belief here in the island that there actually are fairies; and I consider such belief based on an actual fact in nature, because of my own strange experience. About forty years ago, one October night, I and another young man were going to a kind of Manx harvest-home at Cronk-a-Voddy. On the Glen Helen road, just at the Beary Farm, as we walked along talking, my friend happened to look across the river (a small brook), and said: 'Oh look, there are the fairies. Did you ever see them?' I looked across the river and saw a circle of supernatural light, which I have now come to regard as the 'astral light' or the light of Nature, as it is called by mystics, and in which spirits become visible. The spot where the light appeared was a flat space surrounded on the sides away from the river by banks formed by low hills; and into this space and the circle of light, from the surrounding sides apparently, I saw come in twos and threes a great crowd of little beings smaller than Tom

41

Thumb and his wife. All of them, who appeared like soldiers, were dressed in red. They moved back and forth amid the circle of light, as they formed into order like troops drilling. I advised getting nearer to them, but my friend said, 'No, I'm going to the party.' Then after we had looked at them a few minutes my friend struck the roadside wall with a stick and shouted, and we lost the vision and the light vanished.[11]

Kermode acknowledged that the experience was some kind of a vision, which they watched from a distance, whereas the next Isle of Man witness quite definitely claimed to have had an interactive encounter with the fairies, one he would have preferred not to have had. The details were collected in 1887, only three years after the events, so are likely to be accurate, and the collector, William Martin, spoke to the witness.

One evening during the summer months of 1884, the driver of the mail-cart from one of the towns in the island started on his round to collect the mail-bags from the surrounding district in the usual manner. He was due at his destination about half-past one o'clock in the morning, but did not arrive until nearly half-past five, when he appeared dreadfully scared and agitated. Being asked to account for his delay, he solemnly related that when about six miles from home he was beset by a troop of fairies, all of whom were particularly well-dressed in red suits and provided with lanterns. They stopped his horse, threw the mail-bags into the road, and danced around them in the well-known manner usual with fairies. The poor postman struggled with them in vain. No sooner did he succeed in replacing a bag than it was again immediately thrown out. This continued until the appearance of daylight, when the fairies apparently thought it was time for them to take their departure, which they eventually did, leaving the postman in a highly nervous and exhausted state. After resting a short time to collect his scattered wits, he succeeded in replacing the mails in his cart, and reached the end of his journey without further adventures. When I made acquaintance with him some little time afterwards, he did not strike me as a person likely to fall victim to his own fertile imagination. As for doubts with respect to his condition at the time, it can only be said that he had left the post office that night in his usual condition of sobriety, and did not appear the worse for drink when he returned. Moreover, his character for sobriety and honesty was of many years' standing.[12]

In most encounters with the Little People, the witness(es) only see the creatures for a short time, and rarely have any interaction with them. A fairy might acknowledge the presence of the human by looking directly at, even smiling at, him or her, but otherwise usually ignores the surprised onlooker. The mailman's experience just described is the exception rather than the rule. Even more exceptional is the following story (so exceptional indeed that it sounds like a 'story' rather than a relation of true events, even though it was presented as the latter). Told by an old man and his wife to Lady Gregory, W.B. Yeats and Miss Pollexfen in the Wicklow Mountains of Ireland some time during the first twenty years of this century, they were speaking of a time many years before, when they were only recently married. Mr Kelleher said: 'It was in the winter and there was snow on the ground, and I saw one of them outside, and I brought him in and put him on the dresser, and he stopped in the house for a while, for about a week.' Mrs Kelleher interrupted, saying it was more like two or three weeks; then her husband continued, saying:

> He was about fifteen inches high. He was very friendly. It is likely he slept on the dresser at night. When the boys at the public-house were full of porter, they used to come to the house to look at him, and they would laugh to see him but I never let them hurt him. . . . One day I saw another of the kind not far from the house, but more like a girl and the clothes greyer than his clothes, that were red. And that evening when I was sitting beside the fire with the Missus I told her about it, and the little lad that was sitting on the dresser called out, 'That's Geoffrey-a-wee that's coming for me,' and he jumped down and went out of the door and I never saw him again. I thought it was a girl I saw, but Geoffrey wouldn't be the name of a girl, would it? He had never spoken before that time. Somehow I think that he liked me better than the Missus. I used to feed him with bread and milk.

He added that he used to feed him with a spoon, putting the spoon to his mouth. Mrs Kelleher added a description of the creature: 'He was fresh-looking at the first, but after a while he got an old look, a sort of wrinkled look. He was wearing a red cap and a little red cloth skirt. He had a little short coat above that; it was checked and trousers under the skirt and long stockings all red.'[13] Red clothing is often described by those who have seen the Little People, green apparently being the next most popular colour. The significance of the popularity of red, if there is any, is not clear, but green is a colour of nature, and may relate to the creatures' role as guardians of nature, a topic to be more fully considered in Chapter 6.

In 1928 Mrs G.M. Herbert described how, as a seven-year-old girl in 1897, she had seen a 'pixy' on Dartmoor in Devon.

> Though I am a grown woman with three sons, I still firmly believe in pixies and in fairies. When a child of seven I saw a pixie, and in recent years I have been 'pisky-led' on Dartmoor.
>
> I saw the pixie under an overhanging boulder closer to Shaugh Bridge (on the southern edge of Dartmoor) in the afternoon. I cannot say more definitely as to the time, but I remember running in to my mother after an afternoon walk and saying I had seen a pixie—and being laughed at. This was in 1897.
>
> It was like a little wizened man about (as far as I can remember) 18 inches or possibly 2 feet high, but I incline to the lesser height. It had a little pointed hat, slightly curved to the front, a doublet, and little short knicker things. My impression is of some contrasting colours, but I cannot remember what colours, though I think they were blue and red. Its face was brown and wrinkled and wizened. I saw it for a moment and it vanished. It was under the boulder when I looked, and then it vanished.[14]

Although the fairies are generally seen in groups, they do also sometimes appear alone, as this one did. In the following account, too, one solitary fairy was seen. The details were told in 1959 by Jeannie Robertson, grand-daughter of the lady who had the experience, some time in the late nineteenth century I would guess. Aged sixteen or seventeen, she was walking one night through a cornfield somewhere in Scotland, intending to take some corn back to her hungry horse, when she noticed a beautifully dressed 'little lady' jumping from stook to stook. After seeing it she felt unable to steal any of the corn; and indeed the fairy's role may have been to guard the cornfield.[15]

Finally, two Irish accounts dating from some time in the nineteenth century, and both involving horses, though the animals in the first tale were fairy horses. The activity of the first group demonstrates the fairies' close affinity to humans, even to enjoying the same kind of sports. A County Clare man told folklorist Lady Gregory:

I saw them myself one night I was going to Ennis with a load of straw. It was when we came to Bunnahow and the moon was shining, and I was on the top of the load of straw, and I saw them in a field. Just like jockeys they were, and riding horses, red clothes and caps they had like a jockey would have, but they were small. They had a screen of bushes put up in the field and some of the horses would jump over it, and more of them would baulk when they'd be put to it. The men that were with me didn't see them, they were walking in the road, but they heard the sound of the horses.[16]

In his book *Ghostland,* ghost-hunter Elliott O'Donnell described an encounter experienced by a relative of his near Ballynanty in County Limerick.

The horse had come to a dead stop, and was standing still, shivering, whilst the roadside was crowded with a number of tiny shadowy figures that were surging round the car trying to drag the unfortunate driver, who was quite frantic with terror, from his seat. Mr. B., however, concluding that what he saw could only be the fairies . . . of whose existence he had hitherto been very skeptical, seized the reins and urged the horse forward. Meanwhile his servant seemed to be still paralysed with fright, and it was not until they were well out of sight that the man found himself once again in possession of his tongue and normal faculties . . . Then he described what had befallen him . . . He was driving along quite all right, till the horse suddenly stopped, and when he looked down to see what was the cause of it, he perceived a crowd of fairies, who rushed at him, and tried to drag him off the car. He said their touch was so cold it benumbed him. But by praying hard he held on. The cause of the attack was apparent.

'It was all because we came on them, sorr, when they were dancing. They won't be disturbed when they are at their revels and enjoying themselves. Had they got me down into the road, maybe I should have lost my sight or my hearing or the use of my limbs, and in any case my soul.'[17]

From this round-up of pre-1900 accounts, certain patterns have begun to emerge, and it will be interesting to see if those same patterns are also evident in the twentieth-century accounts which follow in the next chapter. The predominant one is that the witness is usually alone, usually out at night, usually in a detached frame of mind which is more receptive to supernatural happenings. When two companions witness the events together, perhaps one will become aware of the fairies first, and his signalling of their presence to the other will trigger a parallel vision, or shared hallucination. Although probably rare, such an event is not impossible, especially if the two have entered a similar receptive frame of mind by reason of their present circumstances and close harmony at that time. The experience described by Mr Kermode in the Isle of Man would seem to fit this description.

Another emerging pattern is in the creatures' behaviour. They are often described as dancing, or performing antics of some kind in the open air. This described behaviour recurs so often that such accounts have the ring of truth to my ear; though I am at a loss to explain why the fairies should so much enjoy dancing at night. Perhaps it is simply that they enjoy it and will take every opportunity to relax in this way; perhaps they are performing rituals of some kind, in a similar way to the witches, who for centuries have been in the habit of congregating at lonely places by night. Perhaps witches have on occasion been mistaken for fairies, and vice versa. The descriptions of fairies dancing sometimes recall the folk dancing still performed so enthusiastically throughout Britain today, especially the so-called Morris dancing whose origins are shrouded in mystery. It is not inconceivable that people centuries ago copied fairy dancing, and adapted it over the years to produce the performances we see today. Certainly the fairies seen by the Reverend Dr Williams and his childhood friends in North Wales seem to have had some similarity in their dancing to modern-day folk dancers.

Perhaps if we were all psychic, and not so preoccupied with the trivia of our lives, we would all see fairies very often and so would be able to establish some kind of relationship with them, whereby we could learn who they really are, and what they are about. Some people claim frequent sightings, and even have talked with them, as we shall hear in the next two chapters. Perhaps the fairies are indeed, as one of Lady Gregory's informants suggested, 'all about us as thick as grass'.[18]

# 3

# 'LITTLE FIGURES
# DRESSED IN BROWN'

## Reports from Great Britain and Ireland During the Twentieth Century

❦

Even in our modern age, when science and technology have ostensibly taken over from superstition and irrationality, people still continue to see the Little People—and the Little People are still dancing. Some time before 1945, as dowser J. Foot White wrote:

> Some years ago I was one of a party invited to spend the afternoon on the lovely slopes of Oxeford Hill, in the County of Dorset. The absence of both trees and hedges in this locality enables one to see without obstruction for long distances. I was walking with my companion, who lives in the locality, some little distance from the main party, when to my astonishment I saw a number of what I thought to be very small children, about a score in number, and all dressed in little gaily-coloured short skirts, their legs being bare. Their hands were joined, and all held up, as they merrily danced round in a perfect circle. We stood watching them, when in an instant they all vanished from our sight. My companion told me they were fairies, and they often

came to that particular part to hold their revels. It may be our presence disturbed them.[1]

Also in the early part of the century, and again in Dorset, a Mr Lonsdale saw the Little People dancing in a garden on the Branksome Park estate, Bournemouth.

Suddenly I was conscious of a movement on the edge of the lawn . . . I saw several little figures dressed in brown peering through the bushes . . . in a few seconds a dozen or more small people about two feet in height, in bright clothes and with radiant faces, ran on to the lawn, dancing hither and thither . . . this continued for four or five minutes. They were frightened away by a servant bringing tea.[2]

Nor does bad weather inhibit the Little People. W.E. Thorner described how on the island of Hoy (Orkney Islands), during the Second World War, he saw 'wild men' dancing in a storm. He was battling his way along a windy clifftop at Torness, with misty rain swirling around him, when he saw 'a dozen or more "wild men" dancing about, to and fro . . .'

These creatures were small in stature, but they did not have long noses nor did they appear kindly in demeanour. They possessed round faces, sallow in complexion, with long, dark, bedraggled hair. As they danced about, seeming to throw themselves over the cliff edge, I felt that I was a witness to some ritual dance of a tribe of primitive men. It is difficult to describe in a few words my feelings at this juncture or my bewilderment. The whole sequence could have lasted about three minutes until I was able to leave the cliff edge.[3]

Orkney-woman Bessie Skea also wrote of little men ('trows') seen on various Orkney islands. She saw one herself, and so did her mother-in-law when a girl. Coming home from school, she and her brother saw 'a small man sitting on the dyke in front of the house. He wore a long grey beard and he was nobody either of them had ever seen before. They were terrified, and went around the back of the house to avoid passing him.'[4]

In her *Dictionary of Fairies,* Katharine Briggs comments that there are constant references to the fairies as dancers from the sixteenth century onwards, and she adds that all types of Little People seem to enjoy dancing, from the tiny, beautiful fairies to the ugly dwarfs.[5] The above quotations illustrate this point very clearly, with the beautiful Dorset fairies and the Orkney 'wild men'. However, it is not only dancing that they enjoy—sometimes they seem to be simply playing around—but whatever they are doing, energetic movement is involved. One theory is that a leaping movement, as in dancing and gambolling, produces energy which helps the crops to grow. Ancient crop-growth rituals employed by human beings in past ages included skipping and dancing.[6] Perhaps the dancing fairies are in this way performing their role of encouraging the growth of plants by energizing the land.

Some areas seem to be known as haunts of the Little People, though why they should prefer some places and not others is not immediately obvious. W.M. Thomas recorded how, in the early 1960s, he had been exploring Mynydd Llangynidir near Brecon (Powys) and had got talking to an old farmer, who told him that one day he had allowed two amateur botanists to camp in the nearby field while they were collecting specimens on the mountain. The farmer talked to them whenever he passed by, and one day came upon them arguing. One of the men insisted that he had seen 'hordes of tiny people playing' around the spot where they were hunting for plants. They were tiny men and women, and he described their clothes. His companion did not believe him, for he had seen nothing. When they showed the farmer on the map where the spot was, he translated the Welsh name for them: Fairies Bog.[7]

Dancing and other fairy activity of a similar kind could be taking place throughout Britain even now, but generally unseen by human eyes. Despite the fact that parts of Britain are very densely populated, large areas are not, except by sheep, and the Little People could be happily going about their business in the remote areas, never seen by human beings. Also, of course, if they are largely invisible, only psychic humans are going to see them in any case: if you were not psychic and so not 'tuned in to their wavelength', you might pass close to a group of fairies dancing in a field, but not suspect anything.

If invisibility were not enough, further concealment may be achieved by restricting their forays in the open to the night-time, so that even in populated areas they could dance largely unseen. Most people are asleep at the dead of night; only people such as policemen are abroad. Sometimes they do see strange things: on 10 August 1977 a police constable on early morning patrol saw three figures dancing in a field, who disappeared as he approached. As reported in the *Hull Daily Mail*, PC David Swift first saw 'a bank of fog' on playing fields near Stonebridge Avenue, East

Hull (Humberside), and then three dancing figures he thought must be drunks. As he got nearer, however, they disappeared into thin air. He described one of the figures as 'a man dressed in a sleeveless jerkin, with tight-fitting trousers'; the other two figures were women 'wearing bonnets, shawls and white dresses'. All had an arm raised as if dancing round an invisible maypole.

Ten years later, in September 1987, several different people including policemen experienced strange happenings at Pearoyd Bridge, Stocksbridge, near Sheffield (South Yorkshire), including seeing ghostly figures. Among these was a group of (apparently) young children seen playing around a large electricity pylon just after midnight. The witnesses drove past and stopped close by. Examining the ground round the pylon, they found no footprints in the fresh mud.[8] Children were unlikely to be playing outdoors so late at night, especially children who left no tracks, and the figures seen could easily have been Little People.

Fairies engaged in dancing and gambolling are almost always in groups—sometimes just a few individuals, sometimes large numbers of them—but the Little People do appear singly, and there are numerous reports of them being seen alone. Mr W.S. Jones, for example, was a boy of eight or nine in the late 1920s, living at Llanystumdwy on the Lleyn Peninsula of Gwynedd, North Wales, when he saw a 'little old fellow' in a circle of trees. The boy was collecting firewood and smoking an illicit cigarette in an orchard near the village, when he saw the little man coming out of some bushes. He was about three feet tall, green from the waist down, and wearing a red cap. Nothing was said, and Mr Jones didn't remember the little man leaving, but he was quite sure that he had not imagined the incident: 'It was there, sure enough, that little old fellow.'[9]

Mr E.J.A. Reynolds of London was evacuated to Horsham in Sussex during the war, and in 1948, aged ten, he was staying there during the school summer holidays. He described what he saw one moonlit night when out setting rabbit traps:

> I decided to sit still and watch, being young I thought that the rabbits would come out and I could see them being trapped. As I sat still and waited I suddenly realised that a small hairy man had stepped out from a blackberry bush. He was no more than eighteen inches high and covered in hair. His face was bare but had a leathery look. The nose seemed sharp. I noticed it when it turned away in profile. It definitely had hands. Its arms seemed longer than a human being's. I did not notice his feet. It was definitely substantial, real. It did not notice me, or if it did it did not show it. It turned and disappeared back into the blackberry bush. When I told the couple I was staying with they laughed at me.

A few days later Mr Reynolds saw the creature again when travelling upstairs on a bus. This was during the daytime, and in a different location in Horsham. He saw the little man walking across the lawn in a large garden.[10]

Only a few years later, in June 1952, Mrs C. Woods saw a little old man three or four feet tall on Dartmoor, Devon. He wore a brown smock tied round the waist with a cord. His legs were covered in a brown material, and he wore a flat brown cap or had brown hair. Mrs Woods was walking on

Haytor with her son on a hot summer's day, and she went off alone, climbing up the stony path, where she saw a little man who seemed to be watching her. When she was forty yards away he turned and went behind a boulder. She fetched her son and together they went back to look for the man, but they found nothing: no little man, no hole, nowhere he could have hidden.[11]

Near St Asaph in Denbighshire, North Wales, in 1961, a man walking his dog had an eerie encounter with a little man only three feet tall. The witness tapped his muddy walking stick several times on a metal roadsign, at which the little man appeared beside it, almost as if the tapping had summoned him—or maybe he was displeased with the disturbance made by the tapping, because the witness felt a malevolent air about the creature, who had a very ugly brown face and was dressed all in green. The dog also felt ill-at-ease, for he growled and raised his hackles. The little man suddenly disappeared after only a short while.[12]

Children's author Mary Tredgold saw a tiny man about eighteen inches tall when she was on a bus on the island of Mull, in Scotland.

> My bus drew into a lay-by and I looked idly at an expanse of peat outside the window. This tiny young man was standing beside a clump of tallish heather with his foot on a spade. He was wearing blue dungarees and a very white shirt. He made me think of a leprechaun. He wasn't a vision from the past because he was wearing contemporary dress; and a mirage would have had to come from a long way away because there was a blizzard and he was in his shirt sleeves.

During this century, the largest number of sighting reports has come from Ireland, where the fairy tradition has lingered longest.

Here are four separate accounts from that country of single fairies being seen, starting with a nine-year-old boy who was bathing with friends in the River Moy at Foxford, County Mayo. This sighting took place at the beginning of the century: the boy later graduated at Trinity College, Dublin, and was an army officer in the First World War. On that hot summer's day, the boy was strolling home with a friend, when he saw a little figure dodge behind a big boulder. Going to look, they saw a little man about four feet tall, wearing a collarless black coat buttoned up to his chin, and a cap that covered his hair. He had a flat face and curly brown whiskers across his chin from ear to ear. He stood grinning at them, but this did not calm the boys' fear: they ran away as fast as they could.[13]

Also apparently unconcerned about finding himself close to a human being was the 4½-foot tall fairy seen by a nine-year-old girl living at Cranagh near Borris in County Carlow, who on that memorable November afternoon early this century was fetching her father's cows home. When she got to the field and was waiting for the cows to come through the gate, she saw the little man, moving quickly in front of a cow. The beast tossed its head, whereupon the little man tapped it lightly on the nose with a switch of wood he was carrying. The girl saw that he had on a bright red coat, buttoned up, tight buff trousers, and a close-fitting black cap turned up at the front. As he came past her, almost touching, the fairy looked at her, then stepped across a ditch and disappeared into a grassy bank, walking into the earth as though it was no barrier, but only a door. Which, of course, for him it may have been. There are other reports in existence of the Little People seen apparently walking through 'solid' objects.[14]

Also in County Carlow, a 'wee red man' was seen about thirty-five years later at Dunroe, not far away from Cranagh. John Byrne was moving a large bush with a bulldozer in November 1959 when the three-foot-tall man ran out from underneath it. Three other men who were present also saw him, as he ran across the field and over the fence. Under the bushes the men found a large flagstone which appeared to be covering a hole. They tried to move the stone, but could not shift it, even using gelignite, which failed to explode. Finally the farmer removed his machinery and stopped work on the site.[15]

A few years earlier, in 1951, a little man dressed in black was seen by two girls walking along a country lane in County Wicklow. When they first saw him he was standing in the road close to an old thorn tree, looking at them. They stopped, amazed, and gazed back at him. They later described him as two to three feet tall, youngish looking, and dressed all in black with a black cap. Realizing he must be a fairy, they opened a gate into a field and ran inside, closing the gate behind them before running across the field. Looking back, they couldn't see the little man, but they did notice something strange, about the size and shape of a kitchen clock, on the top bar of the gate. What this might have been is anyone's guess.[16]

The sightings continue to the present day. Quite recently, probably in the early 1990s, fifteen-year-old Brian Collins was on holiday in the Aran Islands off west Donegal. While out walking early one morning he saw two little men fishing from a bank overlooking the sea. They were about 3½ feet tall, dressed in green and with brown boots. One had a grey beard and a flat hat. They were laughing and talking in Irish, and suddenly they jumped over the bank. When Brian went to look for them, they had gone, but they had left a pipe behind. He took it back to the house where he was staying, but while there it disappeared from a locked drawer. When Brian saw the little men again, he tried to photograph them and tape-record their conversation, but nothing came out.[17]

It seems obvious that sightings of the Little People should happen outdoors, as they seem to be creatures of the natural world—and it is true that most first-hand accounts do describe creatures seen in an outdoor environment—but just occasionally, people have seen them indoors. The fairies are usually alone, and the witnesses are usually children, like the six-year-old who awoke in the middle of the night to see a 'little man'. 'He had no decided clothing on but to me he looked grey all over. He had no age in his appearance, but looked more like a gnome. He had in his hands a great big ball of knitting wool, which seemed to unravel as he backed away across the bedroom and down the stairs. I never saw him again.'[18]

The girl who saw a fairy in the fireplace of her home in Wandsworth, London, was of a similar age, more precisely five, and the events took place probably early in the twentieth century. She was practising her dancing steps in the drawing room when she suddenly noticed a little figure sitting in the fireplace. He was just over half her size, dressed in green, and wearing a red 'jelly-bag' hat. As she knelt down and went to lift him up, he smiled, nodded his head, and then suddenly disappeared.[19]

In 1909 a pair of nine-year-old twin boys, playing alone

in Rosehaugh House near Avoch on Scotland's Black Isle, saw two little men as they climbed the main staircase. The men were coming downstairs, and walked straight past the boys, disappearing into the hall below. About eighteen inches tall, they wore 'loose tunics and small pointed hats'. They had grey hair and beards. Some time later, a strange bootlace was found. It was a leather strip with no metal fasteners.[20] Also in Scotland, a troop of fairies was once seen in a house on Iona. A Norwegian visitor to the island first saw them outdoors; they were about twelve inches tall, and she felt they needed spiritual help, so she gave them a blessing. That evening she saw them again, in a house on the island called Grianan, where they appeared in the so-called Faery Room. They had brought a cross made of twigs and bark, and she believed that this showed they had accepted Christianity.[21]

That case is an example of interaction between the Little People and humans. Interaction does not always occur, and if it does, it is usually only slight: the fairy may look at the witness, or even smile, but rarely speaks. The fairy may flee as the witness approaches, but rarely attacks. However there are a few accounts which describe more definite interaction, like these two from Ireland where the fairies spoke—but only to show disapproval of the witnesses. A farmer from the Mournes described his 1951 sighting in these words:

I seen a fairy myself. We were out on a Sunday evening and up on the ditches—you know what young fellows would be—pulling these haws. Well, I was the smallest—I was only a little tot—and these other bigger fellows was up on this thorn tree just after sunset on a Sunday evening and they were breaking branches with their hands and throwing them down to me. Well, this wee man came at the bottom of the tree and he shouts 'Come down out o' that! Come down out o' that! Come down out o' that!'—and I shouts up, 'Holy Murder—there's a fairy!' And they came down and there was no fairy to be seen. He was gone, and they would make me believe it wasn't so, but I seen the man, a wee man there in a big broad hat on him—that's the God in Heaven's truth—I see it to this day yet![22]

This creature clearly objected to the fairy thorn being damaged. The one John Keely spoke to in 1938 was clearly not about to reveal any secrets. Schoolboy Keely was walking along a road in the west of County Limerick when he met the fairy. He ran to tell his friends, who suggested he go back and speak to it. In fact they were probably joking, and did not believe he had seen any such thing. But Keely did go back, and asked the fairy where he came from, to which the little man replied: 'I'm from the mountains and it's all equal to you what my business is.' Next day, two fairies were seen skipping at a crossroads between Ballingarry and Kilfinney; John Keely went up to them and held the hand of one. He walked off with them, and Keely might have found himself a kidnap victim, had not the Little People seen his friends hiding in the bushes, and taken flight. The fairies were described as about two feet tall, with 'hard, hairy faces' and no ears. They were dressed in red, wore knee breeches, and one had a white cape. Despite being chased through the hedges, ditches and marshland, they looked neat and clean.[23]

Sometimes the fairies find themselves rather too close to human beings for comfort and, as in the previous case, they run away. The Limerick creatures, though smaller than their pursuers, nevertheless outpaced them *and* stayed neat and clean, suggesting there was definitely something supernatural about them. The tiny fairy who strayed too close to a woman in Gloucestershire early this century found himself in an awkward dilemma, if we can believe this strange tale.

> I was staying at an old house in Gloucester, and the garden at the back ended in the forest of Birdlip Beeches which covers part of the Cotswold Hills. It was before the days of the 'shingle', and I had washed my hair and was drying it in the sunshine in the forest, out of sight of the house. Suddenly, I felt something tugging at my hair and I turned to look.
>
> A most extraordinary sight met my eyes. He was about nine inches high, and the most dreadfully ugly, dreadfully misshapen, most wrinkled and tiniest mannikin I have ever seen.
>
> He was the colour of dead aspen leaves, sort of yellow brown—with a high, squeaky voice. He was caught in the strands of my hair. He was struggling to escape, and he grumbled and complained all the time, telling me I had no right to be there, troubling honest folk, and, that I might have strangled him with my hair. Finally, he freed himself and disappeared.
>
> I mentioned my experience afterwards to a professor of Bristol University. He was not surprised and told me that Birdlip Beeches was one of the few places left where there were fairies, and no one could go there because of it.[24]

Very different, but in some ways even stranger, are the following events which took place around 1910 on the island of Muck off the Scottish west coast. The Reverend

Alexander Fraser had the tale from an elder in his church, who was also a lobster fisherman. Two boys, aged ten and seven, were looking for driftwood on the seashore one morning, and found a tin which they tried to open by hitting it with a big stone. As they were thus engaged, two tiny boys dressed in green appeared, and asked what they were doing. The fairies spoke in English, but could also speak equally good Gaelic, and they asked the boys about their home and family. The boys saw a tiny boat lying just offshore, with a tiny woman and a rat-sized dog on board. The woman, who was also dressed in green, invited them to come and take tea, but the boys refused. So she gave them some loaves of bread, as big as a walnut, which they ate and enjoyed. Then the fairies left, saying, 'We will not be coming back here any more; but others of our race will be coming.' The boys were found by their sister sitting by the shore and gazing out to sea. When she spoke, the spell was broken, and they immediately became fearful, though before they had felt happy.[25]

Some of the Little People seem to have ghost-like qualities: they walk through solid objects, and they seemingly disappear into thin air. Some reports emphasize these features, and it is then difficult to decide whether the being seen was indeed a fairy or 'merely' a ghost. In Ireland, earlier this century, a teenage girl who had come over from England to help her aunt to look after her children, saw a little man about four feet tall in the house. One of the little girls had seen him standing by her cot, and had called out. As they both stared at him, he vanished. Afterwards the older girl described him as wearing a green hat without a brim, a close-fitting green coat, yellowish waistcoat and cravat, buff knee breeches, grey woollen stockings, and brogues. He had blue eyes, brown hair, and no beard. She saw him again a few weeks later, just before her return to England. Her uncle, Colonel Henry Jordan, told an old man who worked on the estate about the little man, and he recalled having seen him himself many years before, when he was young. He had been smoking his pipe in a field near the big house. He spoke to the little man in English and Irish, but on getting no reply, he cursed him angrily—at which the little man vanished. When he told his tale in the kitchen afterwards, one of the maids claimed to see the figure often.[26]

Very different was the ghostly old hag seen on a footpath near Pittentian Farm, Crieff (Scotland), some time in the 1980s. Four children, a dog, and an adult, Margaret Mills, were walking along the path one Sunday afternoon when they saw an old lady coming towards them. Alarmingly, she had no feet, and began to disappear as they watched, from the legs upwards. They also heard her speak, and she seemed to be saying 'tee-hee'. This was later interpreted as 'taigh shidhe', or fairy house, and Pittentian itself means 'place of the fairies' or 'fairy mound'. If the interpretation of the ghost's words is correct, she demonstrates clearly what has in other cases only been hinted at: a link between two apparently separate types of being, ghosts and fairies.

So far the Little People have not been particularly little, averaging about three to four feet tall; occasionally smaller creatures have been described. Yet some really tiny fairies are seen on occasions, like the one that got caught in the girl's hair. Here are a few more. Marjorie T. Johnson of Nottingham described in 1936 a childhood experience:

The house in which I then lived was surrounded by a beautiful garden and orchard, and was near woods and fields in a lonely part of Nottingham. On this particular morning I was lying in bed enjoying the early morning sunshine which streamed in through the low, open window, when suddenly I felt compelled to sit up in bed and turn my eyes to the empty firegrate. There, on a filmy cobweb on the bars, sat a strange little creature. It seemed quite unafraid and, from the broad grin on its face, appeared to enjoy my observation. At first I just kept still and stared, and it blinked back at me with a blank expression which showed very little intelligence. Soon I had to satisfy my childish curiosity by climbing out of bed. The elf immediately disappeared. I climbed back, and when I turned round it was perched in the same place. This disappearance and reappearance continued until I brushed away the cobweb. I never saw the nature-sprite again.

I should say it was from 4in. to 6in. in height; its ears were very large, and its body was of a glimmering green colour . . .[27]

Violet Tweedale saw a similar creature around 1915, while walking in Devon. She noticed a swaying leaf of wild iris.

Expecting to see a field mouse astride it, I stepped very softly up to it. What was my delight to see a tiny green man. He was about five inches long . . I had a vision of a merry little face and something red in the form of a cap on the head. For a full minute he remained in view, swinging on the leaf. Then he vanished.[28]

This account was published in an article on fairies by Sir Arthur Conan Doyle who, in the 1920s, was intrigued by fairy lore and along with fellow enthusiast Edward L. Gardner took a close interest in the Cottingley fairy photographs (which will be described more fully in Chapter 6). Some of Gardner's correspondents sent him details of their own fairy sightings, of which the following two accounts are just a sample. It is interesting to note that the photographs of the Cottingley fairies show the tiny, diaphanous kind, and these are the ones with which Gardner concerned himself. His writings contain no mention of the larger, more earthy and human-looking ones, although they are in fact more commonly seen. He was wholly concerned with 'nature spirits', and the questions arise: Are these tiny fairies the same as the three- to four-foot tall beings? Do different people see the fairies differently, or are there several distinct categories of Little People? This tricky question will be tackled again in Chapter 6. Meanwhile, here are two first-hand accounts of sightings of tiny fairies. The first is from the Reverend Arnold J. Holmes, of the Isle of Man.

The startling phenomena occurred on my journey from Peel Town at night to St Mark's (where I was Incumbent).

After passing Sir Hall Caine's beautiful residence, Greeba Castle, my horse—a spirited one—suddenly stopped dead, and looking ahead I saw amid the obscure light and misty moonbeams what appeared to be a small army of indistinct figures—very small, clad in gossamer garments. They appeared to be perfectly happy, scampering and tripping along the road, having come from the direction of the beautiful sylvan glen of Greeba and St Trinian's Roofless Church. The legend is that it has ever been the fairies' haunt, and when an attempt has been made on two occasions to put a roof on, the fairies have removed all the work during the night, and for a century no further attempts have been made. It has therefore been left to the 'little people' who claim it as their own.

I watched spellbound, my horse half mad with fear. The little happy army then turned in the direction of Witch's Hill, and mounted a mossy bank; one 'little man' of larger stature than the rest, about fourteen inches high, stood at attention until all had passed him dancing, singing, with happy abandon, across the Valley fields towards St John's Mount.[29]

Mrs Rose of Southend-on-Sea told Gardner:

I think I have always seen fairies. I see them constantly here in the shrubbery by the sea. They congregate under the trees and float around about the trees, and gnomes come around to protect them. The gnomes are like little old men, with little green caps, and their clothes are generally neutral green. The fairies themselves are in light draperies. I have also seen them in the conservatory of my house, floating about among the flowers and plants. The fairies appear to be perpetually playing, excepting when they go to rest on the turf or in a tree, and I once saw a group of gnomes standing on each other's shoulders like gymnasts on the stage. They seem to be living as much as I am. It is not imagination. I have seen the gnomes arranging a sort of moss bed for the fairies, just like a mother-bird putting her chicks to bed. I don't hear any sounds from the gnomes of fairies, but they always look happy, as if they were having a real good time.[30]

The tiny creatures seen among the flowers and plants may be the nature spirits Edward L. Gardner describes in his book *Fairies*:

The life of the nature spirit, nearly the lowest or outermost of all, is active in woodland, meadow and garden, in fact with vegetation everywhere, for its function is to furnish the vital connecting link between the stimulating energy of the sun and the raw material of the form-to-be. The growth of a plant from a seed, which we regard as the 'natural' result of its being placed in a warm and moist soil, could not happen unless nature's builders played their part. Just as music from an organ is not produced by merely bringing wind-pressure and a composer's score together, but needs also the vital link supplied by the organist, so must nature's craftsmen be present, to weave and convert the constituents of the soil into the structure of a plant.

The normal working body of the fairy sprites, used when they are engaged in assisting growth processes, is not of the human nor of any other definite form, and herein lies the explanation of much that has been puzzling concerning fairies and their kin. They have no clear-cut shape and their working bodies can be described only as clouds of colour, rather hazy, somewhat luminous, with a bright spark-like nucleus . . . Although the nature spirit must be regarded as irresponsible, living seemingly a gladsome, joyous and untroubled life, with an eager enjoyment of its work, it occasionally leaves that work and steps out of the plant, as it were, and instantly changes its shape into that of a diminutive human being, not necessarily then visible to ordinary sight but quite near to the range of visibility. Assumed in a flash, it may disappear as quickly.[31]

Two accounts follow from people who were lucky enough to see nature spirits during some of their brief appearances in human form. Cynthia Montefiore of Somerset wrote in 1977:

I was in the garden with my mother at her home . . . when this occurred. Mother wanted to show me the correct way to take cuttings from rose trees. She stood behind the finest rose tree we had with a pair of scissors in her hand, while I stood in front of it. Thus we faced one another with the rose tree between us.

Suddenly Mother put a finger to her lips to indicate silence and then pointed to one of the blooms. With astonishment I saw what she was seeing—a little figure about six inches high, in the perfect shape of a woman and with brilliantly coloured diaphanous wings resembling those of a dragonfly. The figure held a little wand and was pointing it at the heart of a rose. At the tip of the wand there was a little light, like a star. The figure's limbs were a very pale pink and visible through her clothes. She had long silvery hair which resembled an aura. She hovered near the rose for at least two minutes, her wings vibrating rapidly like those of a hummingbird, and then she disappeared.

'You saw that, didn't you?' asked my mother. I nodded and we both went back to the house astonished and enriched by our mutual experience and having forgotten entirely our rose-cutting.

Perhaps the most surprising aspect of the experience was the way in which the little creature we both saw corresponded in practically every detail to the archetypal fairy of folklore and nursery stories. I know now that these descriptions are firmly founded on reality.

This was proved to me once again by a second experience I had when I was alone in the same garden. I was sitting reading under a tree when my eye was caught by a sudden movement in front of me. A little figure, about 18 inches tall, ran from the lawn on my left, across a path and onto another lawn, finally disappearing under a young fir tree. The sturdily built figure seemed to be dressed in a brown one-piece suit. I was not able to see the face because it was turned away from me. I immediately jumped up to investigate the area around the fir tree but there was no longer any sign of this gnome.

Not long after this episode a man friend of the family, who was obliging my mother by digging in the vegetable garden, saw the selfsame gnome and described it to me . . .[32]

A friend of mine also saw a nature spirit in a rose garden. Sylvia Pigeon was cutting roses in her garden in Hampshire when she looked down and saw a figure on the ground. 'It was all sort of greenish, and light—light, airy—and I have a vague recollection of seeing a little sort of face of some kind, but I have no recollection of any limbs, any arms or any legs, but it was round in some way, and moving, very sort of carefully, almost as though it was looking where it was going.' It was about twelve to eighteen inches tall, 'misty and leaflike . . . it really seemed to me to be a spirit of the roses, and there were some draperies about it, but it was more like petals, you know, curved and intertwined, and flowing.' At the time she saw the creature, Mrs Pigeon was thinking about the imminent wedding of her daughter, and the beauty of the roses, and she felt that somehow the appearance of the creature, the wedding and the roses were all linked. She felt 'love and compassion' coming from the creature, that it was 'looking at me with some delight, I would say, some sort of love, friendliness, as though to say yes, how nice it all is, all friends together, I had a feeling of friendliness and love really.'[33]

Other people's accounts suggest that nature spirits do not necessarily have to be tiny, nor do they always appear in human form. In addition, even though they may be performing the sort of tasks expected of nature spirits, they do not necessarily consider themselves to *be* nature spirits! 'Confusing' is a mild way of describing the information that is coming out of the accounts, but it is only fair to let them speak for themselves, and then later to try and sort them out. Some witnesses claim to have spoken with nature spirits. One such was a man who wrote in the magazine *The Ley Hunter* under the name Circumlibra. In 1973 he wrote:

The incident which has prompted this story took place one delightful day when the trees and all things growing were at their best, a day when it was grand to be alive. I climbed the steep hill from the bridge, out of sight of the busy main road which traverses the floor of the valley, [and] passed by the few houses which are Alderwasley [Derbyshire]. Here the lane is less steep and just above the houses it makes a bit of a twist for no apparent reason which has always intrigued me, and so on this occasion I climbed the stile at this point.

I noticed a slight mound on the hillside and went across to investigate. It told me nothing, and being such a delightful day I chose a spot on the grassy bank to relax. Soon I became aware of a presence beside me and turning saw a rather strange looking creature, a dumpy little chap less than four feet from the ground to the tip of his pointed hat, everything the same colour as the grass which grows around. I was neither disturbed nor excited, just curious to know more about him for he was the first of his kind I had met.

I felt there was a reason for his appearance and perhaps he had a message to deliver. He had, and so we carried on a short conversation. Well, we will call it conversing, but more likely it was an exchange of thoughts which were fully understood by each of us. I gathered his work was in breaking down decaying materials into food for plants. We spoke of other things also but what impressed me most was his assertion that he was a man, a human being, when I thought he was an elemental or nature spirit.[34]

Scotsman R. Ogilvie Crombie (Roc) has also communicated with nature spirits, both at the Findhorn garden and in Edinburgh's Royal Botanic Gardens. One day in March 1966 he saw a half animal, half human creature in the botanic garden: it was three feet tall, had cloven hoofs, gave its name as Kurmos, and told Roc that it helped the trees to grow. Roc took Kurmos back to his flat in the city; and later saw it again in the garden, Kurmos coming when Roc called. The two talked together during their meetings, and it later revealed itself to be the god Pan.[35]

One explanation of these strange experiences is that Roc had an affinity with nature's energy and was thus able to perceive and even to communicate with life-forms not visible to most other people. Those people who are lucky enough to see fairies not just once but often are likewise more sensitive than most of us to emanations passing through the invisible curtain which seems to separate us from the world where the Little People live. Scotsman

Struan Robertson had several encounters with the fairies, as he described in 1936.

The first fairy I met was alone upon a hillside near Aberfoyle, where Robert Kirk wrote his *Commonwealth of Fairies*. She was very friendly, beckoned me to follow her, and eventually showed me the most wonderful of sights. [Unfortunately Robertson does not expand on this. It would have been interesting to know exactly what he saw.]

One afternoon in Arran I saw ten fairies playing out and in among gorse bushes and round about the grazing sheep. The sheep were quite undisturbed except that if a fairy went too near one of them it would trot off for a few yards.

Wandering in a wood in Arran one morning I heard the silvery, plangent accents of fairies, and following the sounds I saw quite a clan of them hurrying along a green footpath. They seemed angry about something. Observing me, they chattered loudly, scattered as one sees a flock of excited sparrows scattering, increased their speed and fled.

Tramping near Loch Rannoch I was attracted by tuneful tones coming from clumps of rhododendrons, and advancing cautiously beheld the most beautiful dancing. I was too interested to count the number of fairies, concentrating upon how close I could get. When I was within ten paces of them one sighted me, and alarming the dancers she shepherded them in among the bushes. I shall never forget the glance she gave me as she disappeared, and the gesture, the grace of her exit, I have seen approached only by the incomparable Pavlova herself.[36]

I have saved until last the most intriguing and detailed encounter with the Little People that has occurred in recent

A drawing of the little green men seen in Wollaton Park, made
by a child witness (Fortean Picture Library).

years. The witnesses were a small group of about four children, aged eight to ten, and the events took place in September 1979 in Wollaton Park, Nottingham. They were in
the park grounds at 8:30 p.m., when it was getting dark but
there was still some light to see by. In a swampy area with
trees, fenced off to stop the public from entering, the children saw around sixty little men, about half as tall as themselves. They had long white beards with red tips (though
one boy was positive the beards were black), and wrinkled
faces. They wore caps on their heads, described as being
like old-fashioned nightcaps, Noddy-style, with a bobble on
the end. They also wore blue tops and yellow tights. For

most of the fifteen minutes that the children spent with them, the little men were in little cars. There were thirty cars, with two men in each. (One child said the cars were green and blue, one said they were red, one said red and white; perhaps they were of mixed colours.) The cars didn't have steering wheels, but a round thing with a handle to turn. There was no sound of engines, but they travelled fast, and could jump over obstructions like logs. The little men chased the children, but didn't catch them, although they could have done. The children were sure it was only a game. They said the men did not talk, but laughed a lot and looked friendly—'joyful', one child said. At no time did they touch the children, nor did the children touch them. They were also seen up in the trees, coming out of and returning to holes. The children felt that they could only come out when it was dark. Despite the disbelief of their parents when told about the little men, the children were adamant that they were not making up stories. They also claimed to have seen the Little People before, during the long summer holiday. Their headmaster interviewed and recorded them separately soon after the events and, despite a few discrepancies in their accounts, and differences of emphasis, the children do sound truthful.

Over six years before the Wollaton fairies were reported in the media, I had corresponded with Marina Fry of Cornwall, who wrote to me giving details of her own fairy sighting when she was nearly four years old, around 1940. One night she and her older sisters, all sleeping in one bedroom, awoke to hear a buzzing noise (one sister said 'music and bells'). Looking out of the window they saw a 'little man in a tiny red car driving around in circles'. He was about eighteen inches tall, had a white beard, and a 'red droopy pointed hat'. She stressed that he was 'very happy looking'. He just disappeared after a while. The similarities between this sighting and the Wollaton Park case are striking.[37]

A fairy boat, fairy cars . . . there is also a report of a fairy aeroplane. In 1929 a five-year-old girl and her eight-year-old brother saw a tiny pilot in a tiny plane. They were in the garden of their home in Hertford when they heard the noise of an engine and saw something like a biplane with a wingspan of twelve to fifteen inches swoop down over the garden fence. It landed briefly, almost hitting the dustbin, and then took off again and flew away. The pilot wore a leather flying helmet, and he waved at the children as he took off.[38] Little People travelling in vehicles leads me to think of other aerial craft from which small beings have emerged: the so-called flying saucers or UFOs of modern twentieth-century folklore. Examples from the many case reports, and discussion as to their links with the more traditional Little People and fairies, will follow in Chapter 5, but first we must leave Britain and Ireland and venture further afield, to discover whether the Little People are also seen elsewhere in the world, or are a peculiarly British and Irish phenomenon.

## 4

# DWARFS, MUMMIES AND LITTLE GREEN MEN

## Little People Around the World

~~~

Belief in the existence of fairies and Little People is by no means confined to England, Wales, Scotland and Ireland. The world's folklore is rich in tales of smaller-than-human creatures who sound remarkably like their British and Irish counterparts. For example, in Russia the domovik or domovoj was a household spirit similar to the brownie. Old and grey-haired, he loved fire and lived behind the stove. He was called 'he', 'himself' or 'grandfather'—a name taboo was clearly in operation, as in Britain. Food would be left out for him at night.

In Europe, the Little People were known in practically every country. In France, Breton lore was full of fairies, Brittany being a Celtic land with close links to the Celtic areas of Britain and Ireland. Its fées and corrigans were once as numerous as the gentry of Ireland.[1]

In Scandinavia, elves, dwarfs and trolls were legion; in Germany and Switzerland also, dwarfs lived in the mountains. Further north, in Iceland, there lived a race of hidden people (huldufolk) with similar characteristics to the fairy folk; and present-day belief in them is still strong. In a mid-1970s survey, 55 per cent of 900 people questioned thought their existence possible, probable or certain.

The construction of new roads in Iceland causes problems, because of the disturbance of fairy ground. When, in the early 1980s, a road was being built at Akureyri in the north, labourers were taken ill and machinery failed to work. The new road connecting Reykjavik to the suburb of Kopavogur was diverted around a hill where elves were said to live, and was called Elf Hill Road. Helgi Hallgrimsson, manager of the Museum of Natural History at Akureyri, has collected many eye-witness accounts of fairies. He commented: 'Those who tell me these stories are honest people, and many of them did not believe in such creatures until they saw them themselves'. In the early 1990s, Reykjavik's planning department published a map showing the main dwelling places of 'hidden people, elves, light-elves, gnomes, dwarves'.[2]

The Little People were also to be found in the hotter countries close to and south of the Equator. In the 1930s G.I. Davys wrote of his experience of fairies in India:

In the lower Simla Hills in the neighbourhood of Dharmpur and Kasauli the fairies are supposed to be small people some seven inches high; in the winter they live in the trunks of the pine trees and in the summer they come out and dance on the flowers. They particularly like bridges of flowers such as flowering creepers or branches trained along palings. Some of these fairies are green and some are blue. I cannot say if they possess wings for none of our gardeners had observed this point. Our oldest gardener said he saw them constantly and always referred to them as of the female sex, they were always happy and always good-natured and we never heard of them as doing any harm. They were very fond of sweets, especially sugar; the gardeners regularly put out sugar for them, placing it beside the flowers. The fairies preferred moonlight nights for their dancing. We never saw them personally. They were always supposed to be beneficent and to bring happiness and good fortune, certainly we were very happy indeed in the lower Simla Hills.[3]

Rather different were the Little People living on the forested hill behind Bawyi in Ghana (West Africa). They were known as the Asamanukpai.

They are dwarf-men, with feet turned back to front, 'a little bigger than a monkey', and either black, white, or 'red' . . . The old dwarfs are the biggest and are bearded. They all eat and dance on outcrops of smooth stone which they themselves polish.

The disc-shaped quartz thunderstones, holed through the middle, of unknown origin, which are plentiful in the district, and are said to have fallen from heaven, are also said to have had their holes made by being caught, on falling, between the finger and thumb of an *asamanukpa*.

Hunters obliged to invade the haunts of *asamanukpai* propitiate them with offerings of rum placed against their dancing-stones, and with the pans of clean water in which they like to bathe and splash. If disturbed or angered they stone the offender, lead him into the depths of the forest and there lose him.

Occasionally they lead a man away in order to befriend him, and during his stay with them they teach him all they know, and squeeze into his eyes, ears and mouth the juice of a plant which enables him thereafter to see and hear all men's thoughts, to foresee all events, and also to sing and talk with the *Asamanukpa* people. On returning to his home after a sojourn of a week or two, he . . . becomes a much revered fortune-teller, and giver of advice on medical and other matters.[4]

Folklore of this kind could be based on fact: there may at one time have been a pygmy race living in the area, which kept apart from the normal-sized population. Indeed, pygmy races may account for numerous tales of Little People from different parts of the world, for example the Australian bush, the jungles of Malaysia, several African countries, and also in South and Central America.[5] Pygmies have also been used as an overall explanation of the fairy phenomenon, so I will discuss them more fully in Chapter 6, where all the theories will be considered together.

Tales of Little People are also widespread in American Indian folklore, and these may hint that pygmy races also once lived on the North American continent. In the far north, in the Arctic Ocean coastal community of Cambridge Bay (Victoria Island, Canadian North West Territories), people in the 1,000-strong community are claiming to have seen in recent years a seventy-strong tribe of Little People who are believed to roam the High Arctic. They are said to be about three feet tall, dressed in caribou skins and carrying bows and arrows, and Sean Peterson, recreational director for the area, added that 'people are leaving food out there, hoping if they were out there they'd take it and come into town and try to be friendly. All the elderly people say they're real. They've come across their camp sites and some people see them on the tundra hunting.'[6]

A report like this highlights the difficulty there sometimes is in drawing a dividing line between fact and fiction. Although at first glance it seems likely the local people could have seen a tribe of genuine Little People, it could just as easily be that a lingering folk belief in their existence has been revitalized. By being passed around from one to another the story has gained a spurious air of realism, just as the 'urban legends' (like the dead granny stolen off the car roofrack, or the microwaved pet) do in the Western world. It's not reasonable for an unprejudiced person to dismiss such accounts out of hand—for it is not impossible that a race of diminutive people might still survive in such a sparsely populated area, just as it is not impossible that Bigfoot/Sasquatch and other tall, hairy hominids may today be living in the forests of North America and Siberia, China, etc.—but neither should we embrace such reports uncritically as providing positive evidence of their existence. We must always be aware that rumour often masquerades as fact.

Further south in Canada and the United States, the Little People have survived in both fact and folklore. The factual reports will come later in this chapter: first let's look at some fairy lore.

On the west coast of Nova Scotia's Cape Breton Island there is a community called Inverness by the Scottish settlers. They also called the area the Shean, from the Gaelic word 'Sithean', meaning house of the fairies, and they believed that the Little People could be seen there. People walking at night would see them, but on approaching the hill, the fairies would vanish. This belief is clearly imported from Scotland, and the link with the home country is clear,[7] but where did the American Indians import their fairy lore from? Or did it grow independently in the same way that Celtic fairy lore developed?

The Cherokee Indians of North Carolina, for example, know the Little People as Yunw Tsunsdi, a race of elf-like Indians. They find small footprints in the snow in winter, but it is dangerous to follow them, for by doing so the Cherokee risk being pelted with stones or put under a spell. In his 1901 book *Myths of the Cherokee*, James Mooney told the story of a hunter who found some of these small tracks in deep snow in the mountains. He followed them and came to a cave where Little People were dancing and drumming. They took him in, gave him food to eat and a place to sleep, and he stayed there for sixteen days. His friends, who had been searching for him, thought he must have died. Mooney continued:

> After he was well rested, they had brought him a part of the way home until they came to a small creek about knee deep, when they told him to wade across to reach the main trail on the other side. He waded across and turned to look back, but the Little People were gone, and the creek was a deep river. When he reached home, his legs were frozen, and he lived only a few days.

In 1987, 77-year-old Martha Wachacha related some of the tales she had heard during her youth. She said the Little People were about eighteen inches tall, with perfect proportions and hair that touched their heels. Some wore gold caps, while others went bare-headed. Lois Calonehuskie, a high-school counsellor, said,

Sometimes at night people will wake up and hear footsteps and voices in their houses. When they get up to see who is there, they find nothing. But in the morning, when they go to the kitchen and they find some food missing, they know the Little People have been there. Other times, you'll be standing by a stream and you'll hear children laughing, but, when you go to look, there's no one there. Then you know the Little People have been there.

The Cherokee treat the Little People with respect; they believe them to be the spirits of Indians from long ago, before the time of man.[8]

Throughout these worldwide tales of Little People, there are certain similarities to Celtic fairy lore, and anyone who could undertake a minutely detailed study of the beliefs from all over the world would surely find clues which would lead to a thorough understanding of why such beliefs should have once been so prevalent. Today much of the traditional knowledge is rapidly being lost, but the fact that Little People are still being seen indicates that despite the encroachment of 'civilization', the impulse behind belief in fairies is a strong one. It may also, of course, indicate that the Little People do have an objective existence, albeit not wholly in our world.

Physical remains would surely prove that Little People exist . . . but as one might expect, the situation is not so clear-cut as that. Bodies of 'little people' have been produced from time to time, but identification is inconclusive. Skeletal remains of people whose average height was under five feet were found in Poland: they were thought to indicate that a pygmy race lived in the Breslau/Sobotka region around the first century BC. In Switzerland, remains of people less than five feet tall were also found, and in Eguisheim in Alsace the height of the people whose remains were found ranged from 3ft 11in to just under five feet. So it seems likely that pygmy races have lived in Europe, and not so very long ago.[9]

The buried remains of dwarf humans were also reported found in Victoria, British Columbia (Canada) around 1890. Excavations in mounds at Macaulay's Point and Cadboro Bay revealed iron weapons, utensils, and stone graves containing 'dwarfed bodies doubled up in a sitting posture'. They were thought to be the remains of ancient Indian tribes.[10]

While it is not too extraordinary to conclude that there have been dwarf humans and pygmies in many parts of the world, these small people being not much shorter than the average person today, the conclusion would have been far less believable had the skeletons been only twenty inches tall. No known pygmy races have been as small as this, yet in 1932 two gold prospectors blasting granite rock in the Pedro Mountains, sixty-five miles south-west of Casper, Wyoming, came across a small cave where they found a mummified little man sitting on a tiny ledge (see page 5 of photograph section). He had dark brown, wrinkled skin, a low forehead, flat nose, and a wide mouth with pointed teeth. X-rayed at the American Museum of Natural History, he was found to have a human skeletal structure. The creature was thought by some to be an adult around sixty-five years old, though Dr George Gill, professor of anthropology at the University of Wyoming, who examined the X-rays in 1979 (the mummy itself had by then disappeared), thought it was an infant or foetus which had anencephaly which could explain why its skeleton had adult proportions. If he is correct, then the mystery is explained. However, the Pedro mummy is not the only one to have been found. In addition to other mummies, small skulls have been found, not only in Wyoming but also in Montana's Beartooth Mountains. The suspicion that the Little People of Indian legends were a race of tiny pygmies has not yet been proved wrong.[11] Another mummy, even smaller, was exhibited in San Anselmo in 1979. Said to have been found in Central America around 1920, this one was only 11⅝ inches long. It was mummified in a sitting position, hands and legs crossed, and X-rays showed its bone structure, but again, further study would be needed to show conclusively whether it was an adult, a child or a foetus.[12]

Finds of tiny arrowheads have fuelled speculation that they must have been made and used by an equally small race of people; but archaeologists believe them to have a more conventional history. Tiny arrows are sometimes known as 'bird points', and may have been used for hunting birds, but this is only speculation. Miniature tools of this kind have been found in many parts of the world, including Egypt, Africa, Australia, France, Sicily and India, as well as in various parts of the United States of America. At the end of the nineteenth century, hundreds of flint tools—scrapers, borers, crescent knives—none more than half an inch long and some smaller than a quarter-inch, were found under peat in the Pennines of East Lancashire in England. Their purpose is unknown, though it was suggested that they might have been used in rituals. The other possibility, of course, is that they were made for normal use by a tiny race of people—the Little People.[13]

Whether or not races of very small humans have ever existed within the reality in which we now live, there are plenty of people around the world who claim to have seen them. German researcher Ulrich Magin has discovered reports describing both large hairy 'wildmen' and small 'earth dwarves' with long white beards seen in Germany in the seventeenth century.

> In 1635 Hans Krepel saw a 'moss woman' near Saalfeld and had a chat with her. On August 18, 1644, Kürfurst Johann Georg I caught a female dwarf 2 feet in height near Chemnitz (today, Karl Marx Stadt). An earthwoman tried to steal a human child and replace it with her own near Saalfeld in 1662. A strange and tiny humanoid creature dwelled in a cellar in Lutzen, and was observed several times in 1665. A year before, an earthdwarf was observed near Dresden. Another dwarf was seen in Torgau in March 1669.[14]

More recently in Germany, the fifteenth-century Wildenstein Castle near Heilbronn was said to have its resident 'goblin' in the 1950s. Strange noises had been heard and ghosts seen during the previous century, and even earlier, but it was in February 1955 that the goblin was first seen, at least in recent years. Maximilian, Baron Hofer von Lobenstein was the castle's owner at the time, and it was he who saw the goblin, late one night when he let the dogs out. About ten feet away lit from behind by a small blue flame was a little man with a beard. He hopped around the Baron, but suddenly disappeared. The Baroness saw him too, on a different occasion. It was about noon when she saw a two-foot tall man in a yellow vest and peaked cap, who turned a somersault in one of the castle rooms. Many other strange things happened in the castle in the 1950s, and a thorough investigation by psychic researchers was undertaken.[15]

In Germany and across eastern Europe, spirits who lived in the mines were called kobolds. They were evil and malicious, and when miners heard them knocking, they took it as a sign not to work in that direction. In Hungary in the last century, a miner named Michael Engelbrecht believed that the knockings indicated to him when the spirits would appear in his hut. One such materialization was witnessed by author Mme Kalozdy: lights were seen, around which were the dim outlines of small human figures, described as black and grotesque. They flitted around before disappearing.[16]

A strange story emerged from Transylvania, an area of Romania, in 1883.

Mrs A.G., of Szemerja, coming home last Friday night, found a little red man sitting by the oven: the moon shone on the oven, and the outline of the little man could therefore be distinctly seen: his size was about that of a man's arm; a black cap crowned his head; his dress was red; his face and hands covered with hair. The woman's blood ran cold, as she stood staring at the strange being, who sat immovable in the moonlight: after some time, the creature advanced a few steps and disappeared. That night was spent in prayer; and in the morning she scrubbed the place where the little man had sat with garlic, and fumigated the whole place: but all in vain, for that very night the little red man sat by the oven again. As the woman entered the room, he approached her; when (either actuated by fright or by returning courage) the woman threw the can she held in her hand at the goblin: in one moment, he was on her back, thrust her head down and scratched her forehead. She fainted! and was bedfast for three days; nor did she recover until she had taken some dust from the place where the goblin sat, and drank of it three times, and she herself and the place had been fumigated three times! The little man was seen by other people last Saturday, after he had left the fainting woman, but has since disappeared. No doubt she must have seen some stray monkey, which had got loose by accident: but the good people of Szemerja are fully convinced that it was a goblin, if it was not the devil himself, as it has left traces of its footsteps behind, which are exactly like those of a goose.[17]

Earlier in the nineteenth century, the Reverend Sabine Baring-Gould (1834–1924), the Devon parson who was interested in folklore, curiosities and strange events and wrote many books, himself saw some Little People when he was travelling in Provence (France) during his childhood. Sitting on the box of his father's carriage on a hot summer's day, he saw a horde of dwarfs, little men in peaked caps, who were running among the pebbles of the stony Cran landscape. The dwarfs seemed to be trying to climb up the horses, as well as jumping over tufts of grass and making faces at him. No one else could see them and gradually he saw fewer and fewer, until he could see them no more.[18] It may be that Baring-Gould was for a short while able to see through the curtain which separates our world from that of the Little People.

Sometimes, as has happened in Britain, the Little People are seen riding their own tiny horses. The following account was written by Mrs Hardy, wife of a settler in the Maori districts of New Zealand, around 1920, following publicity given to fairies by Sir Arthur Conan Doyle and Edward L. Gardner.

After reading about what others have seen I am encouraged to tell you of an experience of my own which happened about five years ago. Will you please excuse my mentioning a few domestic details connected with the story? Our home is built on the top of a ridge. The ground was levelled for some distance to allow for sites for the house, buildings, lawns, etc. The ground on either side slopes steeply down, to an orchard on the left, and shrubbery and paddock on the right bounded by the main road. One evening when it was getting dusk I went into the yard to hang the tea-towels on the clothes-line. As I stepped off the verandah, I heard a sound of soft galloping coming from the direction of the orchard. I thought I must be mistaken, and that the sound came from the road, where the Maoris often gallop their horses. I crossed the yard to get the pegs, and heard the galloping coming nearer. I walked to the clothes-line and stood under it with my arms uplifted to peg the towel on the line, when I was aware of the galloping close behind me, and suddenly a little figure, riding a tiny pony, rode right under my uplifted arms. I looked round, to see that I was surrounded by eight or ten tiny figures on tiny ponies like dwarf Shetlands. The little figure who had come so close to me stood out quite clearly in the light that came from the window, but he had his back to it and I could not see his face. The faces of the others were quite brown, also the ponies were brown. If they wore clothes they were close-fitting like a child's jersey suit. They were like tiny dwarfs, or children of about two years old. I was very startled, and called out, 'Goodness, what is this?' I think I must have frightened them, for at the sound of my voice they all rode through the rose trellis across the drive, and down the shrubbery. I heard the soft galloping dying away into the distance, and listened until the sound was gone, then went into the house. My daughter, who has had several psychic experiences, said to me: 'Mother, how white and startled you look! What have you seen? And who were you speaking to just now in the yard?' I said, 'I have seen the fairies ride![19]

More recently, and also in the southern hemisphere, across the sea on the island of Fiji, children were seeing hairy dwarfs near their school. The details were given in a press report published in the *Fiji Times* in 1975.

According to students from Lautoka Methodist Mission School, about 8 mysterious little figures two feet in height and covered with black hair have been seen near the school. The figures, believed to be dwarfs, hastily moved away into nearby bushes when the children began to approach them. As the news spread, scores of neighbours rushed to the scene. The 'dwarfs' could not be found upon further investigation, and seemed to have jumped inside a pit near a bush.

Since the first sighting, dozens of people have gathered near the pit in the hopes of seeing the dwarfs. Some sat there for hours with sticks and torches, in the event the 'little men' might be harmful.

The head teacher of the Methodist School, Mr Narayan, said he threatened the children with punishment for made-up stories, 'but they remain firm in whatever they have said about the mysterious figures'.

Apparently six different students, ranging in age from 10 to 14, actually saw the figures while returning home from school. One student said: 'I saw his white gleaming eyes and black hair. I was frightened.'

'One showed me his teeth and then ran away,' claimed another student.

David, a student who apparently saw eight of the little people, wanted to speak to them but as he approached them, 'the little ones ran away'.

Mr Peniasi Tora, a long-time villager who went to the scene after hearing the news, mentioned that when his fore-fathers first came to Fiji, they saw little men already living here.[20]

As suggested at the end of the item, these could possibly have been the remnants of a race of very small people living on the island—but if they were, surely more sightings of them would have been made? It is interesting that they were thought to have taken refuge inside a pit. This echoes the many accounts telling how the Little People of Britain lived inside the earth.

Rather different, but very puzzling, is a tale which came out of Cuba. Some time during 1930, a navy captain was driving at around midnight on the Güines road towards the city of Havana when his car headlights lit up a short figure standing in the middle of the road. Thinking it was a lost child, the driver stopped and got out of the car. He couldn't see any detail of facial features, presumably because the car lights were not shining on the being at this point, but it was about three feet tall and seemed muscular. He tried to pick it up, but couldn't move it: it was as hard as a rock and seemed to be made of lead. Very surprised and probably frightened, he ran back to his vehicle and left the place.[21]

South America has plenty of folklore tales of dwarf be-ings, often living in subterranean homes, but from time to time modern reports are published too. In Argentina in the

1980s, for example, there was a spate of reports of dwarfs and gnomes being seen by children. In late November 1983 green dwarfs were seen at Villa Montoro, an old house in La Plata city. They were described as being half a metre (twenty inches) tall, and had big heads, wrinkled human-like skin, and green clothing. Footprints were found, and claw-marks on a tree-trunk; the dwarfs were said to live in tunnels under the house and garden, and to come out of a well in the yard. When someone tried to take a photograph of a dwarf, only dark shapes appeared on the film. A boy who fell into mud while fleeing from a group of dwarfs said that they shouted and whined at him, while one threw a brick at him.

Over the next few years little men were also appearing at various other Argentinian locations. Black hairy dwarfs were seen by children at Roque Saenz Pena in May/June 1985, one trying to kidnap a five-year-old boy. In Parana city in December 1986, three children aged eight to eleven were playing on the banks of a stream when eight to ten gnomes appeared as if by magic. They had claws for hands, not much hair, and two small horns! Having no feet, they appeared to levitate above the water. The boys fled, but eight-year-old Claudio fell, his friends abandoning him to his fate. He threw a stone at a gnome carrying something that looked like an arrow—but the stone went right through him. Strange tracks were found (which is odd, if the gnomes had no feet!) after the creatures shrank and disappeared in a cloud of black, sickening smoke.[22]

These reports are representative of many emanating from Argentina. Although the dwarfs are rarely seen along with UFOs, the reports come from areas where UFOs are often seen, and there is reason to believe the two may be linked, a possibility to be explored more fully in Chapter 5.

Some strange reports of dwarfs have also come out of North America during the past hundred years. The continent is already well known for sightings of the giant hairy man-beast known as Bigfoot or Sasquatch; but despite well over 1,000 sightings this century, there is still no solid proof that the creature exists. No carcase has been obtained for scientific study; the only physical evidence is controversial in some way—footprints and photographs that could have been faked, hairs and excreta that could have come from something else. The situation with regard to the Little People is much the same: despite the existence of serious reports from apparently sane people, and some physical evidence which is controversial (the Pedro mummy, for instance), there is no way anyone can *prove* that Little People exist, either as pygmy races or as beings living in another dimension which closely overlaps our world, or as anything else. It's a frustrating situation, most especially for the people who have seen the Little People and told others, but have rarely been believed. Here is a selection of their stories.

William Allen White was a journalist who began as a newspaper reporter in Kansas City in 1891. About to start his new job, he was at home in El Dorado (Kansas) saying goodbye to friends before leaving for the city. Awaking that August night, he heard music. On looking out of the window, he saw under the elm tree a group of Little People only three or four inches tall, dancing along with the music. He looked away and then looked back, but they were still there. He went back to bed, but later when he looked out again there they were. Then, as he watched, they began to fade until they had disappeared. Writing of the experience in his autobiography, he commented, 'When I recall that hour I am so sure that I was awake I think maybe I am still crazy.'[23]

A little man who turned up on a farm near Farmersville (Texas) in May 1913 got a reception he can't have expected. Three boys chopping cotton were alerted by the barking of the dogs, and went to investigate. What they found was a little man about eighteen inches tall, and dark green in colour. He wasn't wearing any clothes, but his body looked like a rubber suit, including a hat that looked like a 'Mexican hat'. As the boys looked on, the dogs jumped on the little man and tore him to pieces. The boys saw that he had human-looking internal organs, and red blood. Afterwards, the dogs avoided the spot where the remains lay rotting in the sun, and they seemed frightened. Next day, when the boys went to the place again, there was nothing to be found, not even a bloodstain.

One of the witnesses was Silbie Latham, and many years later, in 1978, his grandson wrote to the Center for UFO Studies about the occurrence. He said, 'My grandfather has a most solid reputation for truth and honesty but has never told of this because of fear of ridicule . . . He has agreed to tell this only after much prompting and encouragement from me, his history-oriented grandson. He would take a polygraph or be hypnotized or whatever you need. There is no question in my mind that he is telling the truth.' Mr Latham was interviewed by Larry Sessions of the Fort Worth Museum of Science and History, who described him as 'a remarkable man'. Clearly finding the story difficult to believe, Sessions commented, 'There's no doubt he *believes* it happened, but that doesn't mean it *did* happen. Maybe he has an overactive imagination. Or maybe his brothers played a trick on him and he's sort of unconsciously embellished the story over the years.' Mr Latham vigorously rejected Mr Sessions' suggestion that the 'little man' might have been a large frog.[24]

Little People dressed in green, or green in colour, have already been described in this and earlier chapters, and will appear again later, so the green colouring of Silbie Latham's 'little man' was a convincing detail. The derogatory phrase 'Little Green Men', used to describe so-called men from Mars and other aliens, may be much more accurate than most people realize! An inhabitant of Nova Scotia also saw a little man in green, while travelling from Lisbon to Hillsboro (date unknown, but probably early this century). He described his encounter with a 'lepricorn' as follows:

I seen a little fellow about two feet, two inches high. He had a little green coat on him, and a little red skull cap. He had a stick in his hand. So I wondered who he was, and where he came from, and what his name was. Then I remembered about the lepricorn. He is the fairy guardian of all buried treasures and money. If you can look him straight in the face, and look him square in the eye, you'll get a lot of money. But you must never take your eye off him. I followed him. I said to him, 'Take me to a pot of gold.' He had to take me, because I had my eye right on him. So we went on, but just then a noise in the thicket made me withdraw my gaze just for a moment. When I looked again, the lepricorn was gone. So was the money.[25]

Another undated encounter with a 'little green man' comes from Morongo Valley in California. A man driving his truck up Rawson Road was alarmed when a small green man jumped out into the road just ahead of him. He braked and swerved to avoid him, and saw the little man making a face at him as he stopped. Then he heard a clanking noise, and got out to investigate, carrying his hunting knife. He found the little man underneath his radiator, unscrewing a protective plate with his fingers. The driver jumped back into the truck and drove off. As he did so, he could hear the plate banging on the road. He stopped at a friend's house and wired it up. The next day, he went back down the Rawson Road, and found the missing bolts lying in the middle of the road at the place where the little man had unscrewed them.[26]

The little man seen briefly in Oregon some time in the middle of this century didn't do any damage to the vehicle he was close to. He was seen by Ellen Jonerson of Canby (Oregon) as he walked under the running board of a 1937 Dodge car. He didn't bend at all as he passed beneath it, and she said he couldn't have been more than nine inches tall. He was man-like, dark-skinned, and wearing something like rompers and a plaid shirt. She didn't feel threatened by him, and he just seems to have been passing by. He walked into the grass and she never saw him again.[27]

Plaid was also the cloth favoured by a little man seen in Maryland earlier this century. Details of the encounter were related by the witness's niece.

This happened in Snowhill. My Uncle Sewell was dating a girl who lived in Pocomoke. He went to see her so often that the horse knew the route. On this particular evening he had an argument with her about marriage. He did not want to get married but she did. Finally he left and his thoughts were of her. He slowed down to a thinking pace which is very slow. Suddenly out of the woods appeared a little man in a bright yellow tie and a green plaid jacket. He called to the little man, but the little man just smiled. My uncle used the whip to speed up his horse and the little man started running faster. The little man kept the same pace as the horse did and would give a smile every so often. When my uncle got outside of Pocomoke the little man disappeared. My uncle took this as a warning to stay away from that lady. So he did.[28]

Oak Island, on the western side of Nova Scotia's Mahone Bay, has long been famous as the location of treasure believed to be buried there. Despite many attempts, costly in both money, time and labour, nothing valuable has been found. In recent years, tourists visiting the island have reported some strange experiences: one man collided with an invisible wall, while others have seen a dwarf. A couple from New York saw him in September 1973, while they were walking near the place where the man ran into the invisible wall. They described a small beardless man dressed in white, including his large 'seven league' boots. He was accompanied by a larger man dressed in black, with a cloak and three-cornered hat. Two years later, the odd couple were also seen by two local ladies, but in a different part of the island.[29]

Writing in *Fate* magazine in 1978, Jane Frances T. Woodruff described her two sightings of Little People in Massachusetts. The first encounter took place in spring 1974 in Lexington.

My friend Barbara and I were walking to our high school and enjoying the fine weather. We both happened to glance to our left at a small patch of weeds where a figure about 10 inches tall was sitting with his knees drawn up to his chin and showing us his right profile.

'Did you see that?' we exclaimed in unison. Surprisingly enough, we both described the leprechaun the same way: green clothes, a long thin curved golden pipe between his lips and a flopped-over conical cap.

A year later, in Ashby, Mass., my friend Orin and I both saw a group of elfin creatures no more than five inches tall staring curiously at us. In a field of blue wildflowers we saw hundreds of tiny fairies leaping from flower to flower in an exquisite dance.

I would have thought I was imagining such wondrous sights if my friends hadn't been there to describe the same scenes.[30]

Tiny fairies were also seen in September 1993, by Karen Maralee who was on a camping trip to the sacred site of Mount Shasta in California. She was travelling alone, and revelling in quiet contemplation of life and nature, clearly in the relaxed frame of mind which often seems to facilitate a glimpse into another world. At dusk she heard children's voices singing, and in a small clearing in the trees she saw '11 tiny blue fairies, perhaps one foot tall, and seemingly transparent . . . The blue color was electric, seeming to pulsate or flicker . . . The wings were larger than the fairy bodies themselves and appeared to be particularly delicate and lacy.' She watched without daring to breathe, but when she had to breathe out, the noise alerted the fairies who leapt up and disappeared. On the ground Karen found eleven piles of blue dust she calls 'fairy dust' and collected some to take home. She feels it is magical, and has helped the people she has secretly sprinkled with it.[31]

A good number of the sightings described in this book have been made by children, and it seems to me that a larger proportion of the witnesses are children than one would expect, bearing in mind that there are more adults than children (say, ages five to fifteen). If the majority of Little People seen are 'supernatural' rather than physical beings, then it may be that children, being relatively uncontaminated by earthly concerns, have a higher level of psychic awareness than adults, and thus can see things that their elders do not see, or choose to block out.

The next witness was an eight-year-old boy who, in 1976, saw a little man 'not much bigger than a Coke bottle' near Dunn (North Carolina). Tonnlie Barefoot was alone and playing with a toy shovel in a cornfield. Looking up, he saw a little man watching him open-mouthed. He was wearing black boots, blue trousers and a blue shiny top, 'the prettiest little white tie you ever saw', and a black 'German-type hat'; he ran off fast with a squeal like a mouse. Tonnlie found some small footprints, and took his mother to see them. Others saw them too, including the managing editor of the local newspaper, Fred H. Bost, who said that 'The tracks were definitely those of little boots; cleat marks were easily discernible. I failed to count the number in the first set, but there were 14 in the second set, which was clearer than the first. Individual prints were 2¼ inches long and about 1 inch wide at the broadest point.'

Tonnlie's sighting was made on 12 October, and Bost reported that a fortnight later, on 25 October, twenty-year-old Shirley Ann McCrimmon also saw a little man. He was either wearing a thin garment or was naked, and light brown in colour. He wore no hat, but he did wear boots, and she found a small footprint; Fred Bost found another. He commented, 'The strange part about the footprints were that they led nowhere in any of the locations where they were found. The ground was soft in both areas of the corn-field, yet in both cases the footprints ended abruptly. The ground was hard where the footprints were found at the McCrimmon home; yet around the back where the little man was said to have disappeared, there was a garden area with soft earth—but here no footprints could be found.'[32]

Again it was youngsters who saw what has now become known as the 'Dover Demon'. The first sighting was made during the night of 21 April 1977, when seventeen-year-old Bill Bartlett was driving two friends through their wooded home town of Dover (Massachusetts). Bartlett's headlights lit up a strange creature he first thought was a dog or cat. Then he saw its two round glassy lidless eyes, shining bright orange. The eyes were set in a large watermelon-shaped head; the body was thin, as were the arms and legs, and it grasped with its fingers the rocks on top of the wall where it was standing. Bartlett thought it was about 3½ to four feet tall. Neither of the others in the car saw the creature, and at first didn't believe what Bill was telling them. When he got home, he drew what he had seen. Around midnight, John Baxter, aged fifteen, was walking home alone when he too saw the creature, standing by a tree in a wooded gulley. His description was the same as Bartlett's, but he had not heard of Bill's sighting. Twenty-four hours later, Will Taintor (eighteen) and Abby Brabham (fifteen) also saw the Dover Demon, as they drove past it in a car. Experienced investi-gator Loren Coleman interviewed all the witnesses only a few days afterwards, and brought in other researchers, but

Bill Bartlett's first pencil sketch of the 'Dover Demon' he saw in 1977 (Loren Coleman/Fortean Picture Library).

no conventional explanation could be found, nor was there any evidence that the youngsters were hoaxing.[33]

However much the disbelievers try to eliminate reports of inexplicable happenings by means of ridicule, cries of 'Hoax!' and appeals to scientific reason, people still report strange events; indeed they seem to occur as frequently as ever, even in our supposedly rational and scientific world. Little green men hit the headlines in Nome (Alaska) as recently as August 1988 when more than a dozen people saw them on five separate nights. As reported in the local newspaper, the Nome *Nugget,* the sightings started on 24 August:

The first sightings were by some teenagers out for a drive on the Beltz road after work at Flag Stop. It was approximately 2.00 p.m. [*sic,* but probably should be 2 a.m.] They noticed a glow in the rear view mirror as they headed toward Icy View. The strangeness of it prompted them to turn around and head back toward town. As they drew near the figure, a couple of the guys said their first thought was that it was a lady on the road walking toward Nome—because they could see legs and feet walking. Their eyes almost bugged out of their heads when they finally realized the whole body had a greenish luminescence and was walking somewhat off the center of the road.

When they pulled up behind it the little green man was starting running fast. He was between two and three feet high and appeared somewhat transparent sort of like a hologram. Yet as he ran the boys could see that he possessed a well-developed muscular structure like a trained athlete's, broad shoulders and muscular legs. The kids speeded up the car and clocked the little fella at between 40 and 50 mph. They went past it and in the process ran over it, but they felt no bump or thud. He seemed to flatten out.

The kids got scared at that point and floored it into town. They picked up friends and co-workers for reinforcements and also to shore up their shaken nerves. Then they went back out there. The little green man was not where they left him when they ran over him. He was farther up the road toward Martinson's and standing on the side of the road. At that point, the folks who were picked up in town saw him. They stopped and watched. The thing turned from green to silver before their eyes. Every once in a while his feet got darker.

A couple of the boys left the car and started chasing it on foot. The luminescent entity ran off the road, but had not gone far when it turned on the kids and chased them back to their car. It was then that its red eyes were noticed. They only sound it made was a sort of dry whistling hiss. There was not a total agreement among the observers on the sound or lack of, largely due to the fact that by this time most were slightly hysterical. Everybody made it back into the car; no one else wanted to get out. The little man went somewhere and the carload of folks went back to town.

The second night the observation of one little green man was between 2 and 3 a.m. approximately the same place as the previous night. This time they (the same group as the previous night) brought the KNOM station manager and engineer with them—plus some other folks. There were at least three cars out there. One car ran over the little green man. This was observed by the others. It seemed, they said, as if the car ran through him.

The adult witnesses said they couldn't see as much detail on the small figure as the kids could. Indeed, it seemed from the people interviewed that the older a person was the less detail they could see, even though one adult ran his car over the little green man and was as close as the kids to the glowing figure.

By the third night, a regular rendezvous was established. Three little green men were observed between 2–3 a.m. This time one turned silver, one turned black, and one remained green. Even though the color changed on two of them, some people described the retention of a bluish-green aura.

On the fourth night there was a whole bunch of people at 1.00 a.m. on that same stretch of road. Nothing, but at 2.30 a.m. the little green men made their appearance. One silver, one black, and one blue-green.

The fifth night at 2.00 a.m. two little men both green appeared to be dancing on the road.

The sixth night nothing—no green men. Folks waited and watched to no avail.[34]

Janet Ahmasuk who wrote that article also collected details of other local encounters with Little People over the years. One man who was cod fishing was visited by little men as he sat sheltering from the snow in a snow guard he had built. They had 'pack sacks, seal skin pants, mukluks, almost white skin parkys and they sported miniature mustaches on their faces'. The fisherman spoke to them in Eskimo and they answered in Eskimo, saying they had been hunting and fishing like him.[35] Another informant told how she had followed small footprints in the sand and came upon a little man wearing an Eskimo-style squirrel parky and spearing fish. When he raised his spear as if to defend himself, she ran home.[36] Two brothers were grabbed by Inukins (small wild men with bowl haircuts and wearing caribou skins) one summer day in 1938 when fetching water from the Noatak River: they struggled and managed to escape. In the same year their sister chased away two Inukins who were in the act of stealing salmon drying on her rack. The family has had other encounters since.[37]

The strangest tale collected by Janet Ahmasuk was of

three little men who came to an Alaskan village in a silvery-looking disc from the sky, some time in the past (perhaps around 200 years ago). The little men settled in the village and spoke Eskimo. They told the local people that they could not return home because their craft had broken down and could not be repaired.[38] Were the 1988 visitors from the same place, and did they too come to Alaska in a silvery craft, what we would now call a UFO? The strange quality they exhibited, seeming to be transparent and remaining unharmed when run over by cars, suggests that whatever they were, they were not physical beings. Over the last fifty years many strange stories have been put on record describing the landing of non-terrestrial craft and the emergence of non-human beings. A high proportion of these beings are short in stature, and some of them are green in colour. Are these UFO entities a twentieth-century version of the traditional fairies? Some descriptions of the UFO entities and their behaviour, which are the subject of the following chapter, will reveal what features are shared by the two types of creature.

# 5

# UFO ENTITIES AND FAIRIES

## *Are They the Same?*

'And many such have been taken away by the said spirits, for a fortnight or month together, being carried with them in chariots through the air, over hills and dales, rocks and precipices, till at last they have been found lying in some meadow or mountain, bereaved of their senses.'

> *Discourse upon Devils and Spirits,* added to Reginald Scot's *The Discovery of Witchcraft* (third edition 1665)

UFO researchers who have also taken an interest in folklore have noticed some strong similarities between the creatures sometimes seen to emerge from landed UFOs, and the traditional fairies or Little People. The following case, dating back probably to the early nineteenth century and first published over a hundred years ago, demonstrates this link at a time long before 'UFOs as alien craft' were even thought of. The sole witness of the events was a servant, David Williams, who lived at Penrhyndeudraeth Gwynedd, North Wales and who, on the night in question, was walking some distance behind his mistress, carrying home a flitch of bacon. He eventually arrived back three hours after her, and when questioned said he was only three *minutes* later. He took some convincing of his delayed arrival, and explained what had happened to him.

He observed, he said, a brilliant meteor passing through the air, which was followed by a ring or hoop of fire, and within this hoop stood a man and woman of small size, handsomely dressed. With one arm they embraced each other, and with the other they took hold of the hoop, and their feet rested on the concave surface of the ring. When the hoop reached the earth these two beings jumped out of it, and immediately proceeded to make a circle on the ground. As soon as this was done, a large number of men and women instantly appeared, and to the sweetest music that ear ever heard commenced dancing round and round the circle. The sight was so entrancing that the man stayed, as he thought, a few minutes to witness the scene. The ground all around was lit up by a kind of subdued light, and he observed every movement of these beings. By and by the meteor which had at first attracted his attention appeared again, and then the fiery hoop came to view, and when it reached the spot where the dancing was, the lady and gentleman who had arrived in it jumped into the hoop, and disappeared in the same manner in which they had reached the place. Immediately after their departure the Fairies vanished from sight, and the man found himself alone and in darkness, and then he proceeded homewards. In this way he accounted for his delay on the way.[1]

We must remember that David Williams had not heard of UFOs or flying saucers—even the terrestrial aircraft we now take for granted were unknown to him. So his description of a 'hoop of fire' from which the couple emerged is a reasonable way for him to have described the strange sight which we would now call a UFO. Assuming that the 'men and women' who then appeared were fairies living locally and not themselves from the fiery craft, then this case is probably unique in describing an encounter between little people from a UFO and Little People on earth. An air of unreality pervades this report. I'm not suggesting that the events sound unlikely, but that for the witness an other-worldly aura seems to have surrounded them. The apparent inconsequentiality of the events is strong: what is the reason for this meeting of little people and UFO people, and what compelled them to dance together before abruptly parting again? David Williams thought he watched for only a few minutes, but it was in fact three hours: does this mean that he unwittingly strayed into another world—fairyland— where time runs at a different speed?

A much more recent case from Norway has some similarities to David Williams' experience. Again the events lasted for about three hours, and again a large number of Little People was seen. The Hønefoss case dates from 28 October 1985, and the witnesses were children aged seven to twelve, who were out on a cold night watching an eclipse of the moon. They saw an oval light moving towards them from the sky, and one child shone a torch at it. The light shone a bright glow in their direction, and in this strong light they saw a hundred tiny beings less than two feet tall in the road. They all wore box-like structures on their heads, and were different colours including white, brown and black. They ran away on seeing the children, but were seen repeatedly during the next three hours, sometimes apparently playing a game like hide and seek. (Acting inconsequentially, as did the beings David Williams saw.) Parents were alerted, but none came to look. A jogger passing by claimed only to see a cat! (Maybe he was not on the same wavelength as the children.) Footprints were found, but a dog excitedly pawed at them and they were destroyed. A strange story, but it is one that rings true, perhaps by reason of its strangeness.[2]

UFO landing cases where entities have been seen can be divided into two main categories: those where the entities appeared to be human (the so-called 'contactee' cases), and those where the entities were clearly not human. These latter are often four feet or less in height, with a definite non-human appearance, though just as the Little People do not all look alike, so do the small UFO entities vary considerably in appearance. Although this might suggest that the sightings are hoaxed or imaginary, that is not necessarily the case, and I will discuss the significance of this point further in Chapter 6. From the many reports of small UFO entities seen during the last fifty years, I have selected a few cases which together provide a representative picture of these creatures: what they might look like and how they might behave.

On 24 November 1978, Angelo D'Ambros was gathering firewood near his home in Gallio, north-east Italy. After cutting up a branch, he turned—and saw two creatures around three feet tall hanging in the air about eighteen inches above the ground. They had large bald heads, big pointed ears, sunken white eyes, large noses, fleshy lower lips and two long pointed fangs. They had very large hands and feet compared to the rest of the body, with long fingers and nails, and were dressed in tight dark garments. Terrified, D'Ambros asked who they were and what they wanted, but heard from them only mumbling noises. One came to-

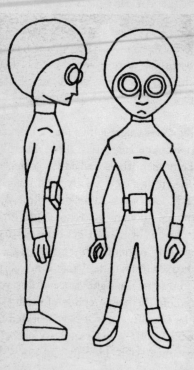

Two depictions of small UFO entities. R.L. Johannis, out paint-
ing near Villa Santina in Italy in August 1947, saw a disc land
and two beings about three feet tall emerge. Their skin was
greenish in colour and, when Johannis waved, one of them shot
a vapour at him which made him fall down. After looking at his
easel, they returned to their craft. This is a very early report of a
UFO sighting with entities, in the year when the modern UFO
era began (Fortean Picture Library).

An artist's impression of the strange events which took place at a remote farmstead near Hopkinsville, Kentucky, in August 1955, when entities three feet tall swarmed around the building and terrified the occupants (Loren Coleman/Fortean Picture Library).

wards him and tried to take his wood-cutting tool, but he held on to it and they struggled for possession. The creature was strong, and D'Ambros felt electric shocks through his hand. When he grabbed a branch, intending to hit the creature, the two entities fled, seemingly aware of his intentions. D'Ambros ran after them along the track, having regained his nerve during the struggle. They went out of sight round a bend, but he ran on, and came to a clearing where he saw a solid metallic disc with a dome, standing on four legs. It was about twelve feet wide and six feet high, and he could see one of the creatures' long arms closing a sort of trapdoor from inside the dome. Instantly the craft took off and silently shot away behind the trees. Later his son-in-law found a circular area with black flattened grass at the landing site.[3]

As in so many reports, the creatures' behaviour is strange with no apparent meaning to it. Why should they want to steal D'Ambros' billhook? The actions of three entities seen in Brazil in 1976 were equally inexplicable. Joao Romeu Klein, a nineteen-year-old farm worker, was walking home on the evening of 3 September when he saw a disc in the sky, about ten feet in diameter. It stopped just ahead of him, about fifteen feet above the road, and a beam of red light shone down from it. Three small beings about three feet tall were slowly descending in the light until they stood in front of him across the road. They spread their arms to stop Klein proceeding, so he threw his big knife used for cutting sugar-cane leaves at them, but it struck an invisible barrier. One of the creatures pointed a 'rod' at him: a blue-white light came from it and touched Klein's leg, after which he fell unconscious, only coming round after being carried home by neighbours. Afterwards his leg was very stiff but he eventually recovered. The entities Klein saw were more human-like than those seen by D'Ambros; they were also heard speaking to each other, but Klein could not understand what they said.[4] Why should they have wished to prevent Klein from walking to his home? They didn't seem to want to communicate with him, and their actions seem inexplicable from a human standpoint.

Italy and Brazil are only two of the many countries where similar inconsequential encounters with small UFO entities have occurred. In France during 1954 a large number of UFOs were seen, many of the witnesses also seeing little entities. On 9 October at Pournoy-la-Chétive, near Metz, for example, three children aged five to twelve saw 'a round, shiny machine' which landed close by.

> Out of it came a kind of man, four feet tall, dressed in a black sack like the cassock M. le Curé wears. His head was hairy, and he had big eyes. He said things to us that we couldn't understand, and we ran away. Pretty soon we stopped and looked back. The machine was going up into the sky very fast.

A man close to the children also saw it take off. Only two hours later, a man driving near Briatexte saw 'two small creatures the size of children of eleven or twelve, who were crossing the road in front of my car. I stopped instantly. But before we had time to get out we saw a red, glowing disc taking off straight up from the meadow next to us, and saw it disappear in the sky a few seconds later.[5]

If all the UFO and entity sightings in France during 1954 really happened as reported, then the alien beings were for some unknown reason devoting a lot of time and effort to

their activities around that country. A thread of purpose-
lessness runs through the whole body of documented UFO
entity activity. Clearly, whatever they are doing is likely to
be incomprehensible to us. Years of study have provided
few clues. Perhaps we should approach the puzzle differently: humans are generally purposeful and so expect that
other beings will be purposeful too, but perhaps they just
do not have such a concept in their world (or worlds—there
may be more than one type of entity involved, from more
than one source).

Small UFO entities have also been seen in Britain. A very
strange case took place on the morning of 4 January 1979 at
Rowley Regis in the West Midlands. Mrs Jean Hingley was at
home, having seen her husband off to work at 6 a.m. Seeing
an orange light by the car port, she went to investigate and
saw a large orange sphere hovering over the garden. Three
small figures shot past her into the house: they were about
3½ feet tall, wore silvery tunics and transparent helmets
'like goldfish bowls' and also had large oval 'wings' seemingly made of thin paper and decorated with glittering dots.
A halo surrounded each figure, and thin streamers hung
down from their shoulders. Their limbs were silvery-green,
and they appeared to have no hands or feet, the limbs ending in tapering points. They spoke and were understood by
Mrs Hingley, but she noticed that they always spoke in
unison. When she asked where they came from, they replied, 'From the sky', and, when she complained about the
light they repeatedly shone at her forehead, told her that
they hadn't come to harm her. They went round the room,
touching things, and it seemed as if they were magnetic, for
the things they touched lifted up. When she saw them looking at bottles of drink left over from Christmas, she asked if

they wanted some, and they said, in unison, 'Water, water, water', so she fetched a tray with glasses of water, plates and mince-pies. They took the water, and later returned the glasses empty, though Mrs Hingley didn't see them drink. When she lit a cigarette, to show them how to smoke, they 'sort of shot back', and she feels they were also afraid of the fire. They then glided out of the house, each taking a mince-pie, returned to their craft which was hovering outside, and took off. Mrs Hingley felt very ill, so she spent the rest of the day lying on the settee and suffered after-effects for some time, including severe headaches. Marks were left on the grass where the craft had been, and various electrical items in the house were damaged, as if they had been affected by a strong magnetic field. The cassette tapes which the creatures had handled were distorted and useless.[6]

However ridiculous Mrs Hingley's experience may sound in its details, the fact remains that something clearly occurred, because the after-effects could not be ignored. It is interesting that although Mrs Hingley could communicate with the creatures, she felt that buttons on their tunics which they pressed before they spoke acted as some kind of translation device. She commented, 'Every word they didn't understand, they did 1-2-3 ever so fast on their chests . . . bleep-bleep, bleep-bleep . . . I said "You'll learn a lot of things from me with that bleep-bleep." And they said "Yes-yes".'

In none of the other cases quoted earlier in this chapter has the witness been able to understand what the UFO entities were saying, and this fact holds true for the majority of cases of this kind. If the witnesses were imagining or making up the events they describe, it is more likely that they would enable their imaginary entities to speak in the same language as themselves, so that they could ask them questions and receive answers. This is exactly what happened in the more dubious contactee cases, where the 'contactee' witness allegedly spoke with UFO entities of human appearance who claimed to come from other planets.

The small UFO entities so far described have all been between three and four feet tall, but sometimes even smaller beings are seen. Early in July 1953, when fourteen-year-old Maximo Munoz Hernaiz was looking after some cows near the village of Villares del Saz in central Spain, he heard a faint whistling noise and turned to find that a machine, which he at first thought was a big balloon, had landed. It was glowing, and Hernaiz estimated it was about four feet high. Still thinking it was a balloon, he walked over to it, but before he could reach it, a door opened and little people started coming out. Three of them jumped down to the ground, and Hernaiz described them as being about two feet tall, with yellow faces and narrow eyes. They were dressed in blue, with flat hats, and a 'metal sheet' on their arms. They approached the boy and spoke to him, but he couldn't understand them. One of them hit him in the face; then they all walked back to their machine. They jumped inside, and the craft took off fast, 'like a rocket'. Hernaiz ran home and told his father, who didn't believe him, but he went out to the place and found footprints, and four holes in the ground.[7]

The fact that, so often, physical traces are found following sightings of landed UFOs with entities, indicates that there is some objective reality to the events reported, and the witness wasn't simply hallucinating or fabricating. It is always possible, of course, that he or she created the confirmatory physical traces by means of psychokinetic (PK)

*Some rural customs were tied up with a belief in fairies. This photograph, taken in 1918 near Moira, County Down, Northern Ireland, shows children hanging up gorse and fern on May Eve to keep the fairies out. (Ulster Folk and Transport Museum)*

*This fairy stone from County Antrim, Northern Ireland, was tied to a cow's horn to stop pixies from stealing the milk. (Warrington Museum and Art Gallery)*

*A fairy thornbush on the grounds of the Ulster Folk and Transport Museum, Holywood, County Down, Northern Ireland (Ulster Folk and Transport Museum)*

*The 'fairy shoe' found on the Beara Peninsula, Ireland, in 1835, compared in size to a thimble (Christopher Somerville)*

*The mummified little man found in the Pedro Mountains, U.S.*
*(John Bonar/Fortean Picture Library)*

*The first photograph of the Cottingley fairies series, taken in England in July 1917 (Brotherton Collection, Leeds University Library)*

*Else Arnhem's photographs of a possible fairy, taken in Germany in the summer of 1927 (Mary Evans Picture Library)*

*Dorothy Inman's fairy photograph, taken shortly after the Cottingley events (Brotherton Collection, Leeds University Library)*

*A tiny entity seemingly clad in knee-length shorts, on the beach at La Jolla, California*

*An enlargement of the same figure (Bill Cox, The Pyramid Guide)*

A photograph of the Little People in Cornwall, England, also showing a member of the group of witches involved in obtaining the picture (S.I.N./ Fortean Picture Library)

*The Ilkley Moor (England) entity, on the path in the center of the photograph (Peter Hough)*

Genii cucullati, *carved on a stone from the Roman fort of Housesteads on Hadrian's Wall, England (Museum of Antiquities of the University and Society of Antiquaries of Newcastle-upon-Tyne)*

This carving of a 'green man' on a sixteenth-century bench end in Crowcombe Church, Somerset, England, may depict an elemental nature spirit. (Fortean Picture Library)

*The Fairy Hill at Aberfoyle, Perth, Scotland, where the Reverend Kirk was captured by the fairies (Fortean Picture Library)*

*Craig-y-Ddinas, South Wales, once believed to be a fairy haunt (Fortean Picture Library)*

*Glastonbury Tor, Somerset, England, where St Collen visited fairy-land (Fortean Picture Library)*

*The village sign at Woolpit, Suffolk, England, depicts the legend of the Green Children. (Fortean Picture Library)*

energy effects (in the same way that some people claim to be able to bend metal without touching it); but this seems to be as unlikely as the landing of alien beings. A third possibility is that an over-eager investigator has mistaken for landing traces something which has a more mundane explanation altogether, such as marks caused by terrestrial machinery like tractors, or human activity. This may happen on occasion, but it is unlikely always to be the explanation. Just think of the tiny footprints found after Tonnlie Barefoot said he had seen a little man in the cornfield (see page 99): these prints showed very clear detail, and are unlikely to have an easy, non-mysterious explanation, unless they were faked—but such fakery would seem to be beyond the capability of a small boy.

The two-foot entities of Villares del Saz were giants when compared with those seen in Malaysia during the 1970s and 1980s. The sightings seem to have begun in 1970 at Bukit Mertajam (State of Penang) where on 19 August six boys saw a blue UFO the size of a soup plate, which landed in bushes near their school. Five entities, three inches tall, came out: four wore blue clothes, the fifth was in yellow. The creatures appeared to be fixing an aerial on a tree branch, and sending out signals. The frightened boys ran away. On the same day, schoolboy K. Wigneswaran saw twenty-five tiny UFOs which landed in bushes near the school. A three-inch entity came out of each, but the school bell rang before the witness could investigate further. He was able to go back to the place on the next day, 20 August, and he saw five three-inch entities come out of a small UFO. The one who was the leader wore a yellow uniform, and also had two projections like horns on his head. When Wigneswaran tried to catch this entity, he was shot at, and

Drawings made by schoolboys in Penang, Malaysia, who in August 1970 saw a tiny UFO with three-inch occupants. The UFO is shown here, and the strange entities (Ahmad Jamaludin/Fortean Picture Library).

fainted. Later a small red dot could be seen on his leg where he had been shot. Another boy was also shot at, with what looked like a small gun. When some boys tried to capture the entities, they just vanished.

Four days later, more horned entities were seen, this time at Rawang in the state of Selangor. Again the UFO landed by a school, and the events were witnessed by children. Between August and November 1970, small UFOs also landed by schools at Alor Star (state of Kedah), Ipoh (Perak), Kampung Pandan (Selangor), and Temerloh (Pahang).[8] Similar events occurred later in the 1970s, including further landings at Bukit Mertajam in 1973 and 1979. At Miti in Sarawak in 1973, six-inch entities wearing white suits were seen. At one time they seemed to be trying to cut fence wire with a powerful beam of light. Holidaymakers also saw similar beings on the beach, six or seven of them altogether, and some may have been females, judging by their long hair. Attempts to capture them were unsuccessful.[9]

In June 1980, tiny entities in white suits were seen at Lumut. These were described by the girl witnesses as two inches tall, very hairy and like monkeys. One was seen which wore a white hat and boots in addition to its white suit. They carried what looked like packs and a long weapon. Two details made the creatures even stranger: their feet did not seem to touch the ground; and one girl saw a big hairy creature which, as she watched it, shrank to just a few inches tall. Clearly these creatures, whatever they were, were not existing totally in our reality. There were claims that they were seen to enter a small UFO which took off, and a UFO was seen over the area three days later.[10]

UFOs were reported again in 1982, and boys near Sarikei

(Sarawak) said they saw tiny beings with large heads near their school. Two days later a UFO as big as a classroom was seen in the same fruit plantation, with tiny entities nearby. At Paka (Terengganu) in October 1985, four-inch entities, including possibly a woman, were seen by children near their school. One child touched an entity, but had to let go its hand when his own suddenly began to itch. Throughout the 1980s, UFOs continued to be seen in Pahang, but I have no further reports of tiny entities being seen.[11] Very tiny entities as reported in Malaysia are very unusual, but the taller ones, three to four feet tall, are common and form a high proportion of the UFO entities seen.

The 1970s onwards have seen a change of emphasis in the activities of UFO entities. Whereas there used to be many reports of landed UFOs with entities seen outside, nowadays few such encounters are reported. Instead, many more people are claiming to have been taken inside UFOs and there subjected to distressing physical examinations by the entities; some even claim that sexual contact with aliens has been forced on them. Argument rages as to whether these so-called abductions actually took place, or happened only in the witnesses' minds.

The abducting entities are often smaller than humans. In the case of PC Alan Godfrey, who may have been abducted while on duty at Todmorden (West Yorkshire) in November 1980, the small figures he saw were the size of five-year-old boys, or about three to 3½ feet tall.[12] Alfred Burtoo, another British abductee who was invited aboard a landed UFO while he was fishing one night in the canal at Aldershot, Hampshire, saw two figures about four feet tall, dressed in pale green.[13]

The entities who kidnapped Liberato Anibal Quintero

from his home near El Banco in Colombia were described as 'less than 1½ metres [4ft 10in] in height. They were white-skinned, with flattened faces, very high cheek-bones, quite thick eyebrows, and round protruding eyes. I don't think they had either eyelids or eyelashes.' There were long-haired women among them. Quintero's case is especially worth describing, for reasons that will soon become clear. He worked as a cowman, and on this fateful evening (probably some time in the early 1970s) he had gone home from work and gone to sleep in a hammock. When he awoke, he felt that something strange was about to happen. He went out-side and walked through the night towards the cowsheds, where he saw a light which seemed to be coming closer. He tried to hide, as he watched 'a big luminous craft, shaped like a hen's egg' coming slowly down, lighting up the ground and giving off a powerful heat. So afraid that he could not move, Quintero saw a number of beings come out of the craft. He tried to escape, but they took hold of him and he lost consciousness. When he came to, he found himself inside a room, and in great pain. His fear turned to amazement as he realized that three naked women were massaging him. One thing led to another, and he spent an exhausting three hours with them. He seems to have moved in and out of consciousness, and eventually found himself lying on the grass with dawn breaking. When he took his colleagues back to the place where the UFO had been, all they found were marks on the ground.[14]

Quintero was one of several men, mainly in South Amer-ica, who have been taken into a UFO apparently for the sole purpose of mating them with alien women. The first known case of this type featured a Brazilian, Antonio Villas Boas, who in 1957 was kidnapped on his farm. The woman with whom he was forced to mate afterwards made signs which have been interpreted as 'I will have your baby out there, on my home planet.'[15]

It has been suggested that the aliens are interested in producing part-human offspring because their own stock is weakening for some reason, and needs an injection of new genes. From some women abductees have also come claims that the aliens have made them pregnant and then later taken away the resulting babies. In addition to the mating of human males with alien females, and taking babies from human females, the UFO people have also reportedly performed gynaecological examinations on a large number of human females, abducted by them apparently for this purpose. Perhaps they have also taken female eggs, fertilized them outside the body, and produced children from them.

So far as I know, no proof exists that male or female humans have genuinely been used for crossbreeding, but the mere suggestion of it takes us right back to the fairies and their penchant for stealing human babies. One explanation why fairies should take human children and leave changelings in their place was given by Professor A.C. Haddon, who wrote that in Ireland, 'dwarf or misshapen children are held to be given to a mother by the fairies in place of a healthy child they have stolen from her to renew the stock of fairies.'[16] This is the very same idea as has been put forward to explain why UFO entities have sometimes shown a sexual interest in humans, and it is intriguing that fairy lore and UFO lore should touch at this point, though it is only one of several features they hold in common.[17]

The fairies, like the UFO entities, also abducted adult humans. However, they were not always successful in their attempts, as in this account from the Isle of Man. The Reverend J.M. Spicer of Malew told Evans Wentz at the beginning of this century:

> The belief in fairies is quite a living thing here yet. For example, old Mrs K—, about a year ago, told me that on one occasion, when her daughter had been in Castletown during the day, she went out to the road at nightfall to see if her daughter was yet in sight, whereupon a whole crowd of fairies suddenly surrounded her, and began taking her off toward South Barrule Mountain; and, she added, 'I couldn't get away from *them* until I had called my son.'[18]

Had this incident been reported more recently, it might have been seen in a UFO context, Mrs K's encounter being with UFO entities.

Fairy lore is full of tales of people being taken away into fairyland, again a popularly believed reason being that the fairies wanted to 'inject the dwindling stock with fresh blood and a human vigour'.[19] As well as being kidnapped, humans might be lured away by offers of fairy food and drink: accepting this put the human in the fairies' power. There are also instances of humans eating food and drink offered to them by UFO entities. Nursing mothers were borrowed to suckle fairy babies; and people with musical talent might be taken to provide the fairies with entertainment. Sometimes people who came across a ring of dancing fairies would join them, and then be unable to leave. When such a person finally stepped out of the circle, or was pulled out by friends, he would be surprised to learn how much time had elapsed while he was dancing. Just one dance (as he thought) could have taken months or even years of human time.

Other similarities between fairy lore and UFO lore include the frequent incomprehensibility of the beings' speech. In the UFO cases given earlier, the entities were not understood by the witnesses unless, as in the case of Mrs Hingley, they 'translated' their words. Other descriptions of UFO entity speech include: 'they said something that sounded like "Dbano da skigyay o dbano" '; 'they spoke with guttural sounds'; 'chattering'; 'shrill sounds similar to a gargle'.[20] Fairy speech was described as 'whistling, clear, not rough' in Scotland by Robert Kirk, writing in the late seventeenth century;[21] while Welsh fairies have been described as talking in a language the witness could not understand, which seemed to be neither Welsh nor English.[22] But sometimes, UFO entities spoke clearly in the language of the witness; and so too did the fairies.

Similarities in appearance have already been noted. Both fairies and UFO entities are often small in size, varying from a few inches to four feet; but there are also human-sized UFO entities, as there are human-sized fairies, and even giant versions of both have been recorded. The frequent use of the colour green is obvious both in UFO lore and fairy lore. The term 'Little Green Man' is used somewhat derisively to describe UFO entities, and most people do not take seriously the possibility that there exist creatures with green skin. Even ufologists, who should know better, have dismissed Little Green Men. Patrick Aimedieu, a French scientist involved in UFO research, is quoted as saying: 'People often talk of "little green men". This is nonsense, because, so far as I know, no eye-witness has ever spoken of little green men.[23] Likewise, K. Gösta Rehn, a Swedish ufologist, said in his book *UFOs Here and Now!:* 'But ufologists have been fighting for twenty-five years, with increasing revulsion, against the pattern of "little green men", repeated intolerably by ignorant opponents of saucers. Perhaps there was a green dwarf in the forties—I have not seen one single case among thousands where the pilot was dressed in green.'

All who dismiss the concept of Little Green Men are certainly wrong to do so, for there are many accounts where eye-witnesses describe UFO entities as having green skin, or green clothing, or both. Interestingly, a number of witnesses were unable to determine whether the green colouring was of skin or clothes, or even whether the entities were clothed at all! A few examples will demonstrate what people claim to have seen.

In August 1956 in Badajoz, Spain, twenty children and ten adults saw a UFO which hovered at a height of ten feet only 150 feet away from them. They ran towards it, gesturing at the two entities they could see inside, who were also gesturing at the witnesses. The craft took off before the ebullient Spaniards got too close, but they saw the head and shoulders of two apparently naked occupants with greenish skin.[24]

The following year a green-clad entity only 2½ or three feet tall was involved in a weird encounter at Everittstown in New Jersey. John Trasco was the main witness. At dusk on 6 November he went out to feed his dog King, and came face to face with a little man dressed in 'a green suit with shiny buttons, with a green hat like a tam, and gloves with a shiny object at the tip of each glove'. He said to Trasco in 'broken language' but obviously in English: 'We are peaceful people. We don't want no trouble. We just want your dog.' As he shouted at the entity to 'Get the hell out of here!', Trasco made a grab at him and got some green powder on his wrist, which later washed off easily; he also found some under his fingernails the next day.[25]

Reports of green skin *and* clothing are rare, but there was one from Brazil in September 1967, when sixteen-year-old Fabio Jose Diniz encountered a landed UFO on the football pitch at Belo Horizonte. Two entities, six feet or more tall, stepped out of the craft and spoke to him in perfect Portuguese. They wore tight-fitting green clothing which covered them from head to toe, and the only skin visible was on the upper part of the face; Diniz described the skin as greenish. Two entities seen at Torrita di Siena in Italy in September 1978 also wore green clothing and had green skin, but they were shorter, only three feet or so tall. Those witnesses who saw beings with green skin described it variously as greenish, earthy green, having a green tone, mossy green, brilliant green, bright green, or simply 'green'.

Little Green Men are not just a phenomenon of the UFO 'heyday' of the 1950s and 1960s, and they have also been reported from countries whence few UFO reports have emerged, that is when compared with the United States. There were sightings of Little Green Men in Poland in 1978: in May, a 71-year-old peasant driving his cart through the woods saw two beings with green faces and wearing tight-fitting black clothing, and in September eight children saw a green-faced being, again in a tight black suit. In August 1981, still in Poland, an artist saw two entities with green faces, standing only six feet away from him so that he was presumably close enough to see them clearly.

There is certainly no doubt that green fairies and green UFO entities have been seen on numerous occasions. However, their visual similarities are matched by their dissimilarities. All manner of physical characteristics and assorted clothing are described by witnesses of both fairies and UFO entities. One explanation for this (apart from the obvious but unlikely one that *all* the witnesses are making up their accounts) is that the creatures are appearing in a human-like form, wearing clothes, because they are consciously taking a form that the human witness will recognize and be comfortable with. In other words, the figure seen is in fact no more than an insubstantial apparition, and the beings can actually appear in whatever form they choose.

Similarly, if the UFO entities are really fairies in modern guise, the craft in which they seemingly travel (called by us flying saucers or UFOs) are only a part of the scenario in which they reveal themselves to humans. When humans see non-human beings, be they 'fairies', 'ghosts' or 'UFO entities', they need to categorize, and to assign an origin, to what they are seeing: it makes them feel in control, even if the category is no more than a label and doesn't add to their understanding of the true nature and source of the being. The people of the twentieth-century Western world have accepted the likely existence of beings on other planets, and are used to space travel. That is why the entities seen usually have a spacecraft lurking somewhere nearby, and sometimes tell humans that they come from planet so-and-so. (For more details of such reports, see an earlier book by myself and husband Colin, *Life Beyond Planet Earth?*[26])

The changing nature of the manifestations is revealed in the following accounts separated by 300 years, yet the essential similarities are still there. In a letter written in 1656, John Lewis of Cardiganshire (Wales) described a then-recent experience of a man he knew:

A man and his family being all in bed, about after midnight, awake in bed, he could perceive a light entring a little room, where he lay, and one after another of some a dozen in the shape of men, and two or three women, with small children in their arms, entring in, and they seemed to dance, and the room to be far lighter and wider than formerly: they did seem to eat bread and cheese all about a kind of a tick upon the ground; they offered him meat, and would smile upon him: he could perceive no voice, but he once calling to God to bless him, he could perceive the whisper of a voice in Welch, bidding him hold his peace, being about four hours thus, he did what he could to wake his wife, and could not; they went out into another room and after some dancing departed, and then he arose; yet being but a very small room he could not find the door, nor the way into bed, until crying out, his wife and family awaked. Being within about two miles of me, I sent for the man, who is an honest poor husbandman, and of good report: and I made him believe I would put him to his oath for the truth of this relation, who was very ready to take it.[27]

This man was visited by the Little People, and maybe he was even taken away by them, for the room seemed to change. Had this experience been recounted by a late-twentieth-century witness, it would surely have been a case of 'bedroom visitants' (UFO entities) and the abduction of the witness into a UFO. If this man had afterwards been hypnotized, as today's suspected abductees usually are, there is no telling what astounding details he might have 'remembered' of his experience.

The 'Little Blue Man' seen in Bedfordshire in 1967 could have been a fairy, except for the technological trappings the child witnesses described. The seven boys, aged ten and eleven, were playing on Studham Common early in the afternoon of 28 January, as they made their way back to school. A flash of lightning and a thunderclap were followed within a few minutes by the first sighting of the entity. Alex Butler saw 'a little blue man with a tall hat and a beard' and immediately alerted his friends. As they ran towards the being, he disappeared 'in a puff of smoke'. The boys searched for him, and soon saw him again, but again he disappeared when they got close. When they saw him the third time, they heard deep voices, strange and babbling. Before they could resolve the mystery and perhaps creep up on him, the teacher's whistle called them back to school. Later, the boys described the little man as about three feet tall, and wearing a tall hat or helmet like a bowler without a brim. Details of the being's appearance were obscured by a greyish-blue glow, but they noticed a black box about six inches square on a broad black belt, and a divided 'beard' which may not have been a beard. The man's arms were short and held close to the body; the legs and feet could not be clearly seen. The boys also said that the 'puff of smoke' was aimed at them, and possibly came from the black box. It was a yellowish-blue mist, and although it cleared quickly, the little man may have hidden in the bushes under cover of the mist, rather than actually disappearing each time.[28]

Changing as the times change, the entities yet stay the same. It is clear even from the few cases briefly outlined in this chapter that there are strong links between fairy lore and UFO lore, and I would go so far as to say that both are manifestations of the same phenomenon.[29]

# 6

# FALLEN ANGELS,
# PAGAN GODS . . .

## Who Are the Little People?

In trying to answer the question 'Who are the Little People', one thing is clear: the answer is neither short nor simple. As has become obvious, the term 'the Little People' covers a wide range of creatures, from tiny, inch-high beings to almost human-sized figures, wearing an assortment of clothing, and doing all manner of (often incomprehensible) things. It would surely tax even the most enthusiastic solver of mysteries to assign one all-embracing solution to this motley crew, yet folklorists (who are the people who have shown a serious interest in the Little People in past years) have tried—and have sometimes succeeded, in their own eyes at least. They have succeeded because they have usually ignored the evidence that didn't fit their chosen explanation; and neither do they usually consider the possibility that their informants have been seeing 'real' creatures.

It is true that the majority of fairy lore told to folklore collectors by country people comprises nothing more than traditional tales, handed down through the generations, with only a handful of informants being able to offer allegedly first-hand accounts of sightings of Little People. In general, folklorists have failed to distinguish between fictional and factual accounts, perhaps believing that as fairies can't really exist, all the stories must therefore be products of the imagination. They may be right in such a belief; but I feel that more credence should be given to those who vehemently claim to have seen an inexplicable phenomenon, whether it be the Loch Ness Monster or a little person only a few inches high. These people may be lying, they may be mistaken—or they may have seen an objectively real 'whatever it is'. And even if only one witness has genuinely seen a tiny being a few inches tall, then there is surely a mystery to be investigated.

Because of the complexity of the Little People, a number of different explanations have been produced over the years, all with some validity but none satisfactorily explaining all the reported sightings. There are clearly different kinds of entity being seen, and each kind may possibly have a different explanation. Therefore I intend to work through them all to try and assess their relevance, all the while bearing in mind Katharine Briggs's wise words: 'On the whole we may say that it is unwise to commit oneself blindfold to any solitary theory of the origins of fairy belief, but that it is most probable that these are all strands in a tightly twisted cord.'[1]

Fantasy ('imagination unrestricted by reality') plays a larger part in many people's lives than we generally realize, and people with fantasy-prone personalities will not only imagine all manner of 'facts' and events, they will believe their imaginings to be true. It seems very probable that such phenomena as UFO abductions will eventually come to be explained as the product of fantasy on the part of most (but perhaps not all . . .) of the alleged abductees. The increase in reported abduction experiences over the last twenty years can easily be explained, not by saying that suddenly the aliens are abducting many more people, but by the growing media publicity given to the abduction experience. Fantasy-prone individuals latch on to the publicized scenarios and weave their own experiences, albeit unconsciously, from the raw material available to them. This explanation is certainly more feasible—and more comfortable—than the realization that alien beings are in control of mankind; though those who argue for the objective reality of UFO abductions will claim that the disbelievers simply cannot cope with that reality. These contrasting arguments point up the difficulty in proving the reality or non-reality of *any* claimed phenomenon, be it UFO abductions or sightings of Little People.[2]

I do believe that some people are prone to fantasize—often without realizing it—and they see things that just aren't there. They may be in an area where Little People are said to have been seen, and if they have been exposed to fairy beliefs earlier in their life, the unconscious mind may activate the data stored in the memory and come up with a fairy image which is seen by the witness as if through his or her eyes, as apparently an objective reality. Rumour can exaggerate such occurrences. For example, in 1964 in Liverpool, rumours spread that 'little men in white hats' were on the bowling green in Jubilee Park, throwing mud and stones at each other. Crowds turned up to see the 'Liverpool leprechauns', and UFOs joined in the fun too, but no one ever seems to have discovered any fire behind the smokescreen of the rumour, which eventually died down.[3]

The process of seeing things that aren't really there may

be helped if the witness has been taking hallucinogenic drugs of any kind. In Ireland there are structures called sweathouses, small stone-built chambers with small doorways which would be heated with a turf fire, and then used by several naked people to induce a perspiration which would cure illnesses. Sometimes water was used to produce steam, as in the Turkish baths, but usually dry heat was preferred. Researcher Anthony Weir, who has made a study of sweathouses, suggested that they might also have had a magical function, and he refers to the Siberian and North American shamans who performed ceremonies inside circular tents which in some ways were similar to the Irish sweathouses. The Siberian shamans employed the red and white spotted fly agaric fungi (*Amanita muscaria*) which affects the mind when ingested; and Weir notes that sweathouses were most often used in the autumn, when 'magic mushrooms' (*Psilocybe semilanceata*) were abundant. Could the users of the sweathouses sometimes have eaten magic mushrooms, as part of the ritual? He concludes:

> Although little mushroom-lore survives in Ireland, unlike Lapland, Siberia and North America, the púcaí (pixies or hobgoblins whose very name derives from Scandinavia) are as much personifications of *Psilocybe semilanceata* with their little pointed caps as of the chthonic feelings of connection which the mushroom induces. Irishmen whom I have talked to—and not old ones either—have claimed to see The Fairies after taking 'magic mushrooms'. It is a pity that no report of sweathouse use has come from an habitué.[4]

Hallucinations can be complex, and collective, as a case from Pennsylvania shows. In August 1963 two men were trapped underground in a coal mine for fourteen days, and during that time David Fellin and Henry Throne experienced some very vivid hallucinations. They saw Pope John, a gold cross, men with lights who came in a vehicle like a chariot and were unreeling wire from a spool, and white marble stairs leading upwards. They both independently saw the same things. Other people appeared at different times, including three men who carried a plaque which bore no names, so Fellin and Throne knew they would get out alive.[5] Compared with this, producing an imaginary fairy would be child's play for the human mind to perform!

Sometimes the mind plays tricks on us by misidentifying what the eye sees. I think we've all had this experience. For my part, I have seen a piece of paper beside the road on a dark night transformed into a dog about to run into the traffic, and a friend of mine regularly sees cows lying across the road at night. 'UFO' witnesses have mistaken the moon for a spacecraft; indeed in many UFO cases it is likely that the witness is seeing an ordinary celestial object like a star or planet and then, alert to the possibility of flying saucers, unconsciously embroiders the sight, seeing windows and perhaps even entities inside those windows. Such cases are widely documented in UFO literature.

Misidentification can also occur in the daytime, especially if the person concerned has faulty eyesight, and it is possible that animals have on occasion been mistaken for Little People. The sighting of a little old man by a French priest near Dijon in 1945 was later explained as having been a marmoset (a type of monkey) which was kept as a mascot by a regiment stationed locally. The priest could not, naturally enough, accept that explanation—yet the fact that a marmoset was kept not far from the spot where the little man was seen, and the sighting only lasted twenty seconds, and the 'little man' was moving fast, all make it very likely that the priest saw a monkey.[6]

Another misidentification may account for the Scandinavian trolls (dwarfs), a possibility suggested by professional mountaineer, author and photographer Hamish Brown:

> Trollval on Rhum [Scotland] is the site of a Manx Shearwater nesting site. They nest in burrows and only come out at night—when there's a wild bedlam. During the day [there are] only little 'voices' occasionally. I'm sure this is the origin of trolls. The name is often allied to Shearwater sites in the Scandinavian countries too. The Vikings were not too happy at night-outings so they'd largely only ever hear the underground voices (very human-sounding sometimes)— and no doubt could only envisage little people. Unless they dug 6 feet down they'd not know birds were in the burrows.[7]

This theory sounds feasible; and it is more than likely that a number of sightings of so-called alien beings have a very down-to-earth explanation. I myself once briefly saw a band of 'aliens' trooping along a country lane, as I passed the end of the lane in a car. I might have wondered to the end of my life if I had really seen aliens, if I had not immediately gone back to the lane-end for another look—and seen a group of walkers exotically clad as protection against the wet and windy weather.

It should not be forgotten of course that some sighting reports might be downright lies: the witness is not *imagining* he or she has seen fairies, he or she knows very well that the report is untrue. Pondering why people would make up reports is not likely to be productive: personal publicity (and perhaps hoped-for financial gain) and a feeling of superiority over those who believe a false story are perhaps the two main reasons. I am sure also that sometimes what began as an outright lie, consciously told, later is believed by its teller to be a true account, especially if the tale has been told many times. Unfortunately it is not always easy to distinguish deliberately untrue reports, or reports based on unconscious fantasizing, from reports of sightings of objectively real events, and we need to bear in mind that some untrue reports are going to be mixed in with the rest. After a while one develops a 'nose' for suspect reports, and I have deliberately omitted some suspicious ones from this book.

In addition to written reports, other evidence for fairies and Little People can be faked. Early in 1989 it was reported in the local press that P.J. O'Hare, who owned a pub in Carlingford, County Louth, saw strange lights on the mountain one dark December morning and went to investigate, accompanied by a friend.

. . . as we reached the mountain gate he too saw the lights. There was no sound; only an eerie silence broken by the bark of a dog coming from the sleeping village below. We walked slowly towards the lights, conscious that darkness was turning to day-break. When we were about 300 yards from them, the lights disappeared. We continued on to where they had been and, to our utter amazement, we found these, what I can only describe as leprechaun clothes. The sovereigns were in the left hand pocket of the trousers. To the left of where the clothes lay, the ground was scorched, and on the scorched ground lay these bones. We gathered them up and headed back down the mountain, and that's it, the whole story.

The finds were later displayed, and Carlingford got lots of publicity. It later transpired that the whole story started as 'a marketing ploy to promote a village', organized by the local tourist association.[8]

This is not a new idea: in Victorian times the village of Beddgelert in North Wales put out a story that caught the imagination of all who heard it, and has since become part of the local folklore. The story concerned the dog Gelert who, in the twelfth century, was mistakenly killed by his master for killing his child, when all the time the dog was protecting the baby from a wolf. The infant, still alive, was only found after the dog had died. 'Gelert's Grave' can still be seen as 'proof' of this tale.[9]

It might be thought that a photograph should be able to provide reliable proof that fairies are real, but sadly few photographs of Little People exist, and those that do are unreliable. Either they are known to be definite hoaxes, or their provenance is unclear or suspect in some way. Considering how many people claim to have seen Little People, it is surprising that there are not more photographs claiming to show them. The most famous ones are of course the Cottingley fairy photographs. These were a series of five photographs, taken between 1917 and 1920 by Elsie Wright and Frances Griffiths, two Yorkshire schoolgirls (aged seventeen and nine respectively in 1917), in the woods by the stream behind Cottingley village near Bradford. They would probably long since have vanished unremarked had they not come to the attention of members of the Theosophical Society. Through them they were seen by

Edward L. Gardner and Sir Arthur Conan Doyle, and thereafter received wide publicity. Many people believed the photographs to be genuine, and the girls did not immediately confess to having faked them. By the time that famous names became involved, it would have been very difficult for the children to own up without causing many people great embarrassment.

So, they kept silent for many decades, until Geoffrey Crawley, editor of *The British Journal of Photography,* embarked on a detailed study of the photographs, the results of which he published in the journal in the early 1980s.[10] Finally Elsie and Frances admitted that they had created a hoax. In view of the fact that these photographs do not show genuine fairies, it is not relevant to discuss them at greater length here, but further details of this fascinating story can be found in Joe Cooper's book *The Case of the Cottingley Fairies.*[11] It is interesting to note, however, that Elsie and Frances claimed to the end that they *had* seen real fairies at Cottingley, and were trying to reproduce what they had seen. The most famous photograph, and the first one taken, is reproduced on page 6 of the photograph section, and two rarely seen photographs of a similar kind are on page 7. Dorothy Inman's photograph on page 8 was taken shortly after the Cottingley events, but she died without revealing her technique.[12]

Sir Arthur Conan Doyle's *The Coming of the Fairies* was published a few years later, and contained intriguing photographs, including those by Else Arnhem (see page 7 of photograph section) taken in Germany in the summer of 1927, which seem to show a figure that is moving (and there may be a second figure to its right). These strange yet inconclusive images are followed by more recent ones dating from the 1970s. A photograph of Gloria Ramsey and her brother-in-law, taken at La Jolla in California, revealed a tiny human figure close to the water's edge (see page 9 of photograph section). Whether anyone present actually saw him is not known. Also during the 1970s, several photographs of Little People have emerged from a group of witches working in Cornwall (see page 10 of photograph section), but precise details of the circumstances in which they were obtained have proved impossible to obtain, and so I can offer no more than an 'open' verdict on them. The same applies to a photograph of a humanoid creature taken on Ilkley Moor (West Yorkshire) on 1 December 1987 by a former police officer (see page 11 of photograph section). He claimed to have heard a humming noise and seen 'a small green creature moving quickly away'; it turned and waved, as if to warn him to keep away, and the witness took a quick photograph before the entity was lost to sight behind a rock outcrop. Continuing along the track, the witness saw a landed UFO, 'like two silver saucers stuck together with a square box with holes sticking out of the top'. He did not photograph the UFO before it shot up into the sky. Later, when hypnotized, the witness described a UFO abduction by green entities. Despite intensive investigation, it has not been possible to determine whether the case is genuine or a complicated hoax.[13] Although the creature was a UFO entity, it was green in colour, and so is certainly relevant in this round-up of fairy photographs, in view of the close links between fairies and UFO entities suggested in Chapter 5. Photographs of UFO entities are as rare as photographs of fairies and photographic evidence for the existence of either is noticeably lacking.

The most recent fairy photograph I know of was taken in

1994 on the Isle of Man, although the photographer did not see the creature at the time. John L. Hall was in Glen Aldyn near Ramsey on Sunday 4 September, walking through the wooded valley with a friend. He experienced 'odd sensations', 'uncanny feelings', and heard 'musical sounds and tinkling voices'—Little People or the rushing stream? He 'sensed movement of something and also being watched by (invisible to me) someone or something'—he felt 'distinctly sick' and decided to turn back. He took photographs of the area which seemed so atmospheric: on one of them, taken while the experience was happening, can be seen what John Hall describes as 'a strange-looking green man on a pedestal' up in the tree leaves. He adds: 'It could be a trick of the light, of course,' and indeed it could—but there's no denying that in enlargements there seems to be a tiny entity among the leaves (unfortunately somewhat clearer in colour than in a black and white reproduction, which is why it is not reproduced in this book).[14]

In Ireland especially, the Little People were often associated with prehistoric sites, mainly forts, and a theory has developed that fairies were a memory, distant or not-so-distant, of a race of small, primitive people who lived in the country before it was occupied by modern men. The latter gradually overwhelmed the former, who retreated back into the remotest countryside before dying out altogether. There is a strong parallel here with present-day reports of Bigfoot or Sasquatch (in North America) and his cousins elsewhere in the world, especially China and the remoter areas of the former USSR (Siberia, Pamir mountains, etc.). It is widely believed among those researchers who take the reports seriously, that there are real creatures out there, that people really have seen tall, hairy, manlike beings, and that they may well represent the last few survivors of an early relative of man, perhaps Gigantopithecus. In the same way, the Little People could have come from another branch of the evolutionary tree: closely related to man, but not exactly the same and not accepted by modern man as a neighbour. Therefore they were gradually pushed back, as modern man's population expanded, until they were existing on the edge, and were nearly pushed over into extinction. Perhaps present-day reports are sightings of a few survivors of this unknown primitive race.

Pygmy tribes have existed worldwide, with reliable information available on those that have been closely studied, and anecdotal evidence being available for many lesser-known tribes, some of which are likely to have become extinct only in comparatively recent times. Examples include: the *agogwe* of Tanzania (Africa) who are four feet tall; the *séhité* of Ivory Coast (Africa) who are reddish hairy dwarfs; the *maricoxi* who were small hairy men living in the Mato Grosso area of Brazil; the *orang pendek* or *sedapa* who was a 'little man' from Malaysia; and the *dwendis* who were long-armed and hairy, living in the Belize forests (Central America). Writing of the Nittavo, the pygmies of Sri Lanka, in 1945, Wilfred Mendis described them as follows:

They were a cruel and savage race of man, rather dark in colour, small in build and living in small communities in Lenama. They built platforms in trees, covered with a thatch of leaves, and in these they lived. They could neither speak the Veddah language, Sinhalese or Tamil, but their language sounded like Telugu.

They would descend in parties from the rocks—men,

women and children—walking like men but covered with shaggy hair, and would eat up the meat spread in the sun to dry, while the Veddahs, who had procured it, hid themselves from fear of attack.

Driven to desperation by the cruelties of these little folk it is said that the Veddahs had rounded them up, driven them into a cave, piled brushwood at its entrance and set fire to it for three days until they were smoked to death. Thus ended the race of Nittavo according to Veddah tradition.[15]

As this description shows, the race of small people is usually feared and disliked by the taller people of the region; the two rarely live in harmony together. The same reactions are repeated in the next quotation, this time describing a tribe of African pygmies.

[the lofty hills of Kwa Ngombe, Kenya] are inhabited, the Embu natives say, by buffalo and a race of little red men, who are very jealous of their mountain rights. Old Salim, the interpreter at Embu, tells with great dramatic effect how he and some natives once climbed to near the top when suddenly an icy cold wind blew and they were pelted with showers of small stones by some unseen adversaries. Happening to look up in a pause in their hasty retreat, he assures me that he saw scores of little red men hurling pebbles and waving defiance from the craggy heights. To this day even the most intrepid honey hunters will not venture into the hills.[16]

Did Salim really see the little red men? Or did the stones have some other origin? They might have been hailstones, or they might have been a poltergeist manifestation, with in both instances the frightened natives seeing the little red men because they expected to see them. When an area becomes peopled with dwarfs, real or imaginary, they tend to be blamed for all negative events; this is human nature all over the world.

There have been ample rumours of pygmies from enough different countries for it to be clear that, at least until recently, they were widespread, but Western anthropologists really only know about a few of the pygmy races in great detail. Some may be closely related to man; others may have more controversial backgrounds. Professor Bernard Heuvelmans suggests that the 'little hairy men' seen widely in Africa could be surviving examples of Australopithecus, who was believed to be about four feet tall, built like a miniature man, and walked upright. They are known to have lived in South Africa around 500,000 years ago. It seems not at all unlikely that these early relations of man (and Gigantopithecus already mentioned, and others) could have survived until recently in unfrequented and unexplored areas of the earth. Whether they still do is doubtful, bearing in mind the way man has systematically ravaged the planet and left few regions untouched.

Supporters of the theory that at least some of the British fairies represent a primitive tribe included Professor A.C. Haddon, who in a lecture in 1894 said:

. . . we may regard many of these fairy sagas as stories told by men of the Iron Age of events which happened to men of the Bronze Age in their conflicts with men of the Neolithic Age, and possibly these, too, handed on traditions of the Paleolithic Age.[17]

Other supporters felt that the brownie, who was so often linked to a household and performed domestic tasks, could have been 'a shaggy aboriginal hanging around the farm',[18] and Elizabeth Andrews saw souterrains or fogous as the chief dwellings of a primitive race. These were underground stone-built tunnels of unknown purpose, surviving still in various parts of Britain and Ireland. She wrote:

> . . . tradition records several small races in Ulster: the Grogachs, who are closely allied to the fairies, and also to the Scotch and English Brownies; the short Danes, whom I am inclined to identify with the Tuatha de Danann; the Pechts, or Picts; and also the small Finns. My belief is that all these, including the fairies, represent primitive races of mankind, and that in the stories of women, children, and men being carried off by the fairies, we have a record of warfare, when stealthy raids were made and captives brought to the dark souterrain.[19]

Andrews also described what she heard about the fort dwellers from the local people:

> The building of the forts and souterrains is ascribed by the country people to the Danes, a race of whom various traditions exist. They are said to have had red hair; sometimes they are spoken of as large men, sometimes as short men. One old woman, who had little belief in fairies, told me that in the old troubled times in Ireland people lived inside the forts; these people were the Danes, and they used to light fires on the top as a signal from one fort to another. I heard from an elderly man of Danes having encamped on his grandmother's farm. Smoke was seen rising from an unfre-

quented spot, and when an uncle went to investigate the matter he found small huts with no doors, only a bundle of sticks laid across the entrance. In one of the huts he saw a pot boiling on the fire, and going forward he began to stir the contents. Immediately a red-haired man and woman rushed in; they appeared angry at the intrusion, and when he went out threw a plate after him.[20]

The Little People may have seemed to 'disappear' into the hills and forts where they dwelt, whereas they may in reality have been retreating through hidden doorways into the underground chambers or souterrains.

Those researchers who supported the theory of a primitive or aboriginal race tried to identify them with peoples mentioned in legends, or to link them with historical peoples like the Picts, but no hard proof has been produced for any of the identifications, nor is there any archaeological evidence that dwarf races ever lived in Britain and Ireland. Also counting against the recognition of the fairies as pygmy races is the fact that known pygmies also have their own fairy traditions. So although the idea of a primitive race of hairy dwarfs skulking about the remoter corners of our lands is an intriguing one, there is no real evidence to support it, and indeed much of the fairy lore, and especially the first-hand accounts I have quoted earlier, do not fit in at all with this theory.[21]

Before Christianity became the accepted religion of Britain, Ireland and the rest of Europe, the people followed cults based on nature-worship. Trees and water were both sacred, and there is evidence to suggest that they were centres of worship way back in time, perhaps even for the earliest people. Because preindustrial man was so reliant on the natural forces for the success of his life, it is understandable that he should have developed ways of encouraging nature to assist him; and so numerous rituals grew up which were performed at a certain time in the annual calendar. Fertility was particularly important, and many rituals which have survived in a degenerate state can be found to have originally had the theme of fertility at their heart.[22]

In nature religions, powerful beings (gods and goddesses) watched over and controlled each aspect of life and the environment. Over the centuries a vast panoply of gods and goddesses grew up, each with their own characters and attributes, and their doings were woven into stories which were passed down the generations and became legends. It seems very likely that at least some of the fairy lore derives from deep-rooted memories of the old gods and goddesses. The fairies' close links with the natural environment, and especially with thorn trees, are pointers to their origins. Those folklorists who have researched into fairy origins have found many other such links.[23]

One example demonstrates the process of change which has occurred. There exist Roman carvings showing figures of hooded men, these beings known as *Genii cucullati*, hooded spirits (see page 12 of photograph section). They might wear short cloaks, with hoods which could indicate invisibility. They are thought to be land spirits; sometimes they are with a female figure who could be a fertility goddess. The hooded men could also symbolize the supernatural world, which is normally unseen by man. They could also be early depictions of what later became brownies, fairy beings who were associated with the domestic scene and helped bring prosperity (i.e. fertility) to the household.[24]

This image of the brownie or dwarf has also survived in the form of the familiar garden gnome.

The priests and priestesses who supervised the pagan cults may also have been turned into fairies. It is not likely that a folk-memory of such people as the Druids could account for the whole range of fairy lore, but it might be one thread in the fabric.[25] Similarly, witchcraft practices could be remembered in fairy tales. Witchcraft itself may have its origins in pre-Christian fertility and nature worship, and witches generally prefer to perform their rites outdoors, close to nature. Their circular rituals are echoed in the many sightings of Little People dancing in rings.

Clearly, pre-Christian religious beliefs and practices have made a strong contribution to the development of fairy life, and these themes can easily be traced in the country people's tales and memories. However, the value of these themes in explaining present-day sightings of Little People is less clearcut; indeed they may be largely irrelevant. There is a possibility nevertheless that, especially in the Celtic lands, 'the old religion' may somehow have imprinted itself on to the natural landscape in such a way that especially sensitive people may at times experience visions incorporating the main elements of the rites that used to be performed there.

The following message came through from Feda, the child control of spiritualist medium Mrs Osborn Leonard in the early years of this century, and sums up neatly the characteristics of the nature spirit category of fairies:

Yes, they do exist. They are the nature spirits and there are many classes of fairies. Clairvoyance is needed to see them.

They belong to another vibration. They don't have quite the same soul as we do. But they have spirits. All forms of life are used again. Nature spirits don't die like us. Some are created out of earth or fire or friction. They are all activity and movement.[26]

Nature spirits represent the life-force of the trees, plants and flowers, and are usually depicted as tiny, gauzy-winged creatures. They are the 'fairies' that most people understand by that word, and have unfortunately become sentimentalized. In reality they are more at home in the garden than on the chocolate box: the use of the fairy as decoration on top of the Christmas tree could be seen as an acknowledgement of her role as nature spirit. All vegetation was peopled with these elementary spirits, who were vital to proper growth and fruitfulness, but the link between nature spirits and the other fairies is by no means straightforward. As Lewis Spence succinctly put it: 'all nature spirits are not the same as fairies; nor are all fairies nature spirits.'[27]

One of the most interesting pointers to fairies being nature spirits is the colour green, which is the colour of plant life. Many instances of green beings will be found among the first-hand accounts quoted earlier, not forgetting the Little Green Men of UFO lore. Two further examples demonstrate the close link these tiny beings have with the plants they live among.

My only sight of a fairy was in a large wood in West Sussex . . . He was a little creature about half a foot high, dressed in leaves.[28]

I was a child of six or seven years, and then, as now, passionately fond of all flowers, which always seem to be living creatures. I was seated in the middle of a road in some cornfields, playing with a group of poppies, and never shall I forget my utter astonishment at seeing a funny little man playing hide-and-seek amongst these flowers to amuse me, as I thought. He was quick as a dart. I watched him for quite a long time, then he disappeared. He seemed a merry little fellow, but I cannot ever remember his face. In colour he was sage-green, his limbs were round and had the appearance of geranium stalks. He did not seem to be clothed, and was about three inches high, and slender. I often looked for him again, but without success.[29]

The idea of elemental spirits living in the foliage has been perpetuated in numerous ways, including the carvings found in churches depicting 'green men': masculine faces with greenery sprouting from them (see page 13 of photograph section). These can sometimes look devilish and frightening, reminding us that the nature spirit is not necessarily pretty and friendly. The folklore custom of 'Jack in the Green' may also embody the belief in living nature. A man would be covered by a wicker framework, into which would be woven green branches, leaves and flowers, and in this costume he would take part in May processions, to celebrate the rebirth of nature at springtime.

Another theory has it that fairies are fallen angels, lost souls or spirits of the dead.

'What are the fairies?' Padraic Colum asked a blind man whom he met on a West of Ireland road.
His face filled with an intensity of conviction.

'The fairies,' he said. 'I will tell you who the fairies are. God moved from His seat, and when He turned round Lucifer was in it. Then Hell was made in a minute. God moved His hand and swept away thousands of angels. And it was in His mind to sweep many thousands more. "O God Almighty, stop!" said Angel Gabriel. "Heaven will be swept clean out." "I'll stop," said God Almighty; "them that are in Heaven, let them remain in Heaven; them that are in Hell, let them remain in Hell; and them that are between Heaven and Hell, let them remain in the air." And the Angels that remained between Heaven and Hell are the Fairies.'[30]

Associating the fairies with the dead embraces several separate yet closely linked ideas, also spanning the pre-Christian and Christian religions. Seeing fairies as fallen angels is obviously a Christian concept; seeing them as the dead is likely to be pre-Christian in origin. The fallen angels were seen as devilish in nature: they were cast out of Heaven along with Lucifer their leader, and condemned to live in the hills and rocks. Devout Christians frowned on the fairies, thinking them evil. Referring to the legalization of certain games and to holidays in Wales, Edmund Jones wrote in 1779:

All Hell rejoiced in it, for there was a dreadful harvest of souls prepared for it. Now did the Fairies frisk and dance and sing their hellish music, for the darkness of ignorance and vice in which they delighted returned again and feasts of sin were made for them.[31]

Katharine Briggs also demonstrated how fairies and the Devil were linked:

The popular traits of the Devil, the horns and cloven hoof and shaggy hide, do not spring from Christian theology, but belong to folk gods or nature spirits. The early Christian missionaries, who had to deal with vast numbers of converts, adopted two methods with the beliefs and practices which they could not quite abolish. All that they felt capable of good they sanctified, building churches where temples had been, placing saints' days upon ancient heathen festivals and occasionally identifying gods with saints. All the gods that they felt incapable of sanctification they denounced as devils or demons, and they did this increasingly as the church gained strength, and perhaps as they found the heathen practices incompatible for Christianity. By this policy the Devil acquired many of the characteristics of the heathen gods and nature spirits.[32]

The link between devils and fairies was personified in the form of Robin Goodfellow (another name for Puck), whose cloven hoofs show him to have had the attributes of a devil. The frontispiece illustration to the seventeenth-century pamphlet *Robin Goodfellow, His Mad Pranks and Merry Jests* shows him with dancing witches . . . or are they fairies? Folklorist Alfred Nutt linked Robin to ancient deities, and he has also been seen as identical to Robin Hood, who may himself originally have been a god of vegetation. The 'green men' and 'Jack-in-the-Green' are again part of this same complex tapestry, being other manifestations of the deities of the woodland.[33]

In addition to being seen as fallen angels, the fairies were sometimes linked directly with the dead. In Ireland, people often believed that those who died had been taken by the Little People, therefore allowing the possibility that they might return or be retrievable. This belief is clearly seen in the story told of the Reverend Robert Kirk, who lived during the second half of the seventeenth century. In addition to his work as a priest, he was a folklorist and collected information on fairy beliefs from the Highlanders around Aberfoyle where he was born and lived. He published his material in *The Secret Common-Wealth of Elves, Fauns and Fairies* (the manuscript of which was produced in 1691, but first published 1815).[34] Kirk is said to have died on the Fairy Hill near his manse at Aberfoyle in 1692 (see page 14 of photograph section), and according to the tradition which grew up afterwards, he appeared to a relative and gave him a message, saying he was not dead but a captive in fairyland. He said he would appear at the christening of his posthumous child, and his cousin was to throw a knife over the apparition; this would break the spell, because iron has physical power against fairies, and Kirk would then be able to return to the world. He appeared at the christening as promised, but in his amazement the cousin forgot to throw the knife and Kirk disappeared, never to be seen again.[35]

An Irish story told to Lady Gregory parallels this account of the failed rescue attempt. A man's wife died leaving a young child. One night she returned to suckle it, but her husband kept silent on seeing her. On the second night when she came, he spoke to her: 'Why have you got no boots on?' She replied that they contained iron nails. (As noted in the Kirk story, iron was believed to have the power to repel fairies, and knives and iron crosses were used to protect against witchcraft and evil magic. Open scissors, in the shape of a cross, were hung over a child's cradle to protect it from fairy abduction.[36]) So he took out the nails for her. On the third night when she came she was still barefoot, and told him he had left a bit of iron between upper and lower sole. She then told him how he could retrieve her. 'Come tomorrow night to the gap up there beyond the hill, and you'll see the riders going through, and the one you'll see on the last horse will be me. And bring with you some fowl droppings and urine, and throw them at me as I pass, and you'll get me again.' He went to the place, and saw her riding past, but his courage failed, and he never saw her again.[37]

The Little People were also themselves sometimes identified with spirits of the dead, not just as beings who held the dead captive. Prehistoric burial mounds were their homes, a clear link with the dead. The fairies were perhaps thought to be small because the human soul was likewise small: in a bas-relief in an Egyptian temple, showing a queen making offerings of perfume to the gods, her *Ka* (soul) stands behind her, in the form of a little creature barely reaching her waist; and on Greek vases the human soul is seen leaving the body through the mouth and takes the form of a pygmy. In other cultures, too, the soul was depicted as a small human figure, often winged. Is it merely coincidence that this is how the fairy has been portrayed in relatively recent times? This association, in addition to folk beliefs linking the fairies with the dead, demonstrates clearly that at least some fairy lore grew out of people's conjectures about, or direct experience of, the afterlife. Sometimes fairies were half-and-half, neither one thing nor the other: 'living beings halfway between something material and spiritual, who were rarely seen'.[38]

Lewis Spence was a strong supporter of the theory that belief in the fairies represented a cult of the dead, and his book *British Fairy Origins* contains all his arguments,[39] some of which I have already outlined here. His ideas are persuasive, but again the theory cannot account for every aspect of fairy lore, and especially people's direct experiences of the Little People. The fairies as the dead form an important pattern in the tapestry, but not the whole design.

Earlier in this chapter I touched on the role of imagination in the creation of sightings of the Little People. People like C.G. Jung, who have studied the depths of the human mind, have found 'little people' appearing in various guises and performing important functions for the wellbeing of humankind. It is possible that these inner dwarfs and fairies have sometimes become externalized and 'seen' in the outer world. They may be archetypes, or symbols from the collective unconscious, and many traditional fairy tales have been interpreted in this way. They embody themes which are important to people's deep-seated needs, like the struggle to understand one's true self, the meaning of life, the fight between good and evil, the cycle of birth and death, and other eternal truths.[40] Jung studied and interpreted people's dreams, and dwarfs in particular sometimes appeared in them. Jung saw the dwarfs as:

> . . . kinsmen of the unconscious, they protect navigation, i.e., the venture into darkness and uncertainty. In the form of the Dactyls they are also the gods of invention, small and apparently insignificant like the impulses of the unconscious but endowed with the same mighty power.[41]

Jung also referred to the dwarf as the 'guardian of the threshold of the unconscious'.

Psychoanalyst Dr Nandor Fodor, on the other hand, developed a theory which centred on the female womb: he saw the 'fairy mound or fairy ring' as a representation of 'the pregnant uterus'.

He who is teleported by the diminutive creatures living in the underground kingdom, is reduced to their size, which is anywhere within the size of the fetus. The enduring feasting, dancing and merry-making in which he joins is also descriptive of the life of the unborn, for whom everything is provided bountifully and without effort on its part. Time does not exist in the womb. It is a postnatal concept. The unborn, at the very best, could feel the rate of its own growth as a form of biological time. Hence, the supernatural lapse of time in Fairy Land is a fetal characteristic, and the motive for fairy fantasies is a psychological one: projection of strength unto the weak (the Little People) whom, in our inadequacy, we wish to dominate, and use thereafter as substitutes for the fulfilment of unattainable dreams of power.[42]

Can the tapestry of fairy lore encompass two so disparate theories: that of the world of the dead and the world of the not-yet-born? It would seem that it can: all the theories in this chapter, however dissimilar and even contradictory they may appear to be, can supply a thread or two to make up the final fabric.

Some witnesses have encountered the Little People only from a distance, and have not interacted with them. Others, however, have experienced a close interaction, sometimes unpleasant (as in UFO abductions), but sometimes decidedly pleasant and beneficial. One woman actually had her own personal leprechaun, whose name was Murgatroyd.

She was a patient of Dr Nandor Fodor, and first consulted him in May 1948. Murgatroyd claimed to be descended from the Tuatha de Danann, an Irish race who eventually became a fairy tribe.

> He was two feet tall and was always dressed in green and tan. He usually stood three to four feet away from her, his body cast no shadow, yet she could not look through him. Once she tried to sketch him. The sketch disappeared. Barring this, Murgatroyd had never taken or brought anything, and he only appeared when she was in great distress or was very elated. He loved to ride in taxis. He was with her when she came to call on me, and approved of her visit, but he stayed below in the taxi and continued to ride in it as an invisible fare.

Through discussion, Fodor realized that the leprechaun was 'a successful device'. Since he descended to the woman after the death of an elderly relative to whom he had formerly belonged, he represented her need to belong to a family.

> The appearance (sensory or extrasensory) of the guardian spirit of the family was unquestionable evidence of the importance of her identity. As Murgatroyd only appeared at times of great distress or elation he was also a protective mechanism against manic psychosis. Beyond that, he could have been the liaison officer between herself and the Family Gestalt. Being handed down after death as an heirloom, Murgatroyd belonged less to the individual than to the family.[43]

*Who Are the Little People?*

The scientist George Ellery Hale (1868–1938) was another adult with his own personal elf visitor. Hale made important discoveries in relation to the behaviour of the Sun, and was also interested in the Egyptian sun-god Ra; he was also a manic-depressive. On one visit to Egypt a little man suddenly appeared in his room, and began to advise him on the conduct of his life. Thereafter he often appeared to Hale in various parts of the world, his appearance being linked to a ringing in Hale's ears. It would seem that the elf was an externalized aspect of Hale's own personality, by means of which he could sort out his problems and take important decisions.[44]

Children could also have their own personal elves which supplied psychological needs. This one visited a child at bedtime; the occurrence is described by someone who heard it in 1976.

While vacationing in Ottawa, Ontario, my wife and I met a charming young woman who told us she was the oldest child in a large family and often wanted more attention than her busy mother could give, especially while lying in bed before going to sleep. One night a little man appeared on the headboard of her bed. He wore bright-coloured clothes which consisted of a crooked hat, jacket, knee britches, woollen stockings and shoes with large shiny square buckles. She particularly remembered his eyes which were black and shiny.

She told us he was not frightening to her and when he began to tell her stories she was delighted. He came every night for a while and told her stories until she fell asleep. Once she reached up to touch him and in a flash he had slid out of reach. He told her never to try to touch him.

Finally one night he said to her, 'This will be the last time I will come to you. Another child needs me more than you do. You will always remember me.' He vanished from her sight completely and she never saw him again.[45]

All three of these Little People are unlikely to have been independent beings but to have originated deep within the minds of the witnesses and to have been externalized by them. In the following two reports the little people also provided a valuable service to the witnesses, but it is not so clear whether these beings were imaginary or whether they in fact existed independently of the witnesses.

In 1977 a Peruvian university student, Jorge Alvarez, claimed to have been saved from drowning by four little creatures. He was going down a river bank to fetch water when he fell into a swamp. He had given up hope of survival and was sinking quickly when 'four scaly little creatures of human appearance, but with three fingers on each hand' suddenly appeared and held out branches to him, with which he was pulled to safety. When he recovered, the creatures had gone. He later described them as less than three feet tall, and covered with green scales. Their hands were cold and clammy.[46]

In September 1988, Ludovico Granchi, who had already had at least two strange encounters with UFOs, found himself one evening investigating some little lights he had seen in woods close to his home near Rio de Janeiro, Brazil. Hearing a sound like grasshoppers, he was surrounded by five little men wearing some kind of uniform. They were carrying 'wands' which had lights on their tips and which lit up the area round about. The men took Granchi into a cave, which was a large chamber with a stone 'bed' where they laid him. They examined him with the 'wands' and especially a large wound on his leg. Although the creatures talked with a sound like grasshoppers chirping, when Granchi asked them if they knew his name, one little man replied in perfect Portuguese. His voice was shrill, like a child's, and he gave the correct name. The little men, who had white skin, fair hair, dark-green eyes and thin arms, were friendly in attitude, and gave Granchi a fruit to eat, something between an apple and a plum. On leaving the cave, he picked up a stone from the floor and took it away with him. Soon after the experience, the wound on his leg healed up, but in himself he felt 'confused and troubled', and a week afterwards still looked pale, though normally he was sunburnt.[47]

This report is similar to a UFO abduction, in that the witness was taken into a bright room, but on this occasion it was a cave, and not an alien spacecraft. Could the 'cave' in fact have been fairyland? The report incorporates several features which are able to be interpreted either as fairy lore or UFO lore: the cave/spacecraft, being taken somewhere/abducted, little men (UFO entities/fairies) and the offering of food which is common to UFO lore and fairy lore. The creatures, however, were kind and friendly, characteristics not normally attributed to abducting UFO entities, and not very often to fairies, either. The feeling of 'floating in thin air' which Granchi noticed for a while after his experience echoes the feeling of unreality supposedly felt by visitors to fairyland, who lose all sense of worldly time. Did Granchi perhaps inadvertently stray into fairyland?

Those readers who were impressed by the numerous first-hand accounts quoted earlier in this book, and are now convinced that at least some of the Little People possess an objective reality, will not have been satisfied by the explanations so far provided. All can be countered by objections, and none can totally account for all the strange events allegedly experienced. My personal view is that traditional fairy lore has developed from various stimuli, namely belief in nature spirits, primitive races, pagan gods and the spirits of the dead. Personal sightings, on the other hand, could be the result of imagination, fabrication, or the externalization of unconscious archetypes. If these were the only explanations, then none of the Little People seen were objectively real.

Can this be true? I honestly do not know, and I am not going to pretend that I do, but if I were to allow myself a flight of fancy, I would speculate that *some* of the Little People *might* be 'real', and that they live in another world which exists parallel to ours. If one cares to interpret it in that way, there is considerable 'evidence' from many sources which supports this idea. The material is so intriguing, at least to me, that I have decided to devote my final chapter to setting it out, so that other people can discuss it, perhaps enlarge on it, and maybe, just maybe, prove conclusively whether or not there is another world into which humans have occasionally strayed or been taken.

# 7

# FAIRYLAND AND
# OTHER WORLDS

If another world operating close to our everyday world really does exist, why is it not well known to us? Why is it not recognized and understood by science, and why cannot we travel from our world to this other world at will? A partial answer to these questions may be that all 'mysteries' in some way violate accepted scientific beliefs; phenomena such as the Loch Ness Monster, ghosts and poltergeists, and fish falling from the sky, do not fit in with the accepted worldview, and are therefore not considered worthy subjects for examination by most scientists. They languish, therefore, in a scientific limbo, from which it is exceedingly difficult for them ever to be rescued. Only those people who have personally experienced such mysteries, or are open-minded enough to consider them possible, show any great interest in them, and by scientists and the general population they are relegated to that area where fact merges into fiction. Being on the fringes of knowledge, they are considered vaguely disreputable, and therefore unworthy of serious consideration.

The problem is that so many mysteries are lumped together and disregarded in this way, and it is likely that some extremely important scientific breakthroughs have been long delayed or even missed altogether as a result of scientists' refusal to examine objectively some of the data that doesn't fit in with their orthodoxy. The idea of a parallel universe, another world close to ours, is one such topic which has so far not been afforded the attention it deserves. Some physicists have theorized about such a possibility, but most are unable to accept that it might actually exist, and even less of them accept that some people have been able to cross over into the other world.

If the transition were easier, and there were more people reporting on their visits to some alternative world, perhaps scientists' interest would be aroused. From the available evidence, the other world does seem to be very close to ours, perhaps even occupying the same space, but the two rarely interpenetrate, and consequently few humans ever step from one to the other. It is also difficult, from the evidence, to give a coherent description of the other world—and there may even be more than one of them, for there is no way of knowing if all the people who describe visits to an apparent other world have been visiting the same place. Similarly it is not always possible to determine whether the place they saw was physically objective, or solely manufactured within their imaginations. So, the search for the other world is fraught with problems, and this is possibly the most compelling reason why its existence is not generally known and accepted.

As this book is primarily about the fairies or Little People, I will first of all describe the 'other world' in which they live, fairyland, and people's claims to have been there. Many descriptions of fairyland come from legend and folklore, which cannot be considered a reliable source of evidence. Nevertheless what country people believed about fairyland may have originally been derived from genuine experiences. It should be clear from the context which accounts in this chapter are factual and which legendary.

Fairyland was most commonly believed to be located somewhere underground, either in hills (natural, or prehistoric burial mounds, or ancient forts) or deep inside the earth. It was entered through holes in the ground, or simply by (apparently) passing through the solid earth, as fairies were sometimes seen to do. (Less widespread were tales of lake-dwelling fairies, though these were quite common in Celtic regions. The lake may have served as an entrance to fairyland, rather than the fairies actually living in the water.) Inside what appeared to be an ordinary green hillock, a different world was found: a subterranean palace, large rooms brightly lit, a pleasant summery landscape even though it might be winter 'up above'. Detailed descriptions can be found in several legends describing visits to fairyland, such as the Cornish tale of Selena Moor, where a man who was lost stumbled into fairyland and there met his dead sweetheart, who warned him against touching her or eating anything or picking any flowers, for if he interacted with the fairies in any way he would not be able to return home. She had herself been captured by eating a fairy plum when she was lost on the moor, and now she had to work for the fairies. All vanished when the man turned his hedging gloves inside out, and he found himself alone in a ruined barn, where searchers later found him fast asleep.[1] Turning his gloves inside out was akin to turning one's coat inside out, once a familiar act performed by someone who felt himself to be 'pixy led' and unable to find his or her way out of a field, for example. It may originally have been done to confuse the fairies, perhaps to make them think this was a different person.

In the story of St Collen, the role of fairy food in capturing humans is also featured. Collen was a seventh-century Welsh saint who spent part of his life in Somerset, living as a hermit at the foot of Glastonbury Tor (see page 15 of photograph section). He was invited to visit the King of the Fairies, who had his castle on top of the hill, and when St Collen accepted he made a point of carrying a container of holy water hidden under his cassock. On top of the Tor he entered a beautiful castle where a banquet was taking place, and the King invited him to join them. He refused to eat, saying, 'I do not eat the leaves of a tree'—not being under the fairy influence, he saw the food for what it really was. Telling the King that his courtiers were suitably dressed—in red for the flames and blue for the ice of Hell—he threw holy water over them all, whereupon the castle and banquet vanished and he was alone on the Tor.[2] If St Collen had eaten the fairy food offered to him, he would have fallen under their spell and been unable to leave fairyland.

A tale from Wales, set 400 years later, describes the boy Elidorus and his frequent visits to fairyland. The details were recorded by the archdeacon Giraldus Cambrensis, who wrote a book about his journey through Wales in 1188, and the story can be dated to the previous century. When he was twelve and a schoolboy, Elidorus was often beaten by his tutor, so he ran away and hid under a hollow river bank.

After fasting in that situation for two days, two little men of pigmy stature appeared to him, saying, 'If you will come with us, we will lead you into a country full of delights and sports.' Assenting and rising up, he followed his guides through a path, at first subterraneous and dark, into a most beautiful country, adorned with rivers and meadows, woods and plains, but obscure, and not illuminated with the full light of the sun. All the days were cloudy, and the nights extremely dark, on account of the absence of the moon and stars. The boy was brought before the King, and introduced to him in the presence of the court; who, having examined him for a long time, delivered him to his son, who was then a boy. These men were of the smallest stature, but very well proportioned in their make; they were all of a fair complexion, with luxuriant hair falling over their shoulders like that of women. They had horses and greyhounds adapted to their size. They neither ate flesh nor fish, but lived on milk diet, made up into messes with saffron . . . The boy frequently returned to our hemisphere, sometimes by the way he had first gone, sometimes by another; at first in company with other persons, and afterwards alone, and made himself known only to his mother, declaring to her the manners, nature, and state of that people.

His mother desired some gold, which Elidorus tried to steal for her, but two of the little people retrieved the gold ball from him, and afterwards Elidorus could never again find the entrance to fairyland. He later became a priest, and told David II, the Bishop of St David's, of his experiences, including details of the fairies' language, which resembled both Welsh and Greek.[3]

Elidorus's tale lays claim to be based on factual events, as also does the story of Anne Jeffries, a Cornish girl who lived in the seventeenth century in St Teath parish. She was a servant and, wishing to make friends with the fairies, she would occupy her free time looking for them among the flowers. One day they showed themselves to her in her master's garden and carried her away through the air to a beautiful land with palaces of gold and silver, and trees full of fruit, where she joined in with the dancing. She was now the same size as the Little People, though previously they had been smaller than her. Eventually they took her home, and she was found lying on the ground, seemingly having suffered a fit. Although she never visited fairyland again, Anne Jeffries continued to have dealings with the Little People, for which she was imprisoned and charged with witchcraft.[4]

Two further seventeenth-century claims to have visited fairyland came from Scotland. A boy from Borgue would be away for several days at a time, visiting 'our folks', as he called them. The priest gave him something to frighten the fairies away: a cross on black ribbon which he hung around his neck; and he was never taken away again. Folklorist J.F. Campbell, who recorded this tale in the 1890s, concluded: 'some of the oldest men now alive remember that boy as an old man. The whole affair is recorded in the books of the kirk-session of Borgue, and can be seen any day.'[5]

A boy from Leith, Edinburgh, also regularly visited the fairies, and he was interviewed by George Burton some time in the seventeenth century. The boy said he played the drum for the fairies every Thursday night 'under yonder hill'. Burton asked him about the fairy people.

There are, sir, said he, a great company both of men and women, and they are entertained with many sorts of musick, besides my drum; they have, besides, plenty of variety of meats and wine, and many times we are carried into France or Holland in a night, and return again, and whilst we are there we enjoy all the pleasures the country doth afford.

Burton also asked how he got into the hill.

To which he replied that there was a great pair of gates that opened to them, though they were invisible to others; and that within there were brave large rooms, as well accommodated as most in Scotland.

Burton tried to detain the boy when the time came for him to join the fairies.

He was placed between us, and answered many questions, until, about eleven of the clock, he was got away unperceived by the company; but I, suddenly missing him, hasted to the door, and took hold of him, and so returned him into the same room; we all watched him, and, of a sudden, he was again got out of doors; I followed him close, and he made a noise in the street, as if he had been set upon; but from that time I could never see him.[6]

In Ireland, several of the people interviewed by Lady Gregory claimed to have visited fairyland. One was an old lady called Mrs Sheridan, who said:

I know that I used to be away among them myself, but how they brought me I don't know . . . Where they brought me to I don't know, or how I got there, but I'd be in a very big house, and it was round, the walls far away that you'd hardly see them, and a great many people all round about. I saw there neighbours and friends that I knew, and they in their own clothing and with their own appearance, but they wouldn't speak to me nor I to them, and when I'd met them again I'd never say to them that I saw them there. But the others had striped clothes of all colours, and long faces, and they'd be talking and laughing and moving about. What language had they? Irish of course, what else would they talk?

Mrs Sheridan also described an important woman with 'a tall stick in her hand', who was 'the mistress', and who touched Mrs Sheridan on the breast with her stick when she cried to go home. Sensibly, Mrs Sheridan refused to touch the food and wine they offered her, though sometimes she would have to breastfeed a child for them.[7]

People accused of witchcraft also sometimes said that they had visited fairyland, including Isobel Gowdie whose story I told on page 29. Another witchcraft connection was revealed when a Yorkshire man was tried for practising white witchcraft. He claimed to perform his healing art by means of a white powder he received from the fairies, obtaining it by going to a certain hill and knocking three times, whereupon he gained access and was given the powder he needed. He explained how he had first met the fairies, and was taken to see their Queen. He described the 'Hall' inside the hill as neither light nor dark but like twilight. Because he had indeed performed reliable cures, the judge and jury acquitted him.[8]

Some early accounts of fairyland have been obtained from medieval chronicles which were compiled by monks, for example the story of Elidorus quoted on page 165. Both

Ralph of Coggeshall and William of Newbridge wrote about
the Green Children of Woolpit in Suffolk (see page 16 of
photograph section), whose journey here from another
world was said to have taken place during the reign of King
Stephen, that is, in the middle of the twelfth century. Because of its strange details, and its obvious link with fairies,
the tale is worth recording in full here, using Ralph's version.

Another wonderful thing happened in Suffolk, at St Mary's
of the Wolfpits. A boy and his sister were found by the
inhabitants of that place near the mouth of a pit which is
there, who had the form of all their limbs like to those of
other men, but they differed in the colour of their skin from
all the people of our habitable world; for the whole surface
of their skin was tinged of a green colour. No one could
understand their speech. When they were brought as curiosities to the house of a certain knight, Sir Richard de
Calne, at Wikes, they wept bitterly. Bread and other victuals
were set before them, but they would touch none of them,
though they were tormented by great hunger, as the girl
afterwards acknowledged. At length, when some beans just
cut, with their stalks, were brought into the house, they
made signs, with great avidity, that they should be given to
them. When they were brought, they opened the stalks instead of the pods, thinking that beans were in the hollow of
them; but not finding them there, they began to weep anew.
When those who were present saw this, they opened the
pods, and showed them the naked beans. They fed on these
with great delight, and for a long time tasted no other food.
The boy, however, was always languid and depressed, and
he died within a short time. The girl enjoyed continual good

health; and becoming accustomed to various kinds of food, lost completely that green colour, and gradually recovered the sanguine habit of her entire body. She was afterwards regenerated by the laver of holy baptism, and lived for many years in the service of that knight (as I have frequently heard from him and his family), and was rather loose and wanton in her conduct. Being frequently asked about the people of her country, she asserted that the inhabitants, and all they had in that country, were of a green colour; and that they saw no sun, but enjoyed a degree of light like what is after sunset. Being asked how she came into this country with the aforesaid boy, she replied, that as they were following their flocks, they came to a certain cavern, on entering which they heard a delightful sound of bells; ravished by whose sweetness, they went for a long time wandering on through the cavern, until they came to its mouth. When they came out of it, they were struck senseless by the excessive light of the sun, and the unusual temperature of the air; and they thus lay for a long time. Being terrified by the noise of those who came on them, they wished to fly, but they could not find the entrance of the cavern before they were caught.[9]

Katharine Briggs notes that 'beans are traditionally the food of the dead', and green is 'the Celtic colour of death'.[10] It is also, of course, a colour very often associated with the Little People, and sometimes with so-called UFO entities.

The entrance to the children's world was through a cave, and the light was like our twilight, as in the witchcraft case on page 169 and also the story of Elidorus on page 165. The girl called her country St Martin's Land and said that the people who lived there were Christians, according to

William of Newbridge's version of the story. St Martin's Land is clearly also fairyland, the other world which sometimes briefly links up with our own world, allowing people to stray from one into the other, but not always giving them time to get back again.

Even though not always agreeing in details, the descriptions of fairyland tend to agree in generalities: it is often reached through a hill or a hole in the ground; and when the fairy world is entered it is a beautiful place with fine buildings, perfect in every way. Those whose descriptions I have so far given, seemed to be able to come and go at will; but usually in folklore, those who were foolish enough to eat any fairy food or in some other way to interact with the fairies were thereafter held captive, unable to return voluntarily to their normal life.

Sometimes it was the fairy music and dancing which at-

A man who foolishly joined the fairy dance is pulled back to safety by a friend (Fortean Picture Library).

tracted the human so that he felt compelled to join the Little People in the fairy ring. Once inside he could not escape—though indeed he rarely wished to, for the experience was so enjoyable. In the folk tales, friends would rescue him some long time afterwards, a year or two even. He would be pulled out by his clothes, the rescuer making sure not to enter the circle, or he would be touched with a piece of iron before being dragged out (the importance of iron as a protection against the fairies has already been noted). The released man would believe he had only been dancing for five minutes, not a year or more: one man was told to look at his 'new' shoes, and saw they were now in pieces. Only then was he convinced of what his friends had been trying to tell him.[11]

Sometimes the visitor to fairyland is away for very much longer, perhaps 200 years of earth time, though only a short time was seemingly spent in fairyland. In a Scottish tale, two fiddlers entered a hill near Inverness and played for a fairy gathering which lasted a few hours, but when they returned home they were amazed to find that a hundred years had passed. They went to church but, when the priest began to read the gospel, they crumbled into dust. This sometimes also happens when the person returns home and eats some food. Katharine Briggs interpreted these events as indicating that fairyland is 'a world of the dead, and that those who entered it had long been dead, and carried back with them an illusory body which crumbled into dust when they met reality.'[12] In one tale, however, a man who spent many happy years in fairyland broke a prohibition when he drank from a certain well, and immediately found himself back in Pembrokeshire (Wales) on the hillside with his sheep. Only minutes of earth time had passed.[13]

Being in a state of trance can sometimes bring about a mistaken concept of the passage of time. People who have been close to death by drowning or other sudden accidents, but are later revived, have claimed that 'their whole life flashed before them' in a very short space of time. Also, drug-taking can cause a person to experience or dream events that seemingly last a long time: nineteenth-century author Thomas de Quincey who took opium and wrote of his experiences in *Confessions of an English Opium-Eater* recorded dreams lasting ten to sixty years. People who have had inexplicable UFO experiences sometimes find difficulty in reconciling the time: they often find that they have 'lost' an hour or two. A journey which normally took, say, two hours, on the day in question took four, and the witness is at a loss to explain what happened during the missing two hours. When he or she is later hypnotized, it may be found that a UFO abduction took place, the details of which have been erased from the victim's memory.[14] This experience parallels that of the visitor to fairyland who found that in the 'real world' more time had passed than he or she seemed to have experienced.

The image of the human happily dancing with the fairies, while outside the ring his friends plan their rescue attempt, clearly demonstrates how close is the world of the fairies to our world. The rescuers can see the dancer, but he is living in a different world, with a different time-scale. The closeness of the fairy world to the human world often occurs in accounts of the Little People, with the difficulty of crossing from one to the other, especially from the fairy to the human world, being emphasized. These features occur in a story told to Evans Wentz by an Irish tailor, Patrick Waters:

Shon ap Shenkin turns to dust on returning home after spending a few minutes, as he thought, but in reality many years
listening to fairy music (Fortean Picture Library).

A girl in this region died on her wedding-night while danc-ing. Soon after her death she appeared to her husband, and said to him, 'I'm not dead at all, but I am put from you now for a time. It may be a long time, or a short time, I cannot tell. I am not badly off. If you want to get me back you must stand at the gap near the house and catch me as I go by, for I live near there, and see you, and you do not see me.' He was anxious enough to get her back, and didn't waste any time in getting to the gap. When he came to the place, a party of strangers were just coming out, and his wife soon appeared as plain as could be, but he couldn't stir a hand or foot to save her. Then there was a scream and she was gone. The man firmly believed this, and would not marry again.[15]

In the modern world, strange events sometimes occur which might be indicative of our world's closeness to an-other world, one which we cannot normally see, but which nevertheless interacts with ours. People who are psychic are the most likely to be able to see events occurring on another level of existence. We may be sharing our living space with all manner of strange creatures that we cannot normally see. Mrs Claire Cantlon, one-time secretary of the Faery Investi-gation Society, told psychologist Dr Nandor Fodor of her own experiences.

My house and garden in Putney are overrun by fairies and gnomes. The other day, Robin, my boy of ten, ran to me in great fright. He thought there was a pig in the room. It was a fat gnome, sitting on the chair, looking very cross and grunting. A few days after I heard the noise myself. It was a blend between the growling of a dog and grunting of a pig. I thought it was the dog going at the cat. Last week I saw the gnome. Just as I was putting out the light, I noticed a queer shape trying to climb up the blind cord and fall with a fearful flop. He glared at me, for I had an impulse to laugh, and vanished.

June, my 11-year-old daughter, who is very psychic, saw some little time ago a gnome in a circle of light, sitting on the knob of a bedpost and hammering at a ring. He wore a cloak and had a long, white beard.[16]

People who are not psychic, however, might still be un-expected witnesses to events which may hint at the existence of another world. We may not all be able to see fairies or the Little People, because they are normally invisible to us, but there may be occasions when they acquire partial visibility and so are seen fleetingly before the conditions become unfavourable again. I regret that for those of a scientific frame of mind I cannot provide any details of the mechanism that allows for invisibility or partial materialization: I will leave that aspect of other worlds for the scientists themselves to tackle. All I can provide are the case histories, the facts as described by the witnesses. For example, in the mid-eighteenth century, the Reverend Robert Hughes was returning home along the Pwllheli road to Llanaelhaearn on the Lleyn peninsula (Gwynedd, Wales) early one morning when he saw fairies riding on tiny horses. He told of his encounter to Dr John Rhys, who retold it in a book of Celtic folklore: 'his recollection is that he now and then mastered his eyes and found the road quite clear, but the next moment the vision would return, and he thought he saw the diminutive cavalcade as plainly as possible.'[17] Similarly in the last century, someone living in the Isle of Man saw the fairies briefly:

About 34 years ago, when he was 23, at 10 a.m. of a brilliantly sunny summer morning he was walking on the short grass below the debris at the west side of the Glen Aldyn slate-quarries, which lie far above the inhabited part of the Glen. Here he came to a sudden stop to avoid stepping on something alive between two and three yards in front of him. It was five little creatures dancing in a ring, hand in hand. They stood a foot or 18 inches high and were greyish in colour like fungus, their bodies seeming to be swollen in front, their limbs and eyes clearly distinguishable, and their heads moving as they danced. He speaks of them as 'little men' because they gave him a strong impression of being of the male sex. After he had watched them for a short time they vanished from his sight, and there was nothing there but the grass. Thinking his eyes or brain might have played him a trick, he went to the same spot a couple of mornings later, and there they were again, just as before. He has hardly ever spoken of it to anyone for fear of ridicule.[18]

Just because the Little People suddenly disappear, or are there one minute and gone the next, and then later return, does not mean that the witness's vision is to blame, or that he or she is imagining things. In fact such sightings, seemingly on the edge of visibility, provide clues to the ways and circumstances in which humans see these elusive creatures. In 1912, Dr Robert Ernst Dickhoff also saw Little People who disappeared, but on this occasion they did it slowly.

An incident that occurred in 1912, when I was eight years old and lived in a suburb of Cologne, Germany, has remained indelibly in my memory. One afternoon I was looking out into the backyard from a window of our apartment.

My mind was in no way keyed to the forces and powers of the paranormal—I was merely looking out of a window to see what could be seen.

Behind me was a large fourposter bed. I was alone in the room, but I felt compelled to turn around. I did so, and saw, sitting against the posts of the bed, two strange creatures which could not have been more than three and a half feet tall if standing.

They looked exactly alike, had features just like humans and skin of a lightbrown texture. They did not smile and therefore I could not see if they had teeth. If they wore clothing, it must have been the same colour as their skin and worn tightly over their bodies. It appeared to me, however, that my strange visitors were naked.

I do not know how long the creatures had studied me before I turned. But after we had gazed at each other for about a minute a fantastic thing happened. Apparently having realised that I was able to see them, they faded slowly into invisibility before my astonished eyes. I never saw them again—but that may be because they have been careful to remain invisible when around me.

I've always wondered whether my strange visitors were extraterrestrials, possibly from a flying saucer, although I saw no saucer anywhere at the time of my experience.[19]

Some UFO experiences seem to suggest that the 'spacecraft', as some people believe them to be, may not be totally solid. Jennifer F. Canfield was sitting on the front porch with her husband at their home at Callicoon on the New York/Pennsylvania border, on 3 July 1977. The sky was overcast and the time was around 7.30 p.m. They saw a 'brilliant light' approaching soundlessly, and Mrs Canfield fetched a pair of binoculars. Through them she could see a solid craft with two huge headlights. It had a 'cockpit' like an inverted cone, and the craft was grey or off-white. She continued:

Several people were lucky enough to see the object through the binoculars. As it came within less than half a mile from our home, my husband remarked, 'Don't tell me I'm finally going to get a ride in a flying saucer!' Almost as if it had been given a stage cue, the saucer disappeared. It did not fly up, down or veer right or left. It simply disappeared! As I said, the sky had been overcast and the clouds were very low. The saucer was below these.[20]

A few years earlier, in the summer of 1972, a man fishing in a stream at Buckingham in England saw a cigar-shaped object reflected in the water—but there was nothing to be seen in the sky. Looking again at the water, he could see the reflection of a pewter-coloured object with rounded ends, and watched it moving. Again he checked the empty sky. Then, after twelve seconds, the object turned and vanished.[21] A somewhat similar experience happened to myself and husband Colin in July 1983. We were standing on a bridge over the Worcester and Birmingham Canal in the English Midlands, taking photographs of the canal, the pub alongside, and the boats on the water. It was a hot day, with a cloudless blue sky. We saw nothing unusual, but days later, when we received the transparencies back from being processed, one had a strange white 'cloud formation' in the sky. None of the frames preceding or following, all taken within a short space of time, showed anything unusual. There was just one frame with an object looking for all the world like a misty cigar-shaped UFO. If it was a UFO, it was not visible to the human eye. If it was a cloud, it came and went within seconds. Nor has anyone been able to explain the image convincingly as a fault in the film or the processing; it remains a mystery. On this occasion, it may be that the film recorded something only visible on a certain wavelength, one not shared by the human eye. Cameras also sometimes capture ghostly figures not seen by the photographer. This suggests that in certain circumstances, aspects of the 'parallel world' may be caught on film, but it is no use going around taking photographs and expecting them to show 'invisible' people—the rarity of this happening indicates that only very occasionally are the conditions (whatever they may be) right for this event to occur.

If the 'other world', the 'parallel world', or fairyland, whatever one likes to call it, is indeed very close, it may be separated from us only by a thin barrier, but that barrier proves almost impossible for mere mortals to penetrate, unless by chance we fulfil the right conditions for a moment or two, and catch a quick glimpse of what is on the other side. There may normally be too much clutter in our minds to allow us to get on to the correct wavelength, or into a receptive frame of mind. Using the 'barrier' image might be a bit misleading, if the 'other world' operates in the same space as our everyday reality, for in that case the barrier takes on a more insubstantial form: our own lack of knowledge of the correct viewing conditions. That is why we sometimes 'see' without expecting to.

Although these ideas are hypothetical, and based entirely on a few strange experiences, similar reports can be found in other parts of the world, and these experiences are suggestive of something unusual occurring: we are tantalized

This old engraving shows a pilgrim discovering another world. To the right is the everyday world, from which the pilgrim has broken through the barrier to a different world, separated from ours, but close at hand (Fortean Picture Library).

by brief flashes of clarity, a momentary glimpse of another existence, and then all is 'back to normal'. Most people can recall at least one odd event that seems to have no logical explanation, however hard they try to find one. Household objects disappear and reappear in a different place, almost as if a mischievous entity is playing games; or sometimes the 'entity' is helpful, like the household brownies of the fairy tales. In the late 1950s a vicar and his wife stayed in a Devon cottage. One day the wife prepared a stew and was going to light the fire and put the stew on, but something distracted her and they went out. On returning home, expecting to have to eat bread and cheese for supper, they found that the fire had been lit and the stew was cooked. They had been within sight of the house all day, and no one had come near, nor had they seen smoke. On another day, she forgot to take the evening meal off the fire. By the time she remembered it, it should have been burnt, but she found that it had been taken off the stove. Another time, while sitting outdoors in the heather to do some sewing in the sun, she lost two needles, and the needlebook also disappeared.[22]

In a similar case, a woman who for years ran a village post office and shop in rural Wales had an invisible helper. Every morning, she would get up to find that the previous day's muddle in the shop had been tidied up. She commented,

> I never really understood the meaning of it. But I was grateful right from the very first, so it became a habit with me never to pry too much into the whys and wherefores. I thanked whoever it was aloud every working morning. I began to call him—if it was a him—Billy, just to give him a bit of personality. And he never let me down once. When I retired, Billy went. No need for his services, see.[23]

These events cannot, of course, be directly attributed to the fairies but they are the sort of things that the fairies would be expected to do. I had a somewhat similar experience myself, while writing this book, and it continues to puzzle me. Our house, in the North Wales hills, was approached along a track across two fields and through three gates. On the morning of 1 February 1991, there was ice on the ground at the 'bottom' gate into the lane, and when I had opened the gate I had to back the car into the lane and take a run at the entrance, because the track goes uphill. Once through the gate I had to keep going, for to stop to close the gate would have meant the car would be unable to move again on the icy ground. I drove across one field and into the next (the gate was open) and stopped on a level area where there was no ice. I was by now out of sight of the lane gate, and had to hurry back to close it before the sheep escaped. Only a minute elapsed between driving through the lane gate and walking back into sight of it: and I was very surprised to see that the gate was closed. I still had to walk down the field to it, to check that the latch was in place, and it was. It was impossible for the gate to have been blown shut by the wind, for there was none, and when open the gate dragged on the ground. I had definitely not stopped to close it myself, and the only possibility is that someone else closed it for me. There had been no one in sight when I drove along the lane only three or four minutes earlier, and as I now stood by the gate pondering the mystery, I looked along the lane and saw no one. They could not have disappeared out of view in such a short time. There was a neighbour from the village who walked his dog along the lane and would open and close the gate for me if he happened to be there when I needed to drive through; but I had not seen him on this particular morning. I did happen to see him the very next day, and asked if he had closed the gate for me the day before, but he said he had not. Until someone else owns up to skulking in the bushes unseen by me, I can only assume that some invisible hand closed and latched the gate.

I say 'invisible' because in addition to seeing no humans I

also saw no fairies—but then I don't claim to possess any greater degree of psychic sensitivity than most of the rest of the population; and the evidence suggests that people who *are* psychic have a greater chance of seeing fairies and also of experiencing other so-called 'paranormal' events. Children tend to be more psychic than adults, and the numerous cases already quoted of children seeing Little People support this belief. Perhaps their minds are less cluttered than adults' and more open to outside influences—they instinctively allow their natural psychic abilities free rein, whereas adults tend to stifle them—so, when children are in the right place to see the fairies, they are likely to do so, though many adults in the same situation would very likely not see anything.

A case demonstrating the receptivity of children occurred in the 1870s on the island of Skye, where three children were being looked after by their grandmother. An old lady came to visit, and she offered to show them something interesting. It was twilight, and she took them along a path by the burn. Stopping, she said, 'Look, do you see them?' On the hillside they saw fairies dressed in green, dancing in a ring around a fire. Next day the children went out to look for the ashes of the fire, but there was nothing to be seen. The old lady who took them was said to possess 'second sight', a Scottish term referring to the possession of psychic powers and the ability to see into the future.[24]

Maybe the children would have been able to see the Little People if no one had been with them, if they had stumbled accidentally across the ring of fairies. Or maybe the old lady was somehow able to pass on to them her psychic ability. There are numerous instances in the literature of people who are psychic being able to transfer that ability by means of some special action. For example, one of Evans Wentz's informants told him:

> There used to be an old man at Newchurch named David Davis (who lived about 1780–1840), of Abernant, [Carmarthen, Wales] noted for seeing phantom funerals. One appeared to him once when he was with a friend. 'Do you see it? Do you see it?' the old man excitedly asked. 'No,' said his friend. Then the old man placed his foot on his friend's foot, and said, 'Do you see it now?' And the friend replied that he did.[25]

The four-leafed clover was also said to be able to help humans to see fairies, and the leaves were also an ingredient of a special ointment made by the fairies which could be used by humans on their eyes to enable them to see the Little People.[26] The fairies however, had ways to prevent humans seeing them: a fairy blew on the face of a man who said he could see them, and he never saw them again.[27] Another fairy spat in the eyes of a man who saw 'a great crowd of little fellows in red coats dancing and making music' near Jurby, Isle of Man. She said to him, 'You'll never see us again'—and he was blinded thenceforth. The man's grandson told his story to Evans Wentz, saying that his grandfather had definitely had good sight in his youth, and was totally blind for fourteen years before his death, but added: 'I am unable to say of my own knowledge that he became blind immediately after his strange experience, or if not until later in life; but as a young man he certainly had good sight, and it was believed that the fairies destroyed it.'[28] It was believed that if you did see the fairies you had to keep looking at them, for if you blinked or looked away, they would disappear. Or as one Irish informant expressed it to Evans Wentz: 'But the minute you wink or take your eyes off the little devil, sure enough he is gone.'[29]

Apart from possessing psychic ability, or being lucky enough to find a four-leafed clover, there are other important requirements to be fulfilled: you have to be in the right place at the right time. You need to know where the fairy haunts are (see the Appendix), and to be there at the good times: twilight, midnight, the hour before sunrise, and noon—the 'four hinges of the day'. Important times of year are May Day, Midsummer Eve, and Hallowe'en, when 'the doors open between the worlds'.[30] Places that were held sacred in ancient times, like stone circles, standing stones and burial mounds, are thought to be 'naturally charged with psychical forces',[31] and so are good places to see the Little People. It may be that the rock used by the ancients to build these sites was very important: quartz is often seen at such sites, for example, and its piezo-electric properties have caused researchers into earth energies to wonder if it was chosen for its special qualities—perhaps its ability to assist those performing rituals at the sites to enter into another dimension of being? Certainly people have reported strange experiences at ancient sites, and in connection with quartz. One was ley researcher Paul Screeton, who wrote of seeing an 'elemental' (a nature spirit or disembodied spirit). He was walking along a road near Carlisle, and he stepped on to a quartz stone on the grass verge. He bent down to look at it more closely.

> I touched it for about half a minute and then walked a couple of paces. Then I saw something move a yard or so in front of me. The thing leapt like a frog and was frog-shaped,

but about three feet high. It was brown but its form was hazy, difficult to describe, but the effect was not dissimilar to a television screen when the lines go crazy. I had the impression that what I had seen was an elemental and that I perceived it at the edge of my consciousness.

He interpreted it as an 'earth gnome', and believed it possible that 'the quartz itself was instrumental somehow in bringing about the sighting, i.e. raising my consciousness while I touched it.'[32]

Quartz rock may also be involved in some electro-magnetic effects which manifest as balls of light, these often being interpreted as UFOs or 'alien spacecraft'. The electro-magnetic energy which is emitted might possibly cause hallucinations in witnesses, so that they 'see' all manner of strange things, including landed craft, entities, etc. Sometimes light or lights are a feature of Little People sightings, and it is conceivable that the same mechanism is in operation: the witness is having hallucinations triggered by the outpouring of energy from the light. Alternatively, of course, the appearance of the Little People might be due to the presence of the light and/or energy, in that the curtain between this world and the other world parts under influence of the energy forces.

A report from Cornwall dating from the mid-nineteenth century may demonstrate the potential link between lights and seeing the Little People. A man returning home from market, and passing between dense hedges, saw a light and heard music and singing. Looking through the hedge, he saw an elf sitting on a toadstool. He held a lantern formed from a campanula flower, from which poured a greenish-blue light. A group of fairies was dancing in a ring. The man described what he did:

> I looked and listened awhile, and then I got quietly hold of a great big stone and heaved it up, and I dreshed in amongst them all, and then I up on my horse and galloped away as hard as I could, and never drew rein till I came home to Morwenstow. But when the stone fell among them all, out went the light. You don't believe me? But it be true, true as Gospel, for next day I went back to the spot, and there lay the stone, just where I had dreshed it.[33]

Clearly he saw something, else why throw a stone, and then return to the spot later? What really happened here? Was what he saw objectively there, with the light simply a fairy lantern? Did he come under the influence of some electromagnetic energy which caused him to see the fairies who were really there, the lantern being the light from the power source? Or did he perhaps hallucinate the elf and dancing fairies when he came under the influence of an electromagnetic discharge?

If electro-magnetism and other forms of energy do have a part to play in so-called fairy sightings, with the events being purely hallucinatory, the variety in the appearance of the fairies is explainable as being an externalization of the fairy image stored within the witness's memory. Another explanation, though, is that the Little People themselves influence how humans see them. They were said to exercise 'glamour'—'a mesmerism or enchantment cast over the senses, so that things were perceived or not perceived as the enchanter wished', as defined by Katharine Briggs. The fairy ointment or four-leafed clover could be used to negate the glamour.[34] Fairies were also credited with being accomplished at 'shape-shifting', changing their appearance at will. This all makes sense if the Little People do indeed live in another world close to ours, where the vibratory rate is different from ours and they need to consciously materialize in our world in order to be seen by humans. We can never see them as they really are, owing to the difference in the rates of vibration in our separate worlds. UFO entities too have indicated that their appearance while on Earth is temporary, or even illusory. One witness was told that he would see the being 'only as I wanted to see it. If I wanted to see the being resemble a duck, it would look like a duck! If I wanted the being to look like a monster, it looked like a monster!'[35]

It is of course difficult (probably impossible) to *prove* that UFO entities, and other unexplained beings like fairies, live in another world close to ours, and can materialize and dematerialize in our world at will in whatever form they choose. The fact of materialization is itself controversial, though there is some convincing evidence, mainly from poltergeist cases, that solid objects, and on occasion even people, have indeed dematerialized and rematerialized somewhere else. In an extraordinary poltergeist case which happened in India in 1928, Miss H. Kohn, of German origin and teaching languages in a Poona college, witnessed many strange events while living with the Ketkar family whose young children seem to have been the focus of the phenomenon. Her sister also saw some of the happenings, as here described by Miss Kohn:

At 9.45 a.m. on April 23rd, my sister says in a letter, the elder boy 'suddenly materialized in front of me in your doorway like a rubber ball. He looked bright but amazed, and said "I have just come from Karjat". He didn't come through any door'. My sister describes the posture of the boy as having been most remarkable. When she looked up from her letter-writing, she saw him bending forward: both his arms were hanging away from his sides, and the hands hanging limp—his feet were not touching the floor, as she saw a distinct space between his feet and the threshold. It was precisely the posture of a person who has been gripped round the waist and carried, and therefore makes no effort but is gently dropped at his destination.[36]

In addition to materializing, the boy had been teleported (carried by unknown means, probably instantaneously, from another location). There are other instances of this occurring, and the two phenomena of teleportation and materialization are probably closely linked. No one can explain how such a thing could happen, and it goes against all our scientific conventions, hence the lack of scientific research into such phenomena.

Perhaps people who claim to have visited other worlds have been teleported there, dematerializing in our world and rematerializing in the other world. Scattered through the vast range of material describing people's brushes with the supernatural are many accounts of visits to what sound like other worlds. Whether these are all the same place, and whether they are also the place where the fairies or Little People dwell, are questions that must remain unanswered for now. Even without being able to solve the mystery neatly, they provide a fascinating glimpse into a possible parallel world. The experiences tend to fall into categories depending on the circumstances, with varying interpretations being placed upon them; though some could not be interpreted at all. The following case is one such.

Early in the morning of Dec. 9, 1873, Thomas B. Cumpston and his wife, 'who occupied good positions in Leeds,' were arrested in a railroad station, in Bristol, England, charged with disorderly conduct, both of them in their nightclothes, Cumpston having fired a pistol. See the London *Times,* Dec. 11, 1873. Cumpston excitedly told that he and his wife had arrived the day before, from Leeds, and had taken a room in a Bristol hotel, and that, early in the morning, the floor had 'opened', and that, as he was about to be dragged into the 'opening,' his wife had saved him, both of them so terrified that they had jumped out the window, running to the railroad station, looking for a policeman. In the *Bristol Daily Post,* December 10, is an account of proceedings in the police court. Cumpston's excitement was still so intense that he could not clearly express himself. Mrs. Cumpston testified that, early in the evening, both of them had been alarmed by loud sounds, but that they had been reassured by the landlady. At three or four in the morning the sounds were heard again. They jumped out on the floor, which was felt giving away under them. Voices repeating their exclamations were heard, or their own voices echoed strangely. Then, according to what she saw, or thought she saw, the floor opened wide. Her husband was falling into this 'opening' when she dragged him back.

The landlady was called, and she testified that sounds had been heard, but she was unable clearly to describe them. Policemen said that they had gone to the place, the Victoria Hotel, and had examined the room, finding nothing to justify the extraordinary conduct of the Cumpstons. They suggested that the matter was a case of collective hallucination.[37]

This strange case reminds me of the 1940s experience reported by the Reverend Dr A.T.P. Byles, who at the time was vicar of Yealmpton in Devon. He and his wife found a hole in the path in the churchyard. It was about a yard wide, and when the vicar threw a stone down it, he heard it hit stonework. They hurried off to fetch planks to cover the hole, but when they returned there was no hole to be found: the path was as normal.[38] In a third similar case, a female student nurse saw a large hole appear in the floor of her room at around 8 a.m. while she was sitting having a cup of tea. The hole took up most of the floor and the edges looked like rock. She couldn't see the bottom, but knew the hole was deep. A voice told her to jump in, but she ignored it and the hole disappeared.[39]

Did these mystified people all suffer from hallucinations? It is clear that the floor or ground in *this world* did not open up . . . but were all the witnesses perhaps momentarily able to see into some *other world*? If they had fallen into the hole, what would have happened to them? In a science-fiction style, we can speculate that they would have dematerialized out of this world and rematerialized in another; but would they then have been able to return at will? Have people who have disappeared perhaps involuntarily entered another world and cannot now get back? I am thinking now of the story of the Green Children of Woolpit (see page 170), who wandered into this world and, unable to return home, had to live here until they died. If the next account is reliable, children in this world have also wandered into another world, and returned to tell the tale.

In the early 1920s, a boy and girl living in Flackton, Arkansas, walked through the silent town one Sunday afternoon when everyone was at the baseball game and took a short cut to the ground, through a pine wood.

About 100 yards in the woods we came to a stream neither of us remembered having seen before. It was narrow and clear and the bottom was no deeper than our knees. Reluctant to turn back, we took off our Sunday shoes and stockings and waded across.

Stepping up on the opposite bank, we saw a scene like nothing we had seen before. Gone was the scrubby undergrowth and knobby pine trees, smelly dog fennel and jimpson weed, the chattering sparrows and screaming bluejays.

The soil seemed wetter and sandier as we pressed our feet in it. We did not recognize any of the plants or low trees but the long graceful fronds of some kind looked like the wind ferns we found in bogs, although dozens of times larger. We saw a bird, somewhat like a goose but with a longer neck and a thinner coat of feathers, that glided from tree to tree with a sort of coiling effect.

Robbie and I were too lost in the wonder of this new place to be afraid. We strolled along, hand in hand, in the direction of the ball diamond [baseball ground]. At the edge of this strange land we topped a small rise and saw, off in the distance, the ball diamond and our friends.

In the languor that pervaded us it looked like a stage with its own familiar setting of pine and sedge. Our friends' voices came to us, thin and disembodied, like the tinny sounds we heard on the worn wax cylinders of our talking machines. Unnoticed by them, we watched until the game ended and they moved out of sight—off the stage it seemed to us.

Pensively we wandered back through the dream world that unaccountably had caught us up; back through the stream that shouldn't have been there; and when we looked back the dream world had vanished.[40]

Forty years later, in 1962, two men on a hunting trip in New York state likewise entered a different world. It was November, there was about a foot of snow on the ground, and it was still snowing as they walked through the lonely countryside.

Crossing a field I noticed a tall stand of pines and thought it would be the perfect place to find deer. Approaching the pines, we were confronted by a thick wall of underbrush; penetrating it was difficult. Finally, entering the pines through a small opening, we were astounded by what we saw. The pine trees stood in perfectly straight rows in an area 500 yards long and 300 yards wide. Only about two inches of snow covered the ground in this area and at the far end the sun was shining. It was unbelievable.

Mystified, I turned back to look at our place of entry; there it was still snowing and the sky was heavily overcast. Then I started to run toward the sunny area with Uncle Sal behind me, shouting for me to stop, but I kept running until I reached the end of the pines. I groped through another wall of underbrush, this one green and flowering, and entered an area of about three to five acres of green grass, flowers, birds singing and squirrels chattering. The temperature was near 80 degrees. Impossible, I thought.

Uncle Sal had caught up with me. I said, 'Sal, do you see what I see?'

Dumbfounded, he said, 'Where the heck are we?'

We took off our heavy winter outer clothing and stretched out on a small hill to enjoy a mid-November summer's day. After about 45 minutes I suddenly realized that Dad and Eddie would never believe us so I told Uncle Sal we had better bring them here to show them. On our return trip to the car we were careful not to disturb our tracks leading in.

When we joined Dad and Uncle Eddie for lunch at the car, we told them what we had seen. Then the four of us followed our tracks to the pines and went through—but this time there was no sunshine at the other end. I ran ahead, thinking that we had left this place only an hour ago and now it had all changed. The others followed me through the underbrush and found me standing in awe. Our tracks leading to the small hill and the impressions of our bodies where we had lain showed that the snow was 12 inches deep.

What had happened? Did Sal and I have the same dream? Or did we step into another dimension? For many years thereafter I searched for that stand of pines but never found it again.[41]

The last two journeys were involuntary and happened outside a recognizable paranormal context. Other people have also visited unknown places, but within contexts which have been categorized. One modern example is the UFO abduction, where people believe themselves to have been taken aboard an alien spacecraft for a medical examination. It is unlikely that they have really been taken into a spacecraft, however; but it is possible that their captors have taken them temporarily into another world. Just one example from the many that could be cited concerns Brazilian soldier José Antonio, who in May 1969, while fishing in a lagoon, was seized by two 4-foot tall beings and taken to a machine like an upright cylinder. After an apparent journey, he was carried to a large room seemingly made of stone, lit uniformly by a very bright light. A number of hairy dwarfs came in, pale-skinned and with green eyes, long thick beards down to their stomachs, and long, red, waist-length hair. Many strange things happened, but at one point José Antonio felt they were asking him to help them in their relations with Earth.[42] Although he felt he went on a journey in a spacecraft before reaching the large room, the craft he saw could have been merely illusory, the aerial journey being fabricated to confuse him as to their real destination. The dwellers in the other world may be keen to avoid humans finding out where they live and how to get there: if we knew their world was close at hand, we might make determined efforts to find the way in, resulting in danger for us and/or for them.

People who have been close to death also sometimes report having visited another world, and naturally enough this world is interpreted as heaven or the afterlife. Some descriptions of the 'transcendental environment' include: 'Just another . . . bright sunny world . . . real beautiful'; 'Beautiful blue sky . . . field of flowers of different colors'; 'A place of beautiful light that pulsated with exquisite music'; 'Beautiful green pasture . . . cattle grazing . . . bright sunshiny day'.[43] Temporary visitors to this world, those going through the 'near death experience' (known as NDE), report having spoken to 'God' and hearing him speak to them, being sent back by 'spirits', meeting 'Jesus', seeing dead relations, and unknown people who greeted them. In 1889 Dr Wiltse of Skiddy, Kansas, was at the point of death and later described in vivid terms his experience of separating from and walking away from his 'dead' body.

I saw a number of persons sitting and standing about the body, and particularly noticed two women apparently kneeling by my left side, and I knew that they were weeping. I have since learned that they were my wife and my sister, but I had no conception of individuality. Wife, sister or friend were as one to me. I did not remember any conditions of relationship; at least I did not think of any. I could distinguish sex, but nothing further.

I now attempted to gain the attention of the people with the object of comforting them as well as assuring them of their own immortality. I bowed to them playfully and saluted with my right hand. I passed about among them also, but found that they gave me no heed. Then the situation struck me as humorous and I laughed outright.

They certainly must have heard that, I thought, but it seemed otherwise, for not one lifted their eyes from my body. It did not once occur to me to speak and I concluded the matter by saying to myself: 'They see only with the eyes of the body. They cannot see spirits. They are watching what they think is I, but they are mistaken. That is not I. This is I and I am as much alive as ever.'

He later travelled through a deserted mountain landscape and reached three rocks which he felt formed the entrance to the next world. He looked through a low archway:

The atmosphere was green and everything seemed cool and quiet and beautiful. Beyond the rocks, the roadway, the valley, and the mountain range curved gently to the left, thus shutting off the view at a short distance. If I were only around there, I thought, I should soon see angels or devils or both, and as I thought this, I saw the forms of both as I had often pictured them in my mind. I looked at them closely and discovered that they were not realities, but the mere shadowy forms in my thoughts, and that any form might be brought up in the same way. What a wonderful world, I exclaimed, mentally, where thought is so intensified as to take visible form. How happy shall I be in such a realm of thought as that.

He was 'tempted to cross the boundary line', but when he decided to do so, he was stopped by a small dense black cloud which appeared in front of his face. 'I felt the power to move or to think leaving me. My hands fell powerless at my side, my shoulders and head dropped forward, the cloud touched my face and I knew no more.'

During his experience, Dr Wiltse noticed that he was connected to his 'dead' body by 'a small cord, like a spider's web, running from my shoulders back to my body and attaching to it at the base of the neck in front'.[44] He was in fact experiencing what is also known as an out-of-body experience, an OOBE. Most people who have had an OOBE have experienced it spontaneously, but a few people have also been able to initiate the experience at will, including Robert Monroe. He has travelled in our present world in his 'astral body', in the world after death, and also in a third type of world, like our present world but yet not the same. He entered it through a hole in a vast wall, and when he ventured through, he found 'a physical-matter world almost identical to our own'. It had people, vehicles, houses, cities, etc., etc., but there were subtle differences between that world and the 'normal' world. There was 'no internal combustion, gasoline, or oil' but locomotives using steam power were seen. Wood and coal were not used to make the steam, and Monroe describes in his book *Journeys Out of the Body* how the engines work, and also how their version of the car operates. Monroe learned much about this other world when he lived there for a while, having merged into the body of an architect. Whenever he found himself in a difficult situation because he didn't have all the necessary knowledge, Monroe would leave the body and come back to this world through the hole in the wall, not wishing to get the architect into trouble. Discussing where this unknown world might be, Monroe suggested:

> It might be a memory, racial or otherwise, of a physical earth civilization that predates known history. It might be another earth-type world located in another part of the universe which is somehow accessible through mental manipulation. It might be an antimatter duplicate of this physical earth-world where we are the same but different, bonded together unit for unit by a force beyond our present comprehension.[45]

In exploring reports of an unknown world we have seen it described in a variety of ways. The worlds described sound similar, but the people who have been there have been influenced by their environment and upbringing when trying to interpret their experience. So, to sum up: there is fairyland, the land of the Little People, seemingly so close yet so difficult for humans to enter (except in fairy lore); there is the near death experience in which people visit the world of the spirit, also known as the astral world; there is the world Robert Monroe visited during his out-of-body experiences; there is the fourth-dimensional world which has been used in the past to explain all manner of paranormal phenomena including teleportation; there is the parallel universe which some people believe lies very close to our world; there is the theory of a multiplicity of universes where any course of events which could occur, does, in one or another of the existing worlds; and there is the 'otherworld' of the North Asian shaman or sorcerer/magician, which is an 'inverted image of this world' with everything taking place in reverse (day here is night there, summer here is winter there, etc).[46] Are these worlds really all one, or is the universe, beyond our tiny part of it, so complex that we cannot begin to understand it? Parapsychologist John L. Randall made a sensible summing up of the situation when discussing the possibility of other worlds:

> What we regard as 'reality'—the everyday world with its three spatial dimensions and linear time-flow—is no more than an abstraction from a much more complex universe. We are indeed like the men in Plato's allegory who, seeing the shadows of a higher reality on the walls of their cave, mistake those shadows for reality itself.[47]

# TAILPIECE

I may not have proved that fairies exist; I may not have proved that there are any other worlds than the one you see around you—but I believe I have shown that there is some mystery to be explored; that there is no simple explanation for people's experiences of fairies and visits to other worlds. If I were asked to interpret the evidence, I would say that it seems to point to a multiplicity of beings living in a variety of 'other worlds' located not far away from ours but to which we do not yet have easy access. However, if you were to ask me again tomorrow for my thoughts on the matter, I might tell you that it is probably all in the minds of the witnesses . . . I would like to think that the Little People do exist and that there are other worlds than this, but I have not experienced either personally, and so I just can't be sure. If *you* have some evidence of your own, to help me make up my mind, please let me know.

# Appendix:
# Some Fairy Haunts in Britain and Ireland

## ENGLAND

**Beedon Barrow, Beedon, Berkshire:** The fairies lived on this round barrow, also known as Burrow Hill. A ploughman broke his ploughshare nearby and went home to fetch tools, but when he returned he found the fairies had mended it for him.

**Blackdown Hills, Somerset:** A man riding over Blagdon Hill in the seventeenth century saw what he thought was a normal fair, but when he rode closer he could see nothing, though he felt a crowd around him. When he got home, he became paralysed and never recovered.

**Cadbury hillfort, Congresbury, Avon:** The fairies used to live here.

**Carn Gluze round barrow, St Just, Cornwall:** Miners returning home at night saw fairies dancing around the barrow.

**Cauldon Low, Waterhouses, Staffordshire:** Fairies were seen dancing on the hill.

**Clint's Crags, near Ireshope, Durham:** The Queen of the Fairies was believed to live in a palace in a cave at the foot of these rocks on the south bank of Ireshope Burn in Weardale.

**Cusop Dingle, Herefordshire:** Fairies were seen dancing under the foxgloves.

**Dartmoor, Devon:** Many locations on the moor were believed to be frequented by pixies, such as a large hut circle on Gidleigh Common, a stone circle on Huccaby Moor, Piskies' Holt in Huccaby Cleave, and the Pixies' Cave which is a grotto below Sheepstor.

**Fairy Bridge, Ballasalla, Isle of Man:** The islanders used to doff their hats and greet the Little People at this bridge on the A5 road; one of their fairy hills was in a round barrow nearby.

**Fairy Hill, Bishopton, Durham:** When this old castle mound was being dug into, a voice was heard, telling the men to leave the hill alone. The work continued, however, and shortly the workmen found a large oak chest. Hoping to find it full of treasure, they broke it open, only to see nothing but nails.

**Fairy's Toot, Butcombe, Avon:** Strange noises have been heard at this damaged burial chamber, and fairies and goblins were thought to live here.

**Glastonbury Tor, Somerset:** St Collen visited the King of the Fairies in his palace on the Tor.

**Harrow Hill, near Patching, West Sussex:** 'The last home of the fairies in England' was the local belief. They lived in the prehistoric flint mines and earthworks on the hill, and when archaeologists came to dig up these sites early this century, the fairies were offended that their existence was denied, and they all left.

**Kenchester, Herefordshire:** The fairies used to dance in the Roman ruins, and Roman coins found here were called 'dwarfs' money'.

**King Stone, Rollright Stones, Long Compton, Warwickshire** (the Rollrights themselves are in Oxfordshire): The fairies used to dance at night around this tall standing stone opposite the stone circle; they came out of a hollow in the mound on which the stone stands. Stones placed over the hole were always found moved next day.

**Lough Goayr, Kirk Bride, Isle of Man:** Said to be one of the last places the fairies were seen on the island. They were cracking

their whips and shouting 'Hoi, son N'herin!' ('Hey, for Ireland!')
Presumably they were retreating to remoter lands.

**Men-an-Tol, near Madron, Cornwall:** The stones' guardian fairy
was believed to be able to perform cures, and this good fairy
could retrieve children who had been stolen by the evil fairies.
The changeling had to be passed through the hole in one of the
stones.

**Nafferton Slack, Humberside:** A large stone on the eastern slope
of the hill was believed to have strange powers. Sometimes it
seemed to be the entrance to a well-lit hall, and one man said he
had heard wonderful music coming from it. He had also seen
fairies going into the hall, some on foot and some in carriages.

**Ogo Hole, Llanymynech, Shropshire:** This cave in the hills was
believed to be an entrance to fairyland.

**Park Mound, Pulborough, West Sussex:** There are the ruins of a
Norman motte (castle) here, and a fairy funeral was once seen.

**Puckaster Cove, near St Catherine's Point, Isle of Wight:** The
fairies were believed to hold their feasts here, on the seashore. A
man who followed a strange light saw tiny people in red and
purple caps dancing to fairy music. They gave him a brown
powder to inhale, and he grew smaller. When they stopped
dancing, they sat on puffballs, which burst and showered gold
dust on them. They gave the man some gold and made him his
normal size again. No one has been able to obtain gold dust
from the puffballs at Puckaster Cove since that time.

**Pudding Pie Hill, Sowerby, North Yorkshire:** By running round
this barrow nine times and striking a knife into the top centre,
you will hear the fairies inside talking, when you put your ear to
the ground, for they built the mound and still live there.

**St Cuthbert's Well, Edenhall, Cumbria:** The now overgrown
well was in the garden of a demolished mansion, and was believed to be a fairy haunt. In Cumbria, a 'luck' was a relic which,
if cared for, would ensure the luck of the family and house, and
the 'Luck of Edenhall' was a glass vase or goblet, said to have

been stolen from the fairies, who prophesied: 'If that glass should break or fall, Farewell the luck of Edenhall.'

**Shan Cashtal (Old Castle), Andreas, Isle of Man:** The fairies used to travel along an underground passage from this earthwork to Maughold churchyard.

**South Barrule mountain, Isle of Man:** The god Manannan, Irish god of the sea who protected the Isle of Man, had his stronghold on South Barrule and worked magic there. The southern slopes were the most fairy-haunted part of the island.

**Tower Hill, Middleton-in-Teesdale, Durham:** The fairies used to go from the hill to the River Tees to wash themselves and their clothes. It was said that a woman found a fairy girl, dressed in green and with red eyes, sitting on a cheese-like stone. She took her home, sat her by the fire, and gave her bread and butter with sugar to eat, but the child cried so bitterly that she took her back to where she found her.

**Trencrom Hill, near Lelant, Cornwall:** The spriggans who lived on the hill were warrior fairies and very ugly; they guarded buried treasure and could call up storms. A man digging for the giant's hoard of gold believed to be hidden on the hill was frightened off when a storm blew up and swarms of spriggans came out from among the rocks, getting bigger as they drew nearer.

**Wick Barrow, Stogursey, Somerset:** A prehistoric round barrow also known as the Pixies' Mound: a man found a broken peel (wooden baking shovel) belonging to the pixies on the mound and took it away to repair it. He then returned it, and later found a cake left for him on the mound.

**Willy Howe, near Wold Newton, Humberside:** A man passing this round barrow at night heard singing, and saw a door leading into the mound. Inside was a well-lit room with people feasting, and a servant offered a cup to the man. He threw away the liquid, not wanting to be in the fairies' power, but ran off with the goblet.

## WALES

*Aberglaslyn Pass, near Beddgelert, Gwynedd:* Last century a man claimed he often saw fairies here: they were like little men, playing in the river.

*Beacon Ring, Trelystan, near Welshpool, Powys:* This prehistoric hillfort, crossed by Offa's Dyke Path, was believed to be a fairy dwelling place.

*Caer Drewyn, Corwen, Denbighshire:* The name of this hillfort means Gwyn's Homestead, and Gwyn was probably Gwyn ap Nudd, King of the Fairies.

*Castell Dinas Bran, Llangollen, Denbighshire:* A shepherd saw 'a little man in moss breeches with a fiddle under his arm' who invited him to join the fairy dance. He did so, and was so excited that he cried, 'Play away, old devil; brimstone and water, if you like!' Whereupon the fairies changed their shape and the fiddler turned into the Devil. The shepherd could not stop dancing, and was found next day by his master, 'spinning like mad' until the master broke the charm.

*Clocaenog Forest, Denbighshire:* The fairies have been seen at several locations in this remote area, now heavily forested, and on nearby Hiraethog (the moors around Llyn Brenig). A man witnessed a fairy dance by Pont Petrual and was taken to fairyland; but next morning awoke on a bed of ferns on the mountainside. The fairies also used to dance on Craig Bron Bannog, a hill in the heart of the forest.

*Craig-y-Ddinas, Pontneddfechan, near Glyn-Neath, Swansea:* This brooding rock face in its atmospheric wooded setting was said to be the last Welsh home of the fairies (see page 10 of photograph section). King Arthur and his knights are also said to lie sleeping in a cave here.

*Fairy Glen, Betws-y-Coed, North Wales:* This atmospheric place, a rocky valley through which the River Conwy flows, just to the south-east of Betws, was a place where the fairies were seen playing.

**Frenni Fawr, Prescelly Hills, Pembrokeshire:** A shepherd boy saw fairies dancing in a ring on the hillside and went to join them. He found himself in a fairyland palace where anything he wanted was his: but he was told not to drink from the fountain in the garden. Curious to know why not, he took a drink, and instantly the palace disappeared and he was alone on the cold hillside.

**Llangua church, Monmouthshire:** Last century, two people passing by the church saw dozens of fairies dancing in the meadows behind; they crossed the bridge in single file and went into the wood.

**Llyn Cwellyn, near Rhyd-ddu, Gwynedd:** A young man who stepped into a fairy circle by the lake found himself in fairyland. He didn't return to the human world for seven years, by which time his sweetheart had married another man and his parents were dead. The man himself died of a broken heart.

**Llyn Morynion, near Ffestiniog, Gwynedd:** A race of fairies lived in the lake, and one day they took back into the water a herd of cows which had been looked after by a farmer, until he displeased the fairies.

**Llyn Rhosddu, near Newborough, Anglesey:** A fairy who brought a regular loaf of bread to a local woman who had loaned her baking grid, was seen to plunge into the water of the lake.

**Llyn y Fan Fach, Black Mountain, Carmarthenshire:** A beautiful fairy maiden from the lake married a human man and they lived near Myddfai for many years, having three sons, but the wife in due time returned to the lake, followed by the cattle she had brought from the lake as her dowry. She later returned to teach her sons medicine and the use of herbs, and this is the origin of the famous Physicians of Myddfai, whose remedies have been preserved in manuscript form.

**Mynydd Llwydiarth, near Pentraeth, Anglesey:** The fairies would sing and dance on the mountain by night, and around the lake. They were 'an invisible race of good little people', who would disappear if approached.

*Pentre Ifan cromlech, near Brynberian, Pembrokeshire:* Fairies like little children in clothes like soldiers', with red caps, were seen around the stones of this prehistoric burial chamber.

*Porth Dinllaen, near Morfa Nefyn, Lleyn Peninsula, Gwynedd:* The fairies would dance and sing in the prehistoric earthworks on this coastal promontory; afterwards they would lift a certain lump of earth and descend to fairyland.

## SCOTLAND

*Broch of Houlland, Shetland:* Fairies playing the fiddle were heard in this ancient stone tower, and the tune was noted.

*Burnswark Hill, Annandale, Dumfries:* A fairy palace lay inside the hill, and the fairies were evilly disposed, abducting young men and women to work for them.

*Carmylie Hill, Glasgow:* A tumulus near the summit of the hill was called Fairy Folk Hillock because the fairies used to dance there at night.

*Dun Borbe, South Harris, Outer Hebrides:* The fairies lived in this ancient fort, and someone stuck an iron knife into the door, which they could not remove because they dared not touch iron. The man who took it out for them was given a quern for grinding salt by the Queen of the Fairies.

*Dun Borve, Snizort, Isle of Skye:* This ancient fort was a fairy dwelling until the local villagers shouted 'The fairies' fort is on fire!', whereupon they all fled. They left for good when they found they had been tricked.

*Dundreggan, Glenmoriston, Inverness:* Fairies lived in this knoll, and they always tried to kidnap mothers of new-born babies to be wet nurses to their own children. A farmer whose wife had just given birth was out tending his cattle, when he heard his wife's sigh in a gust of wind. He flung his knife into the wind, in the name of the Trinity, and she fell to the ground. He had rescued her from the fairies. Another local woman trapped in Dundreggan was rescued by sprinkling holy water on the mound.

**Dun Osdale, Duirinish, Isle of Skye:** A member of the Macleod clan was enticed into a fairy banquet being held in this fort. When they offered him wine in a gold cup, he did not drink it but stole the cup.

**Dunvegan Castle, Isle of Skye:** A tattered Faery Flag is kept at the castle, and there were several stories telling how it came into the family's possession. It was taken into battle by them, because when unfurled, so a fairy maiden said in one account, it would appear like a great multitude of armed men, causing the enemy to flee.

**Eildon Hills, near Melrose, Roxburgh:** Thomas the Rhymer, poet and prophet, saw the Queen of the Fairies while out in the hills, and she cast a spell on him, turning him into her slave. She took him into a cave and into fairyland, where he spent seven years before being allowed to depart with the gift of 'a tongue that could never lie'.

**Fairy Hill, Aberfoyle, Perth:** The Reverend Robert Kirk is said to have been taken into fairyland when he died on the hill in 1692. He was buried in the churchyard, but it was believed the coffin was full of stones. His grave can be seen, covered by a slab of red sandstone.

**Haltadans, Fetlar, Shetland:** Standing stones called 'the limping dance' where trows (the name for Shetland fairies) danced in the moonlight. Once they danced till sunrise, and for punishment were turned to stone.

**Tomnahurich (Hill of the Yews), Inverness:** There was believed to be a fairy living inside the hill; also it was said that Thomas the Rhymer sleeps there with his followers.

## Appendix

### IRELAND

**Ben Bulben, County Sligo:** Evans Wentz collected stories of sightings of the Little People in the shadows of Ben Bulben, like the men who heard music and voices like children's, at night, and the old farmer who saw several thousand 'gentry' in armour shining in the moonlight.

**Dun Aengus, Inishmore, Aran Islands, County Galway:** This magnificent prehistoric clifftop fort was one of the fairies' favourite abodes.

**Hill of the Brocket Stones, Carns, near Grange, County Sligo:** The gentry would come down from this hill like an army; they were like living people, but in different dress—'they were not living beings such as we are'.

**Knockmaa, between Headford and Tuam, County Galway:** This hill was the site of the palace of Finvara (Finbhearra), King of the Connacht Fairies. In the fairies' palace are also people they have abducted. There is an entrance to an underground world inside the hill. The fairy king is buried here in a stone cairn with his wife Onagh.

**Lough Gur, County Limerick:** Fairies were believed to live in the waters of the lake and in the surrounding countryside. Also in the lake is an entrance to Tir-na-nog, the Land of the Young, to which the Tuatha de Danann retreated.

**Lough Neagh, County Antrim:** The town traditionally lying beneath the water was inhabited by a fairy race, and people with the gift of fairy vision can still see the ruins of the beautiful palaces. Boatmen have heard the sounds of music and laughter rising up from the fairy festivals being held below.

**Newgrange chambered tomb, County Meath:** The famous prehistoric burial chamber was a fairy haunt, and people living nearby used to see the 'good people' come out at night and in the morning. Dagda, High King of the Tuatha de Danann, lived in the mound.

**Rathcroghan, County Roscommon:** Owneygat, or the Cat's Cave, is an entrance to the Otherworld.

**Slieve Gullion, County Armagh:** 'The good people in this mountain are the people who have died and been taken; the mountain is enchanted' (according to a local man who spoke to Evans Wentz).

**Slievenamon, County Tipperary:** A famous fairy palace was located on the eastern shoulder of the mountain, where the women of the fairy mound enchanted Fionn mac Cumhail.

# Bibliography

These books deal largely or wholly with fairies and fairy lore.

Andrews, Elizabeth, *Ulster Folklore,* Elliot Stock, London, 1913

Briggs, Katharine, *A Dictionary of Fairies,* Penguin Books, London, 1976

———*The Fairies in Tradition and Literature,* Routledge and Kegan Paul, London, 1967

———*The Vanishing People:* A Study of Traditional Fairy Beliefs, B.T. Batsford, London, 1978

Cooper, Joe, *The Case of the Cottingley Fairies,* Robert Hale, London, 1990

Gardner, Edward L., *Fairies: A Book of Real Fairies,* The Theosophical Publishing House, London, 1945

Gregory, Lady, *Visions and Beliefs in the West of Ireland,* G.P. Putnam's Sons, London and New York, 1920; second edition published by Colin Smythe, Buckinghamshire, 1970

Hartland, Edwin Sidney, *The Science of Fairy Tales,* Methuen, London, 1925 edition (first published 1890)

Keightley, Thomas, *The Fairy Mythology,* 1850; reprint of 1878 edition from G. Bell, London, published by Avenel Books,

New York, 1978, as *The World Guide to Gnomes, Fairies, Elves and Other Little People*

Kirk, Robert, *The Secret Common-Wealth*, edited with a commentary by Stewart Sanderson, D.S. Brewer, Suffolk, and Rowman and Littlefield, N.J., 1976

Logan, Patrick, *The Old Gods:* The Facts About Irish Fairies, The Appletree Press, Belfast, 1981

MacManus, D.A., *The Middle Kingdom:* The Faerie World of Ireland, Max Parrish, London, 1959

Narváez, Peter (ed.), *The Good People:* New Fairylore Essays, Garland Publishing, New York & London, 1991

Owen, Reverend Elias, *Welsh Folk-Lore,* 1888; 1896 edition from Woodall, Minshall & Co., Oswestry and Wrexham, republished by EP Publishing, West Yorkshire, 1976

Rhys, John, *Celtic Folklore, Welsh and Manx,* The Clarendon Press, Oxford, 1901 (two volumes); Wildwood House, London, 1980

Roth, John E., *American Elves:* An Encyclopedia of Little People from the Lore of 340 Ethnic Groups of the Western Hemisphere, McFarland & Company, Jefferson, NC, 1995

Smith, Peter Alderson, *W.B. Yeats and the Tribes of Danu:* Three Views of Ireland's Fairies, Colin Smythe, Buckinghamshire, 1987

Spence, Lewis, *British Fairy Origins,* Watts & Co., London, 1946
———*The Fairy Tradition in Britain,* Rider and Co., London, 1948

Thomas, W. Jenkyn, *The Welsh Fairy Book,* T. Fisher Unwin, London, 1907; University of Wales Press, Cardiff, 1952, 1995

Wentz, W.Y. Evans, *The Fairy-Faith in Celtic Countries,* H. Frowde, London, 1911; Lemma Publishing Corporation, New York, 1973

# Notes

See Bibliography for publication details of those books not fully described here.

## 1. "TWAS ONLY A PACK OF FAIRIES': FAIRY LORE IN GREAT BRITAIN AND IRELAND

1. A fuller explanation of the derivation of 'fairy' can be found in Spence, *British Fairy Origins*, pp.1–2, and in Noel Williams, 'The Semantics of the Word *Fairy*: Making Meaning Out of Thin Air', in Narváez, *The Good People*, pp.457–78.

2. Specific examples can be found listed in Leslie V. Grinsell, *Folklore of Prehistoric Sites in Britain* (David & Charles, 1976).

3. Wirt Sikes, *British Goblins* (first published by Sampson Low, London, 1880; reprinted by EP Publishing, 1973), pp.374–5. Also in Spence, *British Fairy Origins*, p.182. Other examples given on pp.181–4.

4. Lady Wilde, *Ancient Legends, Mystic Charms, and Supersti-

*tions of Ireland* (Ward and Downey, London, 1888; reprinted by O'Gorman Ltd, Galway, 1971), p.235.

5. MacManus, *The Middle Kingdom*, pp.116–17.

6. *Sunday Express*, 13 October 1968.

7. Gregory, *Visions and Beliefs*, p.141.

8. ibid., p.134.

9. MacManus, *The Middle Kingdom*, pp.111–12.

10. ibid., pp.99–100.

11. *Y Cymmrodor*, 7 (1886), p.56.

12. W.B. Yeats, *The Celtic Twilight* (Colin Smythe, Buckinghamshire, 1981), p.93.

13. MacManus, *The Middle Kingdom*, pp.62–3.

14. ibid., p.103.

15. Wentz, *The Fairy-Faith*, p.47.

16. Lewis Spence provides an overview of fairy appearance and costume in Chapter 8 of his book *The Fairy Tradition in Britain*.

17. 'Anglesea Folk-Lore' in *Y Cymmrodor*, 7 (1886), p.196.

18. Correspondence in *Archaeologia Cambrensis* (1886), p.72.

19. Briggs, *The Fairies in Tradition and Literature*, pp.138–9.

20. See entry 'Protection against fairies' for more details, in Briggs, *A Dictionary of Fairies*, pp.335–6.

21. MacManus, *The Middle Kingdom*, pp.119–21.

22. ibid., pp.121–6.

23. Harold T. Wilkins, 'Pixie-Haunted Moor', *Fate* magazine, issue 29, July–August 1952, pp.113–14.

24. See Rogo's books *NAD: A Study of Some Unusual 'Other-World' Experiences* (University Books, U.S.A., 1970) and *NAD: A Psychic Study of 'The Music of the Spheres'* (vol.2) (University Books, U.S.A., 1972).

25. Quoted in Briggs, *A Dictionary of Fairies*, pp.12–13.

26. E. Hamer, *Parochial Account of Llanidloes*, quoted in Owen, *Welsh Folk-Lore*, pp.102–3.

27. Rita Goold, 'Some Notes on Cornfield Circles at Two Sites

in Leicestershire (1988 and 1989)', *Flying Saucer Review*, vol.35 no.1 (1990), p.11.

28. *Coleraine Chronicle*, 26 January 1907, as reported by Sir Patrick Macrory in *SPR Newsletter* no.32, January 1990, pp.11–12.

29. Pierre Le Loyer, *Discours, et histoires des spectres* (Paris, 1605), quoted in Andrew MacKenzie, *The Seen and the Unseen* (Weidenfeld and Nicolson, London, 1987), p.85.

30. Published by Robert Hale Ltd, London, 1990, pp.69–71.

31. *The Countryman*, vol.76 no.4, winter 1971–2, pp.183–4.

32. Spence, *British Fairy Origins*, pp.176–7.

33. Spence, *The Fairy Tradition in Britain*, p.315.

34. MacManus, *The Middle Kingdom*, pp.78–81.

35. John Premnay, 'Small Tales of the Little People', *Country Life*, 24 May 1973.

36. Owen, *Welsh Folk-Lore*, pp.109–10.

37. Collecteana, in *Folklore*, vol.45 (1934), p.344.

38. Forby, *Vocabulary of East Anglia*, vol.8, p.108, noted in Eveline Camilla Gurdon, *County Folklore: Suffolk* (D. Nutt, Ipswich, 1893), p.35.

39. From 'The East Anglian' or 'Notes and Queries', vol.iii p.45, noted in Gurdon, op.cit., p.39.

40. Pennant, *Whiteford*, p.131, quoted in Owen, *Welsh Folk-Lore*, p.111.

41. Henry Morley, Memoirs of Bartholomew Fair (1859), noted in *Fairies*, catalogue of British Museum exhibition, 1980, pp.28–9.

## 2. 'DANCING WITH GREAT BRISKNESS': REPORTS FROM GREAT BRITAIN AND IRELAND BEFORE THE TWENTIETH CENTURY

1. Quoted in K.M. Briggs, *The Anatomy of Puck* (Routledge

and Kegan Paul, London, 1959), p.242; and John Ashton, *The Devil in Britain and America* (first published 1896, republished by Newcastle Publishing Co., Hollywood, CA, 1972), p.294.

2. John Beaumont, *An Historical, Physiological, and Theological Treatise of Spirits* (London, 1705), quoted in Briggs, op.cit., pp.243–5.

3. Owen, *Welsh Folk-Lore,* pp.98–9. Further comment is found in T. Gwynn Jones, *Welsh Folklore and Folk-Custom* (first published 1930, reissued 1979 by D.S. Brewer, Cambridge), pp.72–4.

4. A.W. Moore, *The Folk-Lore of the Isle of Man* (D. Nutt, London, 1891; republished by EP Publishing, Yorkshire, 1971), p.47.

5. Charles C. Smith, 'Fairies at Ilkley Wells', *Folk-Lore Record,* vol.1 (1878), pp.229–31.

6. Hollingworth's *History of Stowmarket,* p.248, quoted in Eveline Camilla Gurdon, *County Folk-Lore: Suffolk* (Folk-Lore Society, 1893), p.38.

7. John Harland and T.T. Wilkinson, *Lancashire Folk-Lore* (first published 1882 by John Heywood, Manchester and London, republished 1973 by EP Publishing, Yorkshire), p.111.

8. Wentz, *The Fairy-Faith,* pp.72–3.

9. Jonathan Ceredig Davies, *Folk-Lore of West and Mid-Wales* (Aberystwyth, 1911), p.124.

10. ibid., p.128.

11. Wentz, *The Fairy-Faith,* p.133.

12. William Martin, Collectanea, III. In the Isle of Man, *Folk-Lore,* vol.13 (1902), p.186.

13. Gregory, *Visions and Beliefs,* pp.219–21.

14. Transactions of the Devonshire Association, vol.60, quoted in J.R.W. Coxhead, *Devon Traditions and Fairy-Tales* (The Raleigh Press, Exmouth, 1959), p.51.

15. Katharine M. Briggs, *A Dictionary of British Folk-Tales in the English Language,* Part B., Folk Legends, vol.1 (Routledge & Kegan Paul, London, 1971).

16. Gregory, *Visions and Beliefs,* p.206.

17. Quoted in Jerome Clark and Loren Coleman, *The Unidentified* (Warner Paperback Library, New York, 1975), p.55.

18. Gregory, *Visions and Beliefs,* p.238.

## 3.  'LITTLE FIGURES DRESSED IN BROWN': REPORTS FROM GREAT BRITAIN AND IRELAND DURING THE TWENTIETH CENTURY

1. Gardner, *Fairies,* p.38.

2. Sir Arthur Conan Doyle, 'The Evidence for Fairies', *Strand* magazine.

3. Letter to Ernest W. Marwick quoted in his book *The Folklore of Orkney and Shetland* (B.T. Batsford Ltd, London, 1975), p.38.

4. Bessie Skea, 'Tales of little people and other isles legends', *Islander (The Orcadian),* (1991), p.4.

5. 'Dancing' in Briggs, *A Dictionary of Fairies,* pp.88–9.

6. See Chapter 8, Janet & Colin Bord, *Earth Rites* (Granada Publishing, London, 1982).

7. Letter in *Country Quest,* vol.14 no.6, November 1973, p.47.

8. David Clarke, 'From My Pennine Valley Notebook', *Magonia,* no.33, July 1989, pp.3–7; Peter Hough, 'Strangeness in Stocksbridge', *Fate* magazine, February 1991, p.55.

9. Robin Gwyndaf, 'Fairylore: Memorates and Legends from Welsh Oral Tradition', in Narváez, *The Good People,* pp.178–9.

10. Personal communication.

11. MacManus, *The Middle Kingdom,* pp.45–7.

12. Letter from Richard Holland in *Fate* magazine, December 1993, p.116.
13. MacManus, pp.38–9.
14. ibid., pp.36–8.
15. *Belfast Telegraph*, 9 November 1959, reported in *Folklore*, 71 (1960), p.53.
16. MacManus, *The Middle Kingdom*, pp.47–8.
17. 'More fairies seen' in 'I see by the papers', *Fate* magazine, April 1993, p.14.
18. Celia Green & Charles McCreery, *Apparitions* (Hamish Hamilton Ltd, London, 1975), p.158.
19. MacManus, *The Middle Kingdom*, pp.48–50.
20. Vivienne Rae-Ellis (editor), *True Ghost Stories of Our Own Time* (Faber and Faber, London, 1990), pp.80–1.
21. Published by Alasdair Alpin MacGregor, and noted in Peter Underwood, *Deeper into the Occult* (Harrap, London, 1975), pp.73–4.
22. Sam Hanna Bell, *Erin's Orange Lily* (Dennis Dobson, London, 1956), p.73.
23. *Irish Press*, 1938.
24. Nandor Fodor, *Between Two Worlds* (Parker Publishing Company, West Nyack, New York, 1964), p.192.
25. Alasdair Alpin MacGregor, *The Peat-Fire Flame* (The Ettrick Press Ltd, Edinburgh and London, 1937), pp.26–8.
26. MacManus, *The Middle Kingdom*, pp.32–5.
27. Letter in *John O' London's Weekly*, 28 March 1936, p.1023.
28. Sir Arthur Conan Doyle, 'The Evidence for Fairies', *Strand* magazine.
29. Gardner, *Fairies*, p.36.
30. ibid., p.38.
31. ibid., pp.40–41.
32. Letter in 'True Mystic Experiences', *Fate* magazine, May 1977, pp.52–3.
33. Personal communication, 1986.

34. Circumlibra, 'The Little Green Man', *The Ley Hunter,* no.40, February 1973, p.2.

35. More details of Roc's experiences are given in David Ash and Peter Hewitt, *Science of the Gods* (Gateway Books, Bath, 1990), pp.100–6.

36. Letter in *John O'London's Weekly,* 28 March 1936, p.1023.

37. Letters from Marina Fry, February 1973.

38. Gordon Creighton, 'A Weird Case from the Past', *Flying Saucer Review,* vol.16 no.4, p.30.

## 4. DWARFS, MUMMIES AND LITTLE GREEN MEN: LITTLE PEOPLE AROUND THE WORLD

1. For more details see Wentz, *The Fairy Faith,* pp:185–225.

2. *Sydsvenska Dagbladet Snällposten,* 5 August 1984, reported in *Fortean Times* no.43, p.45; *Wall Street Journal* (Princeton, N.J.), 13 July 1990, reproduced in *Forteana News,* January 1991, p.19; *European,* 6–9 August 1992, reported in *Fortean Times* no.74, p.16.

3. 'Fairies in the Lower Simla Hills, India', in Collectanea, *Folklore,* vol.45 (1934), pp.345–6.

4. M.J. Field, 'Gold Coast: Ethnography. The Asamanukpai of the Gold Coast', *Man,* 34, December 1934, pp.186–7.

5. For South American little people folklore, see *Strange* magazine, no.11, p.19.

6. Press report dated 11 April 1990 by *Edmonton Journal* writer Laurie Sardadif.

7. Mary L. Fraser, *Folklore of Nova Scotia* (1932), noted in John Robert Colombo, *Mysterious Canada* (Doubleday Canada Ltd, Toronto, 1988), p.31.

8. 'Cherokee "Little People" Legends of North Carolina' by Ron Martz, *Atlanta Weekly* (Georgia), 11 October 1987,

reproduced in *Pursuit*, vol.21 no.1, whole no.81 (1988), p.34.

9.  *Nature*, 66, 12 June 1902, p.151.

10. 'Unearthed Remains of a Dwarf Race': Report from *San Francisco Chronicle*, reprinted in *Toronto News*, 2 January 1891.

11. Information on the Pedro mummy from: John Bonar, *Goliaths of Glenrock* (Jelm Mt. Press, Laramie, Wyoming, 1981), pp.43–5; Ray Palmer, 'Mystery of the Midget Mummy', *Fate* magazine, September 1950, pp.74–6; letter from the Reverend Elvina Colburn of California, who saw the 'midget mummy', *Fate* magazine, April 1951, pp.96–7; 'The Mysterious Little People', *True West*, April 1983, pp.16–18.

12. Frank Farrara, 'Midget Mummy Mystifies Marinites', possibly from *San Francisco Chronicle*, 1 January 1979.

13. 'The Tools of Tiny People', *Mysteries of the Unexplained* (Reader's Digest, New York, 1982 & 1988), p.43.

14. Ulrich Magin, 'The European Yeti', *Pursuit*, vol.19 no.2, whole no.74, p.65.

15. Andrew MacKenzie, *The Seen and the Unseen* (Weidenfeld and Nicolson, London, 1987), pp.77–9.

16. Emma Hardinge Britten, *Nineteenth-Century Miracles* (New York, 1884), noted in Nandor Fodor, *Between Two Worlds* (Parker Publishing Company, New York, 1964), p.193.

17. *Nemere*, Transylvania paper, 16 March 1883, quoted in Wm Henry Jones & Lewis L. Kropf, 'Magyar Folk-Lore and Some Parallels', *The Folk-Lore Journal*, vol.I part XI, November 1883, p.361.

18. 'Dwarfs in the West', Folk-lore Miscellanea, in *Folk-Lore*, vol.4 (1893), p.402.

19. Gardner, *Fairies*, pp.36–7.

20. *Fiji Times*, 19 July 1975, reprinted in *Pursuit*, vol.12 no.3, whole no.47, pp.136–7.

21. Robiou-Lamarche, *UFOs Over Puerto Rico, Santo Domingo and Cuba;* supplied to me by Albert S. Rosales of Miami, Florida.

22. Fabio Picasso, 'Infrequent types of South American Humanoids III: Gnomes & Little Green Men', *Strange* magazine, no.11, pp.19–21.

23. William Allen White, *Autobiography* (Macmillan, London, 1946), described by Glenn Clairmonte in 'William Allen White and the Little People' in *The World's Strangest Stories* (Clark Publishing Company, Illinois, 1983), pp.205–6.

24. Alex Evans, 'Encounters with Little Men', *Fate* magazine, November 1978, pp.83–5.

25. 'Folklore from Nova Scotia', collected by Arthur Huff Fauset, *Memoirs of the American Folk-Lore Society* (American Folk-Lore Society, New York, 1931), p.89.

26. Fred Allen, 'Time Traveler in Morongo Valley', *Elsewhen,* vol.1 no.6, p.8.

27. Kenneth Arnold, 'How it all began', *Proceedings of the First International UFO Congress* (Warner Books, New York, 1980), p.26.

28. Found in Delmarva Historical Archives by Mark Chorvinsky.

29. George Young, *Ghosts in Nova Scotia* (The Lunenburg County Print Ltd, Nova Scotia, 1977), p.13.

30. Letter in *Fate* magazine, March 1978, p.128.

31. Karen Maralee, 'Fairy Dust', *Fate* magazine, September 1994, pp.55–6.

32. Fred H. Bost, 'A Few Small Steps on the Earth: A Tiny Leap for Mankind?', *Pursuit,* vol.12 no.2, whole no.38, pp.50–3.

33. A fuller account is given in Janet & Colin Bord, *Modern Mysteries of the World* (Grafton Books, London, 1989), published in U.S.A. as *Unexplained Mysteries of the 20th Century* (Contemporary Books, Chicago); see also Loren

Coleman, *Mysterious America* (Faber & Faber, London & Boston, 1983), pp.41–56.

34. Janet Ahmasuk, 'Stalking the little green men', Nome *Nugget*, 6 October 1988; reproduced in *Forteana News*, February 1989, p.18. See also Mark Chorvinsky, 'Alaskan Little Green Men', in his regular column 'Our Strange World' in *Fate* magazine, November 1990, pp.19–28, in which he describes and discusses the 1988 sightings.

35. Janet Ahmasuk, 'Little men visit Wales fisherman', Nome *Nugget*, 3 November 1988; reproduced in *Forteana News*, February 1989, p.20.

36. Janet Ahmasuk, 'Little people visit the village', Nome *Nugget*, 27 October 1988; reproduced in *Forteana News*, March 1989, p.18.

37. 'Elder recalls "little people" ', in *Valley Sun* (Wasilla, AK), 29 September 1992.

38. Ahmasuk, *Nugget*, 27 October 1988.

## 5.  UFO ENTITIES AND FAIRIES:
### ARE THEY THE SAME?

1. Owen, *Welsh Folk-Lore*, pp.93–4.

2. Investigated by UFO Norway/Leif Havik, and reported in *The UFO World '86* compiled by Jenny Randles, published by BUFORA (British UFO Research Association), May 1986, p.22.

3. Antonio Chiumiento, 'An Encounter with "Rat-Faces" in Italy', *Flying Saucer Review*, vol.28 no.6, pp.14–18.

4. Dr Walter Buhler, M.D., 'Extraterrestrial Dwarves Attack Farm Worker', *Flying Saucer Review*, vol.28 no.1, pp.5–8.

5. Both French cases from Aime Michel, *Flying Saucers and the Straight-Line Mystery* (S.G. Phillips, New York, 1958), p.154.

6. Alfred Budden, 'The Mince-Pie Martians', *Fortean Times*, no.50, pp.40–4.

7. Antonio Ribera, 'The Landing at Villares del Saz', in Charles Bowen (ed.), *The Humanoids* (Neville Spearman, London, 1969), pp.77–81.

8. Ahmad Jamaludin, 'A Wave of Small Humanoids in Malaysia in 1970', *Flying Saucer Review*, vol.28 no.5, pp.24–7.

9. Ahmad Jamaludin, 'Humanoid Encounters in Malaysia', *MUFON UFO Journal*, no.141, November 1979, pp.7–9.

10. Ahmad Jamaludin, 'Strange Encounters in Lumut', *Malaysian UFO Bulletin*, no.3, October 1981, pp.3–4.

11. Ahmad Jamaludin, 'UFO Reports from Malaysia, 1981–1987', *Flying Saucer Review*, vol.33 no.4, pp.22–3.

12. Jenny Randles, *The Pennine UFO Mystery* (Granada Publishing, London, 1983), p.156.

13. Jenny Randles, *Abduction* (Robert Hale Ltd, London, 1988), p.91.

14. Gordon Creighton, 'UFO, Occupants and Sex in Colombia', *Flying Saucer Review*, vol.23 no.1, pp.14–18.

15. A full report of the Villas Boas case is given in Gordon Creighton, 'The Amazing Case of Antonio Villas Boas', in Charles Bowen, op.cit., pp.200–38.

16. A.C. Haddon, 'A Batch of Irish Folk-Lore', *Folk-Lore*, IV, p.358.

17. For more information on changelings, see 'Changelings' in Briggs, *A Dictionary of Fairies*, pp.69–71; Wentz, *The Fairy-Faith*, pp.244–53; Spence, *The Fairy Tradition in Britain*, Chapter XIII.

18. Wentz, *The Fairy-Faith*, pp.125–6.

19. Briggs, *A Dictionary of Fairies*, p.66; see the entry for Captives in Fairyland, pp.62–6.

20. Jacques Vallee, *Passport to Magonia* (Henry Regnery Co., Chicago, 1969), pp.234, 242, 265, 308.

21. Kirk, *The Secret Common-Wealth*.

22. Rhys, *Celtic Folklore*, p.279.

23. In Jean-Claude Borret, *The Crack in the Universe* (Neville Spearman Ltd, Jersey, 1977).

24. Vicente-Juan Ballester Olmos, *A Catalogue of 200 Type-I UFO Events in Spain and Portugal* (Center for UFO Studies, 1976), case 22, p.5.

25. Bowen, op.cit., p.154.

26. Grafton Books, London, 1991.

27. William E.A. Axon, LL.D., 'Welsh Folk-Lore of the Seventeenth Century', *Y Cymmrodor*, vol.XXI (1908), p.116.

28. R.H.B. Winder, 'The Little Blue Man of Studham Common', *Flying Saucer Review*, vol.13 no.4, pp.3–4.

29. For further discussion of fairy and UFO lore, see Peter M. Rojcewicz, 'Between One Eye Blink and the Next: Fairies, UFOs, and Problems of Knowledge', in Narváez, *The Good People*, pp.479–514.

## 6. FALLEN ANGELS, PAGAN GODS . . . WHO ARE THE LITTLE PEOPLE?

1. Briggs, *A Dictionary of Fairies*, p.394.

2. A useful discussion of the fantasy-prone personality can be found in Keith Basterfield and Robert E. Bartholomew, 'Abductions: the fantasy-prone-personality hypothesis', *International UFO Reporter*, vol.13 no.3, pp.9–11.

3. Nigel Watson, Ian Cresswell, Granville Oldroyd, 'The Case of the Liverpool Leprechauns', *Magonia* no.18, pp.12–16.

4. Anthony Weir, 'Sweathouses: Puzzling and Disappearing', *Archaeology Ireland*, vol.3 no.1 (spring 1989), pp.10–13.

5. Bill Schmeer, 'The Entombed Miners' Staircase to Heaven', in *The World's Strangest Stories* (Clark Publishing Co., Illinois, 1983), pp.99–108.

6. Hilary Evans, 'The Case of the Little Man of Renèvé', *Magonia* no.22 May 1986, pp.9–11.

7. Personal communication.

8. Bob Rickard, 'Fairy Remains at Carlingford', *Fortean Times* no.52, pp.11–12.

9. Janet & Colin Bord, *Atlas of Magical Britain* (Sidgwick & Jackson, London, 1990), p.113.

10. Geoffrey Crawley, articles in issues of *British Journal of Photography* dated 24 December 1982, 31 December 1982, 7 January 1983, 21 January 1983, 28 January 1983, 4 February 1983, 11 February 1983, 18 February 1983, 1 April 1983, 8 April 1983, 24 May 1985.

11. See also Paul Smith, 'The Cottingley Fairies: The End of a Legend', in Narváez, *The Good People*, pp.371–405.

12. *Fairies*, Brighton Museum exhibition catalogue (1980), pp.40–1.

13. Peter Hough and Jenny Randles' investigation into the case is described in *Northern UFO News*, issues 131–136 (1988–9), where Peter Hough's 25-page report for MUFORA is summarized.

14. John L. Hall, 'Expect the Unexpected!': unpublished report dated November 1994.

15. Wilfred Mendis, 'Where the Pygmies of Ceylon Lived', *Loris*, 4 (1945), p.262.

16. S.V. Cook, 'Native Folk-lore. The lepracauns to Kwa Ngombe', *Journal East African Ug. Natural History Society*, no.20, November 1924, p.24.

17. Quoted in Wentz, *The Fairy-Faith*, p.137 note 2.

18. Briggs, *A Dictionary of Fairies*, p.47.

19. Andrews, *Ulster Folklore*, p.vi.

20. ibid., pp.8–9.

21. The fullest description of the pygmy theory can be found in Chapter VII, 'Were fairies a reminiscence of aboriginal races?' in Spence, *British Fairy Origins*.

22. Janet & Colin Bord, *Earth Rites* (Granada Publishing, London, 1982).

23. See, for example, Spence, *British Fairy Origins*, Chapter VIII, 'Are fairies derived from godlike forms?' and Chapter XI, 'Vestiges of cult in fairy tradition'; Wentz, *The Fairy-Faith*, Chapters 4 and 9; Logan, *The Old Gods*.

24. For more information on *Genii cucullati*, see H.R. Ellis Davidson, *Myths and Symbols in Pagan Europe* (Manchester University Press, 1988), pp.108–9; Miranda Green, *The Gods of the Celts* (Alan Sutton, Gloucester, 1986), pp.90–1.

25. Wentz, *The Fairy-Faith*, pp.xxiii–xxiv.

26. Nandor Fodor, *Between Two Worlds* (Parker Publishing Co., New York, 1964), p.191.

27. *British Fairy Origins*, p.110; and see the whole of Chapter VI, 'Fairies as elementary spirits'.

28. An account sent to Sir Arthur Conan Doyle, and used in his *Strand* article, 'The Evidence of Fairies'.

29. Account sent by Miss Hall of Bristol to Edward L. Gardner and used in his book *Fairies*, pp.37–8.

30. H.V. Morton, *In Search of Ireland* (Methuen & Co., London, 1930), p.179.

31. From *Account of Aberystwyth*, quoted in Spence, *British Fairy Origins*, p.164.

32. K.M. Briggs, 'The English Fairies', *Folk-Lore*, vol.68 (1957), p.285.

33. Spence, *British Fairy Origins*, pp.152–4.

34. An edition with a scholarly commentary by Stewart Sanderson was published by D.S. Brewer Ltd, Cambridge and Ipswich, 1976; Rowman and Littlefield, Totowa, N.J., 1976.

35. Briggs, *A Dictionary of Fairies*, pp.252–4.

36. ibid., p.234.

37. Gregory, *Visions and Beliefs*, p.119.

38.  A Welsh informant of Wentz, *The Fairy-Faith*, p.145.

39.  See especially Chapter IV, 'Fairies as spirits of the dead', and Chapter V, 'The ancestral character of fairy spirits'.

40.  See, for example, J.C. Cooper, *Fairy Tales: Allegories of the Inner Life* (Aquarian Press, Northants, 1983).

41.  C.J. Jung, *Dreams* (Ark Paperbacks, London, 1982), p.231.

42.  Fodor, op.cit., p.194.

43.  Dr Nandor Fodor, *The Haunted Mind* (Garrett Publications, New York, 1959), p.139 of Signet Mystic (New American Library, New York, 1968) edition.

44.  Letter in *Fate* magazine, issue 331, October 1977, pp.127–8.

45.  Dennis Stacy, 'An Unsolicited Elf', *Fortean Times* no.64, p.56.

46.  *Buenos Aires Herald*, 12 January 1977, noted in *Flying Saucer Review*, vol.23 no.5, p.iii.

47.  Irene Granchi, 'A pleasant encounter in Brazil with "human-looking" little people', *Flying Saucer Review*, vol.35 no.4, p.21.

7.   FAIRYLAND AND OTHER WORLDS

1.   Briggs, *A Dictionary of Fairies*, pp.141–3.

2.   ibid., pp.345–6.

3.   Quotation from Giraldus, as given in Owen, *Welsh Folk-Lore*, pp.32–6; see also Briggs, *A Dictionary of Fairies*, pp.118–20.

4.   Katharine Briggs, *British Folk Tales and Legends: A Sampler* (Paladin Books, London, 1977), pp.152–3.

5.   J.F. Campbell, *Popular Tales of the West Highlands* (Alexander Gardner, Paisley & London, 1890–93), vol.II,

pp.66–7; quoted in Briggs, *A Dictionary of Fairies*, pp.422–3.

6.  Letter printed in Richard Bovet, *Pandaemonium, or the Devil's Cloyster Opened* (1684) and quoted in Briggs, *A Dictionary of Fairies*, pp.423–4.

7.  Gregory, *Visions and Beliefs*, pp.56–7.

8.  Briggs, *British Folk Tales*, op.cit., pp.165–7.

9.  Translated from Ralph of Coggeshall and published in Keightley, *The Fairy Mythology*, pp.281–3.

10. Briggs, *A Dictionary of Fairies*, p.201.

11. Hartland, *The Science of Fairy Tales*, pp.161–8.

12. Briggs, *A Dictionary of Fairies*, p.400.

13. Hartland, op.cit., pp.225–6.

14. Numerous examples are given in Jenny Randles, *Abduction* (Robert Hale Ltd, London, 1988).

15. Wentz, *The Fairy-Faith*, p.49.

16. Dr Nandor Fodor, *Between Two Worlds* (Parker Publishing Co., New York, 1964), p.192.

17. Rhys, *Celtic Folklore*, p.215.

18. Walter Gill, *A Second Manx Scrapbook* (Arrowsmith, 1932).

19. Letter to *Fate* magazine, November 1956, pp.113–14.

20. *CUFOS Associate Newsletter*, vol.4 no.5, p.7.

21. Case 7235, *Northern UFO News*, no.115, September/October 1985, p.8.

22. Events quoted in the wife's words in Briggs, *The Fairies in Tradition*, pp.137–8.

23. 'Llowarch', 'Ghosts in the Post?' in 'Weird Wonders of Wales' column, *Cambrian News*, 8 March 1991.

24. Briggs, *The Fairies in Tradition*, pp.20–1.

25. Wentz, *The Fairy-Faith*, pp.152–3.

26. 'Fairy ointment', 'Four-leaved clover', 'Seeing fairies', in Briggs, *A Dictionary of Fairies*, pp.156, 180–1, 350–3.

27. Wentz, *The Fairy-Faith*, p.50.

28. ibid., p.131.

29. ibid., p.71 note 1.

30. Briggs, *A Dictionary of Fairies*, p.400.

31. Wentz, *The Fairy-Faith*, p.61.

32. Paul Screeton, *Quicksilver Heritage* (Thorsons Publishers, Wellingborough, 1974), pp.248–9.

33. S. Baring Gould, *The Vicar of Morwenstow* (1876), p.164.

34. Briggs, *A Dictionary of Fairies*, p.191.

35. Cynthia Hind, *UFOs—African Encounters* (Gemini, Zimbabwe, 1982), p.65.

36. Alan Gauld and A.D. Cornell, *Poltergeists* (Routledge & Kegan Paul, London, 1979), p.114.

37. Charles Fort, *LO!,* in *The Complete Books of Charles Fort* (Dover Publications, Inc., New York, 1974; *LO!* was first published in 1931), pp.698–9.

38. Theo Brown, *Devon Ghosts* (Jarrold Colour Publications, 1982), pp.24–6.

39. D.J. West, 'A Pilot Census of Hallucinations', Proceedings of the Society for Psychical Research, vol.57 part 215, April 1990, case 0878, p.176.

40. Ann Boyette, 'Did I travel in time?', *Fate* magazine, May 1956, pp.50–1.

41. Patrick F. Arnone, 'Beyond the Veil', *Fate* magazine, April 1982, pp.59–60.

42. More details and analysis of the case are given in *Flying Saucer Review,* November/December 1973 issue, and Jacques Vallee, *The Invisible College* (E.P. Dutton & Co., New York, 1975), pp.118–22.

43. Michael B. Sabom, MD, *Recollections of Death* (Corgi Books, London, 1982), p.281.

44. Frederic W.H. Myers, *Human Personality and its Survival of Bodily Death* (Longmans, Green, and Co., London, 1903), pp.315–22.

45. Robert A. Monroe, *Journeys out of the Body* (Souvenir Press, London, 1972), pp.94–100.

46. Mircea Eliade, *Shamanism* (Princeton University Press, 1964).
47. John L. Randall, *Psychokinesis* (Souvenir Press, London, 1982), p.216.

# Index

# JANET BORD

has co-authored numerous books on the paranormal

and, with her husband, Colin, runs the Fortean

Picture Library, a pictorial archive of mysteries and

strange phenomena. They live in Clwyd, North Wales.

# DEBBIE MACOMBER

## CHANGING HABITS

MIRA®

ISBN 0-7783-2028-6

CHANGING HABITS

Copyright © 2003 by Debbie Macomber.

Visit us at www.mirabooks.com

**Printed in U.S.A.**

To my cousin Shirley Adler
Who lived the life

Dear Reader,

The question I'm most often asked is where I get my ideas. The one for *Changing Habits* came from a birthday celebration for my cousin Shirley, who is a former nun. Sitting in the sunshine, drinking wine and laughing with Shirley and her friends, I suddenly realized I was the only woman there who'd never been a nun.

Twenty years ago Shirley was a Sister of the Presentation of the Blessed Virgin Mary. She made the difficult decision to leave the order and underwent the transition from religious to secular life. Shirley inspired me, as did her friends; they showed such courage, facing the world after all those years behind convent doors.

Like Shirley, I was raised Catholic and attended twelve years of parochial school. My best friend in high school, Jane Berghoff, entered the convent, with dreams of nursing the sick in India. After three years she, too, made the decision to leave. For a time, I'd also considered the idea of becoming a nun—but I discovered boys, and my interest in the religious life was soon a distant memory.

And now, dear reader—thanks to Shirley's birthday party—you'll meet three special women who each respond to the call. For the sake of their vocations, Angelina, Kathleen and Joanna each abandon the lives they'd led. Later, after Vatican II and the radical changes within the Church, their safe and secure world starts to fray, bit by bit. And then many of their traditions disappear—the habits, the new names they've taken, the routines they've become accustomed to.

I don't think I've ever devoted so much time and effort to research. I read books, from sociological studies to personal memoirs, interviewed nuns and former nuns and visited a monastery, all in preparation for writing *Changing Habits*. I am indebted to Shirley Adler, Sheila Sutherland, Jane McMahon, Diane DeGooyer, Theresa Scott, Mary Giles Mailhot, OSB, and Laura Swan, OSB, for their assistance.

I hope you enjoy Angelina's, Kathleen's and Joanna's stories.

Warmest regards,

*Debbie Macomber*

P.S. I enjoy hearing from my readers. Feel free to write me at P.O. Box 1458, Port Orchard, WA 98366, or visit my Web site at www.debbiemacomber.com.

*prologue*

1973

Kathleen waited in the cold rain of a Seattle winter as her brother placed her suitcase in the trunk of his car. She felt as awkward and disoriented as she probably looked, standing there in her unfashionable wool coat and clumsy black shoes. For the last ten years she'd been Sister Kathleen, high school teacher and part-time bookkeeper for St. Peter's parish in Minneapolis. Her identity had been defined by her vocation.

Now she was simply Kathleen. And all she'd managed to accumulate in her years of service was one flimsy suitcase and a wounded heart. She had no savings, no prospects and no home. For the first time in her life, she was completely on her own.

"I'll do whatever I can to help you," Sean said, opening the car door for her.

"You already have." Tears stung her eyes as her brother backed out of his driveway. She'd spent the last two months living at his house, a small brick bungalow in this quiet neighborhood. "I can't thank you enough," she whispered, not wanting him to hear the emotion in her voice.

"Mom and Dad want you to come home."

"I can't." How did a woman who was nearly thirty years old go home? She wasn't a teenager who'd been away at school, a girl who could easily slip back into her childhood life.

"They'd never think of you as a burden, if that's what you're worried about," her brother said.

Perhaps not, but Kathleen was a disappointment to her family and she knew it. She didn't have the emotional strength to answer her parents' questions. Dealing with her new life was complicated enough.

"You're going to be all right," Sean assured her.

"I know." But Kathleen didn't entirely believe it. The world outside the convent was a frightening place. She didn't know what to expect or how to cope with all the changes that were hurtling toward her.

"You can call Loren or me anytime."

"Thank you." She swallowed hard.

Ten minutes later, Sean pulled up in front of the House of Peace, a home run by former nuns who helped others make the often-difficult transition from religious to secular life.

Kathleen stared at the large two-story white house. There was a trimmed laurel hedge on either side of the narrow walkway that led to the porch. She saw the welcoming glow of lamplight in the windows, dispersing a little of the day's gloom.

Still, she missed the order and ritual of her life. There was a certain comfort she hadn't appreciated: rising, praying and eating, all in perfect synchronization with the day before. Freedom, unfamiliar as it was, felt frightening. Confusing.

With her brother at her side, Kathleen walked up the steps, held her breath and then, after a long moment, pressed the doorbell. Someone must have been on the other side waiting, because it opened immediately.

"You must be Kathleen." A woman of about sixty with short white hair and a pleasantly round figure greeted her. "I'm Kay Dickson. We spoke on the phone."

Kathleen felt warmed by Kay's smile.

"Come in, come in." The other woman held open the door for them.

Sean hesitated as he set down Kathleen's suitcase. "I should be getting back home." His eyes questioned her, as if he was unsure about leaving his sister at this stranger's house.

"I'll be fine," she told him, and in that instant she knew it was true.

PART I

# THE CALL

The harvest is plentiful but the workers are few.
*Matthew 9:37*

# chapter 1

# ANGELINA MARCELLO

## 1948 to 1958

"Angie, come here," her father called in heavily accented English. "Taste this." He held out a wooden spoon dripping with rich marinara sauce.

Obediently Angelina put her mouth over the spoon and closed her eyes, distinguishing the different spices and flavors as they met her tongue. "Not enough basil. You should add fresh chopped parsley, too."

Her father roared with approval. "You're right!" He tossed the spoon into the restaurant's large stainless steel sink. Then he reached for eight-year-old Angie and lifted her high in the air before hugging her tightly. It was 1948, and Angie's world revolved around her father and, of course, the family-owned business, the restaurant named after her. It was a well-known fact that Angelina's served the finest Italian food in all of Buffalo, New York.

Unlike other children her age, Angie's first memories weren't of being plopped on Santa's knee in some department

store for a candy cane and a photograph. Instead, she recalled
the pungent scent of garlic simmering in extra-virgin olive oil
and the soft hum as her mother bustled about the kitchen.
Those were the warm years, the good years, during the big
war, before her mother died in 1945.

Sometimes, late at night, she'd heard giggles coming from
her parents' bedroom. She liked the sound and cuddled up in
her thick blankets, her world secure despite all the talk of what
was taking place an ocean away.

Then her beautiful mother who sang her songs and loved
her so much was suddenly gone; she'd died giving birth to
Angie's stillborn brother. For a while, any hint of joy and
laughter disappeared from the house. A large black wreath
hung on the front door, and people stopped, stared and shook
their heads as they walked past.

Only five years old, Angie didn't understand where her
mother had vanished, nor did it make sense when strangers
crowded into her home. She was even more confused by the
way they put their heads together and whispered as if she
wasn't supposed to hear. A few wept openly, stopping abruptly
when she entered the room.

All Angie understood was that her mother was gone and
her father, her fun-loving, gregarious father, had grown quiet
and serious and sad.

"You're going to be a good Catholic girl," he told her soon
after her mother's death. "I promised your mother I'd raise
you in the Church."

"*Sí, Papa.*"

"Use English," he insisted. "We live in America."

"Yes, Daddy."

"I'll take you to Mass every Sunday, just like your mother
wanted."

Angie listened intently.

"And when you start first grade you'll attend St. Gabriel,
so the nuns can teach you."

She nodded; her father made this sound like a promise.

"It's just you and me now, Angelina," he whispered.

"Yes, Daddy."

"You're going to be a good Catholic girl," he said again. "You'll make your mother proud."

At that Angie smiled, even though she dreamed of being a cowgirl when she grew up so she could ride the range with Hopalong Cassidy. Her hero didn't look Italian but she made him so in her dreams and he ate at her father's restaurant and said it was the best food he'd ever tasted.

In 1948, by the time Angelina entered the third grade, she wore her thick black hair in two long braids that her father dutifully plaited each morning at the breakfast table. He put down the newspaper, giving his full attention to her hair, and when he'd finished, he carefully inspected his daughter. It was the same ritual every morning. Awaiting his approval, Angie would stand tall and straight, arms held stiffly at her sides. She wore her blue and gray plaid school uniform with the pleated skirt and bib front and anxiously awaited her father's nod, telling her she'd passed muster.

"Smile," he instructed on this particular day.

Angie obediently did as he said.

"You're as beautiful as your mother. Now eat your breakfast."

Angie slipped into the chair, bowed her head and made the sign of the cross before and after grace, which she said aloud. Then she reached for her spoon. She hesitated when she noticed her father's frown. Studying him closely, she wondered what she'd done wrong. The worst thing she could imagine would be to disappoint her father. He was her world and she was his—other than the restaurant, of course.

"It's nothing, *bambina*," he reassured her in gentle tones. "I just hope your mother forgives me for feeding you cold cereal."

"I like cold cereal."

Her father nodded, distracted by the newspaper, which he folded back and propped against the sugar canister while Angie ate her breakfast.

"I want to leave early this morning," she told him, struggling to hold back her excitement. "Sister Trinita said I could sing with the fifth- and sixth-graders at Mass." This was a privilege beyond anything Angie had ever been granted. Only the older children were permitted to enter the choir loft at St. Gabriel's, but Sister Trinita, the fifth-grade teacher, was her special friend. She chaperoned the children who attended Mass at St. Gabriel's every morning before school—children who rustled and fidgeted and talked.

Angie knew it was important to show respect in church. Her father had taught her that and never allowed her to whisper or fuss during Mass. She might not understand the Latin words, but she'd learned what they meant, and she loved the atmosphere of the church itself—the lighted tapers, the stained glass windows and shining wood, the Stations of the Cross telling their sacred story. Sister Trinita had commented one morning, as the children streamed out of the church and hurried toward the school, that she was impressed with Angie's respectful behavior.

That first time Sister had spoken to her, Angie knew she'd found a friend. After school the same day, she'd visited Sister Trinita's classroom and volunteered to wash the blackboards. Sister let her, even though Angie was only in third grade.

After that, Angie used every excuse she could invent to visit Sister Trinita. Soon she was lingering in the school yard after classes until she saw Sister leave. Then Angie would race to the nun's side so she could walk Sister back to the convent house, which was situated across the street. Sister Trinita looked for Angie, too. She knew, because the nun would smile in welcome whenever Angie hurried toward her. It became her habit to walk Sister Trinita home.

"You're going to sing with the choir?" her father asked, raising his eyes from the newspaper.

Angie nodded, so excited she could barely contain her glee. "I like Sister Trinita."

"Good."

His curt nod told Angie that he approved.

Scooping up the last of her Cheerios, she set aside her spoon and wondered if she should tell him that she'd started waiting for Sister Trinita outside the convent door each morning. She walked Sister to the church and then slipped into the pew where the third-graders sat.

"Sister Trinita says I'm her favorite." She hesitated, waiting for her father's reaction.

"Who is Sister Trinita?" her father asked unexpectedly. "Tell me again."

"The fifth-grade teacher. I hope I'm in her class when *I'm* in fifth grade."

He nodded slowly, obviously pleased with her acceptance by this nun. Pleased, too, with her daily attendance at Mass— even though he himself didn't like going. He went to Mass on Sundays because he'd promised her mother he would. Angie knew that. He'd made a deathbed promise to the wife he'd so desperately loved. A man of his word, Tony Marcello faithfully escorted Angie to church each and every Sunday and on holy days.

At night when he returned from the restaurant and sent the housekeeper home, he drilled Angie on her catechism questions. And on the anniversary of her mother's death, they knelt before the crucifix in the living room and said the rosary together. At the name of Jesus, they would bow their heads.

This morning, her father smiled as he drank the rest of his coffee. "Ready?" he asked. "If my little girl's going to sing in the choir, then I'll have to get you to church early."

"Ready." With her braids flapping against her navy-blue uniform sweater, Angie grabbed her books, her Hopalong Cassidy lunch bucket, and reached for her father's hand.

For two years, Angelina Marcello walked Sister Trinita to and from the convent each weekday. It broke her heart when Sister was transferred to another school in 1950, the year she entered fifth grade. Angie had turned ten.

After a while Angie stopped thinking about Sister Trinita, but she never forgot the nun from the order of St. Bridget's Sisters of the Assumption—the woman who had lavished her with attention when she'd most needed it.

In the summer of 1953, her father enrolled her in St. Mary's School for Girls. She would always remember that he sang

"That's Amore" as he drove her home following her interview with Sister St. George.

"Your mother would be proud of what a fine young lady you are," he told her, stopping at the restaurant on the way home. At age fourteen, Angie was waiting tables during the summer and cooking with her father, along with Mario Deccio, the chef. She knew the recipes as well as she did her own name. The restaurant was her life—until her senior year in high school.

Everything changed then.

"You *want* to do this?" her father asked, reading the senior class permission slip for the annual retreat. He looked at her carefully. "You want to travel to Boston for this retreat?"

"It's just for the weekend," Angie explained. "Every graduating class goes away for retreat."

"At a convent?"

"Yes. Sister St. George said it was a contemplative time before we graduate and take our place in the world."

Her father read over the permission slip again. "You know your place, and that's right here next to me at Angelina's."

"Everyone's going," Angie protested.

"All the girls in your class?" He sounded skeptical.

"Yes." She wasn't entirely sure that was true, but Angie wanted to be part of this retreat. After attending twelve years of parochial school, she was curious. Convent life was so secretive, and she didn't want to lose this one opportunity to see it from the inside.

"All right, you can go," her father reluctantly agreed.

He was right, of course; her future was set. She would join him at the restaurant and cook or wait tables, whatever was needed. The restaurant was the only life she knew, and its familiarity a continuing comfort.

Early that June, St. Mary's School for Girls' senior class left by charter bus for Boston and the motherhouse of St. Bridget's Sisters of the Assumption. It was three weeks before graduation. The first thing Angie felt when the bus pulled up to the convent was a sense of serenity. The three-story brick structure was surrounded by a tall fence and well-maintained grounds. While traffic sped by on the busy streets surrounding the convent, inside the wrought iron gates there was tranquility. Angie didn't know if her friends felt it, but she did.

Friday evening the sisters served dinner.

"They aren't going to eat with us?" Sheila Jones leaned close and asked Angie. Sheila and Dorothy French were Angie's two best friends.

"Haven't you ever noticed?" Dorothy whispered. "Nuns never eat with lay people."

Angie hadn't noticed, hadn't thought about it until then.

"I wonder if they've ever tasted pizza," Dorothy said.

"Of course they have," Angie insisted. "They eat the same food as everyone else."

"I wouldn't be so sure of that," Sheila murmured.

Angie wondered. She couldn't imagine life without pizza and fettuccine Alfredo and a dozen other dishes. These were the special recipes her father had entrusted to her care.

Later that evening, Angie was intrigued by the Spartan cell she'd been assigned for the weekend. The floors were bare, as were the walls, except for a crucifix that hung above the bed. One small window took up a portion of the outside wall, but it was too high to see out of and only allowed in a glimmer of sunlight. The single bed had a thin mattress and the bed stand could hold a lamp and a prayer book, but little else.

That first night when Angie climbed into bed, the sheets felt rough and grainy against her skin. She'd expected to fall asleep almost instantly, but her mind spun in ten different directions. This was holy ground, where she slept—holy ground on which she walked. Women who had dedicated their lives to the service of God had once slept in this room. This wasn't something to be taken lightly, she realized. She finally fell into a deep sleep sometime after midnight.

The second day of the retreat included an hour of solitary prayer. Each girl was to spend time alone to assess her calling in life. No talking was permitted, but they could speak to one of the sisters if they desired. Angie took pains to avoid her friends because it would be too easy to break silence.

"Angie!" Dorothy French's loud whisper echoed through the chapel as she loped down the center aisle.

Angie cringed and ignored her.

Undaunted, Dorothy slipped into the pew next to her. She rattled her rosary as she lowered her head and pretended to pray. "I'm going to bust if I have to go another minute without talking."

Angie glared at her friend.

"What about you?" Dorothy pressed. She stared at Angie. "Don't tell me this silence doesn't bother you, too?"

In response, Angie shook her head, slid past her and left the chapel. She'd been deeply involved in saying the rosary and resented the intrusion. Fearing someone else would distract her, she walked out of the building and decided to do the Stations of the Cross. The fourteen stations, which illustrated the stages in Christ's journey to crucifixion, followed a path that meandered through the lush grounds. The air was warm and perfumed with the scent of spring, and Angie felt an unmistakable surge of well-being.

It was at the fourth station, where Jesus met His mother on the road to Calvary, that Angie came upon an older nun sitting on a bench, her head bowed and her hands clasped in prayer. Not wanting to disturb the other woman, Angie decided to leave.

Just as she was about to turn away, the nun glanced up and as she saw Angie, a flash of recognition came into her eyes.

Angie took a second look. No, it couldn't be. "Sister Trinita?" she whispered.

The nun smiled. "Is it really you, Angie?"

"Yes…oh, Sister Trinita, I've thought of you so often over the years."

"I've thought of you, too. Are you a high school senior already?"

Angie nodded. "St. Mary's School for Girls."

"The years go past so quickly." Sister smiled gently. "I can hardly believe you're almost grown-up." She moved farther down on the bench, silently inviting Angie to join her.

"I was so disappointed when you were transferred," Angie told her. "I looked forward to fifth grade for two years." After her mother's death, Sister Trinita's departure had been the second big loss of her life.

"It was difficult for me to accept that I wouldn't be your teacher, but it was for the best. The decisions of the motherhouse always are."

Angie didn't agree. Sister Trinita's transfer, her disappearance from Angie's life, had seemed so unfair. "You had no choice?"

"No, but that's not the point. When I became a bride of Christ, I promised obedience in all things."

"I could never do that," Angie told her. She didn't like admitting to such a weakness, but it was true.

Sister Trinita laughed softly. "Of course you could. When God asks something of us, there's no thought of refusing."

Sister sounded so calm and certain, as though there was never any question when it came to obeying God, never any doubt. Angie was sure she'd turned God down any number of times.

"You've grown into a fine young woman," Sister Trinita said, her eyes soft with affection. "I imagine your father is very proud."

Angie shrugged. "I suppose so."

After another moment she asked, "You're assigned to the motherhouse?"

Sister Trinita smiled, but she hesitated before she answered. "For now."

"Oh."

There was a long silence, or maybe it only seemed long to Angie. Just as she started to speak, Sister Trinita rose slowly to her feet, tucking both hands in the capacious sleeves of her habit.

"It's been good to talk to you," Sister said.

"You, too." Angie wasn't ready to leave, and it seemed she was being dismissed. "Sister," she said, "could I ask you about being a nun?" It was the only question she could think of that would prolong the conversation.

Sister Trinita sank back onto the bench. "What would you like to know?"

Angie clasped her hands and gazed into the distance. It was so peaceful here in these gardens. The sound of traffic was muted by the many trees throughout the property. "When did you first realize you had a vocation?" she asked.

"Not until after I graduated from high school."

That surprised Angie. "So late?"

Sister smiled. "I was nineteen."

"But how did you *know?*"

Sister Trinita glanced down at her hands, which she'd removed from her sleeves. "That's not easy to explain. I felt it in my heart." She brought one hand to the stiff white bib of her habit. "I longed to serve God, to follow Him wherever He led me."

"Even if that meant not marrying or ever having children?" This was the most difficult aspect of a vocation for Angie to understand.

"It was what God asked of me."

"I couldn't imagine living without a husband," Angie confessed. "I'm sure I'd feel incomplete."

"I'm married to Christ, Angie. He is the one who makes me whole."

Angie didn't think she could ever feel the same. It wasn't as if Christ was here on earth. She wanted the same things in life that her friends did—a husband, a real flesh-and-blood husband. One who would hold her close and talk with her and…and kiss her. She wanted children of her own, too.

"Has your father remarried?" Sister asked next.

She shook her head. Her father never would. There was no room in his heart for another woman. No room for anyone other than Angie.

"Do you think your father is incomplete?" Sister asked. "He's lived all these years without a wife."

"Not at all," Angie said quickly, aghast at the suggestion.

Her father was content. He owned a thriving business, had his friends—he bowled one night a week with his cronies—and focused his hopes and dreams on her.

"Neither am I," Sister said. "You see, with obedience comes joy, and there is no greater joy than serving our Lord."

*No greater joy,* Angie repeated in her mind. It was at that moment that the idea sprang to life.

"Sister," she whispered, her voice trembling with excitement. "I think God might be speaking to me." It frightened her to admit it, to actually say the words aloud.

"Do you, Angie?"

"Yes, Sister." She exhaled sharply. "Oh, no!"

"No?" Sister asked with a gentle smile.

"My father—he won't like this." God was calling her. Angie felt the desire to serve Him gaining strength in her heart, becoming more real with every minute. When she'd first sat down with Sister Trinita, she'd had no idea where the conversation would take her. God had brought this special nun back into her life at exactly the right moment. It was His way of speaking to Angie and revealing her vocation. As always, God's timing was perfect.

"I have a boyfriend, too," Angie murmured, thinking of the obstacles she had yet to face. "He works part-time at the restaurant and he's cute, but…"

"Are you and this young man serious?"

"No…we're not going steady or anything." The truth was, Ken was more of a friend than a *boy*friend. They'd gone to her school prom together and they talked on the phone once or twice a week, but it wasn't anything serious. Ken would probably understand if Angie announced that she wanted to become a nun. But her father never would.

"Might I suggest you keep this matter to yourself for now?" Sister said.

Angie blinked back tears of joy. "I don't know if I can. I feel like my heart's about to burst wide open." She hurriedly wiped her eyes. "I really think God's calling me to be His bride. What should I do now?"

"Pray," Sister said. "He will lead you. And if your father objects, God will show you the way."

Shortly after she returned from Boston, Angie realized how right Sister Trinita was. She should've kept the call to herself. Instead, she'd made the mistake of telling her father she wanted to enter the convent.

"No! Absolutely not," Tony Marcello bellowed at his only child. "I won't hear of it."

"God is calling me."

Her father slapped the kitchen table with such force, the napkin holder, along with the salt and pepper shakers, toppled to the floor. His unprecedented violence shocked them both, and they stared at each other, openmouthed. Her father recovered first. "What did those nuns say to you while you were in Boston?"

"They didn't say anything."

"You're not entering the convent!" he shouted. "I won't allow it." His face had gone as red as his famous sauce and he stormed out of the house, slamming the door behind him.

Tears pricked Angie's eyes, but she refused to let them fall. Sister Agnes, Mother Superior of St. Bridget's Sisters of the Assumption, had warned the girls that if any of them had vocations, they might encounter resistance from their families. She'd said it was common for parents to have questions and doubts.

Angie had known her father wouldn't be pleased, but she hadn't expected him to explode. In all her life, her father had never even shouted at her. Not until the day she announced her vocation.

Two weeks after graduation, Angie broached the subject a second time.

Her father was in his restaurant office doing paperwork when Angie walked tentatively into the room. She closed the door, sat in the chair beside his desk and waited.

Her father glanced up and seemed to know intuitively what she'd come to discuss. "The answer is no, so don't even think about asking."

"I want you to talk to Mother Superior."

"Why? So I can get even angrier?"

"God is calling me to serve Him," she said simply.

Her father glared at her. "Your mother, God rest her soul, asked me to raise you as a good Catholic. I promised her I would—but I never agreed to this."

Angie's voice trembled. "Please, just talk to Mother Superior."

"No. Your place is here with me. This restaurant will be yours one day. Why do you think I've worked like a slave all these years? It was for *you*."

Although her heart was breaking, Angie held her ground. "I don't want the restaurant," she said, her voice a mere whisper now. "I want God."

Slowly her father stood, his face contorted with rage. "You don't mean that. If I thought you could truly believe such a thing, I—I don't know what I'd do. Now get out of my sight before I say something I'll regret."

Angie's sobs came in earnest as she rushed from the office. Nearly blinded by her tears, she stumbled past Mario Deccio, her father's friend and chef. Despite his concern, she couldn't explain what was wrong, couldn't choke out the words.

For two days Tony Marcello didn't speak to his daughter. For two days he pretended she wasn't in the house.

"Daddy, don't be like this," Angie pleaded on Sunday night. The restaurant was always closed on the traditional day of worship.

Her father ignored her and stared at the television screen while Ed Sullivan announced his lineup of guests.

Disheartened, Angie sat in the chair beside her father's. She started to weep. He'd never been angry with her before and she couldn't bear it, couldn't bear not having him speak to her. "Tell me what you want me to do," she pleaded between hiccupping sobs.

"Do?" he asked, looking at her for the first time in two long days. "What we've always planned for you. That's all I want."

"What *you* always planned for me," she corrected.

Her father's gaze returned to the television. "God took

your mother and my son away from me. I'll be damned if I'll give Him my daughter too."

"Oh, Daddy." Her heart ached to hear him utter such terrible words.

"Enough, Angelina. There's nothing more to talk about."

Defeat settled over her. "All right."

Frowning, he glanced at her. "All right?"

"I won't go."

His eyes narrowed, as though he wasn't sure he should trust her. Then he nodded abruptly and said, "Good." That settled, he returned his attention to the small black-and-white television screen.

She did try to forget God's call. Angie wrote Mother Superior a letter and said it was with deep regret that she had to withdraw her application. Her father would never accept her vocation and she couldn't, *wouldn't*, disappoint him. She was all he had left in the world.

Sister responded with a letter of encouragement and hope, and stated that if God truly wanted her to serve Him, then He would make it possible.

Angie wanted to believe Sister Agnes, but God had His work cut out for Him if He was going to change her father's heart.

To all outward appearances, he was dead set against her joining a religious order.

In July and August, Angie worked at the restaurant every day. At night, mentally and physically exhausted, she hid in her room and wept bitter tears. She feared that if she was unable to follow her vocation, her life would be a waste. She prayed continually and begged God to make it possible for her, as Mother Superior had said. Every night, on her knees, she said the rosary until her mind was too numb to continue.

The first week of September, just three days before the convent opened its doors to postulants, her father burst into her bedroom.

"Go!" he roared at her like a demon. He loomed in the doorway, his shoulders heaving with anger. "You think God wants you? Then go!"

Angie was too stunned to speak. She looked up from where she knelt, the rosary in her hands.

"I can't stand to hear you crying anymore."

Slowly Angie came to her feet. Her knees ached, her back hurt, but she stood there shocked, unmoving.

"Go," he said again, his voice lower. "It won't take you long to realize I was right. You're no nun, Angelina. It isn't God's voice you're hearing... I don't know who put this idea in your head, but they're wrong."

"Daddy."

"You won't listen to me. I can see that. If I make you stay, in the end you'll only hate me. This is a lesson you need to learn on your own."

"I wouldn't do this if I didn't sincerely believe I have a vocation."

He muttered something in Italian that Angie didn't understand. From his tone, she suspected it was just as well.

She wanted to explain that God had taken hold of her soul and she couldn't refuse Him. But she was afraid that if she gave him the slightest argument, he might reverse his decision.

"Thank you," she said, lowering her eyes, humbled that he had given in to her.

He didn't say anything for the longest while, and when he spoke, his voice shook with emotion. "I said you can go, but God help me, I refuse to drive you there."

"I can take the bus."

"You'll have to."

Saying goodbye to her father that September morning in 1958 was the most difficult thing Angie had ever done. He dropped her off at the Greyhound bus depot and hugged her tight. Then, with tears glistening in his eyes, he loudly kissed her on both cheeks.

"You'll be back," he muttered, backing away from her.

Angie didn't argue with him, but she knew otherwise. She'd been born to serve God as a St. Bridget's Sister of the Assumption.

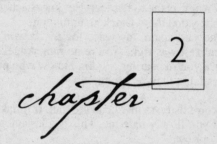

## KATHLEEN O'SHAUGHNESSY

### 1951 to 1963

Kathleen always knew she'd become a nun. She knew it from the day she received her First Communion. She heard her mother say it.

Kathleen stood with three of her cousins for a group photograph. She wore a white dress with a satin sash, a short veil and white gloves. It was the same Communion dress her three older sisters had worn. The same dress her cousin Molly had borrowed a year earlier. Kathleen held the white prayer book, clasped her hands and bowed her head devoutly for the camera.

"Kathleen looks like an angel," her aunt Rebecca said to Kathleen's mother.

Annie O'Shaughnessy nodded. "She does, doesn't she? I have the feeling Kathleen's going to be our nun."

"You think so?"

"Ned and I are sure of it."

Kathleen was sure, too. It was 1951 and she was all of six years old. By the time she entered high school on Boston's east side, there were ten mouths to feed in the O'Shaughnessy household. Kathleen ranked number five of the eight children sired by Ned and Annie O'Shaughnessy, only two of them boys. Everyone old enough to work was employed in the pub owned by her uncle Patrick O'Shaughnessy.

Kathleen and her sisters attended St. Mark's High School and were taught by St. Bridget's Sisters of the Assumption. After school each day, Kathleen and her year-older sister, Maureen, walked to the pub, where they worked as janitors in order to pay for their tuition at the parochial school.

They could have been twins, she and Maureen, they looked so much alike. Both had long thick auburn hair and eyes so blue they sometimes appeared violet. Kathleen's hair fell to the middle of her back and had the sheen of a new car, or so her mother claimed. It was her greatest delight, her hair, and she religiously brushed it a hundred strokes a night.

"Do you think nuns cut their hair?" Maureen asked her as they walked to the pub one cloudy spring day in March of 1962. Her siblings enjoyed riling her about convent life. They were jealous of the special attention their parents gave her because of her vocation.

"They probably do," Kathleen returned, refusing to allow Maureen to upset her. If chopping off her hair was what God asked of her, then so be it, she told herself. Nothing would dissuade Kathleen from her vocation.

"How can you stand it?" Maureen asked curiously.

"Having my hair cut? Don't be silly." Although the remark was flippant, it wouldn't be easy for her to lose her precious locks.

"No," Maureen countered. "How can you give your life to God? Don't you even wonder what sex is like and what you'll be missing?"

"Maureen!"

"Well, don't you?"

In fact, Kathleen thought about sex a great deal. She didn't want to admit it for fear her sister would tease her. Try as she might, she couldn't keep her unruly mind from wandering down that forbidden path. Obviously, anyone who wanted to be a nun shouldn't allow herself to dwell on such profane matters. It worried Kathleen immensely. She was about to renounce sex forever, and she had no idea what she was giving up.

"Don't you?" Maureen pressed, unwilling to drop the subject.

Kathleen increased her pace, but Maureen kept up with her. "I think about it some," she finally muttered.

Maureen slowed her steps and then in a low voice, said, "Robbie and I did it."

Kathleen came to a complete standstill and stared at her in shock. Maureen had lost her virginity? "When?" she gasped. Jesus, Mary and Joseph, her sister was *crazy* to risk getting pregnant.

"Last week… We weren't planning to do it, but his parents were out and we got to kissing, and the next thing I knew we—well, it just happened." Flustered, her sister tucked her schoolbooks tightly against her and looked straight ahead.

Kathleen's mind buzzed with a hundred questions, but she asked the most important one first. "Have you been to confession?"

"Not yet."

"Maureen, you're putting your immortal soul in jeopardy." Without absolution from a priest, her sister was headed for eternal damnation.

"I'll go to confession on Saturday, same as always," Maureen said, casting Kathleen an exasperated look. "Don't you want to know what it was like?"

God help her, Kathleen longed to hear every sordid detail. "Did it hurt?"

Maureen shrugged. "Some, at first. I thought we must be doing it wrong because Robbie couldn't make his…you know…go inside me."

Kathleen could no longer breathe and closed her eyes, mentally fighting off the image of Robbie squirming on top of her sister, pushing into her.

"When he did, I thought he'd ripped me wide open."

"Was there blood?"

"Judas Priest, I hope not! We were in the middle of the living room carpet... Anyway, if there was, Robbie took care of it. He's the one who'd have to explain it to his parents."

Kathleen's head started to pound. She was horrified that her sister had been so careless. "What happened after he put it in?"

Maureen looked away, but not before Kathleen caught a glimpse of her disappointment. "Nothing. Robbie kept saying how sorry he was and how he never meant to hurt me. Then he grunted a little and started to pant and before I knew it, he was finished."

It all sounded rather disgusting to Kathleen. "You'd better not wait until Saturday to go to confession. What if you get run over by a bus before then?"

Maureen rolled her eyes. "I can't go any earlier," she said.

"Why not?" She couldn't understand why her sister would take risks with her salvation, especially when Father Murphy heard confessions every morning before eight o'clock Mass. Maureen could slip into church on her way to school.

Kathleen was about to remind her of that when Maureen announced, "Robbie wants to do it again tonight."

"You can't!" Kathleen was aghast that her sister would even consider such a thing.

"His parents are going out of town and he said he'd pick me up at the pub once I'm finished cleaning." Maureen defiantly flipped her thick red hair over her shoulder. "I already said I would. There's just *got* to be more to it than what we did."

"Are you nuts? You can't take this kind of chance," Kathleen cried. "What if you get pregnant?"

"I know, I know... But Robbie said he'd use something so I wouldn't end up with a baby. And even if I did get pregnant, Robbie said he'd marry me."

"You're not even eighteen. What about college?" Her sister received top grades. She could get a scholarship; Kathleen was positive of that. No one in their family had gone to college yet. Sean had joined the Army when he graduated and

Mary Rose was married and the mother of a two-year-old.
Joyce and Louise shared an apartment and worked at the pub.
Joyce was a waitress and Louise made sandwiches back in the
kitchen. They split the tips. After they'd moved out, Kathleen
had a bed of her own for the first time in her life.

"You're only seventeen," Kathleen wailed. "How do you
know you want to marry Robbie?"

"How do you know you want to be a nun?" Maureen
flared back.

That shut her up. "Just be careful," Kathleen cautioned.

"You won't tell Mom, will you?"

Kathleen promised she wouldn't.

Late that same night, Maureen woke her out of a deep
sleep. Moonlight shimmered in through the sheer drapes, and
the sound of the television traveled up the stairs like distant
whispers.

"Are you awake?" her sister asked, putting her hand on
Kathleen's shoulder and lightly shaking her.

Kathleen propped herself up on one elbow. It sounded like
*Ben Casey* playing downstairs, which would keep her mother
distracted. Maureen's eyes sought hers.

"Did you do it?" Kathleen whispered.

Maureen nodded. "Twice."

"In one night?"

Again her sister nodded.

Kathleen shouldn't be this anxious for details, but she had
to know, despite the fact that she'd never experience physical
love herself. She sat up and wrapped her arms around her bent
knees. "Tell me what it was like."

A soft smile lifted the edges of her sister's full mouth. "I
know why Mom and Dad had eight of us. It feels so good,
Kathleen. It's like…oh, I don't know. It's like nothing else in
the whole world."

Kathleen leaned against the headboard and bit her lower lip,
taking in her sister's words. "Did Robbie use…protection?"

Maureen lowered her eyes.

"Maureen!" Sure as anything, her sister was going to end

up pregnant before graduation and the whole family would be disgraced.

"He put it on, but he said it wasn't as good and—"

"You should've made him do it." Kathleen covered her mouth with both hands, equally dismayed at her sister's foolishness and her own willingness to abandon the Church's stand on birth control. "If you get pregnant, Mom and Dad will kill you."

Indignant, Maureen leapt off the bed. "Robbie said it was a big mistake to tell you. I should've listened to him. Miss Goody Two-shoes. No wonder entering the convent is all you talk about."

"That's not true," Kathleen snapped.

"If you tell Mom or Dad, I'll never forgive you."

"I'm not going to tell."

Maureen hurriedly undressed in the dark. "I could never enter the convent," she whispered, calmer now.

"Because you've lost your virginity?"

"No," she returned with a snicker, "because I could never live without sex. You're better off not knowing, Kathleen. If you did, you wouldn't be so keen to listen to that call from God you're always saying you hear."

Thankfully Maureen wasn't pregnant, although once she and Robbie had started having sex they couldn't seem to stop. Three months after graduation, Maureen had an engagement ring, and all thoughts of attending college were discarded like yesterday's newspaper.

In the last month of her junior year, Kathleen was elected prefect of the Sodality, the society dedicated to the devotion to Mary, the mother of Christ. She felt elated that her classmates had entrusted her with this honor—until her uncle Patrick unexpectedly pulled her aside at the pub one afternoon.

Kathleen was sure he intended to offer her a weekend job as a waitress. She was a good worker and the extra money would mean she could afford a few extras without having to ask her mother.

"Sit down, Kathleen," her uncle said, showing her to a

table at the back of the pub. She wondered why he'd chosen to sit in the shadows.

He pulled out a chair for her, and as she sat, she glanced down at the floor; even in this dark corner it shone. She took whatever task she was given seriously. There wasn't a spot or a speck of dust on the polished oak floor.

"I've never hidden the fact that you're my favorite niece," her uncle said, folding his arms across his big chest.

He wiped the back of his hand across his mouth, and Kathleen wondered if he was already into the beer. Her uncle had a weakness for his own product.

"Since you *are* my favorite, it pains me to tell you this. Damn, it doesn't seem right, but your mother and father said…" He let his words fade, then took a deep breath. "I'm afraid I'm going to have to let you go."

Kathleen thought she must have heard wrong. Let her go? It sounded as though her own uncle was firing her. She couldn't imagine what she'd done to deserve this. Furthermore, without the job, she had no way of paying her tuition. When the shock wore off and Kathleen managed to find her tongue, she said, "You don't want me working at the pub any longer?"

Her uncle stood abruptly. "Back in a minute." With that, he trotted toward the bar and drew himself a mug of Harp. He took a healthy swig before he sat down at the table again. "Let me tell you a story."

Her uncle was the best storyteller she'd ever met. It was one reason the pub was so popular. Boston didn't lack for Irish pubs, but every night her uncle's tavern was filled with music and laughter. And every night, the affable Patrick O'Shaughnessy entertained the crowd with a story or two. He had the gift, and what a gift it was. But if not for her father's handling of the accounts, she feared her uncle would have lost the pub ten times over. Although he was a wonderful host and told a grand story, her uncle Patrick had no sense when it came to money or beer.

"Did I do something wrong?" she asked before he could get caught up in one of the Irish legends or folktales he loved.

"Wrong? My Kathleen? Never!"

"Then why are you telling me I can't work in the pub anymore?" Apparently her mother and father already knew because her uncle had discussed it with them. Come to think of it, her father generally did the hiring and firing for the pub. Not this time, though.

Uncle Patrick leaned over and clasped her hand in his. "Your parents and I talked it over, and we decided it just isn't right for you to be here."

"But why?"

"Kathleen, you've a calling from God!"

"Yes, but…"

"Next year you'll be in a convent. And now that you're head of the Sodality, well…it isn't seemly to have you working in a tavern."

"But Father O'Hara is here two and three nights a week."

"Father O'Hara isn't a nun. It's different with priests. I don't know why, but it is. Now, I realize this comes as a shock—and that you need the money for tuition."

A sick feeling settled in the pit of her stomach. It wasn't her father or even her uncle who'd come up with this outlandish notion. That…that sodden priest must have planted the idea in their minds. "Is this Father O'Hara's doing?" she demanded.

"None of that matters, Kathleen. Just accept that we all want the best for you. This is hard on me, too, you know. Your beautiful face won't be gracing my afternoons any longer, now will it?"

In less than a year she'd be a postulant. When Kathleen entered the religious life, she'd be required to relinquish the things of the world, but that was months away yet. She hadn't thought she'd have to give up her job quite so soon.

"I feel bad about this," her uncle continued.

Kathleen tried not to show her distress. She'd need to make certain sacrifices in order to serve God. She was willing to cut her hair if God asked it of her, although she prayed He wouldn't. Sex was out of the question for her, too, even though

Maureen insisted on filling her in on all the details of what she and Robbie were doing. She hadn't even walked through the convent doors and already she was expected to behave like a nun. It hurt that her only source of income was to be taken away from her, and all because of Father O'Hara.

"Will I have to leave St. Mark's?" It would be a bitter disappointment not to graduate with her friends.

"Now, that would be a sin," her uncle told her, sipping his lager. "Your tuition's been paid up for the remainder of the school year."

Kathleen gasped. "You did that?"

"I can't have my sweet Kathleen worrying about paying her school fees, now can I?" He winked boyishly at her above his mug. "Father O'Hara and I worked out a deal."

He didn't need to tell her what the deal was. Beer in exchange for tuition. Still, she had no complaints as long as she graduated from St. Mark's.

To her surprise, Uncle Patrick's eyes misted. "You're the pride and joy of this family," he whispered. "We all hoped one of the O'Shaughnessy brood would heed God's call. You make us proud."

She murmured her thanks, a little uncomfortable at his emotion.

"You have always been a sweet girl. No wonder God wants you."

The summer of 1963 was the most carefree of Kathleen's life. Knowing that she'd be entering the order of St. Bridget's Sisters of the Assumption in September, she spent lazy afternoons listening to the Beach Boys and Martha and the Vandellas. She even took up the guitar and managed to pick her way through a whole repertoire of songs. The Singing Nun had made "Dominique" popular and for a time Kathleen entertained the notion of forming a band of singing postulants. She wondered what Reverend Mother would feel about that. Maybe nuns could be actresses, too. *Lilies of the Field* had been one of the most popular movies of the year. It would've been far more authentic if they'd used real nuns to act with Sidney Poitier, Kathleen mused.

The highlight of the summer, however, came in August, when her oldest brother Sean was home on leave from the Army. He was so handsome that Kathleen nearly burst with pride when she saw him.

"What's it like being a Green Beret?" she asked, sipping a tall glass of iced tea on the front porch swing. She wore cut-off jeans and a sleeveless blouse and no shoes. This was her last fling before the convent.

"Good." Sean sat down on the porch step and dangled his arms over his knees. "I'd forgotten about summers in Boston," he said, wiping the sweat from his brow.

"Are you enjoying Seattle?"

"Yeah." He leaned against the porch column and stared up at her. "You're absolutely certain about this, Kathleen?" he asked, frowning. "You don't look like someone who wants to be a nun."

She smiled and wondered if he knew what a wonderful compliment he'd given her. "I leave for the convent in two weeks."

"What if you don't like it?"

"I will," she said with utter confidence. She hadn't made a contingency plan because she was sure she wouldn't need one.

Sean reached for his iced tea. "I was thinking back the other day, and I can't remember a time when we didn't know you were going to be a nun."

Kathleen stretched out her bare legs. "First grade I knew."

"At six years old?"

She nodded solemnly. "It was during my First Communion that I heard God calling me."

"Was that God or was it Mom and Dad?" Sean asked with more than a little sarcasm.

"What do you mean?"

"Everyone just kind of assumed this was right for you. Is it something you truly want or did you just accept what the family decided?"

"Oh, Sean, don't be ridiculous."

"Have you ever been kissed?"

"Why do you want to know that?" Answering with a question saved her the embarrassment of admitting the truth.

"You haven't experienced life yet. All you know is home and school and working at Uncle Patrick's place. There's a whole world out there. Don't get me wrong, I love Mom and Dad, but we've lived a sheltered life. Take a few years, travel, go off to college and meet a boy or two before you make your final decision about this nun business."

"This is what I want, Sean. Be happy for me, all right?"

Sean didn't comment for several moments. Then he said, "Promise me one thing."

"What?"

"If you ever decide the convent isn't for you, you won't hesitate to leave."

"Break my vows?" Kathleen had never heard of anyone doing something so dreadful.

"Yes, if that's what it takes."

She was positive he didn't mean that. "Would you ever leave the Army?"

"It's different, Kathleen."

"Is it?"

"Just promise me. I'll rest easier giving my sister to God, knowing that if you change your mind you'll have the courage to walk away."

What an unusual request. She tried to laugh it off, but he wouldn't let her.

"I'm serious," Sean insisted. "I need to hear you say it."

Kathleen weighed her words. This was the strangest discussion she'd ever had with her oldest brother. "I promise." But her decision had been made years earlier. She belonged to God.

# chapter 3

## JOANNA BAIRD

### 1965 to 1967

"Greg, we can't," Joanna managed to say between increasingly deep, urgent kisses. "Not again. We promised." Her boyfriend dragged her mouth back to his. Already his hands were inside her blouse, fumbling with the snap of her bra.

"I can't help it," Greg Markham groaned. "I've missed you so much. I need you, baby."

In the back seat of his 1956 Chevy Bel-Air, Joanna made one last desperate attempt to clear her head. It was too late to reason with Greg, though, and she knew it. She'd missed him, too. Just back from basic training, her high school boyfriend was about to leave for Vietnam, and their time together was limited. Without further protest, she rolled up her skirt and worked off her underwear. Soon he was positioned over her in the cramped car.

Joanna wound her arms around his neck as he slowly sank his body into hers. Closing her eyes, she sighed audibly as she arched up to receive him. She gave herself over to the familiar sensations. Frenzied now, she and Greg churned against each other until his release came in a deep, guttural moan.

Breathing hard, he buried his face in the curve of her neck. "I'm sorry, baby, so sorry."

She didn't know why he felt the need to apologize. She'd wanted him as much as he'd wanted her. Perhaps even more. She might have made a token protest, but she'd been the one who'd purposely set out to arouse him. Using her body to tempt him gave her a sense of power, a sense of control, and she loved it. Loved *him.* Catching his earlobe between her teeth, she relished his body's shiver of renewed arousal. Moving provocatively against him, she whispered, "I haven't even finished my penance from the last time."

"Me neither," Greg said and laughed softly.

When Greg had gone to confession, his penance had been harsh and unreasonable, Joanna thought. Father Kramer had instructed her to say the Rosary six times, but he'd ordered Greg to give up cigarettes for seven whole days. Greg hadn't managed to go without his smokes for five hours, let alone a week. It was unfair of Father Kramer to be so hard on Greg while letting her off so lightly.

Raising himself, Greg awkwardly yanked up his jeans. She heard his zipper close as she struggled to sit upright with her skirt around her waist. He climbed out of the car for a smoke while Joanna tried to rearrange her clothes. She searched for her nylons and sighed with relief when she found them both. The last time they'd made love in the car, one of her nylons had been tucked under the seat. They'd spent an anxious ten minutes looking for it. If she were to walk into the house without it, her parents would know she'd been up to no good.

"Are you dressed?" Greg asked as he opened the car door.

Joanna glanced out. "Is anyone coming?"

Greg chuckled. "Just me."

She groaned. "You know what I mean."

His gaze held hers and the amusement left his eyes. "Oh baby, what am I going to do?"

In a week Greg would be shipping out to Vietnam. In May, shortly after they graduated, he'd enlisted in the Army. His timing was perfect; just a month later, in July, President Johnson had announced the escalation of the war in Vietnam and said that draft calls would be doubled.

"You'll wait for me, won't you?" Greg pleaded.

Joanna didn't understand why he kept asking her that. "You know I will." She'd be starting nursing school at Holy Name Hospital in Providence a few weeks from now. Between her studies, hospital work and writing Greg, she wouldn't have time to meet anyone else. She didn't want to, loving Greg as much as she did.

Stepping out of the car, she wrapped her arms around his middle and wriggled sensually.

"Baby," he moaned and twisted around, backing her against the passenger door. "You know what that does to me."

Joanna sighed and slid her arms around his neck. "I love you, Greg."

"I love you." He leaned away slightly and his eyes held hers. "How am I going to survive an entire year without making love to you?"

"I'll wait for you."

He frowned as though he wasn't sure he believed her, no matter how many times she repeated it.

Then, two days before Greg was scheduled to depart for Vietnam, Joanna arrived home to find him sitting in the living room, talking intently with both her parents.

"Hi," she said, entering the house. She hadn't expected him, but it wasn't unusual for Greg to stop by unannounced. What *was* unusual was to find her parents with him.

"Joanna." He automatically stood when she walked into the room.

Her mother wiped a tear from the corner of her eye and smiled warmly at Joanna.

"What's the matter?" Joanna asked. Clearly *something* was from the way everyone was staring at her. She seemed to be the only one who didn't get whatever was going on.

"Nothing's wrong," her father assured her, steering his wife from the room. "Not a thing."

"Greg?" Joanna asked.

The next moment, he actually got down on one knee. "Joanna," he said, gazing up at her, "will you marry me?"

Joanna gasped as he pulled a small velvet box from his pocket. Greg opened the ring box to display a solitaire diamond in an antique gold setting. They'd talked about the future and decided they wanted to get married, but their plans were for an unspecified date sometime in the future. Marriage would come after she'd received her nursing degree and Greg was settled in with his father's business. Vietnam, however, was about to change all that.

"Greg, yes! Yes, yes, oh yes."

He slipped the ring onto her finger and kissed her. Her parents, smiling broadly, wandered back into the room. Her father wrapped his arm around her mother, who was struggling to hide her tears of joy.

"I came to ask your family for their permission," Greg explained. "I want to do everything right, just the way my father did."

Joanna wiped the tears from her own cheeks. "Mom, look." She held out her left hand so her mother could inspect the small diamond.

"Your father asked me to marry him just before he left to fight in World War Two," she said, hugging Joanna and then Greg.

"What's happening?" Rick, her sixteen-year-old brother, asked as he sauntered into the room, munching a crisp apple.

"Joanna and Greg are engaged."

"Joanna's getting married?" Rick noisily bit into his apple. "I thought you were going to be a nun."

"Rick!" She couldn't believe her brother would bring up that long-ago ambition now.

"A nun?" One corner of Greg's mouth turned up in the start of a smile. Knowing the things he did about her, he had reason to be amused. Joanna elbowed him in the ribs before he could let out their secret.

"You're stealing my little girl away from God," her father said.

"Daddy," Joanna protested, furious that her family would take such delight in teasing her.

"Cut it out, you two." Her mother stepped in to rescue her. "Joanna considered the convent when she was a high school freshman. That's all there is to it."

"Well, God can't have her," Greg said, throwing his arm around her. He kissed the top of her head. "I've got her now."

Rick took another loud bite of his apple. "When's the wedding?"

Greg and Joanna exchanged glances, and then burst out laughing because they didn't know. Soon, they decided. Greg would serve his year in Vietnam and when he returned, they'd get married. While he was off at war, Joanna would make all the wedding arrangements.

Eventually the date was set for September of the following year. That gave Joanna and her mother a little more than fourteen months to plan.

Two days later, Greg left for Vietnam. Joanna rode with him to the airport, where—along with his mother and father—she tearfully saw him off. As the jet zoomed into the sky, she felt a sensation of dread and wondered if this would be the last time she saw Greg.

A week following his departure for Asia, Joanna entered the hospital nursing program. Within a matter of days, her world revolved around her studies, writing Greg and all the planning that went into a big wedding.

"I don't know what I'd do if I didn't have the wedding to distract me," she wrote Greg early in December as her hi-fi belted out "I Can't Get No Satisfaction" by the Rolling Stones. "If I wasn't busy thinking about the wedding, I'd be worrying about you. Now, honey, please take care of yourself. I love you so much."

Greg's letters were full of details about his assignment and his life in Saigon, where he was stationed. He spoke of the squalor and the effects of the war on the people of the Southeast Asian country. He mailed her small things he found in the local shops—a bracelet, silk pajamas, an ivory-handled mirror. He was fortunate not to be in a combat situation; instead, he'd been assigned to desk duty with the Military Police and typed up volumes of paperwork whenever a soldier was sent to the stockade. One bonus to this assignment was that he had plenty of time to write. In the beginning, he mailed a long letter nearly every day.

January 3, 1966
Sweetheart,
    Thanks for sending me the fabric swatches for the bridesmaids' dresses. You sure you want *five* bridesmaids? Never mind, you can have ten if it makes you happy. I like the green one best, but you decide. I'll come up with five ushers, but I'll probably need to ask a cousin or two.
    It was hard not being home for Christmas. I hope you like your gift. A set of bone china isn't as romantic as I would've liked, but that was what you said you wanted. I hope you like the pattern I picked out. Just think—one day you'll be my wife and you'll cook me dinner and serve it to me on those very plates.
    Write soon. I live for your letters.

                                                            Greg

Joanna lived for his letters, too. Each day she hurried home from school and sorted through the mail, suffering keen disappointment if there wasn't one.
    "I don't think there's a letter from Greg," her mother said. It was a cold February afternoon, and Joanna, still wearing her coat, flipped through a stack of envelopes on the kitchen table.
    "I haven't heard from him in three days."
    "I'm sure he's fine."
    "I'm sure he is, too," Joanna said, but she wondered and worried all the same.
    That evening her best friend phoned. "We're going to see *My Fair Lady.* Why don't you come along?"

Joanna was tempted, really tempted. She enjoyed musicals and it would be a welcome break, but she hesitated.

"Everyone's going to be there," Jane urged her. "Bob and Gary and Sharon and just about everyone."

"I can't," Joanna said reluctantly.

"Why not?" her friend asked. "You haven't gone anywhere in months, not since Greg left."

"That's not true. You and I went shopping last week."

"You spend more time with that girl at the hospital than you do with any of us."

"You mean Penny?"

"Whatever her name is. You're always there. Who is she, anyway? It isn't like she went to school with us. You barely know her."

Jane was right. Penny had leukemia and after her classes Joanna often stopped in to visit the teenager. Sister Theresa had introduced Joanna to Penny. These days Joanna had more in common with the hospital patient than her high school friends. Penny's boyfriend was also in Vietnam; they compared notes and discussed news about the war. Sister Theresa had mentioned how beneficial these visits were for Penny, but she didn't understand how much Joanna got out of them, too.

"You're right, we did go shopping," Jane went on, "but that was just the two of us. You haven't gone out with the crowd. We used to all hang out, remember?"

As if Joanna could forget.

"I'm engaged." She didn't feel comfortable meeting her friends in situations that often involved couples pairing up. Not when she wore Greg's engagement ring.

"That doesn't mean you're dead," Jane muttered.

"I know, but it bothers me…." Greg didn't like it either. When she happened to mention running into their old gang, he'd plied her with questions. He hadn't asked her *not* to hang around with their high school friends, but she could tell from his letters that he worried when she was out with the guys. She couldn't find it in her heart to write him long, chatty let-

ters in which she conveniently forgot to mention that she'd
sat beside Paul or Ron at the movies.

Greg was the possessive type, but she didn't mind. She saw
it as proof that he loved her. Besides, it wasn't his fault that
he was in the middle of the war while several of their friends
had gotten college exemptions.

Penny understood Joanna's dilemma on an entirely different level. She didn't want to write Scott, her boyfriend, about
her experiences in the hospital or the progression of her dis-
ease, so Joanna helped her think up cheerful news to convey
to her sweetheart half a world away.

"Do me a favor," Jane said. "Ask Greg. Do you honestly
think he wants you to stay home, pining away for him?"

To Joanna's astonishment, when she did bring it up, casually—with the assurance that she'd stayed home—Greg
protested. "Jane's right. You should be going out with our
friends," he wrote. "I know you love me and I love you. I might
be cut off from everyone while I do this stint in the Army, but
that doesn't mean you have to be, too."

Joanna read his letter a second time, just to be sure there
wasn't any hint of resentment. She detected none and wondered if she would have acted as magnanimous had their roles
been reversed. Still, she wrote him every day, rain or shine,
whether her moods were up or down.

His letters came intermittently now, always with a good excuse about why he hadn't been able to write. "I'm sorry,
Joanna. Has it really been a week? Forgive me, sweetheart,
but it's crazy over here. I promise to look at the wedding invitation samples and get back to you soon." Then he'd remind
her of his love and everything would seem perfect again.

Joanna's studies at the hospital continued. Despite her
fears that Greg's absence would make the time drag, this first
year was flying by.

"Was it hard for you to wait for Daddy?" Joanna asked her
mother as they sat out on the patio in the bright June sunshine.

"The war seemed interminable," her mother said, relaxing
on a chaise longue. "Like you and Greg, we were engaged, I

kissed him goodbye when he left for the South Pacific and then we didn't see each other for twenty-two months."

"I could never wait that long," Joanna said. She sipped her soda and tried to calm her anxieties. There hadn't been a letter from Greg in four days. Lately he hadn't been writing real letters, either. They were more like notes he dashed off early in the morning before he went on duty. But Joanna didn't care; it didn't matter how long his letters were. All she needed was the knowledge that she was in his thoughts.

"You do whatever is necessary," her mother told her. "That's what women have always done."

"Twenty-two months." Joanna couldn't bear to be apart from Greg for almost two years. Already it seemed far longer than that since she'd last seen him—and since they'd last made love.

"I didn't know from one day to the next if your father was alive or not," her mother added.

"I think I'd know if anything happened to Greg." She hadn't meant to say it out loud, but Joanna felt certain her heart would tell her if he was injured…or worse. They were so closely linked, so deeply in love.

"How's Penny?" her mother asked.

Joanna sighed. "Back in the hospital. Sister Theresa called earlier to let me know. I'll go up to see her first thing tomorrow."

The phone rang and Joanna raced into the kitchen. Twice now Greg had managed to reach her stateside and they'd talked, however briefly. Her emotional high had lasted for days afterward.

"Hello," she answered cheerfully. The kitchen radio played the Beatles song "I Want to Hold Your Hand" and she made a mental note to take Penny her transistor radio.

Ten minutes later, Joanna put down the receiver. "Mom, Mom," she cried, so excited she could barely stand still. "That was the fabric store in Boston. The material's in." At fifty dollars a yard, the stuff was horrendously expensive, but her mother had ordered Belgian lace anyway. It was for Joanna's wedding dress, after all, which the best seamstress in town was sewing.

"Did you ask her to mail it?"

"No…I didn't think of it."

"Good." Her mother sat up and removed her sunglasses. "Because you and I will be personally picking it up."

"We're going to Boston?" Joanna shrieked.

"We are," her mother said, sounding delighted, "and we're going to shop. Every bride needs a trousseau."

"Oh, Mom, really?" Joanna felt like crying with gratitude and excitement. The wedding had seemed so far away, but now that the lace had arrived it had suddenly become real.

"I want everything to be perfect for you," her mother said.

"What will Dad say?"

"Leave him to me."

They left the next morning and were away for three glorious days. This trip was exactly the restorative Joanna needed. Sure enough, a long letter from Greg awaited her when she returned. She immediately sat down and wrote him back, describing the shopping spree and the hotel and what a fabulous time she'd had.

Because Joanna and her mother had left on the spur of the moment, she hadn't been to the hospital to visit Penny yet.

Packing up the lacy silk gown she intended to wear on her wedding night, plus her going-away suit and shoes, Joanna arrived at the hospital late on Tuesday afternoon. Penny would enjoy seeing everything, and Joanna was eager to show off her purchases.

Sister Theresa was at the nurses' station when Joanna walked off the elevator.

"Joanna," Sister said abruptly.

"Hello, Sister. I'm here to see Penny."

Sister's face fell and she sighed softly. "I'm so sorry to tell you, we lost her yesterday afternoon."

"Lost her?" The hospital didn't *lose* people. Then it dawned on Joanna. "Penny…died?"

"I'm sorry, Joanna. I know what good friends the two of you became."

A sob broke free from the constricted muscles of her throat. The shock of Penny's death sent the room spinning. Joanna hadn't seen her in two weeks, but they'd talked on the phone and Penny had always seemed so optimistic. Never once had she mentioned her leukemia. Whenever Joanna asked, Penny had brushed aside the question. It was clear she didn't want to talk about her illness and Joanna hadn't pressured her.

"Come and sit down," Sister said, gently sliding her arm around Joanna. "Penny often told me how much she loved your visits. Her other friends had drifted away, but you were there for her."

Only she hadn't been, Joanna realized, sick to her stomach. While Penny had been lying alone and friendless in the hospital, Joanna was off shopping as though she hadn't a care in the world. The guilt tarnished her happiness, made it seem trite.

In Greg's next letter a few weeks later he tried to console her. "You couldn't have known, Joanna. Stop blaming yourself. You *were* there for her. You visited when she needed you."

But even his words didn't help and Joanna didn't know if she could ever forgive herself. She walked around in a daze. She'd never lost a friend before and felt that she'd failed Penny. Sister Theresa talked to her several times, offering both compassion and common sense. The nun's kindness made a real difference.

"I heard from Scott," Sister told Joanna the following week.

"Penny's Scott?" Joanna asked.

Sister nodded. "He knew from the first that Penny wasn't going to recover, but like her he pretended she would. He's taking it hard, but he's a strong Catholic and has accepted the will of God."

Joanna wished she had the faith to be more accepting. Her own relationship with God had suffered since that first time in the back seat of Greg's Chevy. Oh, she faithfully attended Mass every week, sitting in the pew with Rick and her parents. Her brother was bored by church, but he went because he didn't have a choice. Joanna's attitude wasn't much better. Religion had become irrelevant to her. It wasn't only Penny she'd let down; it was God, too.

"If you ever need to talk," Sister Theresa invited, "you know you can tell me anything."

It was as though the nun had read her thoughts. Penny's death had shaken Joanna, and no one else understood that. Not her parents. Not Greg either, although he tried. He seemed to be more and more preoccupied lately. Judging by one or two comments he'd made, he appeared to be involved in some trouble of his own—something to do with his commanding officer. Joanna knew she should ask, but she didn't. School and the wedding demanded all her energy. Then, in July, as Greg's year of duty drew to an end, he wrote to say that it was important for them to talk.

Talk? About what? She wrote and asked, but Greg said he'd explain everything once he got home. And that was fine with her. She needed him, wanted him close. The wedding was less than a month away; she should be excited—in a few weeks, she would be Greg's bride. His *wife*. Instead of making love in the back seat of a car, she would enjoy the luxury of waking in a real bed, wrapped in her husband's embrace.

Just as Joanna finished preparing the wedding invitations, she received word that Greg was flying home. It was early, but she had no complaints. This was the best news she'd gotten in weeks. No, months. She wondered if this unexpected reprieve was linked to his troubles with the military, but Joanna didn't care. Whatever the reason, she was grateful.

"We'll have a long heart-to-heart when I'm home," he wrote again.

"I need you," she wrote back. She craved his arms around her and the release his body would give her. It wasn't only physical satisfaction she sought but emotional, too. With Greg she could be herself. She could let him see her grief over Penny. What had seemed impossible to convey through letters would be easier to explain in person.

Joanna didn't sleep the night before Greg was scheduled to arrive. His mother had called to say—testily, Joanna thought—that Greg's family would meet him at the airport alone. Joanna could see him later. It was as though Mrs. Markham was purposely excluding her from this reunion and Joanna resented it.

"Mrs. Markham doesn't want me there," she complained to her mother.

Her mother didn't bother to hide her irritation. "Greg is your fiancé, for heaven's sake."

"I'm sure he'll be expecting me." Joanna didn't know why his mother was being so unreasonable, but she had no intention of waiting silently at home. "I'm going to the airport on my own."

Her mother nodded. "I think you should. You don't need to ride with Greg's parents."

At the airport, Joanna felt a little silly sneaking behind his parents' backs. She couldn't stay away, though, and considered it cruel of his mother to have suggested it.

When Greg's plane touched down, she saw his parents standing apart from everyone else. They seemed to be arguing. Joanna would have said something, revealed her presence, but she didn't want to embarrass them. His mother took a handkerchief from her purse and dabbed her eyes.

Soon the passengers disembarked, and Joanna strained for a glimpse of Greg. The instant she saw him, her heart leapt with joy. She had to force herself not to run straight into his arms.

It was a good thing she didn't.

Seconds later she realized Greg hadn't traveled from Vietnam alone. There was a woman with him—a petite Vietnamese woman who was obviously pregnant.

Confused, Joanna stared at them. Greg was bringing a foreign woman to the States? A pregnant woman? It didn't make sense.

As if watching a movie unfold before her eyes, Joanna stayed out of view as Greg put his arm around the woman and steered her toward his parents. Mr. and Mrs. Markham stepped forward, and the Asian woman bowed her head at the introduction.

"Greg?" Unable to remain silent any longer, Joanna moved away from the pillar where she'd been standing. "Who is this woman?"

"Joanna." Greg looked at her, and then his mother. The blood seemed to drain from his face.

"Oh, Joanna," his mother groaned. "You should never have come."

Joanna ignored her. "Who is this woman?" she demanded a second time.

Greg exhaled and refused to meet her eyes. "This is Xuan. My wife."

"Your…wife?"

Her question was met with an embarrassed silence.

If the news that he was married wasn't shock enough, Joanna's gaze fell to the small round belly. "She's pregnant?"

Greg swallowed visibly and nodded.

Still Joanna couldn't take it in. "The baby is yours?" That wasn't possible. Greg was engaged to marry *her.* Their wedding was only weeks away. She'd just had the final fitting for her wedding gown, and the bridesmaids had their dresses with shoes dyed to match, and her aunt Betty was flying in from San Francisco to attend the wedding, and… *Of course* there was going to be a wedding.

Joanna read the regret and sorrow in Greg's eyes. "I'm sorry," he whispered.

"You couldn't tell me? You left me to learn this on my own?" Doing something so underhanded was horrible enough, but to humiliate her just four weeks before the wedding was cruel beyond words.

"I *couldn't* tell you," he cried. His eyes pleaded with her for understanding.

"My father important man," the Asian woman said boldly. "He—" she pointed at Greg "—marry me. Take me to America. Big trouble for him if not." Xuan faced Joanna and stared at her. "He love me." She planted her hands on her stomach as if to say she bore the evidence of Greg's love.

"Yes, I can see that he does," Joanna said quietly.

"Joanna, please—this is awkward enough." Greg's mother moved toward them. "Do you think it would be possible to have this discussion elsewhere?" Mrs. Markham glanced self-consciously around her.

His mother was right. This was neither the time nor the place to deal with such—what had she called it?—awkwardness.

"I should never have come," Joanna said in a voice she barely recognized as her own.

"Now you know why I asked you to stay home." Mrs. Markham sounded angry.

"We couldn't say anything," his father said, obviously taking pity on Joanna. "It wasn't our place." He was kind enough to escort her to the parking lot. Joanna followed obediently but it felt as though she was walking in a fog.

"Greg should have explained the situation," he said when they'd reached her vehicle. "He said he couldn't do that to you in a letter. You'd already had one shock this summer."

Joanna stared up at him blankly.

"Your friend died."

"Oh, you mean Penny."

"Perhaps I should drive you home," he suggested, and held out his hand for her car keys.

Joanna stared at his palm. "Did I tell you Mom and Dad got the country club for the wedding reception?"

"Joanna, there isn't going to be a wedding."

She blinked rapidly. He was right. No wedding because there was no groom. Her fiancé was married to someone else. A Vietnamese woman, who'd told them that her father was a powerful government official. So this was the trouble Greg had been alluding to in his letters, the trouble that had involved his commanding officer. His Vietnamese wife was the reason Greg had been sent stateside early.

"I'll be fine," she said and opened the car door herself. Once inside, she pressed her forehead against the steering wheel and waited for the waves of shock and disbelief to dissipate before attempting to drive. When she noticed that Greg's father was still outside, she hurriedly started the engine and drove away.

As soon as the news of the cancelled wedding was out, Joanna's family and friends rallied around her. By the end of the first week of August, there was no evidence that she'd ever been engaged.

The wedding dress disappeared from her closet. The invitations, all stamped and ready to be mailed, vanished. Her family and friends tiptoed around her, and Greg's name was no longer part of anyone's vocabulary.

His wife, Joanna learned, was living with his parents. Their baby was due in three months. That meant Greg had been unfaithful to her soon after he'd landed in Southeast Asia.

No wonder he'd graciously urged her to get out with their

friends. He was "getting out" himself. Oh yes, her fiancé sure had the world by the tail, she thought bitterly. He had a fiancée stateside who loved and missed him, plus a mistress in Vietnam.

The only place Joanna experienced peace was inside church. In the afternoons when she'd finished her classes, she sat in the hospital chapel and absorbed the serenity and peace of the empty room.

After the first couple of weeks, she felt a long-forgotten desire begin to re-emerge. As a high school freshman, she'd considered joining the convent. Every good Catholic girl entertained the idea at some point; Joanna was no different. Perhaps, she reasoned, her broken engagement was just God's way of leading her back to the religious life. She'd give it time, but not discuss it with anyone until she'd made a tentative decision.

A month later, Joanna sought out Sister Theresa. "You said I could talk to you any time I needed."

"Of course." Sister led Joanna into her office and closed the door.

"You heard?" Joanna asked, not wanting to explain her humiliation.

Sister Theresa nodded. "I realize this must be a very painful time for you, Joanna, but God allows these burdens to come into our lives for a reason."

"I believe that, too."

Sister smiled approvingly. "You're wise beyond your years."

Joanna didn't feel wise; she felt wounded and weak. "I've been doing a lot of praying since Penny died and I learned about Greg. I wonder if God is using this situation to point me in a completely different direction."

"How do you mean?"

Joanna figured she might as well be direct. "These days the only place I feel any comfort is in church."

"God is eager to listen to our prayers," Sister said.

"I sense His presence. I pray and afterward I feel better. I've started thinking that maybe God is calling me to a life of prayer."

Sister didn't reveal any emotion. "Are you saying you're considering the convent?"

"Yes…"

"Do you feel you have a vocation, Joanna?"

"Yes."

Sister sighed. "I don't want to discourage you, especially if God *is* calling you to the religious life. But it's important that you enter the convent for the right reasons. Not because you have a broken heart."

Joanna understood Sister Theresa's concern. "I feel God purposely took Greg out of my life. It was His way of asking me to work for Him."

Sister regarded her steadily. "God doesn't want to be your second choice, Joanna. He wants to be first in your heart."

"He is, Sister. He was until…until Greg and I became involved. I want to serve as a St. Bridget's Sister of the Assumption."

Sister Theresa paused. "Nothing would please me more, but I want you to wait."

"Wait?" Joanna was ready to enter that very moment. Greg wasn't right for her. They'd led each other into sin and she so desperately wanted to be at peace with God again.

"Give it six months," Sister Theresa added.

Reluctantly, Joanna nodded.

"Have you mentioned this to your parents?"

"Yes." It hadn't gone well. Her mother insisted that Joanna was just reacting to the broken engagement. Her father, on the other hand, had encouraged her, which only infuriated her mother.

"Give it six months," Sister repeated, "and if you're still convinced this is what you want, then I'll recommend that you be admitted in February as an incoming postulant."

# PART 2

# BRIDES OF CHRIST

As a bridegroom rejoices over his bride,
so will God rejoice over you.

*Isaiah* 62:5

*chapter*

# ANGELINA MARCELLO

## 1958 to 1972

As Angie disembarked from the Greyhound bus that September morning in 1958, she was impatient to start her new life. The farewell scene with her father lingered in her mind. Still, she couldn't allow his disparaging remarks to spoil her first day at the convent. He seemed so sure that entering the order was wrong for her, but if that was true, why did her heart burn with zeal for God?

Her father found it hard to let her go, Angie realized with a swell of compassion. She loved him all the more for his willingness to step aside and allow her to follow her own path, despite the fact that he was convinced she'd made the biggest mistake of her eighteen years.

He'd wept openly as she boarded the bus, the tears streaming down his cheeks. She would always remember her last sight of him: as the bus pulled out of the station, he'd taken the handkerchief from his pocket and dabbed at his eyes. Then with slumped shoulders, he'd turned and walked away.

She'd watched sadly, wishing she could have spared him this grief and knowing she couldn't.

Despite Angie's eagerness to enter the religious life, she was nervous. She arrived in Boston midafternoon and caught a cab that deposited her in front of the motherhouse. She was cheered to see that the wrought-iron gates were open wide as though to welcome her. Carrying her small battered suitcase—originally her mother's—Angie walked resolutely up the brick walkway to the convent's entrance and rang the bell.

"Angelina. I see you made it on your own." A tall nun, so thin and sleek that she resembled a crane, stepped forward to greet her.

Angie didn't recall meeting her before.

"I'm Sister Mary Louise. We met briefly when you made your application. Don't worry if you don't remember me. You met a lot of us that day."

Angie smiled in relief. There'd been so many, and their faces and names were a blur in her mind.

"I'm the Postulant Mistress. We'll be having tea shortly. Now, come inside and make yourself comfortable. Several other girls are already here."

She was ushered to a formal room furnished with a dining table and chairs. Angelina recognized Mother Superior there; she also saw three young women, obviously the other postulants. What surprised her was the immediate sense of connection she experienced. These girls, who sat self-consciously at the table, sipping tea and munching cookies, would become her new community. Her family.

"Mother Superior, I'm sure you remember Angelina Marcello," Sister Mary Louise said, escorting Angelina to the older nun.

Angelina hesitated, uncertain if anything was required of her, such as bowing or genuflecting. She knew priests kissed the Bishop's ring, but she wasn't up on etiquette for meeting such an important woman.

Sister Agnes's smile was warm and encompassing. "Of

course I remember Angelina. You come to us from Buffalo, New York. I'm right, aren't I?"

Angie nodded, holding herself stiff for fear of saying or doing something wrong.

"I thought so. Is there a chair for Angelina, Sister?" Mother asked and Angie was offered an empty place at the table. As soon as she sat, Mother Superior introduced her to the others. "Meet Karen. She's from Boston and Marie is from Columbus, Ohio. Josephine comes to us all the way from California. We're so pleased you're here to be part of us."

By the end of the day, Angelina had been introduced to twenty women ranging in age from seventeen to twenty-two. The postulants were served an early dinner, with only Mother Superior joining them. Because they sat across from each other, Angie and Karen had a chance to talk.

"Did your family bring you?" Angie asked, aware that most girls had been accompanied by their parents and sometimes siblings.

Karen gazed down at the polished tile floor and shook her head. "They were unhappy with my decision." Her hair was dark and straight and fell to the middle of her back. She had a pretty face, Angie thought.

"My father was too," she confessed. This trip to Boston was the first time Angie had traveled anywhere outside of New York State. She'd worried about making the trip by herself but in the end, she'd managed quite nicely. That reassured her, in some small way, that she'd made the right choice.

"I think this is such a beautiful life," Karen told her. Her eyes held a dreamy look. "The habits are lovely, aren't they?"

Angie's smile was vague. She'd never stopped to think about the habits or that she'd soon be wearing one herself.

A few moments later Sister Mary Louise appeared in the refectory doorway and signaled them to follow her. They paraded through the convent, through a series of corridors and passageways, arriving at a heavy wooden door.

"This is the entrance to your dormitory," Sister explained.

Angelina had been a visitor earlier in the year during her high school retreat, but it had all felt so different then.

With the others, Angie slowly entered her new living quarters. The soon-to-be postulants clustered together, their shoes clattering against the stone floor. No one seemed willing to walk all the way inside.

"Come in, come in," Sister Mary Louise encouraged. Then one by one, she led them down the hallway and assigned them rooms.

"This will be your cell," the Postulant Mistress told Angie. "I put you next to Karen."

Angie's eyes linked with the other girl's and they shared a smile. It would be good to have a friend, especially one who understood how difficult it had been to go against her father's wishes. As soon as Sister Mary Louise pointed out her room, Angie moved inside, curious about the place where she'd be spending so many hours. It was stark, with only a bed, table and lamp, similar to the one she'd slept in just a few months earlier. She couldn't help wondering how many other young women had prayed and slept and struggled with doubt and fear in this very room. How many other women had come to St. Bridget's Sisters as she had, with a heart longing to serve? How many had stayed and how many had left? These were things she might never know.

Sister Mary Louise hurried into Angie's cell. "Here are your new clothes." She set a stack of folded garments on the end of the bed.

Angie waited until the nun had left before examining the unfamiliar garb. She could hear nervous giggles coming from the other cells. She discovered black woolen stockings, which she put on after the plain cotton underwear. Next was a dark tunic with long sleeves; they fell past her fingertips and she had to fold them back over her wrists. Then came the black vestlike shirt and pleated ankle-length black skirt, followed by a short cape. Last were the shoes—what she'd always thought of as "nun shoes"—one-inch-thick heels that laced up.

When Angie had finished changing out of her street clothes

and into her new ones, she stood in the cell doorway. Sister Mary Louise nodded approvingly when she saw her. "Does everything fit?"

Everything hung loosely on her, but Angie suspected that was exactly how it was supposed to be. "I believe so, Sister."

"Very good. Now we'll give you a veil." She set Angie down on a stool in the hallway and retrieved a hairbrush from her pocket. With swift strokes, she pulled Angie's hair severely from her face and fastened it in the back with hair clips, then secured a veil to her head. Only a few wisps from her bangs were visible.

Soon all twenty of them were dressed and veiled. "This is your introduction to St. Bridget's Sisters of the Assumption," Sister Mary Louise explained. "During the induction ceremony a few minutes from now, Mother Superior will read a special prayer. I want you to bow your heads and listen carefully. Absorb as many of the words as you can and hold on to their meaning. This prayer is asking God to grant you whatever you need to be a good nun." Sister Mary Louise paused briefly, glancing around at the assembled postulants.

"Let me add," she said, her expression serious, "that this time as a postulant is a period of testing. You are asking for the privilege and honor of becoming a novice. You are studying us and we'll be studying you to ensure that you genuinely belong with us."

The Mistress of Postulants paused for a moment, meeting several girls' eyes. "There will be many questions you will answer in the next year. Important questions. But first and foremost, you must decide if you are ready to set aside your own selfish desires and replace them with a close relationship with God.

"You will learn the lessons of obedience and poverty. From this moment forward, you own nothing. Everything you have, right down to your toothbrush, belongs to the Order. You must be absolutely ruthless in your rejection of the world."

Angie gave a deep sigh. She *was* ready to relinquish the world, ready to cast aside all that she owned and would inherit, including the family restaurant. She wanted this life and was determined to pursue it wholeheartedly.

"For many of you, silence will be your greatest struggle. It is just one of the ways we use to empty out all the clutter in our minds. Silence allows God to fill our heads with His thoughts. Grand Silence begins shortly after dinner at seven-thirty. You are not to speak until the next morning. All of this will be further explained in due course. Now follow me."

Sister Mary Louise led them into the chapel for the short ceremony in which they were officially welcomed as postulants into the motherhouse. After that, they were taken back to the dormitory.

Sister Mary Louise stood in front of them. "I know that most of you are feeling confused and a little numb. It's been a busy day, one that signifies the beginning of an important stage of your lives. You will pray together, eat together and study together. However, you'll be separated from the professed sisters at all times, except in chapel and during meals and Sunday evening recreation."

Angie's head was swimming. There seemed to be so much to remember.

"In the morning the alarm rings at four-forty-five. As soon as you hear the bell, you will rise and immediately kneel beside your bed and recite the Our Father. You are to remain silent from the time you hear the bell until after Mass. The bell indicates silence and offers each of us the opportunity for a short daily retreat as we lovingly prepare for Mass."

All Angie heard was the ungodly hour at which the alarm rang. Everything after that was a blur. Four-forty-five in the morning. But, Angie reminded herself, this time set aside for prayer was the very reason she'd entered the convent. She'd come searching for the way to serve God to the fullest.

"Following chapel and breakfast, you will start your first classes." Angie nodded eagerly; she'd always enjoyed school and these would be the most vital lessons of her entire life.

That night, Angie slipped into the long flannel gown the convent provided and crawled between the coarse sheets of her bed.

The classes that first day were full of valuable information, some of it familiar, some brand-new. Angie took careful notes.

"The history of our order gives us a rich legacy," Sister Mary Louise said, "thanks to the woman who founded St. Bridget's Sisters of the Assumption. I know many of you have already heard the story of Fionnuala Wheaton."

Angie had read about the life of this wonderful Irishwoman before she was accepted into the convent.

"What can you tell me about her?" Sister asked.

The room was silent, and then Karen tentatively raised her hand. "I know she was married to an English landowner."

"She was widowed at an early age," Angie added.

"That's correct," Sister said, smiling appreciatively in Karen and Angie's direction. "Fionnuala and William had a good marriage. They were devoted to each other."

"She was disappointed that they'd never had children," another postulant said.

"Yes, but we know this was all part of God's plan. God had other things in mind for our founder."

Angie was beginning to understand that God's ways were not those of the world.

"After her husband's death, Fionnuala was devastated by grief and turned to the Church for comfort. The priests of St. Bridget's Parish encouraged her in acts of charity. Soon her generosity was widely known throughout the region. It wasn't long before other widows asked to join her. The small group decided to live and work together. It was Fionnuala's intent to heal the sick and educate the poor."

Angie sat up straighter. This was her heart's desire, too—to help the poor, to teach, and endlessly offer herself to whatever work the Church asked of her.

"In 1840, with the approval of Pope Gregory XVI, St. Bridget's Sisters of the Assumption formally received the blessing of Rome and was established as a religious order."

"This was in Ireland?" one of the girls asked.

"Yes." Sister smiled at Bonnie, the girl whose cell was across from Angie's. "These were the days of the terrible potato famine and as you know, many Irish immigrated to the United States. Conditions were deplorable in Ireland and in the United States, too, as the immigrants struggled to make new lives. In an effort to help, St. Bridget's Sisters of the Assumption sent many young nuns to America. They arrived in Boston and established the convent here. Soon the demand for nuns was high, and by the turn of the century more and more women were offering their lives to the service of the Church."

"When was the motherhouse transferred here?" Karen asked. "From Ireland, I mean."

Sister Mary Louise walked toward the blackboard. "Just before the first of the two World Wars. We're proud of our order, which has grown and expanded through the years. As of today, we have ten convents situated across the United States. I'm pleased to tell you that we are one of the most prominent religious orders in the country. God has continued to bless our efforts.

"While the motherhouse here in Boston is our oldest convent, it isn't our largest. That honor goes to our convent in Minneapolis, Minnesota."

Angie had read about the Minneapolis convent in the brochure she'd received at the time of her high school retreat. The Sisters worked as nurses at St. Elizabeth's Hospital and teachers for the thriving Catholic schools within St. Peter's diocese.

Besides attending her classes, Angelina was required to fulfill housekeeping duties around the convent. Her first assignment was in the laundry room, situated next to the kitchen. After several weeks of bland meals, Angie could remain silent no longer, especially when she realized the cook planned to make spaghetti.

"Let me help," she suggested. She'd already finished sorting and folding that day's clean laundry.

"Help?" The cook, an older woman hired from the community, looked up at her in surprise.

"I'm Italian. I know about herbs and spices." She dipped a spoon into the bubbling red sauce on the stove and tasted it, then slowly shook her head. Her father would throw himself in front of oncoming traffic rather than serve anything this bland. "Bring me the basil," she said with such authority that the lay cook hurried to comply.

Searching through the spice rack, Angie added a pinch of this and a handful of that, tasted, tested and wasn't satisfied until she had something that at least resembled the sauce she knew and loved.

That evening the sisters raved about the meal. The two nuns who'd drawn kitchen duty tried to explain that it had been Angie's work, but it was risky to give her credit. Angie had been assigned to the laundry, not the kitchen. Not once was she ever asked to cook, although the other postulants helped prepare meals on a regular basis.

Whenever the mail arrived, Angie searched for a letter from her father, but she never found one. Karen didn't hear from her family, either. Angie's father could come up with no more effective way to discourage her. It was with a heavy heart that she offered up her disappointment to God.

At the end of her first year, in which she'd received only one terse letter from her father, Angie entered the novitiate. This was known as the contemplative year of silence. Speaking was allowed for only half an hour each evening, and all contact with family was prohibited. She never knew if her father wrote during that year but suspected he hadn't. He was still angry with her.

Nor did he write during her second year as a novice. She spent her days in prayer, studying Scripture and Church history and performing household tasks. The slow, peaceful days in this year of silence helped to shape her thoughts. They taught her patience and a willingness to yield her life to the dictates of God and Mother Superior. By the end of her time in the novitiate, Angie was approached by the Mistress of Novices regarding her new name as a professed sister. She was asked to submit three, but final approval rested with Mother Superior.

The Mistress of Novices stopped her one afternoon as

Angie swept the dining room floor. Her eyes brimmed with sadness. "I understand you knew Sister Trinita?"

"Yes," Angie said, keeping her gaze lowered out of respect for the nun's position. The term the convent used was "custody of the eyes." "Sister Trinita was a favorite teacher of mine in grade school," she explained.

"I thought you should know Sister passed on to our heavenly Father last week."

"No," Angie gasped and her hand flew to her throat.

"She'd been seriously ill for some time."

"I...I had no idea."

"Sister didn't wish to burden others. She was suffering from cancer." She paused. "You were a special friend and I thought you'd want to know."

Tears welled in Angie's eyes but she refused to let them fall. The woman who had so greatly influenced her life was gone to be with God. Angie felt the loss as keenly as she had when she'd lost her mother.

"I believe one of the names you chose was Sister Frances?"

Angie nodded. Sister Trinita had long ago told Angie it was her given name before she'd entered the convent.

"I'll talk to Reverend Mother and do what I can to see that you receive the name Sister Frances."

"Oh, thank you," Angie whispered. "That would mean the world to me."

"I can't make any promises, Sister."

When she saw Karen during the recreation period after dinner, her friend knew immediately that something was wrong. "What happened?" she asked, squinting at the needle she was threading. All the second-year novices worked diligently on sewing their own habits, using three battered old machines and doing the finer work by hand. Until they spoke their final vows of chastity, poverty and obedience, their clothing was known as dresses or gowns. Only professed Sisters wore habits.

"Sister Trinita died...she had cancer." Thinking back to their chance meeting on the convent grounds three years earlier, Angie recalled the hesitation in her manner. When Angie had asked about her latest assignment, Sister Trinita had passed over the question. She'd said "For now," and Angie was convinced the nun knew about the cancer then.

"I'm sorry," Karen whispered.

"I am, too… She was so wonderful to me."

That same evening, Angie wrote her father. She expressed her love for him as she inquired about his health and the restaurant. She didn't give him an account of her life inside the convent. It would only rub salt in his wounds. Neither did she tell him the news about Sister Trinita. He wouldn't understand why it affected her so intensely. Just as he didn't understand that the convent's rules and routines now filled her world, and everything she'd once known had faded away. Everything outside these gates represented the world she'd renounced.

In the spring of 1962, Angelina Marcello took the name of Sister Frances as she spoke her first vows. For three long years, Angie had waited for this, and it was a source of deep pain that her father had refused to share such a momentous day with her. The vows were said during Mass, followed by Holy Communion. Forming a procession, the novices came forward, each in a pure white gown and a veil like a bride. Indeed, Angie *was* a bride; she'd agreed to become the bride of Christ. This was a solemn betrothal.

"I am the bride of Him whom the angels serve," Angie said in unison with the other novices.

At this point, the priest ceremonially removed each bridal veil and replaced it with the black veil of St. Bridget's Sisters of the Assumption. When he'd finished, the novices chanted, "As a bride, Christ has adorned me with a crown."

When they turned to face the congregation, all wearing their black veils, Angie felt a surge of triumph. As of that moment, Angelina Marcello became known as Sister Frances.

Her first assignment was teaching in San Antonio, Texas. For ten years, Angie taught high school there, mostly classes in religion and home economics. She heard from her father only once a year on her birthday.

In 1969, after Vatican II, St. Bridget's Sisters of the Assumption were given the option of retaining their chosen names or reverting to their original names. Angie asked to be called Sister Angelina. Her father seemed pleased with her decision when she phoned to let him know.

At the end of the school year in 1972, Sister Angelina learned that she would be sent to St. Peter's High School in Minneapolis. After nearly fifteen years, she'd been assigned to the order's largest convent.

Her time in Texas felt like an apprenticeship, a preparation for this new and special task. And it *would* be special; she was sure of it.

*chapter*

# KATHLEEN O'SHAUGHNESSY

## 1963 to 1972

Kathleen's send-off was a giant family affair with her sisters, aunts, uncles and a multitude of nieces, nephews and cousins all present for the farewell party. Her uncle Patrick closed the pub for a day and unashamedly wept as he hugged her.

"Your smiling face is going to be sadly missed," he said, stepping back to get one last look at the girl he'd always known and loved. Shortly afterward she would no longer be his Kathleen but a nun. Tears glistened in his eyes as he gently clasped her shoulders. "You're making us all proud, Kathleen. God be with you."

Her parents drove her to the convent. Her mother's eyes shone with happiness as Sister Mary Louise, the Mistress of Postulants, led Kathleen and the other young women into the motherhouse to begin their new lives. That first evening Kathleen was given her new garments and taken to the chapel for the welcoming ceremony.

She took easily to the change in lifestyle and enjoyed being a postulant. The concept of owning nothing wasn't new to her; after all, she and her sisters had always shared clothing, makeup, magazines, records—all the paraphernalia of a 1960s teenager. She wasn't allowed to keep anything of her former life, not even the clothes she'd worn the day she entered the convent. Her dress was taken from her, washed and given to the poor.

"Everything we do and ask of you," Sister Mary Louise explained early in Kathleen's instruction, "is for a reason. At times you will understand and agree, and at other times it will remain a mystery. It isn't necessary to understand everything. What *is* necessary is obedience."

Owning nothing was liberating, Kathleen decided. She felt privileged to share everything with her fellow sisters, and her life became much simpler. She no longer wore makeup, had no radio, no books. Nothing. The temptations tied to having such possessions disappeared. It was as though she'd been born into another world.

Kathleen tried to be ruthless in her rejection of the world. She looked forward to emptying herself of all that kept her from loving God. Her sense of righteousness hit its first snag, however, when it came time to cut her hair—her beautiful, waist-length, auburn hair. For easier grooming, she and the others were told, their hair must be cut short.

This was hard. Much harder than any sacrifice Kathleen had made so far. She cringed as she saw several girls with their hair clumsily hacked off. Surely there was some way to forgo this. But when her turn came, she knew it was senseless to ask.

"Sister Kathleen." Sister Mary Louise motioned to the chair. Kathleen bit her lower lip as she sat on the hard-backed chair.

The Mistress of Postulants hesitated, scissors raised. She, too, seemed to regret shearing away such beautiful hair. "It's necessary," she murmured.

"Yes, Sister," Kathleen agreed as she felt the scissors along the side of her neck.

"Otherwise the bulk of our hair becomes too cumbersome under our veils," Sister Mary Louise continued.

The first fat locks fell unceremoniously to the floor. Kathleen closed her eyes rather than watch and swallowed the lump growing in her throat. She felt the second strands drop onto her lap, and despite her best efforts, tears slid down her cheeks.

Her weakness and vanity embarrassed her. It was just hair. It would grow back and later, as a fully professed nun, she could keep it any length she desired. Besides, with her hair hidden under the veil, no one would know or care what it looked like. For all the world knew, she could be bald.

God would find a way to compensate her for this sacrifice, Kathleen reasoned, and He did. With music. Seven times a day, the sisters gathered in the convent chapel to chant the Divine Office. These times of prayer, known as "Hours," were such a spiritually uplifting experience that Kathleen felt transformed. She loved the simplicity and beauty of the music and reveled in the glory of worshiping with her fellow sisters. Losing her lovely hair—her one vanity—was a small price to pay.

That November, President John F. Kennedy was assassinated, and to Kathleen, it seemed like a personal blow. The entire convent reeled with the shock of his death. The president had been the nuns' ideal; not only was he a good Catholic, but he'd once lived in Boston.

Nineteen sixty-four was an eventful year. In February she received a letter—already opened—from her oldest brother, Sean. Although no one ever said as much, Kathleen knew all mail addressed to postulants and novices was censored. Sean wrote to tell her he was engaged to a girl named Loren Kruse. The wedding would take place early that summer, and Kathleen's parents, plus the three youngest O'Shaughnessys, were traveling to Seattle for the event. It went without saying that Kathleen would be unable to make the trip.

She held the letter so tightly that she crumpled it. Family had always been important to Kathleen, and Sean was her favorite. Although he was almost ten years older, there'd always been a close bond between them. He was the only member of her family to question her vocation, and although she'd dismissed his concern, she'd also appreciated it.

Sister Mary Louise knew right away that something was troubling Kathleen. "Distressing news, Sister?" she asked.

"Oh no, this is happy news," Kathleen said and forced a smile. "My oldest brother will be married in June. The family's attending the wedding."

"And you'd like to be there, as well?"

Hope flared inside Kathleen. "If I could… It would mean so much to me, Sister."

Sister Mary Louise frowned, as though Kathleen's response had disappointed her. "Sister Kathleen, you have a new family now."

"But…" She knew instantly that it was both wrong to interrupt and pointless to argue. "I'm sorry, Sister," she said and her voice trailed off.

Sister nodded, accepting her apology. "I realize this is still new to you. You've only been with us for six or so months, and our way of life is still somewhat foreign. But by now you should be willing to make any and all sacrifices to serve God. You must release your family. You belong completely to God now."

"Yes, Sister," she said obediently. But she wanted to protest. She *had* made sacrifices, lots of them, and made them gladly. Her family, though…

"You must die to self before you can be born again."

Kathleen swallowed painfully. She couldn't be with Sean and Loren on their wedding day, at least not in person, but she would be with them in her heart.

That night as she said her evening prayers, Kathleen's conscience bothered her. Her attitude was all wrong. She couldn't allow herself to think she was being cheated because she'd been forbidden to attend Sean's wedding. She'd entered the convent in the hope of living a godly life. If she kept all the rules and obeyed and did whatever was asked of her, eventually she'd find the path that would lead her to God. If she struggled with something as unimportant as a family wedding, it could be years before she broke through the bondage of self. Before she became the kind of nun she truly wanted to be.

Summer passed and with it Sean's wedding. On the day he claimed his bride, Kathleen fasted and prayed and offered this sacrifice up to God. When she went to bed that night, her empty stomach growled and tears dripped from her eyes. As hard as she tried, as hard as she prayed, she couldn't suppress the feeling of loss. Of disappointment. This was a day for celebration, and she'd desperately wanted to share it with her beloved brother.

In August of 1964, Kathleen entered the Novitiate and began her year of silence. In addition to the seven times of prayer each day, which constituted the Divine Office, Kathleen spent a half hour in prayerful meditation, plus two examinations of conscience. Each morning she was required to recite the Rosary; each evening she spent a half hour on private prayer and spiritual reading. All told, her prayers outside chapel took up as much as five hours a day.

In addition to her prayers and her examinations of conscience, Kathleen was assigned kitchen duty. As if Sister Clare Marie, the Mistress of Novices, was aware of her distaste for cooking and meal preparation, Kathleen drew her least favorite task three weeks in a row. Because she was observing the year of silence, she wasn't allowed to speak to Mrs. O'Halloran, whom the convent employed as a cook, unless it was absolutely necessary. It seemed unnatural to Kathleen to work with this woman and not be able to speak to her. The two of them bustled around in the kitchen, where they were sometimes joined by other sisters.

Unfortunately Mrs. O'Halloran was a talker. Even knowing that Kathleen couldn't respond, the cook chatted away.

"I saw my son off to school today," she said as Kathleen entered the kitchen for her chores one September afternoon. "Off to Junior College my Kevin went. He's the first of my brood to take college classes. His father, God rest his soul, would've burst his buttons with pride." She paused in her chatter and dumped a ten-pound bag of potatoes into the sink, then handed Kathleen a paring knife.

Kathleen nearly groaned. Of all kitchen tasks, she hated

peeling potatoes the most. Another sacrifice, she mused, her forehead creasing in a frown.

"We're going to have to come up with the money for tuition," Mrs. O'Halloran prattled on. "But from what I make here cooking for the sisters, plus what I collect from the government for Social Security—God bless Franklin Delano Roosevelt—and Kevin's janitorial job, we should be fine."

Kathleen smiled and reluctantly reached for a potato.

"Being a widow all these years, I've learned how to pinch a penny, I can tell you that."

After peeling the first potato, Kathleen dutifully picked up the next.

"You tell me when you've finished with those, Sister, and I'll set you to work cutting up lettuce for the salad."

Keeping the silence with Mrs. O'Halloran was definitely a struggle, but Kathleen managed. Barely. She found the work mundane and unchallenging. She hadn't entered the convent to peel potatoes, she thought rebelliously. She possessed an active and inquisitive mind.

In the middle of her first year in the Novitiate, Sister Clare Marie asked to speak to her.

"I noticed that the mashed potatoes with last night's dinner were lumpy, Sister. I understand you were the one responsible."

"Yes," Kathleen admitted. If she peeled one more potato she'd scream. Mrs. O'Halloran's favorite side dish was potatoes in one form or another. Kathleen had peeled potatoes every day that week and she was sick of it.

"Do you consider working in the kitchen beneath you, Sister Kathleen?"

"No, Sister… I just don't seem to have the knack for it." Her sewing skills were much better and she was fortunate in this regard because several of the other novices had difficulty constructing their clothes.

"You've always done well in school, haven't you?"

Kathleen lowered her gaze, following the tradition known as custody of the eyes. She was pleased that Sister Clare Marie was aware of her high grades. She'd worked hard to achieve her academic standing and it seemed like a waste not to be partaking in some kind of study, other than simply learning the requirements of the religious life.

"Do you know why you aren't in the classroom this year, Sister?"

Kathleen nodded. "Because of the year of silence." One glance told her that she'd only partially answered the question. "And because mundane tasks help free one's mind for God," she added, knowing this was the answer the Mistress of Novices sought.

Sister Clare Marie seemed to carefully measure her words. "You're answering with your head and not your heart," she finally said. "You seem to think that is what I want you to say, but I want much more from you, Sister Kathleen, and so does God."

Kathleen hung her head. How right Sister was.

"Performing these mundane tasks *is* important work. It is while you are peeling potatoes that you learn to set aside your own will and your own selfish desires. It is while you're holding a peeler in your hand that the demand for self is broken. Remember, only when you are broken can God truly use you."

"But Sister Janice loves to work in the kitchen." Kathleen didn't know why she was arguing. She knew it was wrong to raise objections or to contradict the Mistress of Novices. Kathleen's reaction revealed to her how far she had yet to go.

"You think it would be easier for Sister Janice to work in the kitchen and for you to serve elsewhere. Is that what you're suggesting, Sister?"

Timidly Kathleen nodded. If she could've erased her earlier remark, she would have done so.

Sister Clare Marie sighed heavily. "That's where you're wrong. It's far better for Sister Janice to face her own struggles with a task that challenges her will. I have assigned all of you to work in areas I know you actively dislike. You think this is punishment, don't you?"

That was exactly what Kathleen assumed.

The Mistress of Novices shook her head. "Let me assure

you, Sister Kathleen, it isn't. I'm working hard to help you
be a good nun."

"But Sister, I'm failing. It's a losing battle. The potatoes
are winning."

Sister Clare Marie smiled. "Those potatoes have brought
you to the point of frustration and boredom, haven't they?"

"Yes."

"Then you're exactly where you need to be before you can
die to self."

Kathleen let the words sink in. Her confusion started to
clear and Sister Clare Marie's statement found a home within
her heart.

"I feel you've made significant progress this afternoon," the
older nun said warmly.

Kathleen felt she had, too. What had seemed a burden and
a pointless task earlier now made sense. The convent was
using those mounds of unpeeled potatoes to shape her into a
malleable, useable instrument of God.

That conversation stayed with Kathleen a long time. It
showed her that despite her resolve to the contrary—and despite her own wrongful pride in her sacrifices—the world
still held on to her heart. When Sister Clare Marie had first
mentioned the lumpy mashed potatoes, Kathleen had felt a
small surge of hope that she might be reassigned. Instead,
she'd come away determined to perfect the peeling and mash-
ing of potatoes. Because now she knew that each potato would
bring her closer to God.

As the weeks progressed, the silence that had seemed unnatural in the beginning became the norm. Kathleen didn't
know what was happening in the world. Little outside the convent gates made its way to her ears. Lyndon Baines Johnson
had stepped in as president after the assassination of John
Kennedy; she knew that much but was completely unaware
of his policies. Whatever laws Congress had passed was unimportant to her. Secular music—oh, how she'd once loved the
Beatles—movies and their stars meant nothing. Silence was
her only reality. Everything outside the convent was alien.

Never again did she want to become influenced and corrupted by the world's values.

That summer, just before Kathleen entered her second year in the Novitiate, she was allowed a visit from her family. As the long-awaited weekend approached, Kathleen grew apprehensive. It had been more than twelve months since she'd last seen her parents. Family was considered a distraction in the year of silence. Kathleen wondered if they'd recognize her. She'd changed from the immature teenager who had stepped through the convent doors two years earlier and even from the postulant of last summer.

Her mother and father arrived early and Kathleen nervously met them for a walk around the grounds. She kissed her mother's cheek, but took care to maintain the proper decorum.

"Kathleen," her mother said, searching her face. She blinked back tears. "I always knew you'd make a beautiful nun."

Kathleen lowered her gaze, uncomfortable with the comment about her outward appearance. "Hello, Dad," she said, hugging him lightly. He looked older. His hair was almost completely gray and the wrinkles at his eyes were deeper and more pronounced.

"You seem well," her father said.

"I am well." She buried her hands deep in the sleeves of her gown. "How's Uncle Patrick these days?"

"Good," her father assured her. "He sends his love."

"He was in Ireland this spring," her mother told her.

Her father chuckled. "He kissed the Blarney stone while he was there—not that he needed to."

Her parents laughed at the small joke.

"How's Maureen?"

"Pregnant again. She and Robbie are good Catholics." Pride gleamed in her mother's eyes as she said it. "So many young people are using birth control, but not Maureen and Robbie."

"But Wendy's still a baby." Kathleen didn't know much about family planning, but it didn't seem good for her sister to be giving birth to a second child within a year's time.

"Irish twins, that's what they'll be," her father boasted.

Rather than belabor the conversation, Kathleen changed the subject. "And Sean? How are he and Loren?"

Her parents' eyes met.

Something was wrong, and Kathleen could tell they were hoping to keep it from her.

"Mom? Is everything all right with Sean and his wife?"

"Of course," her father leapt in. "They're very much in love."

Her relief was instantaneous.

"Sean enlisted for another hitch in the Army," her mother said brightly. Her enthusiasm didn't ring true.

"Yes," her father added. "Sean re-enlisted just in time to get shipped off to Vietnam."

"Vietnam?" she repeated as a sense of dread settled over her.

Again her parents exchanged looks. "America's involvement in Southeast Asia is escalating," her father explained.

"Sean's going to Vietnam?" Kathleen was shocked that more news of the war hadn't filtered into the convent. Vietnam had been a minor and faraway conflict when she became a postulant; President Kennedy had merely committed a few troops and military advisors. Surely Mrs. O'Halloran would have mentioned such a significant change in the military's role. The cook chatted endlessly, and Kathleen had learned to tune out much of her trivial conversation, finding the other woman's voice discordant and disruptive. Silence had its own beauty and listening to Mrs. O'Halloran distracted her. Still, she would've noticed and remembered news of this magnitude.

"It's not a declared war," her father said.

"But the president's sending over American men to fight?" Kathleen glanced at her mother and then her father. She was most concerned about one enlisted man, however, and that was her brother Sean.

"Sean sends his love," her mother said, and her voice trembled just enough for Kathleen to detect her worry.

"You're afraid for him, aren't you?"

Her mother nodded. "Loren is, too. She wrote to tell us that Sean's already been in one battle. The fighting was fierce…

We don't know what'll happen. Pray for him, Kathleen. Promise me you'll pray."

"Of course! Of course."

Her parents left shortly after, and while Kathleen had enjoyed their visit, she discovered that she was more than ready to return to the growing familiarity of silence. Sister Clare Marie was right. With time, she'd learned to prefer silence to talking.

Her second year in the novitiate was everything Kathleen had hoped it would be. She excelled in her classes and enjoyed her studies on church history and theology. These were exciting times for the Catholic Church. In 1959, several years before Kathleen entered the convent, Pope John the XXIII had called for an ecumenical council, the first since 1869.

It took place in 1962. Twenty-six hundred cardinals and bishops from around the world had rallied to the Pope's call. So now, in 1965, Vatican II had already been in session for three years and the changes within the Church were gradually making their way down to the people.

Many outmoded customs and rituals were being set aside in favor of a more contemporary worship. For instance, the priest no longer faced the altar with his back to the congregation; instead, the altar was turned toward the people. But the most dramatic change for Kathleen was the translation of the Mass from Latin to the vernacular. It delighted her to hear Mass said in English. Others, including many of the older nuns, felt it was sacrilegious. They were certain these changes would create problems; perhaps they were right.

Only last Sunday, Mrs. O'Halloran told Kathleen that there'd been guitars and tambourines played at Mass in her local parish. A "folk Mass" she'd called it. At first Kathleen found it scandalous to think of such secular instruments in a church—but then again, perhaps it wasn't. After all, Christians were exhorted to "make a joyful noise unto the Lord." What was more joyful than the sound of guitars and banjos and flutes? The more she thought about it, the more she liked the idea. Perhaps in time, this kind of worship could be introduced into the convent's celebration.

Within a few weeks of saying her final vows, Kathleen learned that some religious orders had decided to discard the tradition of wearing habits, substituting secular attire.

To Kathleen, it seemed unbelievable that any woman who'd struggled to separate herself from the world would willingly wish to become part of it again.

"I know you've heard rumors of changes in our traditional habit," Sister Clare Marie announced one afternoon. "After a recent discussion with Mother Superior, I can tell you that St. Bridget's Sisters of the Assumption will not be making any such changes for the time being."

Kathleen was glad to hear it. She'd worked very hard for the privilege of wearing a habit and she didn't want to see it eliminated.

"Mother Superior feels that Pope John's intention was to open the windows of the Church and let in a breath of fresh air. He anticipated a soft breeze, not a tornado."

Again Kathleen was in full agreement.

"We are a large order, one of the most populous in the United States. We welcome small changes, but anything this substantial will develop slowly for us. We have dressed in this same habit since 1840 and we are unwilling to let go of what is most familiar."

Several heads nodded.

"However," Sister said, "one change that might enhance our order has come to the attention of Mother Superior." She smiled as though this was a matter close to her own heart. "Instead of taking a saint's name at the time you say your vows, you may retain your own name if you wish."

That meant Kathleen could be referred to as Sister Kathleen instead of Sister Lydia, the name she had chosen as the first of her three alternatives.

"Think it over carefully and decide within the next week."

As Kathleen deliberated on all the changes, she began to feel a sense of excitement. For three years she had struggled in vain to let go of her earthly family in order to be part of God's. Now she was given the chance to be part of both.

The first person she would tell was Sean. Of all her family, she knew her oldest brother would definitely approve. She wrote him a lengthy letter and, as she'd expected, his response was gratifying.

On August 14, 1966, a Sunday afternoon, Kathleen O'Shaughnessy said her vows. Her parents, four of her five sisters and her youngest brother were in attendance. They watched as the bridal veil was replaced with the full veil of a professed sister.

"Do you know where you're going to be assigned?" her mother asked anxiously. Kathleen knew her family prayed it would be nearby so they could visit on a regular basis.

"I won't find that out until later." Kathleen was as curious as her family. She'd waited three long years for this moment. She'd entered the convent as one of thirty postulants, but over time eleven had chosen to leave. Their vocations hadn't been strong enough to hold them.

A week later, Kathleen learned that she was being sent to attend education classes at the University of Minneapolis. The following September she'd be teaching first grade at St. Peter's School.

Of the nineteen new sisters, she was the only one assigned to the convent in Minneapolis.

*chapter*

## JOANNA BAIRD

### 1967 to 1972

"Joanna," her mother said, twisting around from the front seat of the 1965 Ford Fairlane to look her full in the face. "Are you *positive* that life in a convent is what you want?"

"Mom, please! I've already said it is. I feel God is calling me." She stared out the window, at the softly falling snow.

"Sandra, for the love of heaven, will you leave the girl alone?"

"Mark, don't you see what's happening?" her mother cried. "How can you simply drive our daughter to a convent like this? She's overreacting to what Greg did. Can't you *see* what a terrible mistake she's making?"

Joanna wanted to clap her hands over her ears to block out the angry exchange between her parents. Her mother had been dead set against Joanna's entering the convent from the moment she'd mentioned it six months earlier. Her father, on the other hand, was all for it. His own cousin was a Dominican nun and he'd felt strongly that this was the right decision for Joanna. As her parents, he'd argued, it was their duty to stand by her and support her in whatever she wanted for her own future.

"She's doing this on the rebound," Sandra Baird insisted.

"I'm over Greg," Joanna said from the back seat. She rarely thought about Greg or the broken engagement anymore. He was part of her past. God was her future. Greg's wife had given birth to a robust and healthy daughter they'd named Lily. To prove there were no hard feelings, Joanna had mailed Greg and Xuan a congratulatory letter, in which she told them of her decision to enter the convent.

"Joanna is old enough to know what she wants," her father continued. "You didn't question her decision to enter nursing school, did you? Now she wants to dedicate her life to God. Why are you against that?"

Her mother crossed her arms. "Why?" she cried sarcastically. "Because in my heart I know the convent isn't the place for our daughter, despite what you think."

"If you're right," Joanna said, struggling to remain calm, "I won't stay. Please, Mom," she begged, "try to be happy for me."

"I am, honey," her father said, taking his eyes off the Boston traffic just long enough to send her an encouraging smile. "Your mother and I approve of whatever endeavor in life you choose."

Her mother glanced over her shoulder and pleaded with Joanna one final time. "I'd be happy if I truly believed you belonged in the convent. Just promise me that if you ever decide you want out, you won't be too proud to leave."

"I promise." Joanna hated to be the cause of this struggle between her mother and father. Even today, when they were delivering her to the motherhouse, her parents continued to argue as if it were *their* decision instead of Joanna's.

Once they arrived at the convent, Joanna felt reassured. The quiet, serene atmosphere brought her a sense of peace and renewed her purpose. When it was time to leave, Sandra hugged Joanna tightly. Tears shimmered in her eyes as she released her, then hurriedly turned away.

"I couldn't be more proud of you," her father said, as he handed her over to Sister Mary Louise, the Postulant Mistress.

Joanna didn't see her parents leave. Without another word, Sister Mary Louise directed her to the dormitory and assigned her a cell. The room was stark compared to Joanna's bedroom at home. There she had a canopy bed and a hi-fi set with stacks of albums. But she'd walked away from that life and was eager to embrace another.

"You'll need to change out of your clothes and into these," Sister instructed, giving her the simple garb of a postulant.

"Are there any others entering this month?" Joanna asked. It was mid-January, and the majority of women seeking the religious life came in September.

"Just three. You're the last to arrive. Now I'll let you change into your new clothes," Sister Mary Louise said.

Unexpected emotion swept through Joanna as she stripped off her sweater and skirt. A moment later she realized why. It was as though the sins she'd carried with her since losing her virginity were being stripped away as well. She didn't blame Greg; they'd both been virgins that first time. They'd led each other into sin. But now she was beginning anew.

When Joanna was interviewed by Sister Agnes in November, the head of the convent hadn't asked if she was a virgin. Grateful, Joanna hadn't volunteered the information, either. It was too embarrassing to confess to Mother Superior.

The sin of impurity had already been confessed to her parish priest. She'd received absolution and completed her penance. What she'd done with Greg was in the past and no one need ever know.

As Joanna donned the skirt, blouse, cape and veil, she experienced a feeling of release, a spiritual cleansing. She paused to close her eyes and thank God for His forgiveness and for this opportunity to serve Him.

Sister Mary Louise returned shortly and nodded with approval. "Everything seems to fit nicely."

It was a nice fit in more ways than the obvious, Joanna mused, smiling.

That evening at dinner with the other postulants—both those who'd been there since September and the four who'd come today—Joanna was warmly welcomed. Three of the postulants performed a skit in which a confused new recruit arrives at the convent door. The humor made her laugh so hard, Joanna's sides ached. She hadn't known what to expect from the other postulants, and she was grateful for the laughter and camaraderie. Later, at Compline, the evening prayers, the four women entering as postulants stood before the priest. Joanna willingly surrendered everything to God, her first step toward becoming a bride of Christ.

The glow of welcome lasted all week. But because she was unfamiliar with the rules, adjustment was a bit difficult those first few days. The Grand Silence, which lasted from after evening prayers until breakfast the following morning, proved to be the most challenging. Joanna didn't realize how hard it would be to stay quiet. Each day there seemed to be so much she wanted to share with the others, questions she longed to ask, but there simply wasn't time.

In her first letter home, she wrote confidently about her new life.

February 11, 1967

Dearest Mom and Dad,

I love it here. I really do. You wouldn't believe the welcome the other postulants gave me. There's such laughter and joy at St. Bridget's.

Mom, I know you're worried that this isn't the place for me. Although I made it sound like I knew exactly what I wanted, I confess now that I had my doubts. How could I not? Less than a year ago I was engaged to be married. If everything had gone the way we assumed, I'd be a wife by now.

Sister Theresa suggested I wait six months before entering the convent and that was good advice. Those months helped me deal with my disappointment and recognize my growing desire to serve God. It was important for me to be sure that my vocation wasn't sim-

ply a reaction to what happened with Greg. Today I can
tell you from the bottom of my heart that it isn't.

In a manner of speaking, I'm engaged again. This
time the groom won't disappoint me. This time I don't
need to worry about my fiancé breaking my heart. This
time, I made a better choice.

I'm happy, sincerely happy, and more confident than
ever that I'm making the right decision.

Much, much love,
Sister Joanna

A week later her mother wrote back.

February 18, 1967

My dearest Joanna,

Your letter was just the reassurance I needed. You do
sound happy—almost like your old self once again.
These have been such heart-wrenching months for you.
You can't blame me for doubting this sudden decision
of yours to become a nun.

I want what every mother wants for her daughter, and
that's your happiness. It's been a struggle to put my own
desires for your future aside and accept your wishes. If
you're convinced God is calling you to serve Him, then
I have no right to question your vocation. But, Joanna,
let me ask you for the last time: Have you fully considered everything you're giving up? Are you sure you'll
never want a child of your own? You and Rick have
brought me incredible joy. I hate the idea that you'll
never experience motherhood. Just be aware of what
you're going to miss out on if you go through with this.

FYI, I ran into Greg's mother in the grocery store
yesterday. She tried to pretend she didn't see me, but I
wasn't letting her off that easily. I stopped her to say
hello. When I mentioned that you'd joined the convent

she was shocked. Apparently Greg didn't say anything to her about it. (I still don't think it was a good idea to write him, but that was up to you.)

I understand you're only allowed to receive one letter a month. I'll write a little bit every day so you'll receive an extra-long letter from your family.

Your father and I love you deeply, and although Rick would never openly admit it, I know he loves you too. He misses you, just as your father and I do.

Please think about what I said.

Love,
Mom

The next six months passed in a blur of activity for Joanna. Although she'd entered the convent later than most of the other candidates, she was able to become a novice at the same time as her fellow postulants.

She mentally prepared herself for the year of silence. No letters from home, no contact with the outside world, nothing that would distract from her commitment to Christ. This was her year of contemplation.

Joanna recognized that for her, this would be a true challenge. She enjoyed talking with the others, especially when the postulants gathered around Sister Mary Louise during nightly recreation. That was one of the best times of the day.

Silence for a year. It wouldn't be so bad, Joanna told herself repeatedly. At least it wouldn't be a complete and total silence. Five to seven times a day there'd be singing and prayers. Then, for a half hour each evening at recreation, she'd be permitted to speak to her fellow novices.

One morning as she swept the chapel, Joanna started humming Bob Dylan's "Mr. Tambourine Man." It wasn't a conscious decision. The music that morning had been melodic and lovely, but somehow the Dylan song had entered her mind and refused to leave. She didn't know why a tune she hadn't heard in ages was stuck there, but it was.

As soon as Joanna realized what she was humming, she

stopped, shocked at herself. Although it hadn't been intentional, she felt guilty. Humming Bob Dylan in the chapel was sure to be considered sacrilegious. Still, within minutes she was back at it, keeping her voice low so as not to be heard.

Her own rebelliousness upset her. Humming was bad enough, but breaking silence inside the chapel was that much worse.

Nights were the most difficult for her. After a full day of work, study and prayer, she often fell into a deep sleep without even trying. It was in her dreams that Greg came to her.

The first time she dreamed of him, she woke abruptly, terrified that she might have called out his name. That would've mortified her. Her mind waged battle with her soul as Greg continued to make frequent visitations while she slept.

The dreams disturbed her. During her waking hours she managed to suppress her anger with Greg but these dreams, in which he begged her forgiveness, told Joanna the truth about her emotions. She was furious with him and she *couldn't* forgive him. It got to be so that she was afraid to fall asleep for fear Greg would show up. The memory of his betrayal would linger for hours every morning and she'd have to make an active effort to force it from her mind.

A month or so later, Joanna was summoned to Sister Clare Marie's office. A shiver of apprehension shot through her. Perhaps one of the other sisters had heard her humming while she cleaned the chapel floors. Joanna wondered if her foolish rebellion was about to get her into trouble.

With pounding heart, she knocked politely at the door and waited for a response before entering.

"Sister Joanna," Sister Clare Marie said from behind her desk. "Sit down."

Joanna settled quietly in the chair. She folded her hands in her lap and lowered her gaze as required, although she longed to read the other nun's expression.

"I imagine you're wondering why I asked to speak to you."

"Yes, Sister."

The older nun waited a moment. "Sister, are you happy with your life here?"

"Very much so," Joanna said in a rush. Her panic was immediate. Perhaps the convent was going to dismiss her, send her away.

"I'm pleased to hear that."

Joanna closed her eyes and made herself relax.

"I've noticed a certain…restlessness about you in the last few weeks. Are you sleeping well?"

It would be so easy to blurt out her dreams and beg the older, wiser nun to tell her how to vanquish them. But fear held her back. Fear of rejection if she revealed this unforgiving part of her nature. Fear of what the dreams said about her.

Because the ugly truth was that Joanna wanted Greg to suffer. She wanted him to have a miserable marriage and an equally unhappy life. She wanted him to pay for what he'd done to her.

"Sister?"

Joanna looked up in surprise.

"Are you sleeping well?" the other nun repeated. "I'm afraid the answer is obvious. Perhaps you'd better tell me what's troubling you."

"It's nothing," Joanna answered, hoping to make light of her telltale hesitation.

Sister Clare Marie leaned forward. "The eyes cannot hide what is in the heart, my child," she said gently. "Is this about the young man you'd once planned to marry?"

Keeping her head lowered, Joanna nodded reluctantly.

The Mistress of Novices released a soft breath. "I thought it might be that."

"I've had…dreams about him."

Sister sat back in the hard chair. "Dreams?"

She nodded again. "Dreams in which he wants me to forgive him for what he did—and Sister, I can't make myself do it."

"From your reaction, it appears that your inability to forgive him distresses you."

Joanna wanted to weep. The anger was back and so close to the surface it demanded all the restraint she could muster to remain seated. This nun couldn't know the pain and embarrass-

ment Greg had brought her. Sheltered as she was, Sister Clare
Marie couldn't know what betrayal did to a woman's soul.

"How often do you recite the Our Father every day?"

Joanna gave a quick shrug. "Ten times?"

"Ten times," Sister Clare Marie repeated, then added in the
same serene manner, "and forgive us our trespasses as we forgive those who trespass against us."

In other words, Joanna realized, her inability to forgive
Greg was hindering her own spiritual life. "You don't know
what he did to me," she cried, pleading for understanding.

"But I do," the nun continued undaunted. "I also know that
you love him."

"Loved," she corrected. Joanna felt nothing but disdain for
Greg now. Some days she thought she hated him, and that
frightened her more than anything.

"No, my child, you're still in love with him. Otherwise you
would be able to release him from your mind."

The lump in Joanna's throat hardened. "Are you going
to…send me away?"

Sister Clare Marie smiled faintly. "Not unless you wish to
return to the world."

"No, Sister, I want to stay right here." She'd discovered
what she'd been seeking behind these walls.

The comfort and love of her parents, the loyalty of her
friends and her own righteous indignation had offered little
compensation for her loss. Only when she'd accepted God's
call to become a nun had she found the peace and serenity she
desperately sought.

"The convent isn't a hiding place."

"I know that, Sister." Joanna took a deep breath. "I'll forgive Greg if that's what you want." She choked out the words
with a sob.

Sister Clare Marie's eyes filled with compassion. "You've
read me correctly, Sister. I do want you to forgive this young
man, but not for his sake. You need to forgive him for your own."

Joanna recognized the truth of those words, but she was
emotionally incapable of acting on them.

"Unless you can find it within yourself to forgive this young man…"

*Forgive.* The word reverberated in her mind.

"…and release your anger and bitterness…"

*Anger and bitterness* clashed with *forgive.*

"…I fear you'll be caught in a vicious trap. A trap that will make it impossible for you to progress in the religious life." She paused. "Do you understand what I'm saying, Sister Joanna?"

"I think so. If I can't forgive Greg, then the bitterness will eat away at me until I've lost the very thing I've come to seek."

The Mistress of Novices nodded. "Exactly."

"But how can I do it?" Joanna pleaded. Sister made it sound easy. "I pray for Greg, but I don't *mean* the prayers. I can't stop feeling that he deserves to be miserable after the way he humiliated me."

"We all deserve misery for the sins we've committed," Sister returned.

Of course that was true, but knowing it didn't help Joanna deal with the sense of betrayal. She'd had the wedding invitations all but mailed. Her bridesmaids' dresses had been ordered and paid for, and her own wedding gown with its overlay of Belgian lace had cost her father far too much money. Now it was tucked away in the back of the closet like a forgotten prom dress.

"Pray for him," Sister Clare Marie urged. "Ask God to bless him, his wife and his family."

Joanna swallowed hard. She *couldn't* do this. She couldn't.

"You must." Then bowing her head, Sister closed her eyes and her lips began to move in silent petition.

Joanna couldn't hear her prayer but she felt the effect of it immediately. The resistance, the uncontrollable anger, suddenly seemed to leave her heart. Her eyes flooded with tears as she bowed her own head and asked God to make her willing to forgive Greg. That was the first step and a necessary one if she was to remain part of this life she loved.

When they'd finished praying, Sister Clare Marie looked up. "You may return to your duties now."

Joanna wiped the moisture from her cheeks. "Thank you," she whispered brokenly and started to turn away.

"One last thing."

Joanna turned to face her again. "Yes, Sister?"

"I was just wondering if a Bob Dylan song is appropriate music to be humming in chapel."

Joanna's jaw sagged. Sister knew. Had she heard or had someone told her? "No," she managed to say.

"I didn't think so myself." Sister Clare Marie raised her eyebrows and dismissed Joanna with a nod.

Joanna left the office and leaned against the outside wall. After the shock of the question had dissipated, she began to smile. A nun who had a reputation for being strict and unyielding had treated her with genuine kindness.

Joanna was determined never to forget this conversation. It would be the turning point for her, she decided. The path to God had come to a crossroads and she'd chosen to follow Him. She'd chosen to discard the baggage that impeded her travels and move forward.

That night the dreams stopped. Greg had disappeared into some hidden corner of her mind—and she had Sister Clare Marie to thank for that. She hadn't forgiven him, but she was now willing to believe it might be possible.

In her last year as a novice, the world seemed to be in a state of chaos. It was 1968 and on April 4th, Martin Luther King, Jr. was assassinated in Memphis. Riots broke out across the country. Sister Agnes, the Mother Superior, asked for a day of fasting and prayer.

Then in June, Robert Kennedy was fatally shot in Los Angeles after winning the California primary. His death hit Joanna hard, and she wept openly. After the assassination of his brother less than five years earlier, it felt as though the world had turned into an ugly place. No one was safe, not the president, not the men fighting in Vietnam, not the country. More than ever, Joanna was grateful for the protection of the brick wall around the convent; it gave at least the illusion of keeping the world at bay.

The war in Vietnam was worse than ever and her mother wrote about her fear of Rick being drafted. He'd made it through his first year of college, but if the war continued, his draft number was sure to come up. Joanna worried about him incessantly.

With so many concerns, Joanna found herself on her knees more and more often, praying for the president and the country. After two and a half years in the convent, she felt separate and apart from world events, and yet aware of them. It was as though she was looking on from a distance. She knew from some of the older nuns that compared to even a few years ago, the world was encroaching on the convent and its serenity.

In August of that year, when she took her vows, her brother and parents arrived for the ceremony. Joanna waited with the other novices and prayed fervently that God would use her to touch lives. It had already been decided that she would continue with her nursing program over the summer, but not where.

The ceremony was as beautiful as it was simple. She knelt before Bishop Lawton and vowed to live a life of poverty, chastity and obedience. In her heart, she gave everything to God. She offered up all her romantic dreams and all her hopes for the future.

After the ceremony, her father had tears in his eyes. Her mother looked tired and worried. Rick seemed uneasy.

"Hey, it's me under all these clothes," she teased her brother.

"You don't look the same," he returned.

"I am."

"Are you?" her mother whispered.

"Now, Sandra." Her father placed his arm around her mother's shoulders.

To her credit, her mother attempted a smile. "You look radiant."

"Thank you, Mom." Joanna gave her a hug. Even now— almost three years after Joanna had entered the convent—her mother held out hope that she'd change her mind.

"Do you know where you're going to be assigned?" Rick asked. "Dad said you might come back to Providence."

"I might." But Joanna felt that was unlikely. "I don't know where Mother Superior will send me." It went without saying that she would go without question and serve wholeheartedly wherever Sister Agnes saw fit to assign her.

"When will you know?" her mother pressed.

"Soon," Joanna assured her family.

The next week she received her orders. "Minneapolis," she wrote her family. First to finish nursing school. Later, after she'd obtained the necessary credentials, she'd work at St. Elizabeth's Hospital.

**PART 3**

# LIVING THE VOWS

I have come that you might have life
And have it abundantly
*John* 10:10

*chapter*

# SISTER ANGELINA

## 1972

Angie was thrilled to be assigned to St. Peter's. A progressive high school with co-ed classes, it was the pride of the Minneapolis diocese.

On the first day of classes, Angie entered her homeroom for her last period of the afternoon. She immediately noticed a teenage girl who sat on her desktop, uniform skirt rolled up at the waist and her blue eyeshadow screaming at the world to pay attention.

The class hushed as Angie moved silently toward the front of the class, her habit swishing softly against her legs.

"Good afternoon," she said, tucking her hands inside the wide sleeves. "I'm Sister Angelina, and this is tenth-grade Health. If your class schedule does not show Health in sixth period, then I suggest you find the classroom where you belong now."

She watched as the girl with the long thin legs and the vibrant eyeshadow read over two schedules and dejectedly shrugged her shoulders. She handed the young man she'd been speaking to one of the schedules. The boy reached for his books and slid them off the desk before sauntering out of the room.

"Very well," Angie said in her best teacher's voice. After ten years in the classroom, she'd become proficient at recognizing the troublemakers. Already she could tell that this girl was going to be one of them. At roll call she learned that her name was Corinne Sullivan.

Angie had just started to pass out textbooks when Corinne's hand shot into the air.

"Yes, Corinne?"

"Are we going to learn about sex this term?"

Angie certainly hoped not. "Do you mean sex education?"

Corinne nodded eagerly and smacked her wad of gum.

Chewing gum was an abomination as far as Angie was concerned. Without so much as a pause, she picked up the wastebasket and walked down the aisle to Corinne's desk.

"Regarding sex education, I believe there is a short introduction to the basic facts." Angie held the wastebasket up for the girl, who stared at her blankly.

"Your gum, please."

"Oh." She spat the wad into the basket and Angie returned to the front of the room. "Does anyone else have questions about our curriculum for this term?" When no one responded, she murmured, "Good."

Health class was Angie's least favorite teaching assignment. She preferred the Home Economics classes where she taught food preparation and cooking skills. Her talent in the kitchen made her a favorite with the other nuns and often the parish priests. It wasn't uncommon for Angie to deliver a bowl of her fettuccine Alfredo to the rectory on a Sunday afternoon.

For the remainder of the period, Angie reviewed the curriculum.

Just before the bell rang ending the class period and the day, Corinne waved her arm again. "Is there going to be a lot of reading for this class?"

"There will be some, but no more than your other classes."

Scowling, Corinne sank lower in her seat, as though the thought of cracking open a textbook would be asking too much of her.

The bell rang and Angie walked over to Corinne's desk as the classroom emptied quickly. "Could you stay a few minutes after class?" she asked.

"Sure." Corinne exchanged looks with another girl, Morgan Gentry, if Angie remembered correctly.

"Am I in trouble, Sister?" The words tumbled out. "Because it's only the first day, and I forgot the rule about gum. If I am, I hope you'll give me a break. I don't usually get a demerit until the second week."

Angie struggled to hold back a smile. "Do you deserve a demerit?" she asked.

Corinne appeared to give that some thought. "Just for the gum, and that's a minor offense, don't you think?"

"Your uniform skirt's rolled up at the waist."

Corinne groaned. "Come on, Sister. I have to do that or this thing would drag on the ground." She ran her hands down the hips of the plaid pleated skirt and then flipped back one roll of the waistband. "Better?"

"Much," Angie said.

The girl grinned, her dark eyes sparkling. "Anything else?"

Angie hesitated to mention the eye makeup.

"Most of the nuns object to my blue eyeshadow," the girl cheerfully informed her. "You can complain too, if you want."

"You think I should?"

"Nah." Corinne shrugged. "Why be like everyone else?"

Exactly. "You can wear as much eyeshadow as you want in my class."

"Really?" Corinne smiled sheepishly. "I think you're going to be a lot of fun to have as a teacher."

Angie smiled despite her effort not to. She could see that Corinne wasn't a belligerent girl, just inquisitive and social.

"Can I go now?" Corinne asked.

"Yes, but Corinne…"

"Yes?"

"No more passing notes to Morgan or I'll have to confiscate and read them."

Corinne's heavy sigh could be heard as she walked out the door. "Yes, Sister."

Angie's amusement lasted as she walked home to the convent later that afternoon. She was going to enjoy Minneapolis. The community here was strong and the school staff seemed supportive and dedicated.

To her delight, Angie discovered a letter from her father tucked inside her mail cubicle. She hesitated before opening it. Tony Marcello had never fully accepted her decision to be a nun. Even now, twelve years after she'd professed her vows, he refused to call her anything other than simply Angelina. Not Sister Frances. Not Sister Angelina.

The day she'd entered the convent, he'd stopped attending Mass. It was his private rebellion against the Catholic Church for stealing away his only child. Angie had been praying for years that her father would return to the Church; the thought that he might die without last rites sent a chill through her blood.

Still, a letter from her father was a rare treat and she greedily read the handwritten pages. She hadn't visited him more than four or five times over the last fifteen years. He hated seeing her in a habit; that was obvious whenever she stayed with him. Many of the other orders had modified theirs to a more modern skirt and blouse with only a short black veil to signify their religious status. St. Bridget's Sisters of the Assumption were currently—and reluctantly—considering such a change. It was coming, and soon. Angie wondered if her father would be more comfortable with her if she wore a less restrictive style; somehow, she doubted it.

"News from home?" Sister Kathleen asked, checking her own cubicle for mail.

"Yes," she said, flipping from one page to the next. "It's from my father." Angie smiled and closed her eyes. She could almost smell the marinara sauce. Her grin widened when she noticed that the last sheet of his letter was a handwritten recipe, a new one he was planning to serve at Angelina's. An unexpected wave of homesickness practically knocked her off her feet.

Worst of all was the knowledge that she'd found God, but as a result her father had lost his faith.

*chapter*

## SISTER JOANNA

Joanna loved Minneapolis and the entire state of Minnesota. The first time she heard someone say, "Sure, ya betcha," she laughed outright. Overall, the people were hardworking and dedicated. The Catholics were a tight-knit group. Plenty of good, solid Swedes and Germans had immigrated to the area, and their descendants retained a deep faith and strong family values.

Joanna's assignment as a floor nurse at St. Elizabeth's Hospital was demanding, but rewarding, too. She worked on the surgery floor and cared for patients once they were released from the Recovery Room. Apart from her initial training in Providence, her entire nursing career had been spent at St. Elizabeth's, first as a senior nursing student and then as a registered nurse.

"Sister?" an elderly woman whispered from her bed as Joanna entered the room. She was a recent arrival and gazed up at Joanna. "I thought for a moment you might be an angel."

Joanna smiled and lifted the woman's fragile wrist to take her pulse. Patients sometimes confused the nursing sisters with angelic beings. She supposed it was because of the white habits they wore at the hospital. Older patients often needed their glasses and were disoriented following surgery. More than once she'd been asked if this was heaven.

"You're doing just fine, Mrs. Stewart," Joanna assured the woman.

"I am?" Mrs. Stewart didn't sound as if she believed her.

"Are you in any pain?" Joanna asked.

"Some. If you must know, it feels like someone took a hatchet to my stomach."

"Are you complaining about my sewing technique?" Dr. Murray asked as he entered the room. He stood on the opposite side of the bed, across from Joanna, and gently lifted the blankets. "This is some of my finest stitching, if I do say so myself."

Mrs. Stewart snorted. "I feel like someone ran over me driving a two-ton truck." Her eyes were still dull from the anesthesia.

"It sometimes feels like that. I told you before we went into this that having your gall bladder removed is major surgery."

"So you did, Doc, so you did." Mrs. Stewart's eyes fluttered closed as she drifted back into a drug-induced sleep.

Dr. Murray replaced the blankets and then reached for the chart at the foot of the bed to read Joanna's latest entry. He glanced up and caught her eye. "Could I have a moment of your time, Sister?" he asked.

"Of course." She followed him out of the room. She hadn't known Dr. Murray long, but she liked him better every time she saw him. Certainly better than Dr. Nelson, with whom she'd clashed earlier in the week. Dr. Murray had recently finished a stint in the Army, she'd heard via the hospital grapevine. Word was, he'd served in Vietnam, although he'd never mentioned it himself. His dealings with her had always been strictly professional; however, Joanna knew that several of the younger nurses were vying for his attention. It must have flattered his ego, but, as far as she knew, Dr. Murray had done nothing to encourage them one way or the other.

He stopped at the nurses' station. Mrs. Larson, the day-shift lead nurse, glanced up from the large wraparound desk as Joanna and Dr. Murray approached.

"Mrs. Larson," he said, leaning against the counter, looking relaxed and at ease. He grinned boyishly. "Would it be possible to assign Sister Joanna to care for my surgery patients? She's got half of them convinced she's an angel and it doesn't do any harm to let them think they've reached the pearly gates. Keeps down the complaints."

Joanna was amused by his remarks—and surprised by his request. She knew half a dozen nurses who would envy her the position.

The shift lead looked equally amused. "I'll see what I can do, but I don't think that'll be a problem."

"I'd appreciate it," the surgeon said. "Do you have any objections, Sister?"

"None," she murmured.

"Good." With that, the conversation was over and he turned to leave.

Mrs. Larson's gaze followed Dr. Murray down the polished corridor. "Now, that's one mighty talented surgeon."

Joanna nodded; she certainly couldn't disagree.

"He's a master of tact, too," the other nurse added with more than a hint of admiration.

"How do you mean?"

"Dr. Murray's young and single. Frankly, he's not hard on the eyes, either."

Of course, Joanna had noticed that Dr. Tim Murray was tall and dark-haired and that he possessed classic features with enough ruggedness to give his face unmistakable masculinity and character. But she'd noticed all this objectively, without personal interest. Dr. Murray's social life, or lack of it, wasn't any concern of hers. They had a professional relationship; he was a physician and she was a nun. He apparently approved of her nursing skills and that pleased Joanna. And it hadn't hurt her ego any that he'd asked for her to attend to his patients. Although ego should be sublimated, she reminded herself. It remained one of her greatest challenges.

"But why do you say he's a master of tact?" Joanna asked curiously. What did his looks have to do with it?

"He asked to work with you, didn't he?" Mrs. Larson said. "By having you assigned to his patients, he isn't offending any of the nurses who've requested the privilege."

"Oh." So much for the boost to her ego. Dr. Murray was using her as a shield against unwanted female attention. In requesting Joanna, he hadn't been acknowledging her skills, but protecting his own interests.

"It's more than the fact that you're a nun," the lead nurse added thoughtfully, almost as if she'd read Joanna's mind. "I'm sure he genuinely admires your work. He asked me earlier who'd been assigned to the care of Mrs. Masterson and Mr. Stierwalt. When I said it was you, he commented on what a good job you'd done."

Joanna instantly felt better. She didn't recall those two people, but surgery patients usually stayed on her ward only three or four days. With so many, it was easy to lose track of their names.

"Is it true that Dr. Murray was recently discharged from the Army?" Joanna asked.

Mrs. Larson nodded. "I hear he's been through quite a bit. He doesn't talk about it, but there've been rumors." Then, as if she realized she'd overstepped her bounds, the other nurse shook her head. "Such carnage...so many lives lost."

Joanna tried not to think about the war, even though the headlines had screamed of little else for nearly seven years. She could only imagine the butchery Dr. Murray had seen in his years of duty. His skills were exceptional, and she suspected that was the result of working on the mangled bodies of America's young men.

Following her shift, Joanna returned to the convent. After dinner the nuns partook in a half-hour period of recreation. Then later, before bedtime, there were the nightly prayers.

That evening several of the nuns watched the Summer Olympics taking place in Munich, West Germany. While the convent had a television set, it was hardly ever turned on. Evenings were usually spent in meditation, prayer and quiet pursuits. There wasn't much interest in what television had to offer, but the Summer Games were an exception. Why, only the day before, an American swimmer by the name of Mark Spitz had won an incredible seven gold medals.

Joanna recalled carefree days as a teenager spent at the local swimming pool. Greg was part of those memories, but she could think of him without bitterness now.

As she said her Rosary that evening, Joanna's mind drifted from the Hail Marys to Dr. Murray. It was vain of her to be this pleased—an impulse she should try to curb—but she couldn't help it.

Joanna closed her eyes and forced herself to concentrate on the words of the prayer. *Hail Mary, full of grace, the Lord is with thee. Blessed are thou amongst women and blessed is the fruit of thy womb, Jesus...*

She paused and bowed her head at the name of Jesus.

Briefly she found herself wondering if Tim Murray had returned from Vietnam with wounds of his own. Outwardly it didn't seem so, but men often concealed their emotions. She had the feeling that there was more to Dr. Murray than met the eye.

chapter

9

## SISTER KATHLEEN

Kathleen was one sister who'd have no objection when St. Bridget's order finally got around to making changes to the habits. Every day it became more of a trial to hide her thick auburn hair beneath her veil. Her hair was long again, almost the same length as when she'd entered the convent.

The habit was due to be altered soon. In a few months—perhaps as little as a few weeks—the modified habit would allow the professed nuns to stop dressing like nineteenth-century Irish widows.

With the last of her afternoon bookkeeping classes at the high school dismissed, Kathleen was technically finished for the day. She sat at her desk and graded her students' papers, becoming absorbed in her task. Amazing how easily these kids could forget basic concepts like—

"Sister Kathleen."

At the sound of her name, Kathleen jerked her head up. Father Sanders, the parish priest, came into her classroom, looking a bit disgruntled. The pastor was medium height and middle-aged, with thinning hair and a bit of a paunch. A jovial sort, he was known to liven up his sermons with a joke or two, just to keep the congregation alert and in good spirits. He reminded Kathleen of Father O'Hara, who'd been a friend of the family while she was growing up.

For years Father Sanders had been the only full-time priest serving St. Peter's, but the demands on his time were too much for one man. Only recently had a second full-time priest been added to assist him. Father Brian Doyle, barely two years out of the seminary, was young and idealistic and had a genuine heart for God. Kathleen viewed him as the perfect priest. Never had she met any man more comfortable in a collar. His sermons touched her, although delivered in the self-conscious, faltering manner of an inexperienced speaker. Still, it was obvious that he'd spent hours working on each one. Father Sanders's chatty style was more popular, but in her opinion there was far less substance to his words. Few parishioners, however, appeared to notice.

"What can I do for you, Father?" Kathleen asked.

The older priest crammed himself into one of the student desks with their attached chairs and stretched his legs out in front of him. He leaned back, wearing one of the most forlorn looks she'd ever seen. "Bookkeeping is a job fitting for the saints," he mumbled.

Like her father, she'd always had an affinity for practical mathematics. Over the last few summers she'd taken college-level courses in business math and as a result was now teaching ninth- and tenth-grade bookkeeping. It was a challenge she welcomed, although her actual experience was limited.

Kathleen grinned. "You think so, Father?"

His brows rose toward his receding hairline. "I know so." He straightened, sitting upright in his cramped seat. "Sister Kathleen, I'm here to throw myself upon your mercy."

It was hard not to laugh when Father Sanders had such a flair for drama. "I *desperately* need your help," he said, widening his dark eyes.

Kathleen held her red pencil between her open palms. "What can I do for you, Father?" she asked again.

The priest's shoulders fell. "Mrs. Stafford, who's been doing the books for the parish for the last twenty-five years, is on an extended vacation. She suggested a couple of replacements to keep the books during her absence, but fool that I am, I didn't think getting someone in for such a short time was necessary. I figured I could assume the task myself." He glanced pleadingly in Kathleen's direction. "Just how difficult can it be to enter the weekly collection amounts and write a check whenever necessary?" he asked.

"Not difficult at all, if you know what you're doing," Kathleen assured him with a grin.

"My point exactly." With a hopelessly lost expression, he turned up his palms. "Frankly, Sister, I *don't* know what I'm doing. There, I've admitted it." He continued to stare at Kathleen as though he expected her to comment.

Kathleen wasn't sure what he was asking, although she was beginning to suspect. "What would you like me to do?"

"Could you...would it be possible for you to lend me a hand for the next few weeks?" He gave a helpless shrug. "Just until Mrs. Stafford returns. She's only been gone two weeks, and will be back—" he hesitated "—about a month from now. Could you do that, Sister?"

His request presented something of a problem. While she was willing to assist where she could, nuns and priests generally didn't work together. The priests had little or no say over the nuns' duties and assignments. "I'd be happy to help, but I'll need to check with Sister Superior." Sister Eloise would need to approve before Kathleen could take on any assignment other than her teaching duties, which had to be her first priority.

"Leave Sister Eloise to me," the priest said, brightening considerably as he slid out of the desk. "I can't thank you enough."

He was gone so fast, it almost seemed that he was afraid she might change her mind.

That very night, after the evening meal, Sister Eloise asked to speak to Kathleen.

"I understand Father Sanders visited your classroom this afternoon."

"He did," Kathleen admitted.

"Father says he needs help keeping the church books until Mrs. Stafford is back from her vacation. Apparently he's already spoken to you?" Her frown suggested disapproval. "Is this a task you feel comfortable undertaking?"

"I think it would be good for me," she said honestly. Her own experience was limited to occasionally counting out cash from the till at her uncle's pub. All other bookkeeping knowledge had come from a textbook.

"Do you have time for this?"

"I'll make time," Kathleen told her, eager to accept the assignment. It was an opportunity to accumulate some real experience, and she couldn't imagine that the parish books would present any significant problems.

She knew there must be an office at the rectory, although she hadn't seen it; presumably that was where she'd work. She'd been as far as the front hallway a couple of Sunday evenings, when she'd gone with Sister Angelina to deliver dinner to Father Sanders and Father Doyle. That was all she'd ever seen of the place.

Sister Superior's frown deepened.

"I wouldn't do it at the expense of my prayer life," Kathleen said quickly.

Sister's brow relaxed, and she eventually nodded. "Father asked if you could walk over to the rectory after school three afternoons a week. I agreed, with the stipulation that you be back in time for dinner."

That meant Kathleen would need to bring her students' papers to the convent and grade them at night. "That's fine," she said. The experience she'd gain from working on the books, Kathleen reasoned, would be worth any lost personal time.

"I hope Father Sanders appreciates your sacrifice."

"I'm sure he does," Kathleen murmured.

"Somehow I doubt it, but let's hope so."

The following day, Kathleen arrived at the rectory shortly after her last class. Her briefcase was filled to overflowing with papers she'd have to grade that evening.

Mrs. O'Malley, the housekeeper, greeted her. The scent of simmering beef wafted into the church office.

"Irish stew?" Kathleen asked as she sat down at the big desk the housekeeper had shown her.

"It is. Me own mother's recipe."

Kathleen hadn't tasted authentic Irish stew since she'd entered the convent. The aroma reminded her of home and family, of childhood, and her mouth all but watered as she closed her eyes. For a moment, it was as if she'd slipped back in time and sat at the large kitchen table, between Joyce and Maureen....

Her mother wrote regularly, filling her in on the details of family life in Boston. Over the years Kathleen had visited a number of times, but nothing was the same. How could it be? She was a different person from the young girl who'd walked through the convent door nine years earlier. The changes weren't only with her, either. Her three younger siblings were like strangers to her, and the four older ones had all married and made their own lives. Their letters were few and far between. Only Sean made the effort to keep in touch with her.

"I see my salvation has arrived," Father Sanders said, bursting into the room. He carried a large cardboard box and set it on a corner of the cluttered desk.

"Hello, Father." She stood courteously. "What's that?" Kathleen was almost afraid to ask. She'd assumed that Mrs. Stafford had left the books in good order and she'd merely be stepping in for a brief period.

The priest didn't answer. "I can't tell you how much I appreciate your help in this matter, Sister Kathleen."

She peered inside the box and found a large green ledger, numerous wadded-up receipts and a stack of checks. Kathleen had the uncomfortable sensation that she was about to plunge into water well over her head. Eager as she was to help, this favor suddenly felt overwhelming.

"I don't think this should take long, do you?" Father Sanders said hopefully. "You're a bright one and seeing that you teach bookkeeping, you should have this mess cleared up in a couple of hours."

"It might take me a little longer than that," she muttered, sinking into the padded leather chair.

Father nodded solemnly. "You take all the time you need."

"Would you care for a cup of tea, Sister?" Mrs. O'Malley asked.

Kathleen shook her head. As she started to empty the box, both the priest and the housekeeper disappeared.

Kathleen worked steadily, identifying and sorting collection receipts, hardly looking up from the desk. When she lifted her head, she was shocked to notice that it was past six.

Her heart nearly exploded with urgency as she placed the receipts, now tidied and tallied, in envelopes and set them aside. Then she flew out of the room and almost collided with Father Doyle, who was walking in the front door.

"Oh, Father! I beg your pardon."

"Sister Kathleen?" He was clearly shocked to find her at the rectory.

"I'm sorry, Father, but I have to get back to the convent right away," she said breathlessly. "I'm helping Father Sanders with the bookwork while Mrs. Stafford's on vacation." She edged away from him, walking backward and gripping her briefcase.

"I'll walk you."

"No, no, that isn't necessary, but thank you." She didn't have time to walk at a normal pace; she had to hurry. In her rush it might appear that she was being rude and Kathleen didn't want to risk that.

"You're sure?"

"Oh, yes."

"Have a good evening, Sister."

"You too, Father." Without prolonging her departure, she grabbed her long skirts and raced down the short flight of wooden steps outside the rectory.

A nun was standing by the convent entrance. Kathleen dashed past her, rosary beads clattering at her side. She stopped abruptly when she realized it was Sister Eloise.

"You're late, Sister."

"I'm sorry, Sister," she said, shoulders heaving. "The...the time got away from me."

Sister Superior wasn't pleased and it showed. "I was afraid something like this would happen. I should never have agreed to Father Sanders's request."

"I won't be late again," Kathleen promised her, and she sincerely hoped that was true.

The other nun walked ahead of her. Kathleen paused a moment to catch her breath and placed a hand over her pounding heart.

chapter 10

## SISTER ANGELINA

Corinne Sullivan hurried past Angie on the way to her desk just as the bell rang for class. The heavy stench of cigarettes clung to the teenager like cheap cologne. Corinne had obviously been smoking, which was strictly prohibited while in school uniform.

Angie liked Corinne, even if the girl was something of a challenge. She enjoyed pushing the limits, testing Angie's authority and asking outrageous questions. It was all for the sake of attention. A brief look at Corinne's school records confirmed that she was the second child of three and the only girl. Experience in the classroom had taught Angie to recognize the characteristics of a middle child.

"Corinne," Angie said as she stepped to the front of the room. "Could I speak to you after class?"

"Again?" Corinne said with a low moan.

"Again," Angie echoed.

"Is it about the smell of cigarette smoke?" The teenager slid gracefully into her desk. "I wasn't smoking, Sister, I *swear.*"

"We'll discuss that later, but it's interesting you should mention cigarettes because that's the very subject we'll be discussing in class this afternoon."

A couple of the students opened their textbooks and stared up at Angie, confused. There hadn't been anything about smoking in the chapter she'd assigned them as homework.

"Aw, Sister," Corinne groaned, "are you going to tell us smoking's bad for us?"

"As a matter of fact I am." Recent studies had proven that smoking was detrimental to one's health. Despite that, cigarettes were more popular than ever, especially among teenagers. Angie considered it a disgusting habit, even though her father had smoked for years and as far as she knew, still did.

A low protesting moan rumbled through the class.

"Why do people smoke?" Angie asked, genuinely curious as to what her students would tell her.

Loretta Bond raised her hand. "It helps relax you." Then, as though she realized what she'd said, she added, "That's what my mother told me. She's been smoking since I can remember."

"Cigarettes taste good," one of the boys offered.

"How many of you have ever smoked a cigarette? Just once, just to try it out." Nearly every hand in the room went up.

Corinne Sullivan's hand was one of the first to shoot into the air. She glanced around and looked absolutely amazed. "Wow."

That was Angie's reaction as well. The class was made up of sophomores, fifteen- and sixteen-year-old students. They seemed too young to be smoking.

"Okay," Angie said, as her students lowered their arms. "Loretta, tell me why you lit up the first time."

Loretta appeared to be unsure about answering. "My mom threw away a pack and there was one cigarette left in it, so I decided to see what smoking was like. I thought it might be cool."

"How old were you?"

Loretta cast down her eyes. "Ten."

Angie swallowed a gasp. When she recovered, she asked, "And how was it?"

Loretta laughed. "I nearly choked to death."

"They're nasty-tasting," Morgan added. "At first, anyway."

"Tell me about *your* first cigarette," Angie said to the girl who'd been exchanging notes with Corinne at the beginning of the year.

"I lit up for my boyfriend," she said, glaring at Mike Carson. "He was busy driving and asked me to get out a cigarette for him. I did and it tasted awful, but after a while—I don't know, they kind of grow on you."

"One lady saw me smoking and thought I was twenty," Cathy Bailey inserted proudly.

Angie wasn't surprised. "In other words, you assume that if you smoke you'll look more mature?"

Several heads nodded.

"Everyone smokes, Sister," Corinne said.

"But not you?"

Corinne sighed and reluctantly admitted, "Okay, okay, I smoke, but not every day, just sometimes."

"But not today?"

"No, it was Jimmy's smoke, I swear." She snapped her mouth shut as if she'd said more than she should have.

"Jimmy," Morgan echoed, her eyes round and horrified.

Angie didn't know what that was all about, but she couldn't ask right then. "Next question," she said, resting against the edge of the desk. "Who in this class has never smoked?"

Three timid hands went up. Only three out of a class of thirty students, and all girls.

Angie nodded, acknowledging their response. "That was very interesting," she said. "I appreciate your honesty."

"Sister." Corinne's hand snaked up over her head. "We were honest with you, but will you be honest with us?"

"What do you mean?"

The teenager beamed a smile. "Have *you* ever smoked?"

The question stunned Angie. In all her years of teaching, not a single student had ever inquired about her life outside the convent. But it was plain that every one of these kids was eager to hear her answer. They leaned forward in their desks.

"Once," Angie said. "I was about sixteen and my father smoked. I tried it, thought it tasted vile and that was the end of it."

The class stared at her with astonished expressions, apparently finding it impossible to imagine her as a teenager. "It might surprise you to know that I was once very much like you."

"I want to know what you were like before…" Corinne insisted.

"Before what?" Angie said. "Do you think that because I wear a nun's habit I've never had a life?" She laughed at the teenager's stricken look.

"What about boys?" Morgan asked.

Angie shook her head. "This is Health class, not Ancient History."

A few of her students laughed.

"It's hard for me to think of you as someone my age," Corinne said, propping her chin in her hands.

"Let's return to our discussion," Angie suggested.

"Did you always want to be a nun?" Morgan asked.

Angie could see that the class wasn't going to be satisfied until she gave them a small detail of her life before the convent. "All right, if you must know, I did have a boyfriend once, a hundred years ago. He worked part-time in my father's restaurant."

"Your father has a restaurant?"

"What kind?"

"With a name like Angelina, you need to ask?" Corinne twisted around to mock her classmates.

"You're Italian?" Cathy Bailey cried, as though Angie had told them she walked on water.

"Enough," Angie said and picked up the textbook. "Open your books to page 56. Cathy, would you please read the opening paragraph?"

Her class reluctantly complied. Books could be heard opening and pages flipping. Cathy read the text and Angie reverted to her original plan for the class.

Holding the book in both hands, Angie paced the classroom and directed the discussion, which concerned early childhood development. Angie gave them their homework assignment and then the bell rang, signaling the end of the school day.

"I want you to answer all the even-numbered questions at the end of the second chapter. Anything else before we finish?"

Charlotte Chesterfield, who was also in Angie's Home Economics class, raised her hand. "Sister Angelina, I'd love to learn how to cook a few Italian dishes. Are you going to share any family recipes with us?"

"We'll discuss that in Home Economics, Charlotte."

"But…"

"My mom says that the way to a man's heart is through his stomach," Corinne inserted, as though this were an insider's secret.

"You have plenty of time to think about finding a husband later on," Angie told her as the rest of the class gathered their books.

"No, I don't," Corinne muttered. "I'm looking for one right now."

Angie's shock must have shown, because Corinne said, "I plan to get married the year I graduate."

"But why?"

"Oh, Sister, don't you know? Can't you guess? I don't care if I ever go to school again. I'm not much good at it. All I want is a man."

Angie wanted to argue with her, to explain that there were so many options and possibilities other than tying herself down in a relationship at such a young age.

"Do you still want to talk to me?" Corinne asked, walking backward toward the open door.

Angie shook her head. Everything she'd planned to say had already been discussed in class. "You can go."

Corinne's face brightened with a smile. "Thanks."

Just before she left for the day, Angie walked past the principal's office. "Sister Angelina," the lay secretary called out, stopping her. "What happened in Health class today?"

"What makes you ask?"

"Corinne Sullivan, Loretta Bond and about five other girls came in and requested transfers from study hall to Home Economics."

Sister Kathleen, who taught bookkeeping, chuckled as she moved past Angie in the wide hallway. "Word must've gotten out about your marinara sauce."

Angie answered with a groan, and the other nun broke into an outright laugh.

Soon Angie was smiling, too. She was dismayed about her Home Economics class filling up with young women trying to lure men into early marriage. She didn't understand it, especially with women's rights issues prominent in the headlines. Nevertheless, she had to admit she was pleased to be so popular with her students.

*chapter*

## SISTER JOANNA

Joanna was sitting at the nurses' station going over the medication records when Dr. Murray strolled up to the desk. He folded his arms along the top. "Good afternoon, Sister Joanna."

"Dr. Murray." She looked up and was struck anew at what an attractive man he was. That wasn't something she consciously wanted to notice, but it would be impossible not to. Despite his smile and the friendly expression in his intensely blue eyes, she felt a lingering sadness in him. For some inexplicable reason, she wanted to console him…. "Uh, is there anything I can do for you?"

He shook his head and straightened, almost as if he'd read her thoughts and was embarrassed by her sympathy. "I notice Mrs. Stewart is doing better this afternoon. She'd like to go home, but I'm inclined to keep her an extra day."

Joanna approved. The widow didn't have anyone to help her at home and wouldn't until the weekend. It was often like that with older people. Joanna was grateful that the physicians took home care into consideration before releasing a patient.

"She said you sat with her late yesterday afternoon when your shift was over and read to her."

Now it was Joanna's turn to be embarrassed. Like many patients, Mrs. Stewart was bored, eager to get back home to what was familiar, but still weak and slightly disoriented. Joanna had sat with her for a couple of hours.

"She said she'd been wanting to read *The Godfather,* seeing how popular it is," Joanna said, feeling somehow that she should justify her time, even though it had been after her shift. "She said she didn't know if she'd live long enough to see the movie."

Dr. Murray continued to study her. "You should know she sang your praises for a good ten minutes. It was very thoughtful, what you did."

Joanna dismissed his praise. "It was nothing." The older woman craved companionship. She was alone and away from family and had recently lost her husband of fifty years.

Dr. Murray started to turn away and then seemed to change his mind. "Would you mind if I asked you a personal question?"

"I...no, I guess not." Joanna stood so she could meet his eyes. Unaccountably, she could feel her pulse quicken.

A slight frown came over his face. "What happened? I mean, what makes someone like you decide to become a nun?"

Joanna hid her embarrassment behind a laugh. "Someone like me?"

"*Something* must have happened."

Joanna didn't know whether to be insulted or flattered. "What do you mean?"

Dr. Murray seemed to regret having said anything. "Trust me, when I was in school I never had any nun who looked like you. They were all old and crotchety."

Joanna felt heat invade her cheeks.

"That probably isn't something one's supposed to say around a nun. Sorry." He shook his head. "Listen, do me a favor and forget I said anything. I just figured you must've had a reason for entering the convent."

"I did," Joanna confirmed. "God asked it of me."

Her answer appeared to confuse him even more. "You mean there was never a boyfriend?"

"I didn't say that."

He brightened and raised his index finger. "Ah ha, so the truth comes out. You did have a boyfriend."

"Once, a long time ago."

"And he dumped you."

"In a manner of speaking." She reached for another chart and sat down, indicating that the conversation was over. This subject was far too uncomfortable—far too personal.

"He dumped you, broke your heart and you decided to join the convent," he said, as though this was what he'd suspected all along.

"Wrong," she said. "Yes, I was hurt, but it was for the best that we split up. It would never have worked. It was while I was working through my pain that I felt God pulling me toward Him. I answered His call and I've never regretted my decision."

He stared at her as though absorbing her words.

"My turn to question you," she said.

He held up both hands. "Okay, I'll admit it—I'm a lapsed Catholic. But don't try to bring me back, Sister, because I have no intention of resuming any kind of relationship with God."

That hadn't been her question, but now that he'd raised the subject, she was curious. "Why not?"

He glanced at his watch. "We don't have two or three days to debate this. Suffice it to say, the Church and I had a parting of the ways about three years ago."

"When you were in Vietnam?" she asked, standing once more.

All the teasing laughter left his eyes. "Yes," he said curtly, "but—"

"But?"

"There are plenty of subjects we can discuss, Sister. Vietnam isn't one of them."

"Can you tell me why?"

His gaze narrowed and for a long moment it was as if he'd been transported to a time and place he no longer wanted to remember. "I think it was the closest I'll ever get to hell on earth. Yet even with death and devastation at every turn, there was honor and decency and bravery above anything I'm likely to witness again." He looked away and seemed chagrined by the power of his feelings. "Is that enough?" he said in a mocking manner.

"That's enough," she said gently and then to her amazement she did something completely out of character. Joanna felt compelled to touch him. Almost against her will, she leaned toward him and placed her hand on his shoulder. With someone else it might have made her feel self-conscious, but not with Dr. Murray. She didn't quite know why that was.

Now, more than ever, she was determined to pray for the young surgeon. To lift him before God and plead for the salvation of his eternal soul. After a few seconds, she dropped her hand and said quietly, "Several of the boys in my high school class went to Vietnam."

"Anyone special?"

She must be easy to read, Joanna decided. "I had a boyfriend who went over there."

"Did he come back?"

Her laugh was tinged with a note of bitterness. "He did, only he returned with a pregnant Vietnamese wife."

"I see."

"Like I said, it was for the best. Greg and I were never meant to be." She'd already said more than she wanted and hoping to end their conversation on a subject other than herself, she asked, "What about you? Did you leave anyone behind when you went overseas?"

"I had a whole slew of lovers waiting for me," he returned flippantly.

Joanna snickered softly.

"What? You don't believe me?"

"All nurses, no doubt."

He shook his head and seemed grateful that the conversation had taken a lighter tone. "No, not a one."

"I suppose you left a string of broken hearts in Vietnam, too."

"Sorry to disappoint you. Actually I wasn't nearly as good-looking then as I am now."

Joanna rolled her eyes.

"It's true. I was the class brain and what prom queen wants to date a guy who's more interested in science than in her bra size?"

Joanna knew exactly the kind of girl he was talking about. There'd been some in her high school class, too.

"Later, while I was in med school, I met someone special. We might've gotten married if things had turned out differently."

"What do you mean?"

Dr. Murray pointedly checked his watch again, implying it was time to go.

"You'd better confess now."

He sighed and she could tell he didn't want to discuss it, but she wasn't letting him off that lightly. "Come on, you dug around until you got the information *you* wanted."

"All right, all right. Don't ever try to escape a nun." He smiled as he said it, taking the edge off his words. "If you *must* know, I'll tell you."

"I must."

"After I shipped out to Nam, she met someone else."

It was the reverse of her story. Greg had married a girl from Vietnam, and Dr. Murray's sweetheart had left him for someone stateside.

"Do these sorts of things happen often?" he asked, sounding disgruntled. "Do people come up to you and immediately start confessing their deep, dark pasts?"

"On occasion." A couple of months ago, on a rainy Sunday after the last Mass of the day, a young soldier had stopped her outside the church and asked her to pray for him. That was all he'd said, but there had been tears in his eyes and emotion throbbed in his voice. She could only speculate about why he'd asked, but she'd remembered him in her daily prayers for weeks after that chance meeting.

"If it's any comfort, I've never mentioned Greg to any-one else."

Dr. Murray nodded solemnly.

Despite his casual attitude, he'd been hurt by this woman in med school, just as she'd been devastated by Greg's actions. That pain had shaped them both into the people they were, Joanna mused. The people they'd always be.

*chapter*

## SISTER KATHLEEN

Kathleen was exhausted from teaching all day and then rushing over to the church office, but she gave Sister Eloise no cause for concern after that first night. She made sure she was always on time for dinner. Knowing Sister Angelina would be cooking on Friday, Kathleen eagerly anticipated the evening meal.

Sister Angelina had arrived that summer and quickly become a favorite of Kathleen's. The newest convent member had bonded easily with the other sisters, as well. She was a talented cook, and anyone fortunate enough to sample any of her dinners wasn't likely to forget it. She had a gift for adding whatever a dish needed to make it special. The instant one of the sisters sought her advice regarding a new recipe, Sister Angelina tore into the spice cabinet with enthusiasm and a dash of adventure.

Sister Angelina did the same thing to their lives, Kathleen reflected. She added spark and wit and joy. And she'd quickly become one of the most popular teachers in the school. They were only a few weeks into the school year and already there'd been a number of requests for transfers to her classes. The students loved her.

Kathleen didn't know Sister Joanna well, but she appreciated her sense of fun. Because the other nun worked on the postoperative floor at St. Elizabeth's Hospital, they'd had only a few opportunities to get to know each other. Five nuns worked at the hospital, two fewer than the previous year. Sister Penelope and Sister Barbara had both taken sabbaticals. It was rumored that they were thinking about leaving the convent. That seemed to be happening more often in the years since Vatican II, to the point that Kathleen had become alarmed.

The bell rang signaling dinner, and the nuns formed a silent line, walking with their heads bowed and hands folded into the dining room. They took their places at the long tables and waited to be served. As with all domestic tasks at the convent, they cooked and served meals on a rotational basis. The following week it would be Kathleen's turn to carry the plates from the kitchen out to the waiting sisters. Exhausted as she was, she didn't relish the additional duty. It was difficult enough to manage her high school bookkeeping class and the parish finances.

Once the food was arrayed on the table, Sister Superior stood, and with one voice they said grace. Whatever Sister Angelina had cooked smelled heavenly. Kathleen closed her eyes and drew in a deep breath, appreciating the scent of fresh garlic and a blend of herbs she could never hope to name.

Even after six years of convent life, Kathleen wondered if she'd ever grow accustomed to silence at meals. In the beginning it had so unnerved her that she'd been half-tempted to stand up and shout that this was unnatural.

Meals at home had been boisterous affairs with her mother leaping up from the table, rushing over to the stove and back. Her brothers and sisters chatted incessantly, usually all at once. Kathleen had never thought she'd miss the "infernal racket," as her mother used to call it, but she did.

After the main course—a delectable lasagne—Sister Joanna and Sister Angelina brought the dessert plates to the tables. They set down big round platters piled high with fresh-baked brownies, three per table. Kathleen eyed the brownies, which oozed with melting chocolate chips. She reached into the middle of the table and grabbed one. It was everything she'd hoped it would be. However, Sister Martha seemed to be having trouble biting down on hers. After one bite, she yanked the brownie out of her mouth and examined it, then spat out the offending bit. A piece of half-chewed rubber fell on her plate. Kathleen immediately realized that the two nuns had played a joke on them, mixing fake brownies in with the real ones.

She couldn't help it; she burst out laughing. Knowing she'd contravened the rules of conduct, she covered her mouth. A moment later, someone else started to laugh, and then another, almost hysterically.

In the meantime Sister Angelina and Sister Joanna sat with straight faces.

"Sisters, Sisters." Sister Eloise bolted to her feet and looked around the table, but Kathleen could see that she was struggling to hold back a smile herself.

The laughter faded. Kathleen reached for a second brownie and realized it was made of rubber. Maintaining silence was nearly impossible and small bursts of giggles continued to erupt here and there. Kathleen could see that the other nuns were having as much trouble keeping silent as she was.

Friday evenings, after dinner, were set aside for what was known as the Chapter of Faults. Once a week, the Sisters were to come before their Superior, in front of their fellow nuns, and confess their weaknesses and faults. It was a time for humility, for self-examination—a time to openly acknowledge one's failings that week.

One at a time each nun would kneel before Sister Eloise. Head bowed and hands piously folded, she would state, "Before God Almighty and you, Sister Superior, I confess the following list of faults."

When it was Kathleen's turn, she knelt before Sister Eloise and lowered her head. As hard as she strived for perfection, Kathleen knew she continually failed. She was never at a loss for failings and weaknesses.

All the convent rules, including custody of the eyes and silence at mealtime, served the function of shaping her into God's faithful servant. To an outsider, they might appear harsh or, as she'd once thought, unnatural, but every rule had a purpose.

"Sister Superior," Kathleen began, "I have been weakened by pride in assuming that I could help Father Sanders. Pride was what led me to believe I might be of service to the parish."

Sister Eloise nodded. "I was afraid you were stretching yourself too thin. Be careful, and remember that pride goeth before a fall."

"Yes, Sister." Kathleen quickly rose and returned to her place.

Sister Jacqueline stepped forward and knelt. She bowed her head.

"Sister?" Sister Eloise said when the nun hesitated.

As though to offer assistance, Sister Ruth, one of the older nuns, spoke up. "Sister Jacqueline displayed a lack of charity toward Sister Mary Catherine. Sister Catherine had asked for the scissors and Sister Jacqueline used them herself before passing them on to the one who had asked."

Sister Jacqueline reddened.

"Is this true?" Sister Eloise asked.

The nun in the center of the circle nodded. "It is."

"Very well. I would urge you to be more charitable and patient in the future." Sister Eloise glanced toward Sister Ruth and frowned as if to say that when it came to charity, the other nun had a few lessons to learn herself.

"I will," Sister Jacqueline murmured.

She was one of the youngest nuns in the convent. Kathleen had noticed that fewer and fewer young women had stepped forward to seek the religious life—just as more and more were seeking to return to secular life. There had been much discussion as to why.

Kathleen had her own conjectures. The Church was torn

by controversy over the issues of birth control and women's rights. The religious life, she feared, was losing its appeal and that saddened her.

Then there was the way women left the convent. It was always done in such secrecy. One day a chair at breakfast would be empty, but nothing was ever said or explained. They all knew, however. Another sister had decided to leave them.

With so many nuns reverting to their given names and some orders altering their habits, Kathleen felt that those who'd chosen the religious life had lost part of their identity. At the same time, she herself often craved a less restrictive life. Many of the older nuns, steeped in tradition, were adamantly opposed to any and all changes, while the younger ones welcomed them.

Aware that her feelings—a reverence for tradition on the one hand, and a desire for more freedom on the other—were contradictory, Kathleen didn't know what conclusions to draw.

She'd entered the convent with high ideals. Those ideals had felt poignantly beautiful when she was eighteen, and in fact, they continued to be. Still, there were times, like that very evening, when she would've given anything to laugh freely and joke with the other nuns. She suspected her fellow sisters felt the same way, but the rules were not to be broken.

"Sister Joanna, meals are a time of silence, and with your childish prank, you disobeyed that precept."

Caught up in her thoughts, Kathleen had missed Joanna's confession and part of Sister Superior's rebuke. The rubber brownie incident had been funny, but their order frowned upon such frivolity.

In spite of Sister Eloise's sharp words, Kathleen was sure she detected a note of humor in her voice. Could it be that Sister Superior longed for the free exchange of conversation at meals, like Kathleen did?

Some answers didn't come easy.

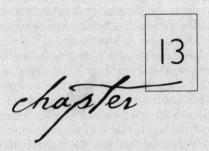

## 13

## SISTER JOANNA

Joanna didn't know why she'd done something as silly as set out those rubber brownies. Sometimes she couldn't help herself. It had been childish, just as Sister Superior had said during the Chapter of Faults.

Saturday was a rare day off from the hospital, and Joanna devoted herself to prayer. She needed to focus on her calling and her ongoing struggles with pride and vanity. After Mass on Sunday, during which she sang with the other nuns in the choir at St. Peter's, she returned to the convent and spent time in the chapel.

Of all the nurses he could have chosen, Dr. Murray had asked *her* to be assigned to his surgery patients. Joanna had allowed his request to go to her head. He had other reasons for requesting her; she knew that. Because of her status as a nun, she was a safe choice. Still, she'd been unable to prevent a feeling of pride. Then there had been that brief discussion later in the week. She was astonished now that she'd told him about Greg and that she'd actually touched him. She sighed. It was wrong to feel this way about a man.

In retrospect, her feelings for Dr. Murray could have been the very reason she'd pulled that ridiculous stunt with the brownies. She'd taken the attention away from her real weakness and cast it on yet another fault.

As soon as she realized that she'd concealed one weakness by exposing another, Joanna sat in the chapel and spilled out her heart to God, asking His forgiveness and pleading for insight into her sinful nature. Even in the convent, devoting her life to God, she struggled with obedience. Joanna sometimes wondered if she would ever become the woman God wanted her to be. Would she ever gain the maturity to win the constant battle she waged against self? At times such as these, the answers to her questions were in doubt. It wouldn't get better, she acknowledged, especially when the order implemented the coming changes.

Rumors had whispered through the convent about the imminent redesign of their habits. The modification itself would upset some of the sisters; what concerned Joanna was the fact that it symbolized shifting attitudes about the religious life and its role in the world.

That Sunday evening, Sister Superior stood before them. "I heard from Boston this afternoon. The modernization of our habits is now complete. Sister Angelina has agreed to model it for us." She turned and waited while Joanna's friend walked slowly into the room, wearing the new shortened habit of their order.

Several of the nuns shifted in their seats for a better look. Joanna was impressed. The skirt was definitely shorter, hitting just below the knee. The veil, which had fallen over their shoulders, was now the approximate length of a scarf. It fit the back of the head with what seemed to be a simple clip. For the first time in their hundred-and-thirty-three-year history, St. Bridget's Sisters of the Assumption would display their hair, part of their arms and their legs.

Murmurs rippled across the room, but they were immediately silenced by a look from Sister Eloise.

"Are there any questions?"

Sister Josephina raised her hand. She was in her seventies and had joined the convent in the 1920s. She stood on shaking legs and glared at Sister Angelina, as if seeing the other nun for the first time. For a moment, she had trouble speaking. "These…these new habits have received the approval of the motherhouse?"

"Yes, Sister." Sister Eloise didn't seem eager for the changes, either, but she had stepped forward in obedience and submitted to the decisions made by her superiors.

Joanna understood Sister Josephina's unspoken concern. For the last fifty years, the other nun's hair had been cropped and hidden beneath yards of heavy fabric. Now she was being asked to display what had once been considered intensely private. It wasn't only her hair that would be revealed to the world, but her legs too. For someone who had worn the same dress for fifty-odd years, this was a drastic change.

"I…I don't know how to style my hair, Sister," another of the older nuns said, her voice trembling.

"Which of us does?" Sister Eloise returned, gesturing in a forsaken manner.

The nuns looked at each other with despair.

"Will we be required to wear nylons?" Sister Margaret asked. "Or can we continue to wear our cotton stockings?"

Sister Superior seemed at a loss as to how she should answer. "I believe the choice will be an individual one."

There were so few individual choices in convent life that this was a revolutionary thought to many of the sisters.

"Our arms will show," Joanna heard Sister Charlene whisper to Sister Josephina. She tucked her hands deep into the bulky sleeves that marked their habit, as though to hide them from view.

The discontented murmurs continued well into the evening. Joanna recognized that many of the older nuns were shaken by the changes. She would adjust easily enough, but then she was young and had worn the current habit only six years; some of the others had worn it for fifty and sixty. Some orders had made the changes optional, but for whatever reason, Sister Agnes, their Mother Superior in Boston, had decided against that.

At the hospital the following afternoon, Joanna ran into Dr. Murray.

"Good afternoon, Sister," he said when he swiftly passed her in the corridor.

She acknowledged him with a polite nod, but her heart raced at the sight of him. Either he was late for his rounds or he was covering for another surgeon because he rushed past her.

Joanna struggled with disappointment. Despite all her prayers and promises, she wanted to see him. She'd hoped for another chance to chat, to know him better; apparently he wasn't interested. This was wrong, this desire of hers. It had to stop. Her awareness of him was too personal, too intense. She had to bring it under control.

At lunch, Joanna joined the other nuns in their private dining room. She'd never understood why they weren't allowed to eat with the seculars. At one time she'd asked about the practice and been told simply that it was tradition. Questioning further would have shown a lack of faith and a rebellious attitude.

Dr. Murray drifted into her mind again. She couldn't help wondering what he'd think when he saw her in the new habit. Her legs were long, and at one time she'd considered them her best feature. After entering the convent, she'd given up all thoughts of her physical appearance. As a postulant, she'd been homesick and turned to food and quickly gained ten pounds. It hadn't bothered her. Anything to do with personal appearance was forgotten. Eventually she'd lost the weight, but not because of any diet. She wasn't even sure how the extra pounds had disappeared.

Now she'd need to shave her legs again. The idea of wearing her cotton stockings was ludicrous. After going through the washing machine two or three times, those stockings were faded and pilled. No, she would wear white nylons the same as the other nurses.

Mirrors! My goodness, the sisters would require mirrors if they were going to style their hair. Joanna wondered if Sister Eloise had thought of that. Knowing how concerned Sister Josephina and several of the other nuns were, Joanna had offered to help with their hair. However, it had been so long since she'd fiddled with rollers and hair spray, she was afraid her fellow sisters might end up resembling the Supremes. That image made her laugh.

After lunch, Joanna returned to the floor to find Dr. Murray out of surgery. He still wore his greens.

"I have another patient for you," he said as she approached the nurses' station. His manner was professional and none of his earlier banter was in evidence now. "His name is Fredrick Marrow. He just had his appendix out. Unfortunately his appendix ruined a perfectly good afternoon—his *and* mine."

"A date, Dr. Murray?" she asked, then wished she could withdraw the words. It had been unethical of her to ask.

"A hot one," he said. The sudden smile he flashed her could have melted concrete. "I'm in a rush to get back to my golf game. Take care of Freddy for me, will you?"

"Of course." Joanna instantly felt better. His date had been on the golf course with a set of clubs. But he should be dating, should have an active social life. That was what she wanted for him, she told herself, but the small voice in the back of her mind claimed otherwise.

# chapter 14

## SISTER ANGELINA

"How are you going to style your hair, Sister?" Corinne Sullivan asked, cocking her head as she studied Angie.

Like the rest of the Health class, she'd been assigned to read her textbook in silence. "I'll give you a few hints, if you want," she offered excitedly. "I'm good with hair. I styled Megan's." Turning around in her desk, she looked at her handiwork while Megan pretended to be reviewing the chapter.

"Read," Angie whispered in warning, not wanting to disturb the others. While most had their heads obediently bowed over their reading assignment, Corinne continued to assess Angie as she walked down the aisles between the rows of desks.

"I'm just interested," Corinne said in a low voice when Angie glared at her.

Corinne might be interested, but for Angie the whole subject of hair was a source of anxiety rather than pleasure. In the past fourteen years Angie had done nothing more than run a brush through her hair. She'd noticed the other day that there were several gray hairs in her brush. It didn't surprise her. For most of her life her father had been completely gray; in fact, the last time she'd seen him, his hair had gone white. Premature graying ran in the family. Which brought up another question: would...should Angie color her hair? Would that be allowed? Somehow she doubted it. Vain and contradictory though it was, she didn't want to appear old—or, at least, any older than thirty-two. She sighed at the prospect of all these decisions she didn't feel equipped to make, all these changes she wasn't ready for.

Redesigning the habit was a sign of the upheaval taking place within the Catholic Church, an upheaval that would profoundly affect the religious life—was already affecting it. Angie felt more and more uncomfortable with the loss of traditions that had defined the order for more than a century.

"Didn't you ever think about marriage?" Corinne pressed, still watching Angie, who paced up and down. "I'm sorry, Sister, it's just that I've never really thought of you as a *woman* before, you know?"

That was understandable enough, Angie mused. For that matter, she didn't consider herself one, either. Her menstrual cycle was a nuisance and her breasts were useless appendages she struggled to contain and minimize.

"We heard you're going to be wearing dresses just like everyone else!"

Before Angie could hush the girl a second time, the class bell rang and the students, including Corinne, surged out the door. Weary after the last class of the day, Angie sat down at her desk and flipped absently through the homework papers she'd collected earlier.

"You busy?" Sister Kathleen asked as she stepped into the classroom. Tiredly she leaned against the doorjamb. "Were you drilled about the new habits all day? I don't understand it. You'd think we were about to break a hundred-and-thirty-year-old tradition or something," she teased.

Angie chuckled. "I got my share of questions."

"If it's this bad now, can you imagine what it'll be like once we actually start *wearing* the habits?"

The students were merely curious, whereas Angie was worried. In all the years she'd spent in the convent, every bit of individuality had been methodically stripped from her. And now…

"I'd better get over to the rectory," Sister Kathleen said with a noticeable lack of enthusiasm.

Angie encouraged her with a smile. The church books must be a disaster if Father Sanders had requested Sister Kathleen's help. Angie liked both parish priests. Father Sanders, who often celebrated Mass at the convent, was congenial in that bluff, hearty way, and from personal experience, she knew it was hard to refuse him. Father Doyle was younger, obviously idealistic and more serious in his manner. Angie suspected he never would have made such a request.

"I'll see you later," Sister Kathleen said as she left.

As Angie gathered up her papers and placed them inside her briefcase for the short walk back to the convent, she glanced out the window overlooking the parking lot below.

She immediately found Corinne, who was talking to a young man sitting in a car. Angie didn't have a clue what kind it was, but it appeared to be new. The driver's window was rolled down and his elbow rested on the edge. He took a puff on a cigarette and offered it to Corinne. Angie was relieved that the girl shook her head and declined. That relief was short-lived, however. A moment later, Corinne shrugged and reached for the smoke. Looking carefully around, the girl leaned close to the car and took a deep drag on the cigarette before handing it back to the young man.

Angie picked up her briefcase, and feeling mildly depressed, headed out of the classroom. Generally she walked directly to the convent, which was down the street from the school. However, at the last minute, she decided to take a more circuitous route and went around the back of the building, toward the parking lot. Corinne had probably left with her boyfriend already, but if not, maybe Angie's presence would

remind her of their earlier discussion about smoking—and the
fact that it was forbidden on school premises.

She was in luck, she saw. Corinne was half in and half out
the car when Angie sauntered past.

"Good afternoon, Corinne," Angie said casually, as though
she often took this out-of-the-way route.

"Sister Angelina?" Corinne's eyes went wide with shock—
and then guilt.

Without waiting for an introduction, Angie nodded in the direction of the driver. The young man was quick to avert his gaze.

"This is Sister Angelina. She's my Health teacher... I tried
to get into her Home Ec class, too, but I haven't heard if
there's room yet. Everyone wants Sister to teach them how to
cook a real Italian dinner."

"I got the paperwork this afternoon. I guess you'll be joining us, after all," Angie told her.

"I'm in?" Corinne nearly exploded with excitement.

"I don't believe I caught your name," Angie said to the boy.
He was attractive enough, with dark hair and eyes, and he
didn't seem particularly tough-looking. That reassured Angie.

"Oh, Sister," Corinne said eagerly, "this is Jimmy Durango, my steady."

"Do you attend school here?"

"No." Jimmy shrugged. "I'm not a Catholic." He said this
as though he expected her to disapprove. He was studying her,
though, and trying not to be obvious about it. Angie understood his curiosity; this was possibly the first time he'd ever
seen a nun up close.

"Where do you go to school, Jimmy?" she asked.

"Garfield High in Osseo."

"Isn't that quite a ways from here?"

"He comes to town to see me," Corinne put in.

"And your parents have met Jimmy?"

"Oh, yes." She gave her boyfriend her hand and they entwined their fingers, expressions fervent. "Mom wants me to
date a Catholic boy," Corinne said, "but I don't like any of the
guys around here." She made it sound as though any boy at

St. Peter's couldn't possibly meet her exacting requirements, although Angie distinctly remembered a young man who'd followed Corinne into class that first day.

Jimmy's eyes narrowed; he seemed to assume that Angie would agree with Corinne's parents and discourage the relationship. She wouldn't. That wasn't her job. Angie was a teacher, not a counselor. She liked Corinne a great deal; the girl had spunk and a sense of humor, and she didn't hesitate to question what she didn't understand. Those were traits Angie admired. She'd just have to hope that Corinne had enough common sense and self-respect not to do anything foolish.

"Nice to meet you, Jimmy."

"You, too…." He hesitated, apparently uncertain about how to address her.

"Oh, just call her Sister Angelina."

"Even if I'm not Catholic?" Jimmy asked.

Angie nodded. "Of course."

"You aren't going to change your name when you get your new habit, are you, Sister?" Corinne asked.

"No, I'll still be Sister Angelina Marcello."

"You have a last name too?"

"Yes, Corinne, most of us do." Try as she might, Angie couldn't keep the amusement out of her voice.

"I know that," Corinne said with a sheepish grin. "It's just that I've never heard yours before. Wow, that is so cool! Sister Angelina Marcello," she repeated reverently.

Angie was about to turn away, but Corinne stopped her. "Jimmy sometimes has questions I can't answer about the Church. Would it be all right if I asked you, Sister?"

"Corinne." Jimmy's voice was low and full of warning.

"Jimmy?" Angie smiled at the young man, thinking he might be more comfortable asking her himself.

"It's nothing important," Jimmy insisted, looking pointedly at Corinne. His face had gone red, as though his girlfriend had betrayed a confidence. When he realized that Angie was studying him, he grew even more flustered. He turned abruptly and started the engine.

"You coming?" he asked Corinne.

She looked torn. "I don't know yet," she said, holding her books tightly.

The nuances of what was happening were beyond Angie. It was time for her to leave. "Once again, it was a pleasure to meet you, Jimmy."

"Thanks, Sister. You too."

"Bye, Sister," Corinne said. She suddenly raced around the front of the vehicle and slid into the passenger side next to Jimmy.

Remembering years ago when she'd been a teenager herself, Angie stood back and watched as the two of them roared off. She liked Corinne's boyfriend, she decided.

*chapter*

## SISTER KATHLEEN

"Sister, I was wondering when you'd arrive," Mrs. O'Malley said when Kathleen stepped into the rectory. A blast of chilly air followed her inside. "I have tea brewing if you'd care for a cup."

Kathleen didn't have time to spare. The housekeeper was an inveterate talker—like Mrs. O'Halloran back at the motherhouse—and if Kathleen took the time for tea, the woman might easily waste an hour with her chatter.

"Thanks for the offer, but I can't today. I'd better get to work," she said grimly. Kathleen had come to realize that her being at the rectory, accepting this task, was a sign of weakness—not the kindness and generosity she'd first thought. Well, it was in part, but she knew that generosity wasn't her primary motivation. She was eager for recognition, eager to leap in and save the day for the parish priest, eager for praise.

"I'll just go into the office," Kathleen said.

With a disappointed nod, the housekeeper returned to the kitchen.

The church office was quiet. After Father Sanders had given her the books and his receipts that first afternoon, Kathleen hadn't seen him again. Father Doyle wasn't around much, either. Even when she did happen upon them, they exchanged only the briefest of pleasantries.

In the back of her mind—and Kathleen was embarrassed to admit this—she'd assumed that once she was in the rectory she'd have the opportunity for interesting discussions about theology and various church matters with one or other of the priests. Friendly discussions, because no nun would dare question a priest or challenge him in any way. She reminded herself that even entertaining the notion that any priest would care to hear her philosophy was to assume a higher opinion of her own intelligence and position than warranted.

Taking her chair, Kathleen opened the ledger and penciled in the deposit from Sunday's collection. That was easy enough. The monthly bank statement had arrived, so Kathleen sorted the checks by number and marked them off as having cleared. This was the first statement she'd seen. Previous ones must have been destroyed or stored elsewhere; they hadn't been in the box with the other material.

The first problem she encountered was a discrepancy in the deposits. It wasn't much—twenty dollars in the first deposit and fifteen in the second. The ledger showed one thing, while the bank statement noted a lesser amount.

Kathleen set the statement aside until she had a moment to ask Father Sanders who, she assumed, had deposited the Sunday collections. Normally Mrs. Stafford would have seen to the task first thing Monday morning, but she'd been on vacation since mid-August, when Father Sanders had assumed her duties.

Kathleen worked diligently for the next hour, reconciling the accounts, but she found one small discrepancy after another. It was as though whoever was making the deposits had skimmed a bill or two off the top each time. She couldn't imagine Father Sanders doing such a thing, but he was the one who made the deposits. It didn't make sense. She also discovered that receipts for rectory expenses didn't tally with amounts deducted in the ledger.

The bell above the rectory door chimed and she glanced up just as Father Doyle strolled down the hallway toward the kitchen. He paused when he noticed Kathleen.

"Good afternoon, Sister. Beautiful day, isn't it?"

Kathleen smiled in agreement. She did enjoy these lovely autumn afternoons, when the air was crisp with intimations of winter. They reminded her of Boston and the big leaves falling from oak trees on the street outside her family home.

"Father," she said, stopping him before he disappeared. "Do you happen to know where Father Sanders is?" If she could have ten minutes of his time, she might be able to clear up these discrepancies. She was certain he'd have a logical explanation.

"Father is out for the rest of the day. Can I help?" he asked, moving into the office.

"No, no... I have a few questions I need answered, but they can wait for another day."

"You're sure I can't be of assistance?"

She appreciated his willingness but she needed the older priest. "No, unfortunately, I have to discuss this with Father Sanders."

Father Doyle shrugged, then said slowly, "I'll ask him to be available for you the next time you're here."

"Thank you." Kathleen glanced up and saw that Father Doyle was frowning. She'd never really looked at him before. Or rather, had never looked beyond his collar. Although he bore a solid Irish name, his facial features betrayed none of the typical signs of being from Ireland. He might be one of the so-called Black Irish, she decided. It was said that Spaniards had settled in Ireland at the time of the Armada, which accounted for the blue-eyed, dark-haired men.

Loud jovial singing could be heard coming from the kitchen. "That must be Father Sanders now," Kathleen said.

She wanted her questions answered as quickly as possible. Otherwise she might be held up for several days.

"I'll check and see." Father Doyle hurried toward the kitchen and left the door between the rectory and the private dining room open in his rush. The singing became louder and more boisterous.

Father Sanders joined her a moment later, obviously in an expansive mood. "Good day to you, Sister Kathleen."

"Good afternoon, Father."

"I understand you have a question for me?"

"I do." As simply as possible, she explained the differences between what the bank statement had noted for the deposit and the amount he'd entered in the ledger.

"I must've written the deposit amount incorrectly," the priest said. "Like I explained earlier, this accounting business is beyond me. Just change what you need to so it comes out right."

His advice shocked her. "Father! I can't do that."

"You can if I say so."

"But…but what will Mrs. Stafford think when she returns?"

Father sighed sharply, and she caught a whiff of mint on his breath. "She won't think a thing of it, seeing I was the one who made the mistake. Mrs. Stafford makes allowances for my many flaws and you should, too."

"Yes, Father." He was growing impatient with her, but Kathleen hesitated to alter the books simply because Father told her to. While it wasn't a lot of money, she had no moral or legal right to do that.

"Anything else?"

Kathleen hesitated.

"I don't have all day, Sister," Father said.

Kathleen felt properly chastised. "Just one more thing," she said, drawing in a deep breath. She could feel the embarrassment redden her face. "I'm afraid the receipts you gave me for expenses don't reconcile with—"

"Reconcile?" Father's voice was too loud. "Speak English. How am I supposed to know what that means?"

"I...I—"

"Father." The younger priest appeared, almost as though he'd been waiting in the wings. "Perhaps it would be better if you discussed this later."

"Yes, yes, it would," Father Sanders mumbled, suddenly deflated. He stared down at the floor in apparent confusion.

"I believe Mrs. O'Malley has coffee for you, Father."

"Coffee?" Father Sanders repeated with a scowl. Father Doyle artfully steered the older priest back toward the kitchen. He glanced over his shoulder at Kathleen. Feeling his gaze, she looked up and read the apology in his eyes.

It was then that she knew. At that moment she recognized what should have been obvious from the first. Father Sanders was drunk. It'd been years since she'd seen anyone in that condition. And yet, now that she was aware of it, she wondered how she could have missed all the signs, from the mouthwash or peppermints masking his breath to the too-careful enunciation and mood swings.

Just as she was clearing off the desk, Father Doyle returned. He hesitated, evidently unsure of what to say.

When he finally did speak, his voice was regretful. "In the future it might be better if you came to me with your questions, Sister."

"Perhaps you're right." Father Doyle preferred to handle the situation on his own—preferred not to involve her—which was understandable, she supposed. Understandable and very kind. What he probably didn't realize was that she was already embroiled in Father Sanders's troubles.

Father Doyle was the most honest and ethical man she'd ever known and if he wanted to protect Father Sanders, then she could only agree.

"As Father said, he doesn't have a head for numbers."

Kathleen offered him a weak smile. "So it seems," she murmured.

Father Doyle was studying her, as if to gauge how much she'd discerned from the other priest's behavior. She considered explaining that she'd been around a tavern most of her growing-up years, but Father Sanders's drinking was a subject that needed to be handled with discretion.

Singing exploded from the kitchen again, loud and badly off-key.

Father Doyle's gaze sought hers.

Kathleen recognized the song from her uncle's pub. "My uncle used to sing that," she said in a whisper.

"Your uncle?"

They were tiptoeing around each other, neither wanting to say what was obvious. "He's...a favorite uncle of mine. My father works at the pub my uncle owns. Uncle Patrick doesn't have a head for business, either, and so my dad helps tend the bar and he does the books."

Father Doyle's relief was unmistakable. "Father Sanders is a good priest," he said seriously. "He has his struggles, as we all do, and I'm sure he'll...improve."

Kathleen was relieved, too. Father Doyle was taking care of the situation. She needn't worry. "I'm sure he will."

The younger priest grinned. "So it appears your uncle Patrick and Father Sanders share a certain weakness for... numbers."

Kathleen grinned back. She could keep a secret and she wanted Father Doyle to know that. As far as she was concerned, the fact that Father Sanders liked to drink would stay between the two of them.

*chapter*

## SISTER ANGELINA

"What did you think of Jimmy?" Corinne excitedly asked Angie the following Monday when she arrived for her first Home Economics class. It was the twenty-fifth, and the last week of September.

"He seems very nice," Angie said, busy setting out all the ingredients for the recipe her class would be working on.

"Are we cooking today?" Corinne asked, glancing at the kitchen countertop, laden with plum tomatoes, olive oil, onions, garlic, parsley and fresh basil.

"We are. I'm going to teach you how to make a proper red sauce."

"Red sauce?" Corinne wrinkled her face as though she'd never heard of it before.

"Better known as spaghetti sauce here in the States," Angie qualified.

"Oh, good," Corinne said as the other class members slowly filed into the room. "When I told him about the class,

Jimmy said he couldn't wait to have me cook for him. Mom and I are going to Italy this summer. I want to learn as much about Italian food as I can." She looked over her shoulder to see who'd entered the room before lowering her voice. "Jimmy says Italian women are hot-blooded."

"Hot-blooded," Angie repeated, making sure Corinne heard the displeasure in her voice.

"Not you, Sister," Corinne said quickly with a horrified look.

"I should hope not," Angie said with a small irrepressible laugh. Hot-blooded, indeed!

"Sorry, Sister. It's just that…well, Jimmy's special and I want to be the perfect wife for him."

Angie struggled to keep her voice calm. "You two don't need to think about marriage for a long time."

"Uh-uh." She shook her head. "I'm going to marry Jimmy."

"And how does Jimmy plan to support you?"

Corinne's face hardened. "He has a part-time job at the lumber-yard and he thinks pretty soon they'll take him on full-time."

"But what about school?" Angie certainly hoped Corinne's young man hadn't dropped out of school. That was a sure way to mess up his future and possibly Corinne's.

"He didn't drop out, Sister, if that's what you're worried about."

"No," Morgan Gentry said, joining Corinne and Angie, "he got expelled. A week ago."

Corinne glared at her best friend. "That wasn't Jimmy's fault and you know it."

"I don't know any such thing and if your mother finds out you saw Jimmy again, you'll be grounded until graduation."

Furious now, Corinne whirled around to confront her.

Just then, thankfully, the class bell rang and cut off their disagreement before it could develop into a full-blown fight.

Home Economics went faster than any of Angie's other classes. It was a subject she held dear, especially the food and cooking sections. Her father had taught her well, and she'd become an inventive and confident cook.

The one drawback of teaching these classes was the memories they stirred of her youth. She'd spent so many hours with her father at his restaurant. *Her* restaurant, she mused sadly. It would've been hers if she hadn't entered the convent. In some ways Angie wished she could be two women. She wanted to serve God; she also wanted to earn her earthly father's love and praise by giving Angelina's the same passion and dedication he had all these years.

"Sister?" Morgan looked at her, face slightly tilted. "I was asking about the red pepper flakes. Aren't they hot?"

"Very, so they should be used sparingly."

"Simmered in the olive oil?"

"Yes."

Another hand shot into the air. "Does it have to be extra-virgin olive oil?"

The girls giggled as if this were a smutty joke.

"The term extra-virgin signifies the first run of the press. And no, it isn't necessary." It would be a sin to use anything else, but only in her father's kitchen. In a high school class, where every penny was carefully considered, less costly oil would do. "You can use any good oil." She nearly choked on the words. "But olive oil *is* preferable."

"Fresh parsley?" One of the other girls threw out the question, taking notes as she did.

"Fresh," Angie repeated. "Always fresh whenever possible. Use dried only if you have no choice."

Her students leaned over their notebooks and scribbled furiously. This recipe was the most popular of all the ones she'd taught over the years.

"Why do you call it red sauce instead of spaghetti sauce?"

"Because it's used on more than pasta."

Her students glanced quizzically at one another. "Like what?" Corinne asked.

"Like pork roast or spread over top of a meatloaf. My family had at least a dozen dishes that required red sauce. A good Italian cook will make up a large batch on Saturday."

"Every week?"

"Without fail," Angie said. "And the sauce is used for the

next few days." She tried to think of a comparison. "It's a little like hot sauce. Some people put Tabasco on their fried eggs, right?"

"Maybe some people, but not me," Morgan said, shaking her head.

"Well, ketchup then." Angie shuddered.

"Red sauce isn't a condiment, is it, Sister?"

"Not exactly…" The bell rang and her class moaned with disappointment.

Lunch period was next and the girls hurried out. All except Corinne. She walked over to Angie's desk. "I don't want you thinking the wrong things about Jimmy," she said.

"It isn't my place to judge another." Angie gathered up her books.

"I know, but Morgan made him sound bad."

Angie hesitated. "Is it true that Jimmy was expelled?"

Corinne frowned and nodded reluctantly. "But it's not like it sounds. He wasn't the one at fault, but Garfield's principal has it in for him and…" She let her voice fade. "I love him, Sister. I really, really love him."

Angie gave the girl her full attention. "What do your parents think of him?"

Again Corinne looked uncomfortable. "My dad doesn't like him, and my mom thought he was all right until he got expelled. Now they don't want me to see him anymore."

That explained a great deal.

"But you're continuing to see him?"

"Only sometimes. We tried to stay away from each other, but it's no good. We were meant to be together." Her face held that dreamy look of young love. "When you saw us the other day, it'd been more than a week since we talked and it just wasn't any good, Sister. Not for Jimmy and not for me."

"Is it good to meet behind your parents' backs?"

"No," Corinne agreed quickly enough. "We hate it. Jimmy's going to talk to my dad, face-to-face. He said it's the way a man does things."

Angie's estimation of Jimmy went up a notch. "Good. And he's asking you questions about the Church?"

Corinne looked at the floor. "Some." She looked back at Angie, smiling widely. "We went to Mass together last Sunday."

No doubt without her parents' knowledge. If they *had* known, they would've disapproved.

"I wish Morgan hadn't said anything," Corinne said as she walked out of the room. "I hate it when people hear something about another person and then judge that person without even knowing the details. It's so unfair."

"Yes, it is," Angie agreed. "But unfortunately that's the way it is in life." If Jimmy didn't return to school for his diploma, he'd carry that stigma wherever he went.

"He was talking about going into the Marines, but they said they wouldn't take him until he graduated." She continued to hug her books.

Morgan was waiting for Corinne at the end of the hall. "Gotta run. See you later, Sister."

Angie smiled as the girl ran down the hall. Parenting must be an extremely difficult task—much more so than teaching, she decided. She prayed God would grant Corinne's parents wisdom in dealing with their daughter.

# chapter 17

## SISTER JOANNA

Joanna was all aquiver. That was how she'd describe her feelings, although "quiver" was certainly an old-fashioned word. She'd come across it in an ancient novel she'd found in the convent library, the kind written by an "authoress" a century ago. Nevertheless, *aquiver* summed up her emotions perfectly. Because this was the first day of her modified habit with its short veil. Her naturally blond hair was artfully styled around it.

The nuns were required to make the modifications to their own habits. The sewing machines at the convent had been humming all weekend. Joanna had never seen such chaos. It was crazy and funny and exciting in ways that baffled her.

Her hair. She'd spent an inordinate amount of time fussing with it, positive that any style she wore would be ridiculously outdated. Joanna wasn't alone in that; many of the nuns had complained about having to find time for personal grooming in their rigid schedules.

The shorter skirts and veils were only the beginning of what was going to be a difficult adjustment for them all.

As she stepped on to the city bus that would drop her outside the hospital, Joanna felt breathless, full of mixed emotions. She couldn't help wondering if Dr. Murray would comment on the change in her dress. Perhaps he wouldn't notice.

She shouldn't be thinking about him. It was a matter of discipline. A matter of obedience. She had no right, no possible excuse, to allow a man to linger in her thoughts. It was flirting with danger, and Joanna knew that as well as she knew her own name.

She hurried into St. Elizabeth's, and as she'd feared, her appearance on the third floor attracted immediate attention. It seemed that everyone, right down to the maintenance man, turned to stare at her. This was decidedly unnerving.

"Sister?" Lois Jensen, a lay nurse, blurted out when Joanna awkwardly approached the station. All of a sudden she didn't know what to do with her arms and tucked them behind her.

"You look…" Lois was obviously at a loss for words.

"Different?" Joanna supplied, hoping to ease the other woman's discomfort—and her own.

"Yes! Different."

"Let me have a look," Julie Jones, a hospital volunteer, said eagerly. She came around the front of the nurses' station to get a better view.

Julie took Joanna by the shoulders and turned her slowly around, studying her from head to toe.

"You two are embarrassing me," Joanna said, feeling herself blush.

"So this is the new habit we've heard so much about," Julie said. "It's quite a change, isn't it?"

Flustered, Joanna nodded. Thinking it would help if she immediately got to her work, she moved toward the tray of prescriptions to be dispensed to her patients.

"Come and look, Dr. Murray," Julie called.

Joanna wanted to grind her teeth in frustration. The last

person she wanted to see right now—or be seen by—was Dr. Murray. She'd hoped to avoid encountering him until the unfamiliarity of this new habit had worn off. Clearly, that was not to be.

"Well, well," the physician said, joining the small group of onlookers. He crossed his arms and gave her a thorough inspection. "What have we here?"

"Sister has legs," Lois said.

"Good ones, too," the doctor added appreciatively.

"Would you kindly stop," Joanna pleaded.

"And hair," Julie felt obliged to point out. "I didn't know you were a blonde, Sister."

Joanna's hand involuntarily went to the side of her head. "You three might have time to waste, but I don't." Eager to escape, she reached for the tray and headed down the corridor.

Dr. Murray caught up with her ten minutes later, when she entered the room of one of his patients. Mr. Rolfson had undergone extensive cancer surgery. No one needed to explain to Joanna that his time on earth was limited. He was receiving massive doses of medication and was in a lot of pain. He was asleep when she walked in.

Dr. Murray glanced up. "Let him sleep," he instructed.

She nodded and was about to turn away when he stopped her. "I didn't mean to embarrass you earlier."

"You didn't," she said wryly. "Lois and Julie already took care of that."

"You look very nice." His gaze held hers a moment longer than necessary.

Joanna immediately dropped her eyes. The silence that followed was rife with a tension she didn't understand, but she resisted looking up. It wasn't hard to guess what he was thinking.

"Why do you do that?" he asked, sounding irritated with her.

"Do what?"

"Refuse to look at me."

"It isn't anything personal," she said quickly. "Actually it's part of our religious training."

"Why?"

With the woman's movement in full swing, the concept of "custody of the eyes" must sound hopelessly outdated. Nonetheless, she explained as simply as she could.

He listened and then in a lower voice said, "I don't like it."

She didn't respond.

"It isn't you," he added.

She couldn't keep from smiling. "Unfortunately, Fionnuala Wheaton didn't clear the practice with you when she founded St. Bridget's Sisters of the Assumption."

"You aren't the meek and mild kind of woman."

"You don't know me," she countered, impatient with him now. She wasn't sure why they were both angry, but it was difficult not to raise her voice. Dr. Murray apparently had no such qualms.

Joanna looked over at the sleeping patient. He seemed oblivious to their conversation, but it distressed her that their words might be invading his rest. "I don't think this is the place for a…a personal discussion."

"You're right. We'll continue in the hall." He reattached the clipboard to the foot of Mr. Rolfson's bed and moved out of the room, then waited for Joanna to follow.

With dread, she joined him. "This conversation is unnecessary."

"I disagree." He raised his eyebrows. "You're a fraud, Sister."

"I beg your pardon?" How dared he say such a thing to her! She glared up at him, unable to hide her outrage.

Delighted, he laughed and clapped his hands. "There," he said, nodding with satisfaction. "What about this 'custody of the eyes' business now?"

"I am allowed feelings." For the most part, however, displays of emotion must be controlled. Dr. Murray seemed to enjoy exposing her failings and weaknesses.

"I am not a fraud," she said, struggling to hide the hurt his words had inflicted.

"Do you know why I asked that you be assigned to my patients?" he asked abruptly.

She did know. "I was a compromise so you could avoid encouraging any of the single nurses."

"Wrong. I asked for you because I saw you argue with Dr. Nelson. You stood up to that pompous jackass and wouldn't let him discharge a patient. You were right. The woman wasn't anywhere close to ready for discharge. You were fearless and unwavering, and eventually he backed down. All it took was someone with enough courage to confront a man who ranks himself right up there with God Almighty."

Joanna recalled her impassioned plea for Mrs. Brock in vivid detail. Dr. Nelson was indeed a jackass, but unfortunately he had no idea how others viewed him. She'd risked his anger that day, but considered it a risk worth taking. Perhaps it was her religious status that had made him listen and eventually concede. Whatever the reason, Joanna was grateful on behalf of the older woman.

"And where was 'custody of the eyes' *that* day?" Dr. Murray asked.

"I…" Joanna bit down on her lower lip, afraid of what he might read in her if she allowed him to meet her eyes.

"My point exactly," he added, his voice softer now. "I knew then that you were the one who should be caring for my patients. Someone who's both fearless and gentle. It didn't have anything to do with diplomacy toward the other nurses. I simply wanted you on my team."

"And I want you on mine," she murmured.

He frowned. "What do you mean?"

"Dr. Murray, it's time you started attending Mass again." As a lapsed Catholic, he'd turned his back on God and Joanna couldn't remain silent any longer.

His short, derisive laugh didn't really surprise her. "Are you trying to save me, Sister?"

"I'm looking out for the care of your eternal soul." She was serious and she hoped he saw her determination.

Dr. Murray shook his head. "Like I told you, I gave up on the Church a long time ago. I appreciate your concern, but this ploy of yours isn't going to work."

"What ploy?"

A slow and far-too-sexy smile slid into place. "I know what you're doing."

It was her turn to ask, "What do you mean? I'm doing exactly what I told you."

"You're diverting attention away from yourself by focusing on me and my relationship with the Church. It isn't going to work. We were discussing *you*."

Joanna was bored with that subject. She had her own rounds to perform and a long list of tasks that would consume the next eight hours. She couldn't allow herself to be distracted from what was important—her work.

"I can't," she insisted. "I have duties, the same as you do."

He raised his hands as though in surrender. "All right, all right. Go, but we aren't finished."

She retreated two steps, walking backward. "Yes, Doctor, we are. And don't think I've given up on getting you back to church. I'll be praying for you."

He chuckled and rolled his eyes. "You go right ahead. Oh, and Sister—" that sexy grin was back "—I like the changes in your habit."

Joanna self-consciously glanced down at her shorter skirt and absently smoothed her hand along her side.

"It's long overdue."

She nodded, agreeing with him, but the order hadn't asked her opinion and she hadn't been foolish enough to offer it.

"What a sin," Dr. Murray muttered.

"A sin?"

"Keeping those legs of yours hidden all these years." Then he whirled around without another word and walked resolutely away.

Despite her best efforts, Joanna experienced a warm glow from his compliment. Just as she was getting ready to leave for the day, Gina Novak approached the nurses' station. Gina was young and pretty and possessed a quick wit and easy laugh. Joanna liked her.

"Good afternoon, Sister," Gina said, pulling out a chair and sitting down next to Joanna. She gave her the once-over just as everyone else had that day. "So, how do you like the new habit?"

"Oh, I'm getting used to it," Joanna said, hoping to bring the conversation to a quick close.

Gina seemed to accept her remark. She nodded, then asked, "Did you hear about my date last night?"

Joanna finished making a notation. "No. Who's the lucky guy?"

"Dr. Murray." She sighed as she said it.

"Our Dr. Murray?" Joanna's stomach twisted and a chill raced down her arms.

"The one and only. I think he's *wonderful*." Gina gave a dreamy smile. "I've wanted to go out with him for ages and ages. I dropped subtle hints, but he didn't seem to notice, and then out of the blue he asked me out."

"Apparently he got your message." Joanna didn't imagine it had been a subtle one, either, and immediately chastised herself for unkind thoughts.

"I'd just about given up," Gina continued.

"I hope you had a good time." God would forgive her for the lie.

"We did."

"Where did he take you?" Joanna hoped she didn't sound inappropriately curious.

Gina rolled her chair back from the desk. "To dinner and a movie. He's very interesting, you know?"

"Will you be seeing him again?" she asked.

Gina shrugged. "I hope so. He hasn't asked me yet, which is fine. Since we sometimes work together, it'd probably be best if we played down our relationship."

"I think that might be a good idea," Joanna said, trying hard to sound unaffected by the news.

"I will tell you this, Sister," Gina said, lowering her voice. "He's a great kisser."

The thought of Gina and Tim Murray kissing fixed itself in her mind. Dear heaven, she was *jealous*. She longed to be the one he was holding, the one he was kissing. This was all wrong, but that knowledge did little to settle her stomach and even less to settle her heart.

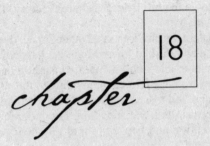

## 18

*chapter*

## SISTER KATHLEEN

On her way to the rectory the following week, Kathleen walked through the elementary school playground during the last recess of the day. Laughter and shouts filled the air as the first-through-sixth-graders scrambled about. The children, dressed in their school uniforms, took eager advantage of their fifteen minutes of freedom. There was a lively dodge-ball game going on, some of the girls were jumping rope, while others played hopscotch on the pavement. It reminded her of her own early years at St. Boniface, the grade school where she'd first been introduced to teaching nuns.

Just then a stray ball rolled in Kathleen's direction. "Sister, Sister, throw me the ball."

"No, me! Sister, throw it to me!"

Kathleen lifted the ball over her head and lobbed it toward the group. The children loved to see her join in, and she was much freer to do so in the shortened skirt. She suspected the kids purposely sent the ball in her direction for the pleasure of seeing her react. The ball landed halfway between the two boys, and both raced after it.

"Not a bad shot for a nun," Father Doyle commented as he walked down the hill from the church rectory. The wind ruffled his dark hair.

The instant the children saw Father Doyle, they abandoned their game and dashed toward him. He laughed into the October sunshine and good-naturedly caught a ball one of the boys threw him. He feinted, pretending to throw it back, then spun around and tossed it at another boy behind him.

Kathleen smiled, watching him. The children were thrilled by his attention and begged him to play for "just one more minute."

It'd been a week since their talk. A week since she'd learned the carefully hidden truth about Father Sanders. Both priests had been absent from the rectory when she'd arrived Monday afternoon; Kathleen had done what work she could and left feeling thwarted. She could only do so much when a number of serious questions remained unanswered. Handling the church's accounts was difficult enough without this additional complication. She'd considered mentioning Father Sanders's weakness to Sister Eloise but feared that might only make things worse. Sister had been against her working on the church books as it was. No—much better to leave the matter in the capable hands of Father Doyle.

Suddenly in no rush to get to the rectory, Kathleen held one end of a jump rope and turned while the eight- and nine-year-old girls leaped in and chanted the same playground songs that had been part of her own childhood.

*On the mountain stands a lady*
*Who she is I do not know*

*Not last night, but the night before*
*Twenty-four robbers came knocking at my door*

The rope slapped against the pavement as the girls jumped in and out. Kathleen recalled how she and her sister had loved to jump rope at this age. Now Maureen was a divorced mother of three and working two jobs to make ends meet. She rarely wrote and when Kathleen had visited Boston the previous summer it seemed that the sister who'd once been her closest friend was a stranger.

All too soon the bell rang, and the children were gone. Kathleen found herself on the playground alone with Father Doyle. Seeing the hopscotch squares, she couldn't resist and tossed her marker into the center, then hopped through the numbered squares.

"Way to go, Sister," the priest called out. "Not only are you a whiz with numbers, but you're a master at childhood games."

Kathleen laughed. "I can see you're easily impressed."

"Oh, not really. But I do think kids can show you how to enjoy the moment."

"I do, too." Kathleen tucked her hands inside her sweater pockets. Speaking of moments, she should be at the rectory by now, but she dreaded another afternoon of trying to understand a situation she couldn't explain.

"Are you working today?" He nodded toward the rectory.

"Yes." Kathleen realized her reluctance must be obvious.

"More problems?" His question was tentative, as though he was afraid of the answer or perhaps already knew it.

The bank deposit was off again. Father Sanders had made the deposit and then forgotten to enter it in the ledger, or so he claimed. He'd left her a note apologizing and promising to do better.

Kathleen had thought it would be a simple matter of phoning the bank and getting the information she needed. She'd done that and the bank had been completely accommodating. How she wished it had ended there, but once again the deposit was short.

The head ushers had tallied the collection, taking the weekly donations from the envelopes. Part of her duty was to record donation and envelope numbers for income tax purposes. The ushers had given the weekly donations to Father Sanders to deposit—only the amount deposited was a hundred dollars short of what had been counted. This was the largest discrepancy yet, and she didn't know how to handle it. She explained the situation to Father Doyle. "What should I do?" she asked, hoping he could provide a solution.

Father Doyle's expression was sad. "I'll speak to Father Sanders and suggest I make the deposits from here on out."

That might solve one problem, but it didn't help Kathleen with the discrepancy in the account books.

But even knowing what she did about Father Sanders, she couldn't help liking him. It was the same with her uncle Patrick. Both were generous, happy-go-lucky men who were often a pleasure to be around. Especially when they were sober…

"Is he worse?" she whispered, although no one could possibly overhear.

Father shook his head. "No." But he sounded unsure.

"Have you spoken to Mrs. O'Malley?" Surely the housekeeper knew, although she, like Father Doyle, seemed bent on silence. Kathleen understood it, but she wasn't convinced secrecy was the best approach. However, she couldn't think of any other.

"Mrs. O'Malley and I have talked," Father Doyle admitted. "Her husband, God rest his soul, was an alcoholic and I'm afraid she's grown accustomed to handling Father Sanders's…moods."

Kathleen swallowed hard and wondered if the older woman had been buying alcohol for the priest. She was a gentle soul who strived to please, and if she'd been caught in that same trap in her marriage—well, there was no telling what she'd do. It wasn't inconceivable that she was supplying Father Sanders; Kathleen couldn't imagine where else he was getting the booze.

As far as she knew, Father Sanders didn't drink outside his room in the rectory. If he went to liquor stores or bars, people in the community would recognize him. She was beginning to feel that this situation couldn't remain hidden much longer.

"The bishop knows," Father Doyle said, walking with his hands clasped behind his back.

"Bishop Schmidt?" Kathleen had been sure the parish was destined for trouble if word of Father Sanders's weakness leaked out, and to the bishop of all people. But if he knew...

"I believe that's the reason the bishop assigned me to St. Peter's." Their steps slowed as the rectory came into view. "I shouldn't be talking to you about this, Sister."

But there obviously wasn't anyone else he could talk to.

"I feel I've failed Bishop Schmidt."

"Failed him?" This made no sense to Kathleen.

"Father Sanders is in spiritual trouble. I was assigned to St. Peter's to steer him away from alcohol and back to God, and I've fallen short of accomplishing my task."

Father Doyle was a good priest, devout and dedicated to God. Kathleen understood why the bishop had given him this assignment. He was a man of prayer, and if anyone could influence Father Sanders, it would be Father Doyle. But that was a lot of responsibility to place on one priest's shoulders, Kathleen mused. Was it really fair?

"I don't think you can blame yourself," she said, looking down at her feet, wishing she knew what to say.

"I can't—"

Father Doyle's words were cut off in midsentence as a car careened around the corner with such speed that for a few seconds it balanced precariously on two wheels. Kathleen gasped, horrified, as the vehicle narrowly missed two parked cars before it fell back onto four tires again. The car landed with such force that it actually seemed to bounce.

Kathleen released a shaky breath, thinking the worst was over, but she was wrong. As though momentarily stunned, the blue Dodge sat in the middle of the street, then turned and aimed for the driveway leading to the garage behind the rectory.

"It's Father Sanders."

Kathleen couldn't believe her eyes as the priest steered the car into the rectory driveway. Unfortunately he missed the

driveway and drove across the lawn, leaving deep tire tracks.
The car quickly disappeared behind the priests' residence.

Father Doyle raced toward the rectory. He outdistanced
Kathleen, but she caught up with him at the car. Father Doyle
had opened the driver's side door and had apparently gotten
the keys out of the ignition and away from the older priest.

It terrified her to think of Father Sanders driving drunk—to
think of what could have happened, what *might* have happened.

While Father Doyle assisted the other man from the vehicle, she hurriedly inspected the car for signs of an accident or
a hit-and-run. She thought her heart was going to roar straight
out of her chest, it was beating so fast. Fortunately, there was
no sign of any impact.

"I need help," Father Doyle shouted, struggling to keep the
other priest upright with one arm around his waist. Father
Sanders, who outweighed Father Doyle by a good fifty
pounds, was leaning heavily against him. Drunk, he seemed
incapable of walking.

Kathleen hurriedly wrapped her arm around him from the
other side, and using her shoulder for leverage, offered him
as much support as she could.

"Mrs. O'Malley, put on coffee," Father Doyle shouted as
they carefully made their way up the back steps. At the top,
Father Sanders turned to get a look at his rescuers. Kathleen
gasped as he nearly sent all three of them crashing backward.
She was convinced the angels must have prevented the fall,
because there was no other explanation.

"Mrs. O'Malley's…gone for the day." Father Sanders
badly slurred his words.

"Gone?"

He laughed as though this had been a brilliant idea. "I gave
her the day off."

Kathleen could guess why. "I'll make the coffee," she said,
once they were safely inside and away from prying eyes.

The younger priest pulled out a chair at the kitchen table
and with Kathleen's help managed to lower Father Sanders
onto it.

Once he was settled, Kathleen started opening and closing cupboards until she located the coffee grounds. In a few minutes she had a pot brewing. No one spoke and the silence seemed to expand in the large kitchen.

When the coffee was ready, Kathleen poured Father Sanders his first mug. She set it in front of him. He stared at it as if he didn't know what to do with it. His eyes were rheumy, with deep pockets beneath. He looked lost and sad and frightened.

"I'm so sorry," he whispered brokenly after he'd finished the coffee. He couldn't look at Kathleen as she refilled the mug.

"I know, Father." And she did. When her uncle Patrick gave in to his weakness for drink, he was regretful and melancholy for long days afterward.

"Did you hurt anyone?" Father Doyle asked.

Silence returned as Kathleen and Father Doyle awaited his reply.

Father Sanders buried his face in his hands. "Just me." He wept openly into his palms. "Forgive me, forgive me," he pleaded.

Father Doyle was suspiciously silent.

"It won't happen again," Father Sanders vowed. Lowering his hands, the older priest lifted his head and large tears rolled unrestrained down his cheeks. "Never again. I swear it, never again. I've hit rock bottom, and God as my witness, I don't want to go back there."

"You've said this before," Father Doyle told him.

"I know," the older priest sobbed piteously. "I do. I'll never touch another drop. This time I'm serious. I swear by everything holy that I'll never drink again."

Father Doyle's eyes met Kathleen's and she could tell that he badly wanted to believe the priest. "This is the end," he said finally.

"The end. Yes. I'm sorry. I'm sorry." Then Father Sanders started to weep in earnest.

Standing with her back against the counter, Kathleen found herself fighting tears. This was hard, so hard. Father Doyle had a terrible decision to make. He should probably bring the matter to Bishop Schmidt; Father Sanders's drinking today—and his subsequent behavior—was out of control. But the older priest sounded sincere and repentant. And they both liked him, *wanted* him to succeed.

She was glad she wasn't the one making the decision.

# 19

*chapter*

## SISTER ANGELINA

Thursday night after school, Angie wrote her father a long newsy letter, telling him about the new habits. Ever since her Health class had learned she was Italian, Angie's head had been full of childhood memories. In the convent you weren't Italian or French or American; nationality was ignored. All nuns were considered children of God who'd come to dedicate their lives to His service.

As she wrote, Angie brooded on what had happened this afternoon. Her Health class had gone poorly. The discussion had gotten out of hand and Angie blamed herself for the resulting chaos as she'd lost control of the class.

She sat at the table and stared down at the letter, realizing that she'd always turned to her father when she was bothered by something. It was a childhood habit. He rarely answered her letters, though. He had a good command of the English language, but his writing skills were poor and it embarrassed him that he had such trouble spelling.

Even though he didn't write, she felt his love. He'd never recovered from the disappointment of losing her to God. He discounted her happiness and still insisted that she'd made a mistake in entering the convent. She wondered if he worked as many hours at the restaurant as he had while she was growing up and what he thought of all this election fuss. It seemed to her Nixon would surely beat McGovern, but she was no judge of that. The nuns always voted Democrat.

"You're looking thoughtful, Sister," Joanna said, sitting in the chair across from her. She pulled out her cross-stitch—of a stylized sailboat—and carefully worked on one of the sails. It was a Christmas gift for her brother and his wife, she'd told Angie.

Angie set her fountain pen aside. She wasn't aware that she was so transparent. "We discussed birth control in class this afternoon. I did a poor job of explaining the Church's position." In retrospect, she wished she'd invited Sister Joanna to come as a guest speaker. As a nurse, Joanna would have presented the information in a manner that was far more enlightening than her own awkward approach.

Sister Joanna's gaze briefly left the fabric. "That's not a subject I'd want to discuss with teenagers, especially these days."

So much for that idea! The more she thought about this afternoon, the worse Angie felt. If she had more knowledge of male-female relationships, more experience, it would help, but she'd dated so little and when it came to sex she knew even less.

"When I was a teenager, sex was something that simply wasn't discussed," Sister Joanna said, concentrating on her cross-stitch.

"I feel so inadequate talking to my students about anything having to do with it," Angie murmured. "But it isn't like I can avoid talking about birth control when we're ordered to discuss it." Sister Superior was adamant that all Health classes hear what the Church had to say on the controversial subject. Corinne's insistence on answers complicated everything; she wanted to know what other forms of birth control worked if the pill was forbidden. Angie didn't feel she should even mention the rhythm method, the form of birth control acceptable to the Church, to teenagers who shouldn't be engaging in sex in the first place.

"The girls giving birth seem to be getting younger and younger, too." Sister Joanna put down her cross-stitch project and leaned back in her chair. "Dr. Murray assisted Dr. Nelson with a cesarean on a fifteen-year-old who was having twins. At fifteen! It's hard to believe a fourteen-year-old girl would be sexually active."

At that age, Angie was listening to records and the radio and laughing on the phone with her girlfriends. The thought of having sex so young—and dealing with diapers and bottles—was beyond the scope of her imagination.

"What did you tell your class?" Sister Joanna asked.

"Well..." Angie mulled over the question. "I said the same things Sister told us."

"That the pill is against God and nature?"

Angie nodded. "I thought it was important my students understand that the medical community doesn't know what effect the pill will have on a woman twenty years down the road."

"Personally I think what the Church is most worried about is that the pill will promote promiscuity."

Angie looked around to make sure no one was listening. "I think a few of the girls might already be...active with their boyfriends." She had her suspicions, especially concerning Corinne.

"That wouldn't surprise me."

"It does me," Angie cried. "They're so young, and they have their whole lives ahead of them."

"Don't you remember this age?" Sister Joanna asked. "Everything was so urgent. So crucial. I was constantly afraid that life was going to pass me by. My biggest fear was that I wasn't going to experience any of it."

Angie shook her head. "I didn't feel that way. My father and I were close. I knew that no matter what happened, he'd be there for me." A childhood friend who lived on the same street came to mind. Maria Croce. Angie hadn't thought about Maria in years. Her friend was constantly afraid her house would catch fire. There'd been a fire down the block and although the family escaped, the dog had died. From that point forward, Maria lived in constant fear of a house fire. Angie never gave the possibility a second thought because she knew nothing would prevent her father from rescuing her. He would walk through flames to save her, and she knew it. With that kind of love and security, Angie hadn't felt the same sense of urgency about life that Joanna had.

"Frankly, my class didn't *want* to hear the Church's opinion on birth control," Angie continued, thinking back.

Corinne was the worst offender; in fact, she had openly scoffed. "One girl," Angie murmured, "said she didn't think it was any of the Church's business whether or not a woman practiced birth control."

"More and more women feel that way," Joanna said as she resumed her cross-stitch.

Angie couldn't get the class out of her mind. Especially Corinne. The girl was quick to state her opinion and often critical of others when they disagreed. Rarely, though, did anyone take offense.

Corinne seemed to revel in being outrageous, but beneath all the show was a good heart. Angie usually enjoyed their talks and looked forward to the days Corinne hung around after class so they could visit.

Today hadn't been one of those days. Corinne couldn't get out of the room fast enough. Sure enough, when Angie looked out the window to the school parking lot, she recognized Jimmy's car.

Corinne ran across the lot and threw herself inside as if she'd been waiting for this moment all day. Angie couldn't tell exactly what was happening in the car, which didn't leave for several minutes. She guessed Corinne hadn't been sharing the quadratic formula with her boyfriend.

"You said you thought a few of your students are sexually active," Sister Joanna said. "Is this something you feel comfortable talking to them about? Privately, of course."

Angie's eyes widened with dismay. *Her* talk about sex?

She didn't even know how to approach the subject. And what could she possibly have to say about it?

Sister Joanna glanced up, looked at Angie and then started to laugh. "God *is* the one who created sex, you know."

"Not to talk about." Angie was sure of that.

"Just discuss it with them the same way your mother talked to you," she advised.

"My mother died when I was five. My father's the one who explained the birds and the bees."

"Your dad?" Sister Joanna lowered the cross-stitch to her lap.

"Dad told me everything. He got books from the library, drew me a picture and explained the way a woman's body works."

"He wasn't embarrassed?"

At the time Angie had been so caught up in what he was telling her that she couldn't remember. "I don't think so."

"But you are?"

She nodded. After years of living in a convent, in which every aspect of her femininity had been ignored, Angie could no more discuss the matter of physical intimacy than she could perform brain surgery.

"It might be a good idea if you did talk to these girls, Sister."

Angie marveled at Sister Joanna. She seemed to believe such a discussion should come naturally—and for her, it probably would.

"I...couldn't."

"I didn't think I could put a needle into someone's arm, but I learned," Joanna said briskly. "We do what we have to. Your students respect you, and I'm sure they'd welcome the opportunity to speak freely with you."

Angie rested her spine against the back of the chair as she considered talking to Corinne about such a deeply personal subject.

"They'd feel safe with you, I think," Sister Joanna went on. "For one thing, you aren't their mother."

"Wouldn't they worry about me judging them?"

"You're not like that and they know it."

Maybe she *could* talk to some of the girls, Angie mused. Maybe she could have a frank and honest discussion with Corinne, just like her father had with her when she was a teenager.

*chapter*

## SISTER JOANNA

Singing with the choir at Sunday morning Masses had never been Joanna's favorite task. Music wasn't her gift and she struggled to stay on key, but Sister Martha insisted Joanna's talent or lack of it didn't concern her. All the choir director needed that Sunday was another voice. It didn't matter that Joanna's undisciplined singing drifted between alto and second soprano, sometimes within the same musical bar.

Her attention drifted too as she sat through the eight, nine and now the ten o'clock Mass. Father Sanders had said the eight and nine o'clock Masses but he'd been replaced by Father Doyle for the ten o'clock.

Sitting at the organ, Sister Martha played the multi-tiered keyboard, and the church echoed with the crescendoing tones. Joanna raised the hymnal and joined her fellow nuns in song as Father Doyle entered from the back of the church with a small procession of altar boys. The first carried the six-foot-tall crucifix, with two of the younger boys behind him, followed by Father Doyle, who held a large Bible.

Joanna was more impressed with the younger priest than ever. His sermons focused on the importance of God in the contemporary world, and he wasn't afraid of difficult concepts, which he tried to explain in clear and relevant ways. Granted, his delivery was a bit dry and sometimes faltering, but he was improving every week. Not long ago he'd quoted the lyrics to a popular song Joanna remembered from her own teenage years. *To know Him is to love Him.*

The priest's words had stayed with her, and she knew they had with others, too. To take something as simple as the lyrics of a familiar song and to use that as the basis for a sermon on God's unconditional love struck her as divinely inspired. The tune ran through her mind for days and she knew she'd never think of it the same way again.

Sister Kathleen had casually mentioned how helpful the younger priest had been to her, too. Joanna worried about her friend, who was burdened with the task of sorting out the church books. It seemed to be weighing heavily on her, although she never complained.

As Father Doyle approached the altar for the beginning of the ten o'clock Mass, Joanna noted that the church was far more crowded than it had been for the previous two. Father Doyle was becoming popular with the parishioners; she hoped that wouldn't cause problems for him with Father Sanders. Joanna quickly rejected that thought. Father Sanders was such a friendly, likeable priest, she doubted he'd care one way or the other.

As the organ music faded, Joanna saw a lone male figure move up the side aisle, searching for space at the end of a pew. If she didn't know better, she would've thought it was Dr. Murray, although of course it couldn't be.

She peered closer, or tried to without being obvious. The man, whoever he was, certainly resembled the doctor, she decided absently. Their gait was similar and—

It *was* Dr. Murray.

Once he'd found a seat, he turned around and glanced over his shoulder. She gazed down at his face. Dr. Murray, the lapsed Catholic who'd emphatically stated that he had no intention of attending Mass again, was in church.

At first Joanna was dumbstruck, and then so excited she nearly dropped her hymnal. Dr. Murray had actually come to Mass! This was what she'd been praying for since their first conversation, what she'd wanted more than anything. He *had* been listening to her, had felt her concern for him. He'd come back to church!

The rest of the hour passed in a blur. She couldn't remember what she sang, or even if she did. Nor did she recall more than two words of the sermon, or climbing down the stairs with the other nuns when it came time to receive Communion.

The minute Mass was over, Joanna set aside the hymnal and hurried down the stairs, hoping to catch Dr. Murray before he left. Unfortunately, she was caught in the crowd of parishioners as they exited. For one frantic moment, it was impossible for Joanna to move.

People stopped to greet her and Joanna couldn't be rude. She smiled and remarked how good it was to see them, then quickly excused herself in an effort to find Dr. Murray.

Once outside, she paused at the top of the church steps, certain she'd missed him. Disappointment flooded her as she scanned the crowd and didn't see him.

"Looking for someone?" the familiar deep-throated voice asked from behind her.

"Dr. Murray!" Joanna whirled around and breathlessly placed a hand over her pounding heart. She stared up and smiled at him, so pleased that for a moment she couldn't speak. "I'm *so* glad you're here."

He looked different without his hospital whites. Good. Better than any man had a right to look. So handsome it was a sin for her to even notice—yet she couldn't help herself.

"I figured you'd be at this Mass," he said.

"I was at the eight and nine o'clock Masses, too."

"I thought we Catholics were only required to attend one a week."

"You are, unless you're singing in the choir. Sister Martha needed an extra voice and—" She stopped, wanting to kick herself for rambling. "What made you decide to come to Mass?" She blurted out the question without even a hint of finesse.

His expression mildly uncomfortable, Dr. Murray shrugged. "I don't know. I woke up, there weren't any emergencies and I decided what the hell, why not? I kept thinking about you praying for me and it seemed the least I could do." He grinned. "By way of thanks, I mean."

Apparently he hadn't been on any Saturday-night dates, which pleased her even more.

Then, because she wasn't sure what to say next, she asked, "Have you met Father Doyle?"

He shook his head and didn't seem especially interested.

"You must," she insisted. "He's wonderful." On impulse she reached for his hand, clasping it in her own as she led him toward the priest. It felt...odd, being linked with him like this. It meant nothing, and yet Joanna felt his touch ripple though her in a way that was all too sexual. Almost at once, the need to be held and touched and loved felt overwhelming. It'd been so long since she'd had any physical contact with a man, so long since she'd been wrapped in a man's arms. Her breath caught in her throat and she suddenly jerked her hand free. Trying to cover for her uncharacteristic actions, she gave him a weak smile and said, "Father's right over here."

Father Doyle stood at the main doors, exchanging greetings with his parishioners. Since he was busy talking, they had to wait a few minutes. Joanna felt awkward standing there, afraid to say anything for fear Dr. Murray would comment on the fact that she'd pulled her hand away from his.

"Are you all right?" he asked, his voice lowered.

Her face was flushed and she could feel the heat in her cheeks. "I'm fine," she said, forcing a light note into her voice. "What about you?"

When he didn't answer she was compelled to look at him. His eyes met hers. "I don't know."

In other circumstances, she might have delved into the question, but right now she was afraid of where the conversation would take them.

As if Tim realized he'd said more than he should, he changed the subject completely. "I liked Father Doyle's sermon."

"I did, too," Joanna said automatically, grateful to escape the tension between them. The truth was, she didn't remember the sermon. She'd tried to listen, honestly tried, but her mind refused to concentrate while Dr. Murray was in the church.

"I didn't know they ordained men that young," he added.

"He's older than he looks."

"Really. And how old are you?"

"Me?" Joanna glanced up at him, wide-eyed with shock. Age wasn't something she thought about, especially her own.

"You don't look much older than a teenager yourself."

"And you're so ancient?" Joanna teased.

"I'm thirty-two and I feel forty."

"Ooh, that's old," she said with a laugh.

"You're not kidding. Now answer my question. How old are you?"

Joanna had to stop and calculate her age. "Twenty-six. I think."

His eyes narrowed. "Good grief, you're just a kid."

"I don't feel like one." Especially just then. What she felt like was a woman, with a woman's heart and a woman's desires, and frankly it terrified her. Since entering the convent, she'd ignored the fact that she was a woman. But unlike a virgin, she'd experienced the delights of the flesh, and the memories refused to leave her.

At just that moment, Father Doyle turned his attention to Joanna. His smile revealed his pleasure at seeing her. "Good morning, Sister Joanna." His gaze slid from Joanna to Dr. Murray and he nodded.

Joanna stepped closer. "Father Doyle, this is Dr. Tim Murray, who's a surgeon at St. Elizabeth's Hospital."

Father Doyle extended his hand, which Dr. Murray gripped firmly. "I don't believe I've seen you in church before."

"Good eye, Father," Dr. Murray said. "I told Sister Joanna that I was a lapsed Catholic and she took it upon herself to pray for me."

Father nodded approvingly toward Joanna. "The effective prayer of a righteous nun availeth much," he said, grinning boyishly.

"You're telling me," Dr. Murray muttered. "Now every Sunday morning I wake up and the first thing I think about is Sister Joanna praying for me. Then I start thinking about all those years I attended Mass as a kid." He shook his head. "To tell you the truth, Father, I gave up on religion a long time ago."

"You were in Vietnam?"

Dr. Murray reluctantly nodded.

"Perhaps we could talk about it one afternoon. Are you free anytime this week?"

Dr. Murray shrugged. "Wednesday. Although I'm not sure you're going to want to hear what I have to say."

"Maybe, but I've got a good ear—as well as a good eye. I'll put you down on my calendar for two o'clock, if that works for you."

"All right. Do you want to meet here?" He gestured in the direction of the church.

"No, come on over to the rectory," Father Doyle said, "and I'll have the perfect excuse to ask Mrs. O'Malley to bake up a batch of her ginger snaps."

"I'll look forward to it, Father."

"So will I." There was no doubting the sincerity in his voice.

Sister Martha and Sister Kathleen, followed by three other nuns, came out the side doors of the church. It was Joanna's signal to leave and return to the convent.

"I have to go." She couldn't quite hide her disappointment.

"So soon?" Dr. Murray sounded equally dejected. "I thought I'd take you to lunch."

Sadly Joanna shook her head. Other, less conservative religious orders had relaxed their rules with regard to these situations. But eating with laypeople other than family remained strictly prohibited for the nuns of St. Bridget's Sisters of the Assumption.

"I can't," she said.

"Perhaps another time then," he suggested, almost flippantly.

Again she shook her head. "That isn't possible. I'm sorry."

"Right," he said, his own voice impatient.

He was drawing away from her. Physically and emotionally.

"I keep forgetting you're Sister Joanna, not nurse Joanna," he muttered.

He wasn't the only one with the memory problem, Joanna thought. She kept forgetting it herself.

*chapter*

## SISTER ANGELINA

Late Wednesday afternoon, as she left the school, Angie saw Sister Kathleen walking from the rectory to the convent house. She sped up to join her friend. Angie was worried about Sister Kathleen and had been for some weeks. Apparently her work at the church wouldn't last much longer, which was a blessing in Angie's opinion.

The normally good-natured, fun-loving Kathleen had become introspective and subdued in the last little while. Twice now, Angie had seen her in conversation with Father Doyle. Angie hadn't been close enough to hear what was being said, and even if she had been, she would've moved away. Whatever the topic, it appeared to be of deep concern to them both. Their body language said as much—their heads were lowered and their voices had dropped to a whisper. Father Doyle stood with his hands behind his back and Sister Kathleen was leaning toward him, hands clasped in front of her.

Father Doyle hadn't been himself lately, either. It seemed

that he, too, was preoccupied by some serious matter. Angie's thoughts came to an abrupt halt. No, it couldn't be—but stranger things had happened. Could Father Doyle and Sister Kathleen have fallen in love? That would make sense, since Sister Kathleen was at the rectory three afternoons a week and it would only be natural for the two of them to talk and get to know each other. They shared a love of God, and well…oh dear, this could be trouble. Angie swallowed hard and considered all the difficulties such a relationship would bring to both the diocese and the convent.

These were trying times for the Church. Nuns, and priests, too, were leaving the religious life in record numbers. Already five nuns had left the Minneapolis convent that year. Five! Unfortunately, there weren't any replacements, and the school had been forced to hire lay teachers, which automatically raised tuition. Many families were already burdened by the expense of private school. Angie feared that these added costs might threaten the very existence of the parochial school system.

Angie worried about the nuns who'd chosen to reject their vows. They were walking into an uncertain future without savings and without jobs. She prayed that God would direct their lives.

"You look a little troubled," Sister Kathleen said as they walked side by side toward the convent.

"Me?" Angie asked with a short laugh. "I was just thinking the same thing about you. Is everything all right?" She hoped Kathleen would be honest with her—not that there was anything Angie could do to help.

Sister Kathleen took so long to reply that Angie wanted to stop and grab her by the shoulders and look her full in the face. Finally the other nun said, "Everything will work itself out soon."

*Soon,* Angie repeated mentally. Then, risking Sister Kathleen's rebuke, she said, "These things sometimes happen when a man and a woman work together." She took a deep breath, hoping she wasn't embarrassing them both as she broached the uncomfortable subject. "Through no fault of their own, of course."

Sister Kathleen gave her an odd, puzzled look. Her face was blank. "Sister, what are you talking about?"

Angie instantly regretted opening her mouth. "It was nothing. Forgive me."

Sister Kathleen grew quiet, frowning as they quickened their pace. "You think Father Doyle and I are…attracted to each other?" At that, she burst into delighted laughter. "Father Doyle and I are *friends,* nothing more. Nothing else, either, I promise you."

Angie's relief was intense. She hated the thought of Sister Kathleen leaving the order because she'd fallen in love with a priest. But her amusement was quickly cut short.

As they neared the convent, Angie recognized Corinne Sullivan sitting on the low brick wall outside the door. When Angie approached, Corinne, agile and athletic, leapt down to the sidewalk, landing solidly on both feet.

"Hello, Sister. Have you got a minute?" The girl's eyes were ablaze and Angie could only speculate about what was on her mind.

"Go ahead, Sister," Kathleen told her, stepping a few feet away to give them privacy.

"What's the problem?" Angie asked, focusing on Corinne.

"It's not you, Sister. I think you're great. It's the Church. You're going to lose us and all the girls in the high school if they continue with this nonsense about birth control and—"

Angie held up her hand. "I can assure you, Corinne, that the Church's stand isn't nonsense."

"But it *is,* Sister," Corinne insisted. "What right does a bunch of old men have to tell a woman what she can and can't do with her own body?" she blurted out. "A married couple should be able to decide how many children they want—not some pope who's never been married and doesn't know a thing about raising a family. It's just *wrong.*"

Angie was still marshaling her thoughts when Corinne asked, "Sister, do you know who Gloria Steinem is?"

Angie shook her head. "Sorry, no."

"Then you've never heard of *Ms. Magazine,* either, have you?"

Again Angie shook her head. She wasn't sure what this other woman had to do with the conversation, but Corinne apparently had a high opinion of her.

"It's all so confusing, Sister." Corinne stared at her intently. "Gloria Steinem is a feminist and she believes…" She paused and made an exasperated gesture. "Never mind, you'd never agree with her anyway, so there's no use arguing."

"I'm willing to listen," Angie assured her, although she privately felt that Corinne might have chosen a better time and place for this discussion.

Corinne slumped her shoulders in a gesture of defeat. "I'd rather talk to you about the Church. I have a lot of questions. Jimmy's parents are Baptists and he says Mary wasn't a virgin her entire life and he even showed me what the Bible says."

Angie stiffened, prepared to defend the truth of the Gospel. "We know it's true. Scripture tells us that our Savior was born to a virgin and—"

"But *after* Jesus was born, Sister," Corinne inserted. "Mary was married to Joseph, remember? According to what Jimmy showed me in the Bible, Jesus had brothers and sisters, the children of Mary and Joseph. They were married and they had sex, and if…if the birth control pill had been around then, they probably would've used it."

"I'm sure Jimmy has misinterpreted the Bible," Angie said in what she hoped was a calm and collected voice.

"The entire book of James was written by Jesus's brother—that's what Jimmy says."

"Corinne, please, I think you're getting all upset over nothing."

"Sister, think about it! What kind of man—and Joseph was a man—would live with a woman he loved and behave like her brother? It doesn't make sense to me. If the Church is wrong about something this important, then I have to question everything else it teaches."

"I don't believe the Church is wrong, Corinne," Angie told her. She couldn't imagine why Jimmy would put such ideas into Corinne's head—unless he wanted to undermine the girl's faith. Of course, Mary had remained a virgin! Angie's whole life was modeled on the Virgin Mother. She'd taken the vow of chastity, accepted virginity for life, based on the ideal of the Lord's earthly mother.

"Don't you *see,* Sister?" Corinne pleaded, wide eyes staring up at her. "If the Church is wrong about this, it could be wrong about other things too."

Angie was speechless.

"Jimmy says—"

"Corinne," she said, snapping out of her stupor. "Jimmy isn't a religion expert. He isn't even Catholic. It's obvious that he's been raised with a number of misconceptions."

"Maybe it's us who have the misconceptions, Sister. Did you ever think of that?"

Frankly, Angie hadn't. "I'll tell you what I'll do. I'll ask for a meeting with Father Sanders and have him answer your questions. Then I'll report back to you what he says."

"While you have his attention, you might ask him about purgatory too." Corinne's tone was skeptical.

"Purgatory?" Was nothing sacred anymore? It was a mistake to date a boy outside the faith, but Angie hesitated to mention that for fear of driving Corinne away completely. She had to wonder what Corinne's parents were thinking to let her get involved with a Protestant boy, but then she remembered that they weren't fond of Jimmy and had discouraged the relationship.

"There's not one single word in the entire Bible about purgatory, Sister. I asked Jimmy's mother after he told me that, and she said the same thing. Not a single mention in all those pages. The Church just made it up so people will think they're going to suffer when they die."

Angie raised both hands, ending this discussion before it went any further. It was best saved for another time. Once she'd talked to Father Sanders, Angie would be able to reassure Corinne; as it was now, the girl was too emotional and in no mood to listen to reason.

"The thing is, Sister, I *want* to be a good Catholic."

"I know you do," Angie said, not doubting her sincerity.

"My parents are both strong Catholics and so are my grandparents. It would hurt them if I turned my back on the Church, but I have to honestly believe in its teachings. I have to know deep in my heart that the Church wants what's best for me, that it won't force me to have more children than my husband and I can support."

"Corinne, you're worried about things that shouldn't be troubling a girl of your age."

"Sister, oh, Sister." Corinne closed her eyes and then she shook her head in a small, knowing way.

"I have to go," Angie said. She had mixed feelings about ending the conversation—regret at not helping Corinne find a way to resolve her doubts, and relief at escaping, for the moment, these uncertain waters.

"When I was in grade school," Corinne said, her voice low, "I used to dream about being a nun one day."

"Did you?" Angie said, touched by her words.

"I can't do it. I realize that now. I just can't."

"Not everyone has a vocation," Angie said, thinking a girl like Corinne would certainly add a bit of energy to convent life.

"Not everyone has the ability to accept what's told to them without ever asking a question," the girl added. "I couldn't deal with that. I'd never be able to do it, Sister, no matter how much I love God."

22

*chapter*

## SISTER JOANNA

Joanna sat across from the shocked, grieving husband, wishing there was something she could say or do to ease his pain. She'd come to comfort Richard Dougal after Dr. Tripton had informed him that his wife, Maryanne, had died. This father would have to raise three young children by himself. He'd have to remain strong for their sake and—somehow—survive her loss.

"I'm so very sorry," she whispered, her heart aching at the unmasked grief she read on the man's face.

Richard Dougal glanced up. "I don't understand. She's only thirty-one. How could this happen? I should've been here. I thought everything was all right after the surgery. Then the hospital called and said there was a…complication." His voice caught and he paused to compose himself before continuing. "I had to get a baby-sitter. I hurried, but by the time I got here, it was too late."

Joanna was well aware of the details. The physician had

already explained the medical reason for the young woman's death. It was a rare heart condition no one had known about and no one could have anticipated. As a result, she'd gone into cardiac arrest following the hysterectomy.

"Is there someone I can phone for you?" Joanna asked.

As if in a stupor, he shook his head. "My neighbor's watching the kids. My mother-in-law was going to fly out to help once Maryanne got home from the hospital. We don't have any family in the area." His voice cracked and his shoulders shook with the effort not to break down.

"Would you like me to pray with you?" she asked softly.

He nodded.

Joanna knelt and briefly raised her eyes to heaven, pleading with God to give her the words to comfort this man. As soon as she bowed her head, Mr. Dougal broke into deep, mournful sobs.

Joanna spent an hour with him, until he'd calmed down and the neighbor's husband arrived to drive him home. Richard Dougal thanked her, his voice a monotone, and let his neighbor lead him away. He was numb with grief; Joanna knew that numbness would get him through the next few days, but afterward... All she could do was pray for him and his family.

Returning to the nurses' station, Joanna felt emotionally depleted. She barely noticed when Dr. Murray approached. He took one look at her and said, "You need a cup of coffee."

She needed something, but she didn't think caffeine would help her any more than it would that poor, grieving husband. To her surprise, Dr. Murray took her into the doctors' lounge on the second floor and then poured coffee for her. She noticed that he'd added a liberal amount of sugar.

"I'm not in shock," she protested.

"No, but you just might be when I tell you who's here."

"Someone's here?" she asked in confusion. "But..."

Dr. Murray pulled out a chair and sat across from her. He met her eyes and placed his hand on hers. He waited a moment as they both stared down at their linked hands, then asked, "Do you know a Greg Markham?"

"Greg?" Joanna nearly swallowed her tongue. Was Dr. Murray telling her that Greg, her one-time fiancé, was at the hospital? That seemed completely improbable. "What's he doing here?" she demanded.

"You'll have to ask him that yourself."

"But…" Joanna was too flustered to think clearly.

"He's in the staff lounge and he insists on talking to you personally. He won't take no for an answer."

She stared at Tim Murray, silently begging him for advice.

"This is the man you once mentioned, isn't it? The one who went overseas?"

She nodded. "We were engaged. He met a woman while he was stationed in Vietnam." She lowered her head, surprised by the flood of memories. They came and went with incredible swiftness, leaving her shaken in their aftermath. He'd been an important part of her life at one time—but now he didn't belong in her life at all.

"Do you still have feelings for him?" Dr. Murray asked. His gentleness rocked her as much as knowing that Greg was down the hall waiting to see her.

"No." Her response came automatically.

"He wants to talk to you. Are you up to it?"

Joanna wasn't sure that meeting Greg would be right for either of them. With some embarrassment she recalled the hours of torrid passion in the back seat of his car. They hadn't been able to keep their hands off each other. They'd lost their virginity together, shared a time in their lives that would be impossible to recapture.

"Sister?"

Joanna raised her eyes and blinked, not knowing what to say.

"As I said, he insisted that he speak to you personally." Dr. Murray frowned. "Do you want to do this? Because if you don't, I'll get rid of him."

Joanna knew that Greg wouldn't leave until he got what he wanted. She also knew he hadn't found her without help. She was fairly certain that assistance had come from her mother.

"I'll talk to him," she said, her voice gaining confidence.

Dr. Murray escorted her to the lounge, where Joanna found Greg pacing the room with his hands clenched at his sides. He stopped abruptly when she entered the room.

"Joanna." He breathed her name as though he were praying.

She felt his look in a physical way. His gaze wandered up and down her body, lingering on her face and then her short veil.

"You're as beautiful as I remember," he said, his voice filled with awe. "I wondered…" He closed his eyes, perhaps to chase the image of a younger Joanna from his mind. When he opened them again, he seemed to be comparing his memory with reality.

"I'll leave you two alone for a few minutes," Dr. Murray said, sounding gruff and none too cordial.

"That was one unpleasant fellow," Greg said, scowling after him. The scowl quickly turned to a smile as he looked back at Joanna. Striding toward her, he reached for her hands. "I don't care, though. He brought you to me and I'm grateful for that."

Joanna pulled her hands free of Greg's clasp.

"It takes some getting used to seeing you in a habit," he said.

A habit that had only been modified a short while ago, she wanted to tell him, but didn't. He wasn't here to discuss the changes in convent life. "How are you, Greg?" she asked instead.

"We need to talk." He gestured for her to sit on the sofa. The coffee table beside it was littered with used cups and old newspapers.

Joanna sat sideways on the very edge, while Greg sat next to her, a little too close for comfort.

He didn't speak for a few minutes, apparently trying to gather his thoughts. "I assumed that once I saw you, I'd know what to say," he muttered. "Now that I'm here, it's damn hard not to hold you."

Joanna stiffened. "You can't do that."

"I know…" He dragged in a deep breath. "Xuan and I are getting a divorce."

Although her mother hadn't told her, Joanna had read be-

tween the lines. There'd been a letter recently in which her
mother had mentioned that she'd seen Greg and his wife having an argument in the grocery store. According to rumors—
which Sandra was happy to pass along—the marriage was a
troubled one.

"Is Lily with her mother?"

Greg nodded. "She's a beautiful child." He pulled out his
wallet, opened it and removed a picture of his daughter for
Joanna to examine.

The child had dark, almond-shaped eyes and a lovely
smile as she stared into the camera. Joanna saw nothing of
Greg in the little girl. In the blending of two backgrounds,
the mother's heritage had clearly been favored. Joanna
handed back the photograph. "You're right, she *is* a beautiful child."

"I miss her a lot," Greg said, tucking the photo inside his wallet. "Lily's the only good thing to come out of the relationship."

"I'm sorry to hear about you and Xuan."

Greg smiled weakly, and when he spoke, his bitterness
was obvious. "So am I, but our marriage was doomed from
the first. Xuan was looking for a way out of Vietnam and I
was a convenient fall guy."

"I'm sorry, Greg," she said, noticing that he accepted none
of the responsibility for his own actions. She *was* sorry about
the divorce; the failure of any marriage was a tragic thing. And
although Greg had badly hurt her, Joanna no longer held any
ill will toward him—and hadn't in years.

"I'm afraid I'm the one to blame for the divorce," he said
next, surprising her.

"In what way?"

"Xuan knew." At her questioning gaze, Greg continued. "She
realized almost right away that I never stopped loving you."

"That's all water under the bridge now."

"Is it, Joanna?"

"It is for me."

"But not for me. I love you. I've always loved you."

At one time Joanna would have given anything to hear

those words. Now they just seemed too little, too late—an avowal that had nothing to do with her.

"You're going through a divorce, Greg," she said calmly, her hands neatly folded in her lap. "It's wiped you out emotionally and you're hoping to return to the past. But that's impossible."

"It isn't, Joanna," Greg said, moving even closer to her. "We *can* have it all, the way we once did. I screwed up, but I swear to you it'll never happen again."

"Greg… You don't know what you're asking."

"I do know," he said firmly. "I want you to marry me."

"Marry you?" She bolted upright before sitting back down. "That's out of the question!"

He ignored her protest. "Leave the convent." He seemed to have everything worked out. To him, it was obviously a simple matter—once she was free, he'd be there to sweep her away. "You shouldn't be here. We both know you're a passionate, loving woman. Closing yourself off from life, from love—it just isn't you."

Joanna tried hard to hold back her irritation. "You're completely discounting the last six years of my life as if they mean nothing."

"They mean everything."

"Not if I listen to what you're suggesting," she said tartly.

"You kept yourself pure for me."

*"What?"* The man was living in a fantasy. "I kept myself pure for God. I think it's time you left." She stood, giving him little option but to stand, too.

"Joanna, please listen…"

She'd already heard more than enough. "I can't help you, Greg. I'm sorry, sincerely sorry that your marriage has fallen apart, but it's too late to recapture what we once had." Six years too late.

His eyes held a look of loss, of loneliness, and she understood why he'd tried to regain something that no longer existed.

Although she'd never said anything to her family, as the years progressed, Joanna realized she'd made a lucky escape by not marrying Greg. If he'd betrayed her once, he would again. She'd been young and naive and ruled by adolescent dreams and raging hormones. Those days were over. She was a woman now, a woman who'd made choices that had taken her life in a completely different direction.

Greg reluctantly left after two more attempts to change her mind. After the door closed, she needed a minute to calm her pounding heart.

She assumed that Dr. Murray had hung around to discover how her conversation with Greg had gone. As suspected, she found him leaning against the nurses' station, chatting with Mrs. Larson.

When Tim saw her, he slowly straightened. He searched her face for signs of what might have happened.

"Are you okay?" he asked.

Joanna smiled and nodded.

"He wanted to lure you away, didn't he?"

She neither confirmed nor denied his statement. "He was a good friend at one time."

"Is he sticking around for a while?"

Joanna laughed. "I certainly hope not."

"Yeah, me too. You've got enough on your mind without him following you around like a lost puppy."

The lead nurse's interest was piqued. She glanced at Joanna, her eyebrows raised in question. "What's this all about?"

"I had an old friend stop by to say hello," she explained.

"An old *boy*friend," Dr. Murray elaborated.

"The relationship died a painful death a long time ago."

"It's over?" he asked. "You're sure of that?"

Joanna nodded again.

Their eyes met and a flash of awareness darted through her. Greg, the boy/man she'd once loved, had asked her to leave the convent for him, and she'd turned him down flat. She hadn't needed to think about it, hadn't so much as considered his request.

Joanna wondered what her reaction would be if Dr. Murray were to ask her the same thing.

*chapter*

## SISTER KATHLEEN

It came as no surprise to Sister Kathleen that there were discrepancies in the bank deposits for the first two Sunday collections in October. The first week it was only twenty dollars, but by the second week it had grown to a hundred and forty, an amount that shocked Kathleen. Father Doyle had made up the difference out of his own pocket, but this couldn't continue and they both knew it.

"Is Father Sanders upstairs?" Father Doyle asked, coming into the rectory late Wednesday afternoon. Kathleen was just getting ready to leave. His eyes met hers and she understood the real question he was asking. He wanted to know if Father Sanders was drinking again.

The truth was, Kathleen hadn't been able to tell. After the drunk-driving incident, the older priest seemed to be making a genuine effort at sobriety. Or perhaps he'd gotten better at hiding his addiction. Kathleen wasn't sure which. However, with money missing from the bank deposit, she realized he was spending that cash on *something*.

"You talked to Mrs. O'Malley?" she asked.

Father Doyle nodded. "She swears she's no longer buying him booze."

"Then he must be getting it himself," she said.

"Or he's found someone else to pick it up for him."

Kathleen was certain of one thing: Father Sanders hadn't taken that money to feed the poor.

"He didn't say much," she told him, meaning she hadn't been able to detect if the other priest was drunk or not. Father Sanders had become very good at avoiding her. It was only in conversation that she was able to hear the slur in his words. And only when she had the opportunity to see him walk for more than a few feet could she observe any flaws in his gait. These days, if he saw her at all, it was briefly and only when absolutely necessary.

"Allow me to walk you back to the convent, Sister," Father Doyle said. Without giving her an option, he handed Kathleen her jacket, then waited by the front door.

As they left the rectory, Kathleen carefully weighed her words, fearing she might be overstepping her boundaries. "I think perhaps it would be a good idea for us to speak openly, Father."

"Perhaps we should," he agreed. It seemed to her that he was relieved to have someone to talk to, someone who shared his concern for the older priest.

Kathleen chewed on her lower lip, a habit she'd had as a child and only reverted to in times of stress. "With you replacing the missing cash, I'm afraid we've created a protective environment for Father Sanders."

"In other words, I'm giving him permission to drink," the priest murmured, and it sounded as though this was something he'd battled with more than once.

"It isn't fair to you *or* Father Sanders if you add money to the collection every week," she blurted out. "Father Sanders doesn't know what you're doing and he obviously assumes

I'm so stupid I don't understand what's going on." She hadn't meant to be so blunt, but it all made sense to her now. This talk about Mrs. Stafford being away on vacation was wearing thin, too. Thin enough for Kathleen to see through it. No wonder Father Sanders had asked her to deal with the books. And no wonder things had been left in such a mess. He knew she had no practical experience and had figured she wouldn't pick up on what he was doing.

"I phoned Mrs. Stafford's house this afternoon," Father Doyle announced, his hands clasped behind his back as he matched his pace to hers.

Kathleen knew what was coming. "She isn't on vacation, is she?"

"No," Father admitted reluctantly.

"She quit," Kathleen supplied for him.

"I'm sorry to say you're right."

"Why do you feel you have to protect him?" she asked after an uncomfortable moment.

Father was silent for a long time. "The bishop has placed his trust in me to handle the situation with Father Sanders. He expects me to bring Father back to God and to a serious understanding of his responsibilities within the parish." He sighed. "I don't want to fail His Excellency—or Father Sanders."

"Bishop Schmidt told you all this?"

"No," he said. "But once I got to St. Peter's, I understood the situation and why I'd been transferred here." Then, as if he'd said more than he wanted, he murmured, "This is my problem, Sister. You shouldn't worry about it."

But she did worry; she couldn't help it. Kathleen was involved now, and she refused to abandon the younger priest. Her admiration and respect for Father Doyle and her anxiety about the burdens he carried grew stronger every day.

"You're right, of course," he said thoughtfully. "I have no option but to take the matter to Bishop Schmidt. I've let my pride stand in the way of doing what's right." His voice fell, and it was clear to Kathleen that he'd agonized over this dilemma for far too long. The bishop obviously knew that Father Sanders had a problem but exactly how much he knew remained unclear.

"Would you like me to go with you?" she offered.

Father Doyle shook his head. "That isn't necessary."

Instinctively she recognized that he was protecting her, although she wasn't entirely sure why.

"What about Sister Superior? Perhaps I should mention it to her?" Kathleen felt honor bound to do something, to help in some way. She was convinced that the head of the convent suspected something, but Sister Eloise hadn't pressured her for information.

"I'd prefer if you kept this to yourself, at least for now."

Feeling the heat of his gaze but not daring to look him in the eye, Kathleen nodded.

"Is that a problem?" he asked at her silence.

"No," she said quietly. She hadn't decided what she'd do or say if Sister Eloise did ask about Father Sanders; Kathleen didn't want to lie, but at the same time she'd given Father Doyle her word.

"I appreciate that, Sister," he said.

The distress in his voice gripped her heart. Kathleen knew she'd do anything she could to take this burden from him. Father Sanders's problem was a constant source of anxiety. For her own part, she hadn't slept a full night since discovering Father Sanders drunk behind the wheel of a car. Twice now she'd woken with nightmares about the priest causing an accident. She worried that he might hurt himself or some innocent bystander and she worried about the scandal such an incident would cause. Father Sanders's actions might do irreparable damage to the Church in Minneapolis.

"I'll call and ask for an appointment with the bishop first thing in the morning," Father Doyle told her as they approached the convent.

"I'll be praying for you," Kathleen assured him.

"Thank you, Sister. I value those prayers."

"What will happen to Father Sanders?" She hadn't wanted to ask, but she needed to know.

The priest sighed heavily. "I'm hoping the bishop will send him to a facility that will give Father Sanders the professional help he needs."

That was Kathleen's hope, too. "Have you known of other such…cases?" she asked.

Father Doyle shook his head. "No. Based on my own admittedly limited experience, I don't believe this is a common problem with priests."

"Father's drinking has gotten worse in the last six months, hasn't it?"

"I'm afraid so. He's worse than when I first arrived, although he's much cleverer about hiding it. The thing is…" Father Doyle paused and his face twisted with a look of torment as they reached the convent steps. "He tries so hard not to drink."

"What about Alcoholics Anonymous?" Kathleen couldn't believe she hadn't thought of that sooner.

The priest dismissed the idea with a shake of his head. "I suggested it once and Father wasn't open to attending the meetings." His shoulders slumped noticeably. "His greatest fear is that someone in the community might recognize him."

They paused outside the convent door, almost like teenagers saying good-night at the end of a date—lingering, not wanting to end the conversation.

"My prayers go with you, Father," Kathleen said when she realized she couldn't delay another moment.

"I can't thank you enough, Sister, for all your help and for your friendship."

Kathleen felt she had done so little, but she was warmed by his gratitude.

"It's such a relief to be able to discuss the problem honestly. I don't know what I would've done if I'd carried this burden alone for even one more day." He turned to leave, then turned back to say, "Thank you, Sister."

"God go with you," she whispered, watching him walk away. Her own heart was oppressed by the weight of their secret.

Kathleen entered the convent and was prepared to hurry into chapel when Sister Eloise stopped her.

"Sister," the older nun called sharply, "could I have a moment of your time?"

"Of course, Sister." Kathleen's heart sank as if she'd been caught doing something wrong. She stood motionless with an impassive expression on her face.

"You're still working on the church books, is that correct?"

"Yes, Sister."

"It was my understanding that the church treasurer was on vacation and would be back within a month. It's been more than that, hasn't it?"

"Yes, Sister." Kathleen kept her eyes lowered.

"Do you have any idea how much longer this *temporary* situation will last?"

Kathleen swallowed hard and shook her head. "Unfortunately, I don't."

Sister Eloise narrowed her eyes. "How is Father Sanders?" she asked.

"Father Sanders?" Kathleen repeated. "He...he seems to be doing well."

Again a lengthy pause, in which the older nun assessed Kathleen's response. "You're sure about that, Sister?"

"Oh, yes," she said quickly—perhaps too quickly, she thought, as soon as the words had left her lips.

The head of the convent considered her answer for minutes that seemed to stretch into hours. "There have been...rumors about Father Sanders. I wonder if you've seen any evidence proving these rumors?"

"I'm sure I haven't," Sister Kathleen said in what she hoped was a reassuring voice.

"No evidence of Father Sanders having a...certain weakness?"

"None." Father Doyle's request that she keep the news of Father Sanders's problems a secret from Sister Eloise rang in her mind. The echo of his words blocked out any other thought, any other consideration.

"You have never seen Father Sanders with a drink in his hand, is that what you're telling me, Sister Kathleen?"

"No, I've never seen that."

The tightness in her throat almost prevented Kathleen from talking as she forced out the lie. In fact, she'd never actually seen Father Sanders with a drink in his hand. Technically she *wasn't* lying, she told herself, although it was certainly a lie of omission because she'd seen the effects of his drinking.

"Never, Sister," Kathleen said again, uncomfortable with her superior's long silence.

Sister Eloise's lips thinned. "Very well."

*chapter*

## SISTER ANGELINA

Her tenth-grade Health class dragged all week and Angie couldn't put her finger on the reason until Thursday afternoon. Corinne. The girl had been quiet and introspective for days. She was usually so inquisitive, asking questions, disputing assumptions, challenging Angie at every turn. Often, the entire class revolved around something Corinne had brought up. This week, however, she had remained oddly silent.

"Can I see you after class?" Angie asked as she strolled past Corinne's desk. She'd given the class ten minutes to start their homework assignment.

Corinne reluctantly looked up from the textbook and stared at her with unseeing eyes. It was as though the girl looked straight through her.

"This should only take a few minutes," Angie assured her in case Corinne planned to meet Jimmy in the parking lot after school, as she often did.

"I can stay," the girl mumbled.

Angie moved down the aisle between the desks and frowned as she glanced over her shoulder. She noticed Morgan Gentry studying Corinne, and she, too, wore a troubled expression. Angie decided then and there that she'd try to find out what the problem was.

The bell rang and the class disappeared from the room with a swiftness that never ceased to amaze her. Only Corinne remained. She slouched against the back of her desk chair and waited with her head lowered.

"You wanted to talk to me, Sister?" she said in the same lackluster tone she'd used all week.

"Yes." Angie slid into the desk across from Corinne. "Is everything all right?" she began.

"Sure, why shouldn't it be?" A defensive edge marked her words.

"You don't seem yourself."

Corinne shrugged.

Angie hesitated, wondering if she should pursue the issue. She didn't know whether it would be worth risking their fragile friendship. If Corinne had something on her mind, perhaps it was better to let her bring it up.

"Is that why you wanted to talk to me?" Corinne asked defiantly. "I can't stay if you're going to interrogate me like this."

"Actually I have another reason," Angie said, refusing to be hurt by the girl's remark. "I wanted you to know that I took your questions seriously."

"Questions?" Corinne repeated. "Oh, you mean my little tirade a couple of weeks back. It's no big deal, Sister. I was on one of my soapboxes. I get like that sometimes. Don't worry, I've forgotten all about it."

"Perhaps you've forgotten it, but I haven't," Angie said. She didn't believe for a moment that Corinne had put the issue out of her mind. "I took your questions to Father Sanders."

The girl's eyes lit up with interest and she straightened. "You did? What did you ask him?"

"My first question concerned what you said about James being the biological brother of Christ."

"Mary and Joseph's son. It's right there in the Bible," Corinne insisted, showing more life than she had all week. She leaned toward Angie, eager to learn what the priest had said.

"It's exactly as I assumed," Angie said, almost sorry to burst the girl's righteous bubble. "Mary and—"

"The Church is asking us to believe that Mary and Joseph lived like brother and sister all those years," Corinne said loudly. "You've got to know it didn't happen. They were in love! I told you before, Sister—Jimmy showed me right in his Bible where it says James was Jesus's brother."

"Corinne," Angie said stopping her before she could leap onto another soapbox.

"But Sister, anyone who's ever been in love will tell you that's impossible. I know Mary was the Virgin Mother and all that, and Joseph was a saint, but he was a man too, and Mary was human. They were in love and they were married. You can't make me believe they weren't intimate. Just think about it."

"Father said you were obviously reading a Protestant Bible and that their Bible is full of inaccuracies."

"Sister!" As if consumed by frustration, Corinne closed her eyes and shook her head.

"I'm sorry you're having a hard time accepting Father's explanation, but it's the truth."

Corinne continued to shake her head in disbelief. Sighing audibly, she crossed her arms and said, "I'd be curious to hear what Father Sanders had to say about purgatory."

His answer had come as a surprise to Angie. "You're right about that. There isn't a single word in the Bible about purgatory."

"See!" she cried.

"Purgatory and limbo might not be spelled out in Scripture, but the Church, under the divine direction of the Holy Spirit, has made these truths clear through the Holy Father."

"The Pope?"

"The Holy Father is our earthly guide."

"He's the same one who says it's wrong for Catholics to practice birth control, isn't he?"

Angie was sure she saw Corinne roll her eyes. "Why do you have such difficulty with Church doctrine?"

"Because it doesn't add up," the girl said. "I want to be a good Catholic, Sister. I make Jimmy attend Mass with me every Sunday and we try to do the right thing." Her gaze skirted away from Angie's, as if she was too embarrassed to meet her look. "It isn't easy because—" She stopped and drew a deep breath. "It just isn't easy, and now…"

"Now?" Angie pressed when the girl let her words fade.

Corinne's closed expression indicated she didn't have anything more to say. "You know what, Sister? I don't believe Father Sanders."

"I'm sorry you're disappointed," Angie said, hoping her soft tone would soothe the girl.

"He's a man, and it's time women in the Church began to think for themselves. These priests and bishops and the Pope aren't married. They don't have families to support. Even you, Sister—your vow of poverty and whatever else you vowed are no real sacrifice."

Before Angie could reply, Corinne started talking again, and the anger seemed to rush out of her. "You have everything given to you. You're provided with a home and all your meals and everything you need. The priests are the same. You don't know what it's like in the real world, where people have to make life-and-death decisions."

"Corinne—"

"I think I've already heard more than I want," the girl muttered as she grabbed her books and stood up from her desk.

"I can't allow you to use that tone of voice with me," Angie said. She'd been patient long enough.

Corinne's eyes narrowed. "I used to think you were someone special, Sister. I used to enjoy your classes and do you know why?"

Angie wasn't sure she was up to having her pride shredded. "I believe you've said too much already, Corinne. School's out. Perhaps it would be best if you left now."

Eyes glittering, Corinne stared her down. "Okay, but I

want you to remember this conversation, Sister. Think about it, think about all the brainwashing that's been going on for the last two thousand years by men like Father Sanders." With that she whirled around and marched out of the room, filled with righteous indignation.

Oh, teenage girls and all their angst, Angie mused. She recalled that period in her own life and how everything had gone smoothly until the one time she'd stood up to her father and announced she wanted to enter the convent.

As Angie cleaned the blackboard, she heard someone behind her and turned to find Morgan standing in the doorway.

"Oh hi, Sister. I thought Corinne might still be here."

Angie lowered the eraser to the ledge in front of the blackboard. "She left a few minutes ago. I'm sure you can catch her if you want."

Morgan shrugged. "She's been a real pill lately."

Angie murmured something noncommittal.

"She's on restriction," Morgan said. "Did she tell you?"

Angie shook her head.

"She hasn't seen Jimmy all week and it's driving her crazy."

"I see."

Morgan nodded. "I think this is the first time Corinne's parents ever put her on restriction."

"Really?" Angie's curiosity was piqued now. "What happened?"

Morgan lifted one shoulder, but Angie could tell the other girl was delighted to tell tales on her friend. "Corinne has a midnight curfew just like me, and her father caught her sneaking into the house at four in the morning last Saturday. He was furious, too."

"I can imagine," Angie muttered.

"She's grounded for a week, so she's only gotta go three more days before she can see Jimmy again."

"No big deal, right?" Angie said casually.

"Right," Morgan agreed. "It isn't like the end of the world, and anyway, that's what Corinne gets for stepping over the line."

It wasn't only with her parents that Corinne was pushing the boundaries, however. She had serious problems with the Church, too.

## SISTER JOANNA

Dr. Murray pulled up to the bus stop in front of St. Elizabeth's Hospital in his shiny red Corvette. He was directly in front of Joanna, who stood waiting for the bus. Leaning across the passenger seat, he rolled down the window, despite the crisp October afternoon.

"Hi," he said, giving her the full effect of his smile.

Joanna's heart skipped with excitement at the sight of him. "Hi, yourself."

"So, have you decided to run away and marry your high school sweetheart?"

"I wouldn't be taking the bus if I had," she said with a laugh. Despite everything, Joanna couldn't disguise how pleased she was to see him, even if Tim Murray teased her at every opportunity. She hadn't seen much of him in a while. They'd both been busy—or pretended to be. It was the oddest thing, this…non-relationship of theirs. Joanna couldn't deny her growing attraction to Tim, and yet, she had to. For the first time since entering the convent, she'd begun to question her vocation. But that brought an avalanche of unpleasant questions, questions she preferred to ignore. As a result, she hadn't spoken to him, other than to exchange information about patients, for almost two weeks.

"Can I give you a ride, or is that forbidden too?" His voice rang with challenge.

Joanna bit the inside of her cheek and glanced down the street. The bus wasn't due for ten minutes, but she really shouldn't go with Dr. Murray. It went against all the convent's rules of propriety. If anyone found out, Joanna would have to answer for her actions. Still, even knowing the risk she was about to take, she found she couldn't refuse.

"Is it really such a difficult decision?" he asked.

"All right, I'll go, but you have to drive me directly to the convent," she said. She didn't wait for him to agree, but walked eagerly toward the car. All her life, she'd longed for a ride in a red Corvette, but the sports car was only a small part of the temptation.

Dr. Murray leaned across the bucket seats again and opened the passenger door. The vehicle was impossibly low to the ground. Joanna slid into the soft leather seat and automatically reached for the safety harness.

"So, heard from Mr. Markham lately?" he asked, keeping his eyes on the road.

"Would you kindly stop?"

"No. I find it interesting that lover-boy would show up wanting to steal you away from the convent."

"You find it interesting, do you?" Joanna was enjoying herself too much to let him provoke her. The Corvette drove oh-so-smoothly, rounding the corners with the ease of a race car.

"You mean to say you weren't tempted?" he pressed. "I'd think any woman would be flattered to have an old boyfriend seek her out."

Joanna *had* been flattered—and dismayed. Five or six years ago, she'd dreamed of this happening, and now that it had, all she felt was pity for Greg.

But she hadn't been tempted. At least not by Greg Markham. She sighed and could see that she was in for a lot of teasing until she explained herself. Although Tim Murray appeared to be joking, there was an undercurrent of seriousness in his remarks.

"His coming here wasn't a joke and it wasn't for old times' sake," Dr. Murray continued. "He wants you back. I'm having a hard time believing you didn't at least consider his proposal."

"Greg is part of my old life," she said simply.

Tim's gaze briefly met hers before he returned his attention to the road. "You mean to say you're a nun now and the religious life is all you care about?"

She nodded and intuitively realized it was a lie. She'd found serenity and peace in the convent, and there was comfort in the rituals of her daily life, but it was her work as a nurse that fulfilled her. Lately, at the end of the day when she returned to the convent, she'd become aware of a new longing—a deep, unspoken, barely recognizable part of herself that hungered for something more. The stark life, the repetitive prayer regimen, the lack of human touch was beginning to lose its meaning for her. In part, she suspected it was her growing attraction to Tim that was responsible for these feelings; she hoped that eventually it would pass. She didn't *want* to feel the things she did, and yet she couldn't help herself.

"Greg sought me out for his own reasons," she said. "He was trying to recapture his youth. What he didn't understand is that there's no going back, not for either of us."

"You sound very wise."

Joanna smiled, pleased by the compliment. "Do I?"

He nodded. "And sincere."

"Greg's hurting just now, feeling the pain of his divorce. He's looking for what used to be comfortable and easy. In his view, I entered the convent because of him. He actually believes I've been waiting for him all these years. He's free now, so of course he assumed I'd want him back."

"It must've been a shock when you turned him down."

"Yes," she agreed, "I imagine it was."

"In other words," he said, inhaling sharply, "you never have any doubts about being a nun?"

She hadn't said that, and she wasn't willing to make such a confession now. "There are days," she said, feigning a lightness of tone, "that I'd give it all up for a gooey hot fudge sundae."

"Really?" He glanced away from the road and his grin broadened to a full-blown smile. To Joanna's surprise, Tim roared past the convent and down the street.

"We just passed the convent," she said, looking over her shoulder and watching the building disappear in the background.

"I know," he murmured as though it didn't matter.

"Where are you taking me?"

"You'll find out."

She wasn't sure she liked the sound of this.

"You don't trust me, Joanna?"

She noticed the *Sister* was suspiciously absent. "Should I?" she asked.

"That depends," he said and pulled up to the drive-in window of a Dairy Queen. "I have a weakness for hot fudge now and then myself."

"Oh…" was all Joanna could manage to say. It'd been years and years since she'd indulged in anything so decadent, but that didn't concern her nearly as much as the implication behind Tim Murray's words.

"So, what would you like?" he asked, studying her before placing his order. The teasing light was gone from his eyes.

Joanna hesitated—and then asked for the largest hot fudge sundae they had. With whipped cream.

By the time she returned to the convent, she was sure there was chocolate fudge smeared across her face. They'd sat in the parking lot and must have talked for an hour. As if she needed to convince him—and herself—she'd told him about her experiences as a nun and the peace she'd discovered in the religious life. He asked her a lot of questions and his interest seemed genuine. In the process, she'd succeeded in reassuring herself of her vocation, of her calling to work for God.

When Joanna finally glanced at her watch, she felt immediate alarm. Arriving back at the convent this late was certainly going to raise eyebrows.

Because of her tardiness, she had to rush to the chapel. If Sister Superior noticed when Joanna slipped into the pew with her fellow nuns, she didn't indicate it in any way. Following chapel, they went in to dinner.

Another space at the table was empty that night. Sister Julia was gone as if she'd vanished by some magician's hand. No one needed an explanation. Sister Julia, like five others that year, had decided to leave the religious life. Joanna felt her absence profoundly. Had she pursued the possibilities she sensed with Tim, she might have found reasons to leave herself.

That night she removed her simple habit, and tired though she was, knelt on the hard floor and reached for her rosary. Her mind drifted as she slid the beads through her fingers and recited the Our Father followed by ten Hail Marys. It took a determined effort to finish without falling asleep right there on the floor, with her head resting against the side of the mattress.

When Joanna finally climbed between the cool, coarse sheets, she closed her eyes and almost instantly fell asleep.

The first thing Joanna felt when Tim came to her in her dreams was that he shouldn't be with her. But he refused to leave. He said he'd given careful thought to all her talk about being a nun and her reasons for staying in the convent, but frankly he wasn't buying it.

He told her she was just as attracted to him as he was to her. He sat next to her in his red Corvette, looking so intense and so handsome she couldn't force herself to glance away.

Then, because she knew he was right, she nodded. Yes, she was attracted to him, but— She wasn't allowed to finish. With a small shout of triumph, Tim kissed her. Really kissed her.

At first Joanna resisted, telling him such contact was strictly against the rules. But he wouldn't listen, because they both knew how desperately she longed for his kisses.

He tasted so good, just as she'd feared. It was everything she remembered and had missed so much. Again and again his mouth sought hers. Again and again she gave him all that she was, all the woman she longed to be.

At some point he took off her clothes. Joanna was embarrassed that he'd see her nude. But when she saw the look of admiration and wonder in his eyes, she lowered her arms and stopped trying to conceal her body from him. How they'd ended up in bed together she couldn't figure out. Everything seemed to be happening so fast; first they were in the Corvette and then they were in bed. Tim's eyes had filled with love as he stared down at her.

She smiled up at him and wove her fingers into his hair. She didn't need to urge his mouth to hers; he released a small, soft moan as his lips met Joanna's.

He made slow, thoughtful love to her, revealing tenderness and care. It was so beautiful that she struggled to hold back the tears. Then he gently placed his arms around her and held her close.

An alarm rang, so loud and piercing that Joanna panicked. Throwing him off her, she leaped out of bed and glanced wildly around, certain they were about to be discovered.

It was then that Joanna realized she stood in the middle of her darkened cell in the convent of St. Bridget's Sisters of the Assumption in Minneapolis, Minnesota.

She wasn't in Dr. Tim Murray's arms, but in the convent. The alarm that had so terrified her—announcing her sin to the entire world—was merely the bell calling her to pray.

Joanna fell to her knees beside the bed, her eyes misting with guilt and regret. She was a nun and such dreams, such longings, were forbidden to her.

And yet her body felt warm and she ached with the deep need to be loved, to be touched. To be treasured.

*chapter*

## SISTER KATHLEEN

"Oh, Sister," Mrs. O'Malley said the moment Kathleen entered the rectory on Monday afternoon. "I'm glad I caught you. Father Doyle needs to speak to you right away."

The housekeeper's face was drawn, her voice low and hoarse. Something must be very wrong.

"What is it?" Kathleen asked.

The older woman reached for a wadded handkerchief in her apron pocket and dabbed at her eyes. "It would be best if Father Doyle told you himself. He went to the church to pray a few moments ago. He's waiting for you there."

Her heart thundering with alarm, Kathleen hurried out the door and swiftly walked down the hill toward the large Catholic church. The sky was dark and leaden, and it felt cold enough for snow. It was early yet, mid-October, but in Minnesota winter sometimes arrived before Halloween.

She hurried into the church, but her eyes didn't adjust to the dim light for a moment or two. Gradually a lone figure took shape, kneeling at the railing in front of the altar, bent over, his head in his hands.

It was Father Doyle and he appeared to be in some spiritual distress. Kathleen's imagination went wild. Father Sanders was nowhere to be seen and she couldn't help wondering if this problem involved the other priest.

Tentatively Kathleen stepped toward Father Doyle, unsure if she should interrupt his prayers.

He must have sensed her presence, because he raised his head and slowly turned to look her way. Kathleen saw such anguish in his eyes that she automatically stretched out her hands to him, in an overwhelming urge to comfort.

"What happened?" she whispered.

Father Doyle took her fingers in his and together they moved to the front pew. They sat angled toward each other, so close their knees touched. The priest squeezed her hands and then released them. Kathleen placed them in her lap, missing the warmth and reassurance of his touch.

"I've been transferred."

"Transferred?" Sister Kathleen couldn't take it in. There had to be a mistake. "But why? Where?" She knew Father Doyle had gone to the bishop about Father Sanders and his drinking problem, but surely Bishop Schmidt wouldn't send him away because of that. None of this made sense.

Father Doyle nodded. "I'm afraid I've been ordered to leave."

The questions crowded her mind and she couldn't get them out fast enough. "You went to Bishop Schmidt? You told him about Father Sanders? What did he say? How could he do this?" The lump in her throat thickened.

Father Doyle seemed resigned to this news, whereas she had yet to deal with it. "I'll try to answer your questions," he said, and his eyes held a distant look. "I did speak privately to the bishop regarding Father Sanders."

"What did he say?"

He hesitated, then shook his head "Perhaps it would be best if I kept that to myself, but suffice it to say that I have failed Bishop Schmidt just as I'd feared."

"But *how?*" Surely the bishop understood that Father Doyle could do only so much on his own.

"It doesn't matter now," he whispered. "The last thing I want you to do is worry."

How could she not? Kathleen was deep in this mess. She was certain Sister Eloise knew of Father Sanders's weakness for the bottle, but if her superior discovered that she and Father Doyle had covered for the priest, there was no telling what would happen.

"I know what you're thinking, Sister," Father Doyle said, "but I want to assure you I didn't mention your name."

At this point Kathleen no longer cared. "How could the bishop do this?" she demanded, her raised voice echoing in the church.

"There's an emergency," he said flatly, revealing no emotion. "Father Wood from Holy Family in Osseo has died suddenly and the parish is desperately in need of a priest."

"What about right here at St. Peter's?" she asked. Surely the bishop wouldn't leave the parish in the hands of an alcoholic priest, a priest who was more often drunk than sober?

This all seemed so unfair. Father Doyle hadn't gone running to the bishop to report on Father Sanders; in fact, he'd waited until the situation had reached crisis proportions, and prior to that, he'd done everything humanly possible to help the older priest. Father Doyle was well aware of his mission at St. Peter's, but what did the bishop expect him to do? No one could protect Father Sanders forever.

"A new priest has been assigned to St. Peter's," he told her.

"Why didn't Bishop Schmidt send the new priest to Holy Family? You belong here. I don't want you to go." She recognized that she was being selfish, but she didn't know what she'd do without Father Doyle.

From the anguish she read in the priest's eyes, Kathleen knew he didn't want to leave the parish, either.

"Sister," he said and he gripped her hands once again. "I want you to tell Father Sanders that you can no longer manage the books. Make up whatever excuse you want, but you must promise me you'll disentangle yourself from this matter as quickly as possible."

She nodded. "What...what about Father Sanders?" she asked, her eyes pleading with him for answers she knew he didn't have.

He shook his head as though he had nothing more to tell her.

This was so wrong! "He could injure or kill someone if he gets behind the wheel of a car," she said urgently. "Not to mention the harm he might do himself."

The priest's jaw tightened. "I have my orders and this parish is not my concern anymore." He said those words as though he was repeating what he'd been told. "I've been given a new assignment."

"You *can't* leave us," she protested.

"Sister Kathleen," he cried. "I have no choice! Do you understand what I'm saying? I can't do anything, and neither can you. It's in the hands of Almighty God now."

"Oh, Father." Kathleen blinked back tears. "I can't believe this." Mortified that the priest would see her weep, she covered her face.

"I'm so sorry," he said and gently laid his hand on her shoulder. "So very sorry."

Kathleen was, too. After a moment she composed herself and raised her head. "When do you have to leave?" Surely the bishop would give Father Doyle a few days to put his affairs in order before forcing him to move to another town and another church.

"Tonight."

"So soon?" She was aghast.

"Holy Family..." He let the sentence dwindle into nothingness. He was obviously as aware as she that this new assignment was just an excuse to get him out of the picture and the sooner the better.

"Who'll be replacing you?" she asked.

"Father Yates. Donald Yates."

Sister Kathleen had never heard of him. "Do you know Father Yates?"

The priest nodded. He offered no assurances about the man, no words of advice.

"What's he like?" she asked, needing all the information she could get.

"He taught me in the seminary," Father Doyle said guardedly. Then he added, "I didn't know he was serving as a parish priest. I...wouldn't think it was his calling."

This was worse than she'd imagined. In all the time she'd worked with and known Father Doyle, she'd never heard him utter a disparaging word about anyone. His intimation that Father Yates wasn't a suitable parish priest was the strongest warning he could have given her.

She realized Father Yates was the reason he'd told her to find a way out of the bookkeeping task as quickly as possible. He was worried about what would happen to her. A chill raced up her back.

"Why is Bishop Schmidt sending you away and not Father Sanders? Does he honestly believe this new priest will do any better than you did? I don't—"

He stopped her with a raised hand. "Father Yates is more...exacting." He sighed. "I can't delay leaving any longer," he said and started to rise.

"No, not yet!" She astonished herself with the demand. "Please," she added softly. "Stay for just a few more minutes."

He nodded and sat back down.

But now she didn't know what to say and fought down the urge to weep. "Will I ever see you again?" she whispered. Father Doyle had become a friend. He was everything that was good about priests and the Church. His genuine love for God and his parishioners exemplified what the religious life should be.

"I don't know," he told her. "Perhaps our paths will cross again."

Kathleen had said farewell to those she cared about before this, but she'd never experienced such a profound sense of loss as she did in that moment. "Is there anything I can do for you, Father?" she asked.

After a few seconds, he said, "Pray for me, Sister."

"I will," she promised. "Every day."

"I'll pray for you, too."

"Thank you," she whispered.

He stood to leave and this time she didn't stop him. As he walked away, she bowed her head in sorrow. The lump in her throat made it difficult to choke back tears.

"Sister," he said, his voice calm now and reassuring, as though he'd found peace within himself. "If there's an audit or if Father Yates decides to check the books and you need me, then all you have to do is pick up the phone. Call me at Holy Family. Call me anytime you need my help. Understand?"

"Yes."

He smiled softly. "God be with you."

"And with you," she returned. But it seemed that God had abandoned them both.

*chapter*

## SISTER JOANNA

Joanna didn't see Dr. Murray again until Friday of the following week. Halloween skeletons decorated the nurses' station, along with giant orange pumpkins. All the talk was of the upcoming presidential elections.

Joanna passed Dr. Murray in the hall and kept her gaze averted. It was an obvious attempt to pretend she hadn't seen him, which appeared to suit his purposes, too. Irrational though it might be, Joanna felt slighted. The least he could do was acknowledge her even if *she* chose to ignore him.

It was all too apparent that Dr. Murray had taken her words to heart. God had called her into His service, she'd told him over and over. She knew now that she'd worked so hard to convince him because she feared what would happen if she admitted otherwise. It was chilling to realize how strongly she was attracted to him. The dream had made that completely clear—her subconscious at work, although her conscious mind tried to suppress the attraction. This flirtation had gone on long enough. For both their sakes it had to end. And yet...

They'd walked past each other when Joanna heard him call her name. "Sister Joanna?"

Despite her resolution to the contrary, relief rushed through her as she turned to face him. She was unable to hold back her smile. "Hello, Dr. Murray," she said, and wanted to kick herself for sounding as perky as a Dallas Cowboys cheerleader. That wasn't how she'd *meant* to sound. She'd hoped to appear sober and professional.

If he noticed anything was amiss, he didn't comment.

"When was the last time you checked Mrs. Wilson's blood pressure?"

"I just did. I made my notations on the chart." Her tone was perfect this time.

"Good." He nodded once, and without another word, continued down the corridor.

So much for that, Joanna mused as she entered her next patient's room. As far as the doctor was concerned, their outing had been time shared between friends. That was the way it should be. She was the one obsessing about it, the one who'd built it into this wildly romantic fiasco.

"Did you hear the latest?" Lois Jenson asked Joanna at the end of her shift. Joanna was preparing to go off duty and head to the bus stop.

"Hear what?" she asked. Lois took delight in passing on rumors, usually adding a comment or two of her own.

"About Dr. Murray and Jenny Parkland. Jenny's that sweet maternity nurse."

"They're dating," Joanna said casually. She hadn't heard, but it wasn't a guess. Somehow she knew—and understood. She was off-limits to Tim. He was right, of course. She was a nun; this was the life she'd chosen, the life she wanted.

Lois seemed unaware of Joanna's drifting thoughts. "Three nights this week."

Joanna returned her attention to the other woman.

"Dr. Murray and Jenny," Lois repeated. "They had three dates last week alone. They're seeing each other every day now."

"That's great," Joanna said, forcing a smile. "It's about time he made the rounds."

Lois laughed. "Cute, Sister, very cute. A little play on words there."

The joke was a pitiful attempt to disguise how the news had made her feel. But Joanna had no right to feel anything whatsoever regarding Dr. Murray. He was a handsome, eligible bachelor and she was as good as married. Her vows had been spoken and she was wedded to the Church, a bride of Christ.

"I'm pretty sure Jenny's had her eye on Dr. Murray, too."

Frankly Joanna didn't blame the other nurse. He was everything a woman could want in a man.

That night Joanna knelt before Sister Superior for the weekly Chapter of Faults. Her heart was heavy, the load of guilt weighing upon her shoulders.

Although Joanna knew she couldn't be held responsible for her dreams, she suffered from repeated pangs of guilt. She'd invited Dr. Murray—she refused to call him Tim again—into her thought life. In the process, she was risking serious trouble, jeopardizing her vows and her emotional health. Furthermore, she was setting herself up for major disappointment.

"Sister Superior, I confess before you and Almighty God a weakness in my thought life." She paused, debating how much to elaborate. She heard herself say something vague about "inappropriate reactions" and then all at once, on her knees with the entire convent looking on, she broke into huge sobs. She didn't know why she was weeping or how to stop.

An hour later, Joanna was called before Sister Eloise. "Tell me what has upset you so much," the older nun said gently.

Joanna reached for her handkerchief and blew her nose. Her eyes were puffy and her nose felt raw. Still, the tears came and she couldn't seem to make herself quit.

"Sister." Once more Sister Superior urged her to speak.

"Oh, Sister Eloise, I'm afraid I've done something foolish."

The other nun waited patiently as Joanna struggled for words. "There's a physician at St. Elizabeth's—and…and I've let my attraction for him build in my mind." She hid her face, fearing the revulsion the other nun might feel toward her.

"Sister, you are still a woman. It's only natural for you to be attracted to a man. We took a vow of chastity, but that doesn't mean we have no heart or no feelings."

Joanna hadn't expected Sister Superior to be sympathetic to her predicament.

"Does this physician return your feelings?"

A week earlier she might have answered yes, but now she knew better. "No…he's involved with another nurse."

"I see," Sister Eloise said after a long pause. "And that upsets you, doesn't it?"

Joanna felt torn. She wanted Dr. Murray to be happy and to have a good life. He was a talented surgeon, but more than that he genuinely cared for his patients. She knew, too, that one day he'd be a wonderful husband and father. He'd marry someone else, someone free to return his love, and that awareness brought an ache to her heart she dared not examine.

"I want him to be happy," Joanna whispered, her voice ravaged with emotion.

The other nun nodded approvingly. "How can I help you?"

Joanna didn't think anyone could help her through this. She felt sick to her stomach now, as though she was coming down with a bout of the flu.

"You see this physician routinely, do you?"

Joanna inclined her head.

"If you worked in a different part of the hospital, would that help?"

So her Superior was going to have her transferred to another floor. Perhaps that would be for the best; perhaps then Joanna might get her life back into perspective. "I think…that would be a good thing, Sister."

The other nun promised to see to it.

Although Joanna knew that a transfer was in motion, she didn't expect it to happen quite so quickly. On Monday she learned she was being sent to work in the Emergency Room, assigned to the swing shift. Her entire schedule had been altered. She wasn't given the opportunity to tell the other nurses she'd worked with about the change or to say goodbye. More importantly, she didn't see Dr. Murray again.

Two days later he sought her out. "You might have said something about a transfer," he said, interrupting her as she dressed a young woman's wound. He completely ignored her patient. The woman, a housewife who'd cut herself with a bread knife, stared up at him.

"I apologize," Joanna said to the woman. "Dr. Fuller will be in to give you the stitches in a moment." She turned to glare at Dr. Murray.

He followed her out of the room.

"What are you doing here?" she demanded.

"Why'd you ask to be transferred?"

"The answer to that should be obvious."

"Unfortunately it isn't that easy, so spell it out for me."

She wasn't sure he could handle the truth any more than she could admit it. "I don't believe it's a good idea for us to see each other again."

"Fine, you want to skip the occasional stop at the Dairy Queen, that's perfectly all right with me. But there's no reason to drop out of sight for three days."

"I didn't drop out of sight."

"No, you disappeared."

Joanna couldn't remember ever seeing him this angry. His face was red and he obviously had to make an effort to keep his voice controlled.

"You don't understand," Joanna whispered.

"Explain it to me."

"I can't see you again. Not at the Dairy Queen, not here, not anywhere."

"What the hell are you talking about?"

She knew he'd ask but she didn't have an answer for him. Not one she could live with for the rest of her life. "Please don't ask me that—just accept that I wanted this transfer."

"Are you *sure* this is what you want, Joanna?"

"Sister Joanna," she corrected.

He didn't say anything for a while. "Sister Joanna," he repeated, frowning darkly. "That's all the answer I need." Then he was gone. The way he left told her he would abide by her wishes.

She'd never see him again.

# chapter 28

## SISTER KATHLEEN

On All Saints' Day, a week after Kathleen gave notice that she could no longer work on the church books, she stopped at the rectory to find out if a replacement had been hired. There was information she needed to convey to the new person—if there *was* a new person. Father Sanders had had plenty of time to hire a bookkeeper, but thus far she'd seen no evidence of anyone stepping into her role.

She refused to let him talk her into continuing in the position; a few words of praise and encouragement weren't going to persuade her to stay on.

She carefully rehearsed her speech in case she needed it. Father Doyle had insisted she get out before she became so entangled in the mess that escape would be impossible. She'd taken his advice and spoken to Father Sanders right away. The older priest had pleaded with her to reconsider, but Kathleen had held her ground. She wanted out—and the instant she met Father Yates she was even more sure of it.

Unfortunately Father Sanders was gone when she arrived and, despite his promise the week before, there was no replacement for Kathleen to train. Now she'd have to talk to Father Yates, a prospect that sent shivers of apprehension down her backbone.

As Father Doyle had implied, the new priest was an unpleasant man who seemed to find little in life with which to be happy. He was often harsh and unfriendly toward parishioners. His manner bordered on rude.

He'd been at St. Peter's a little more than a week, and already Kathleen had heard a number of complaints. She didn't think he was a bad priest, just an angry one, and that anger seemed to come in the form of a sharp tongue and judgmental attitude.

"Father Sanders is out?" Kathleen asked the housekeeper in a tentative voice.

Mrs. O'Malley nodded. "I'd disappear myself if I could," she said. She glanced toward the ceiling and shuddered. In a conspiratorial whisper, she added, "He doesn't like my cooking."

The housekeeper didn't need to identify whom she meant. "My meatloaf is too salty, my mashed potatoes taste like library glue, and he complained about my pumpkin pie. At lunch today he said he'd tasted better black bean soup out of a can." Her voice quavered with indignation as she repeated the criticism.

"You're a wonderful cook," Kathleen told her. The housekeeper made melt-in-your-mouth biscuits and cooked delectable meals for the priests. Her Irish stew rivaled the best Kathleen had ever tasted. Feeding the priests well was Mrs. O'Malley's mission in life, so Father Yates's complaints had deeply wounded her pride.

"Thank you for saying that," Mrs. O'Malley said, sniffling. "It's a shame, you know, about losing Father Doyle. It won't be the same around here."

"How's Father Sanders?" Kathleen asked.

The cook met her eyes. "Poorly, I'm afraid," she said with a sigh.

The message was clear. Father was drinking again, more

than ever. Losing Father Doyle and having to deal with Father Yates had tipped the scales for the priest.

Footsteps could be heard coming from the priests' living quarters. Mrs. O'Malley leapt as if someone had pinched her from behind and hurried back to the kitchen.

Kathleen returned to her small office and sat at the desk, thinking she'd better speak with Father Yates today. She waited for him to acknowledge her. However, he continued down the hallway without as much as a nod in her direction.

After another moment, Kathleen approached him, knocking politely on his office door.

The priest glared up at her from his desk. "Can't this wait?" he asked, frowning.

Kathleen stiffened at his lack of welcome but forged ahead. "I need to speak to you this afternoon. At your convenience, Father."

Scowl lines marked his otherwise attractive face. "What is it?" he demanded.

"Today's my last day doing the church books," she said. "I told Father Sanders a week ago that I could no longer continue to teach full-time and do the bookkeeping, too."

"Overburdened, are you, Sister?"

She detected more than a hint of sarcasm, but chose to ignore it. "When Father Sanders asked me to take on this task, I was told it would be temporary. But apparently the previous bookkeeper has decided...not to return." The woman had resigned in August, but Kathleen didn't want to expose Father Sanders entirely.

"Now you're walking away as well."

"I did tell Father Sanders of my intentions two weeks ago. He's had that period of time to hire a replacement."

The other priest refused to look at her. "Which he hasn't done, now has he?"

"I...I wouldn't know."

"Fine, you can be on your way."

"Thank you." Relief rushed through her. But when Kathleen turned to leave, he stopped her.

"To be honest, Sister, it doesn't surprise me that you've quit."

She made no comment but clasped her hands in front of her as he continued to write.

"As it happens, I had a chance to go over the books this morning," he said. "I don't suppose you know of my own bookkeeping background?"

Kathleen froze. He must have noticed the discrepancies between the donations and the deposits. She'd hoped that with Father Doyle making up the difference, the matter would settle itself.

"There appear to be a number of small...*deliberate* errors."

Kathleen didn't agree or disagree.

He glanced up and met her eyes before she had a chance to lower her own. In those brief seconds, Kathleen read his contempt. He was about to say more when the rectory door opened and in strolled Father Sanders.

The priest staggered a couple of steps, then paused in the office doorway. She could smell the liquor on him and immediately noticed his unfocused gaze.

"I'm happy to see you, Father," the other priest said with open disgust. "You're just in time for this rather unfortunate discussion with Sister Kathleen. As you know, she's chosen to give up the bookkeeping."

"Fine job she's done, too," Father Sanders said approvingly.

"I disagree, Father."

"There's a problem?" Father Sanders sounded shocked. As though he found it difficult to remain standing, he leaned against the doorjamb. The stench of liquor seemed to permeate the office; she was sure Father Yates smelled it, too.

The new priest sat back in his chair. "Your silence doesn't do you credit, Sister Kathleen." He waited, obviously expecting her to speak. She didn't defend herself and wouldn't.

"I believe you owe this parish an explanation."

Her head lowered, Kathleen bit her tongue to keep from defending her actions. She had done nothing wrong. If there *was* a crime, it was in not reporting the shortfalls to the bishop.

Little good *that* would have done her, she reasoned sadly. Father Doyle had tried, and look where it had gotten him.

"I don't know what possessed Father Sanders to ask you to work here in the first place," he said, turning his scowl on the older priest. "It was a bad idea from the first."

How nice to know her efforts were appreciated, Kathleen thought to herself, struggling to hide her irritation. For two months, three and often four times a week, she'd spent hours balancing the church's books, and this tongue-lashing was all the thanks she received.

"Seeing that you have nothing to say, you leave me no option," Father Yates said in a way that told her this would bring him plea-sure rather than regret. "I'm going to have a talk with Sister Eloise regarding the questionable methods you've employed."

She nodded, hoping, praying, that Sister Superior would realize she was in an impossible situation. Perhaps it had been wrong to protect the older priest, but she'd followed Father Doyle's lead. His name, however, would not pass her lips. He'd already paid dearly for his efforts to fulfill the bishop's expectations of him and to help Father Sanders.

"May I go now, Father?" she asked her voice small despite her attempt to conceal her reaction.

"By all means," he said, standing. "You're a disgrace to the good name of St. Bridget's Sisters of the Assumption."

Kathleen nearly ran out of the rectory, so desperate was she to leave. The afternoon was cold and she was chilled to the bone by the time she arrived at the convent. She'd barely stepped in the door when Sister Eloise asked to see her.

"Is what Father Yates told me true?" she demanded the moment Kathleen entered her office. Before Kathleen had a chance to reply, she was hit with a second question. "Did you alter the books?"

The answer wasn't easy. Kathleen *had* altered the books, but only slightly and only to correct the discrepancies once Father Doyle had replaced the missing cash. "I...it isn't as bad as it looks, Sister."

The older nun was clearly angry. "Is it true you took money for your own purposes and then repaid it at a later date?"

"Absolutely not!" Kathleen cried, aghast that anyone would believe such an outrageous lie.

"That's what Father Yates says happened. He has proof."

"I'm not the one who took the money," Kathleen said reluctantly. "I wasn't the one who made the deposits." The fact that Father Yates had blamed her when he *knew* Father Sanders had done it was shocking to Kathleen. She hadn't expected behavior so…so calculated, so unconscionable, from a priest.

Her defense didn't appear to placate her superior. "Are you telling me you know who did and you said nothing?"

Kathleen nodded.

"This is even worse than I imagined. Father Yates is right. Disciplinary action is necessary. I'm going to sleep on this, Sister, but I think it would be best if you returned to the motherhouse for a period of contemplation to acknowledge your sins."

Kathleen couldn't take in what she was hearing. "You're sending me away?"

"You've disgraced us, Sister."

"But…but you haven't heard my side of it." Tears clogged her throat as she struggled to get the words out.

"Nothing you say will change the fact that you were dishonest in dealing with the church's books. You have ridiculed us all."

Kathleen opened her mouth to explain, but Sister Eloise was too angry to listen. Dragging Father Doyle's name into this mess would do more harm than good. He was her friend, her confidant and he'd done what he could to protect her. Now she had to return the favor.

Still, the unfairness of the situation was more than Kathleen could endure. "I don't deserve this, Sister."

The older nun frowned at her. "As I recall, you were certainly eager to accept the job. 'Practical experience' would benefit you, or so I remember you saying. This is what you wanted. I let you do it against my better judgment. I was not in favor of the idea, but in the spirit of cooperation between the rectory and the convent, I gave in.

"I knew it would end like this, and I blame you, Sister, for your refusal to tame your ego and for surrendering to foolish pride."

The silence that followed seemed deafening.

"Very well, Sister," Kathleen whispered.

"You will do without dinner and be ready to leave tomorrow."

"Yes, Sister."

Kathleen left the office and had to find a chair so she could sit down, she was trembling so badly. The shaking didn't seem to abate as she burned with anger and humiliation.

For almost ten years Kathleen had given her life to the church and to God, and *this* was the thanks she'd received. The priests were paid decent salaries but because she'd taken a vow of poverty, as all nuns did, she worked for a pittance. Kathleen taught school, sewed her own clothes, cooked, cleaned and lived a Spartan life. Her reward was loneliness and a variety of thankless tasks. For the first time since she'd entered the convent, Kathleen began to question the rightness of staying.

That night, unable to sleep, her stomach growling, Kathleen packed a small bag. She could only imagine what the other nuns would say or what they'd be told once she was gone. It would soon be apparent that she was leaving in disgrace.

The doorbell chimed in the distance. Then again, more insistently. Two long peals followed by a burst of short ones.

She didn't know who was on duty, but obviously whoever it was had gone to bed. Since she had yet to disrobe, Kathleen took the task upon herself.

To her surprise, an agitated young man was pacing on the other side of the door.

"How can I help you?" Kathleen asked, opening the door a crack.

"I need to talk to Sister Angelina."

"I'm sorry, but the sisters have all gone to bed."

"It's important!"

"I'm sorry," Kathleen said again. She was sympathetic, but there were strict rules about admitting visitors, and she didn't have any choice. "Come back tomorrow and Sister will speak to you then."

"No—I have to talk to Sister Angelina now."

"I'm truly sorry," she said and without waiting for him to argue further, she closed the door.

*chapter*

## SISTER JOANNA

At ten, Joanna had another hour to go until the end of her shift and already she was exhausted. Normally she didn't drink coffee this late at night, but she needed a jolt of caffeine to help her adjust to her new schedule. Working in the Emergency Room was exhausting—periods of boredom alternating with bursts of frantic, high-adrenaline activity.

With only a couple of days until the national election, all the talk around the hospital was of Nixon and McGovern.

"McGovern hasn't got a chance," one of the nurses, Gloria Thompson, said as she added sugar to her coffee.

"Have you checked the price of bread lately?" another complained. "You can thank Nixon for that. He sold our wheat to Russia, and fifty cents for a loaf of bread is the result." She rolled her eyes and nodded when Joanna strolled past. "Good to have you with us, Sister."

"Thank you," she said. It would take time to adjust, not

only to this schedule but to the staff. She missed Sylvia Larson, Lois Jenson, Julie and the others.

And she missed Dr. Murray with an ache that refused to leave her. Countless times each day, her mind drifted to him, despite her efforts to discipline her thoughts.

When she'd finished her coffee, she returned to the Emergency Room. It'd been a slow night, with several minor injuries and one serious situation—a teenage girl who'd been brought in by her boyfriend. The girl had apparently been to a backstreet abortionist and was hemorrhaging badly. Dr. Barlow, the attending physician, was working on her while Gloria and two other staff members rushed to meet his demands.

"Sister Joanna," Dr. Barlow called out when he saw her. "Would you find out what you can from her boyfriend?"

"Right away," she said. She'd just started toward the waiting room when a tall, solidly built teenage boy came barreling through the swinging doors.

"I want to be with her," the boy said belligerently. "Let me see her!"

Two orderlies restrained him from advancing farther.

"Will someone shut him up?" Gloria yelled.

"Where are the parents?" one orderly asked.

"Corinne. Corinne! It's going to be all right, baby." The youth strained against the two men holding him back. "Hang on, Corinne. Hang on." His young face was twisted with torment as he struggled. When he caught sight of Joanna, he went slack. "Sister! Sister."

"Can I help?" Joanna asked.

"Get me Sister Angelina," he pleaded. "Corinne begged me to get her. She needs to talk to her."

The young man didn't know what he was asking. "That's impossible."

"That's what the nun at the door said, but Corinne wants to talk to her. Please, Sister. They'll listen to you."

"You went to the convent?"

The boy nodded, tears brightening his eyes. "Corinne says she has to talk to Sister." The tears came in earnest now, washing down his pale face. "She was bleeding so much and she was afraid… I didn't know she was pregnant. I didn't even know."

The orderlies released him and Joanna took him into a vacant cubicle. The young man collapsed onto a stool and sobbed openly. Joanna laid her hand on his shoulder, trying to comfort him.

"She never wanted me to use any protection—she said it was against the Church and Corinne wanted to be a good Catholic."

Joanna sat with him for several minutes and let him talk. She couldn't imagine how a teenager could rationalize not using birth control and then decide on abortion. How desperate this girl must have been.

"Sister, find out what's happening. I need to know. Please, Sister, please."

Joanna left him for a moment and learned that Corinne Sullivan had been rushed into surgery in an effort to stop the bleeding.

"It doesn't look good," Dr. Barlow said as he peeled off his blood-smeared plastic gloves. "She waited too long to get here. Are the parents on their way?"

A knot in her stomach, Joanna nodded. "Admissions called them."

"Make sure they have privacy when they arrive," he said, and with sadness in his eyes, he turned away.

Joanna recognized that forlorn, hopeless look. It was too late. Nothing more could be done. She wanted to shout at the injustice of it all, to scream how terrible it was that a girl so young would waste her life. Didn't she realize how precious life was? Hers and that of her unborn child.

About ten minutes later, as Joanna passed the Emergency Admissions desk, a middle-aged couple hurried in, looking shaken and unsure. "I'm Bob Sullivan. Where's our daughter?" the man asked.

"Mr. and Mrs. Sullivan." The teenage boy went over to Corinne's parents.

"We've been so worried," Corinne's mother cried. "She

didn't come home after school. We've been phoning everyone, and no one knew where she was."

"None of that matters now, Sharon," the father said. "For the love of God, tell us what happened!"

"Yes, Jimmy, tell us what happened," Sharon echoed. "The hospital phoned but they wouldn't give us any details."

"She was—she was pregnant," Jimmy said in a faltering voice.

"Pregnant?" Bob Sullivan grabbed the teenage boy by the shirtfront and rammed him against the wall. The boy's feet were suspended two inches from the floor before Joanna could get the older man to release him.

"Shall we discuss this privately?" she said, steering them to an area the hospital had set aside for families. Once inside the room, the parents huddled together on the sofa and Jimmy stood by the door, as though ready to flee. Joanna sat in the remaining chair.

"Is Corinne suffering a miscarriage?" The question was directed to Joanna by the girl's mother.

Joanna shook her head. It was hard to even say the words. "Apparently Corinne decided to…abort the baby."

The blood drained from the mother's face. "An abortion? Corinne decided to get rid of the baby?"

Joanna nodded reluctantly.

"You arranged this?" the father asked Jimmy, his eyes narrowed and his face reddening.

"No! I swear I didn't know anything about it! Corinne told me she was going to see a friend and had me drop her off at a street corner downtown."

"You didn't know what she was doing?"

"I didn't have a clue. How could I, when she didn't even tell me she was pregnant." He hung his head and his tears dripped onto the tile floor.

"Why would she go to a backstreet abortionist?" Sharon Sullivan asked her husband, wringing her hands in shock. "Why wouldn't she talk to me about this?"

"How did she pay for it?" Bob asked Jimmy.

"I don't know," he told them. "I don't know anything."

"She was saving her money for Europe this summer," Corinne's mother whispered, gripping her husband's hand. "Where is she now?" she asked. "I want to be with her."

"Corinne's in surgery," Joanna explained.

"Surgery?" the mother repeated. "She'll be able to have other children, won't she?"

"I don't know," Joanna told them.

They sat in silence after that. Perhaps fifteen minutes later, the surgeon entered the room. He was dressed in surgical greens, a protective mask hanging around his neck. From the look in his eyes, Joanna knew. The girl was gone. She'd bled to death.

"I'm sorry," he said, and exhaled sharply.

Corinne's parents and Jimmy stared at him in confusion.

"Sorry?" Sharon Sullivan repeated. "Corinne can't have babies?"

The physician's gaze sought out Joanna's and she saw his regret and his sadness at relaying such horrific news to these parents. "Your daughter died on the operating table," he said. "We did everything we could."

A few seconds passed and then came an unearthly wail of anguish and disbelief. Corinne's mother buried her face in her hands and sobbed loudly.

"There's been a mistake. I'm sure this is all a mistake." Bob Sullivan stood and looked first to the physician and then to Joanna. He clenched his fists at his sides. "Corinne sat at the breakfast table with us this morning. She had a test in her Health class this afternoon. It was the only thing she talked about—this test was important. Now you're telling me my little girl is *dead?* No. There's been a mistake. Something isn't right. Corinne can't be dead."

"I'm sorry," the doctor said again. "She'd lost too much blood. It was too late."

Jimmy seemed close to shock. "She said I had to take her to Sister Angelina first," he whispered, his voice barely audible. "She should've told me, she should've talked to me about the baby." Turning away from them, he slammed his fist into the wall. He howled in grief and pain, then collapsed in sobs, huddled in agony on the floor.

Joanna felt tears pricking her eyes, unable to bear witnessing their pain.

"She can't be gone—this can't be happening," Sharon burst out. "Corinne and I are going to Europe this summer. We've been planning the trip for months."

"She's only sixteen," her father said to no one in particular.

"Is there someone I can phone?" the physician asked.

Bob Sullivan looked up as if he hadn't heard. "My baby girl can't be dead. She sat at the breakfast table with us this morning."

"Sister," Dr. Johnson whispered. "Perhaps you should call the rectory and ask that one of the priests come down to be with the parents."

Joanna nodded and wiped the tears from her own cheeks.

"I'll phone Father Sanders," she murmured, wrapping her arms around Sharon Sullivan. If there was any way she could take this pain away from them she would, but that was impossible. Death had struck again like a thief in the night, stealing what was most dear.

*chapter*

## SISTER ANGELINA

The November morning was clear and crisp, and Angie's spirits were high. The day before, she had received a letter from her father. His letters were so rare that she cherished each one and read them countless times. He seemed to be doing well and his news, as always, was about the restaurant. Angie had written back immediately. Knowing it would please him, she suggested she fly home to Buffalo that summer if it could be arranged. Her summers were often full of college classes and other commitments, but it had been far too long since she'd seen him.

That night she'd dreamed she was cooking in the restaurant kitchen, adding spices to a large pot of red sauce. When she woke that morning, she could almost smell the garlic cooking.

Humming to herself, Angie walked to the high school. She wasn't inside the building ten minutes before she heard the terrible news.

"Corinne? Dead?" she repeated, shocked, as Morgan Gentry came to her weeping hysterically. Surely there was some mistake. Corinne *couldn't* be dead.

"It's true, Sister, I swear it's true. My mother woke me up to tell me. She's with Corinne's mother now. They're at the funeral home picking out the casket."

Instant tears sprang to Angie's eyes.

As students filed into her first-period class, Angie noticed that a number of them were crying. Several came to her looking for consolation, but Angie had none to give. She assigned pages to be read and then sat at her desk numb with disbelief and pain. By noon she realized she could no longer teach that day.

With Sister Alberta's permission, she returned to the convent and sought out Sister Joanna.

"She was in your class?" Joanna asked, sitting in the chapel with Angie after they'd prayed together.

Angie nodded, still numbed by the pure shock of the news. "She was...just a child, with an inquisitive mind. I...can't accept this." She listened with horror as Joanna relayed the events of the night before. "Jimmy was there?"

"Yes," Sister Joanna said. "He took it hard. It would help if you talked to him," she told Angie. "He blames himself, but he didn't know. He would never have let her go through with the abortion if he had, I'm convinced of that."

"The abortion..." Even now, Angie couldn't absorb the fact that Corinne had done this. In class, they'd talked about the physical hazards of such actions, as well as the legal and moral questions. Corinne had voiced her opinions loud and clear, repeating the popular secular cry of a woman's right to control her own body. Angie had been dismayed by her attitude. The child she'd carried was a precious life. No less than her own...

"Talk to Jimmy," Sister Joanna advised again. "He badly wanted to speak to you. He came here looking for you. Apparently Corinne was desperate to find you before going to the hospital."

Angie jerked her head up. "He was here? Last night?" she

whispered. "*Jimmy* was the one who came to the door. Sister Kathleen told me there was a young man asking to see me, but I couldn't imagine who it might be." She wanted to kick herself now because the answer should have been obvious.

"I'm sure it was him," Sister Joanna said, confirming her suspicions. "He mentioned your name and said Corinne had insisted on talking to you."

Angie's heart ached, and this news did nothing to ease that pain. The girl had looked for her, and Angie had been un-available. The agony of knowing this settled on her with an almost unbearable weight.

That same afternoon, Angie was able to speak to Jimmy when he showed up at the convent a second time. The boy's right hand was in a cast, but when Angie questioned him about it, he shook off her concern.

"Corinne wanted you, Sister. Instead of letting me take her directly to the hospital, she begged me to drive to the con-vent and get you first. I should never have agreed but I didn't have any idea she was bleeding so much. She didn't want me to know."

"Oh, Jimmy." Tears streaked Angie's face as she tried to understand the reasons Corinne might have wanted to see her.

Jimmy wept too as he sat with her in the convent's visitor area. Looking away, he drew in a shaky breath. "I didn't know she was pregnant. I swear it, Sister!"

"I believe you." It seemed important to tell him that.

"Corinne insisted we couldn't use any protection," he mut-tered. "She wanted to live up to the Church's rules, even when she didn't agree with them."

"Why would she get an abortion then?" Angie cried.

Jimmy hung his head and the tears slipped from his eyes. "I don't know, Sister. I honestly don't know, but I think it was be-cause of her parents. I...I don't think she could face her mother or her father. She didn't want to disappoint them or...you."

"Oh, Jimmy." This was not something Angie wanted to hear.

"We did try to be careful, Sister...." He lifted his uninjured hand to his face and rubbed his eyes.

The young man left soon afterward, and Angie sat in shock and grief as she tried to make sense of what she'd learned. Sister Joanna had been so sure that talking to Jimmy would help the boy deal with his sorrow, but it had the opposite effect on her.

If anything, her own feeling of loss had grown worse. This young girl was dead. Corinne had challenged Angie constantly, forcing her to defend the Church and her own beliefs. But in the end, Angie had let the girl down. Without ever meaning to, Angie had hurt Jimmy, too.

Angie's tears began in earnest then. Not knowing where else to go, she went into the chapel, knelt at the altar and buried her face in her hands. It felt as if her world was askew, as if nothing was right and never would be again.

She didn't know how long she stayed there, but when she raised her head, afternoon shadows loomed against the chapel walls. Angie had grown emotionally numb, unable to feel, unable to react.

She returned to her cell and collapsed onto her bed. In all her years of serving Christ she had never experienced anything like this sense of emptiness. Corinne had asked Angie if she'd ever questioned authority. The girl had challenged Angie to reconsider Church decrees against birth control. She'd bombarded her with questions and when she didn't like the answers, she'd scoffed at what she saw as outdated views.

To Corinne it was ridiculous that priests couldn't marry and have families. She'd startled Angie once by suggesting that nuns should be able to celebrate Mass. Such thinking was sacrilegious. Angie couldn't imagine a nun being allowed to administer the Holy Sacrament.

Lying on her side on the bed, Angie saw a shadow outside her room. She'd assumed she was alone in the convent's sleeping quarters. She sat up. Perhaps someone had come looking for her.

Standing, Angie went to the doorway and glanced in both directions. "Sister Kathleen," she called when she saw the other nun who wore her coat and carried a small bag. Her veil was missing. Alarm bells rang in Angie's head.

Kathleen turned to face her, dropping her suitcase at her feet. "Sister Angelina," she said in a rush of sympathy. "I'm so sorry."

Angie bit her lower lip in order to keep fresh tears at bay. "Thank you," she whispered. "You're…leaving?"

Sister Kathleen nodded. "Yes, Sister. I'm going away."

"But where?"

Sister Kathleen leaned against the wall and searched her pocket, pulling out a tissue. It took Angie a moment to realize the other nun was weeping.

"What happened?" Angie asked. "What's wrong?"

Kathleen straightened. "It doesn't matter now… I'm going to Seattle. My brother lives there, and he told me years ago that he'd help me if ever I decided I had to walk away from this life. I phoned him."

"You're leaving the order?" They'd lost so many sisters already this year.

"I don't know…I need to think all of this out." Sister Kathleen dissolved into sobs. "I've been ordered to return to the motherhouse, but I can't go back to Boston and disgrace my family. I'd never be able to look my parents in the eye if they believed I'd…" She let the rest of her words fade.

It was clear to Angie that her friend was in agony over leaving. "Is there anything I can do to help?" she asked, although she doubted she was in any state to lend assistance.

Sister Kathleen shook her head. "Nothing. No one can… Sister Angelina, I'm sorry about not waking you last night. Had I known…"

"You did what was required." Had the situation been reversed, Angie would've done the same thing.

The other nun's relief was unmistakable.

"God be with you, Sister Kathleen," Angie whispered.

"Thank you," she whispered as she started down the corridor, carrying her small suitcase.

"Will you write and let us know what's happening with you?" Angie asked.

Sister Kathleen shrugged. "I will if I can. Goodbye, Sister."

"Goodbye," Angie returned. It seemed to be a day for farewells. First Corinne, and now her friend.

*chapter*

## SISTER JOANNA

Joanna was concerned about Sister Angelina, who'd taken Corinne Sullivan's death hard. When she first heard the news, Sister Angelina, like so many others, had reacted with shock and disbelief. Joanna had suggested Sister Angelina speak with Corinne's boyfriend; he needed emotional support and counseling to help him deal with his role in this tragedy. In retrospect, Joanna realized that while Sister might have consoled the young man, the conversation had only made her feel worse.

For reasons she couldn't fathom, Sister Angelina blamed herself for what had happened to Corinne. She wasn't sleeping, wasn't eating and hadn't been able to return to school for a week following the funeral.

All Sister Angelina seemed capable of doing was staring at the wall and weeping. Everyone was worried, including Sister Superior, who'd called in a physician.

Joanna didn't know what was said, but she suspected the doctor had prescribed tranquilizers. Now, as she sat in the hospital chapel, Joanna prayed for her friend, prayed for Corinne's parents who'd suffered such a grievous loss. She prayed for Jimmy whose life was forever altered by the death of his girlfriend and his unborn child.

While she was whispering her prayers, Joanna prayed for herself. More and more she'd grown dissatisfied with her life. For six years she'd constantly reassured her mother that she hadn't entered the convent on the rebound. Yes, if Greg had come home from Vietnam without a wife they would've been married and by now she would have produced the requisite two point five children and lived in a house with a white picket fence. But Greg hadn't come home to marry her, and Joanna's future had taken a detour.

In her pain and humiliation, she'd turned to God for comfort. She'd believed with all her heart that He was calling her to the religious life. She had trusted to the very depths of her soul that becoming a Sister of St. Bridget's was the right decision for her.

Then she'd met Dr. Murray and everything changed. For six years she'd ignored every part of her femininity. Yet God was the one who'd created her as a woman. He'd been the one who'd given her breasts and a womb, who'd given her sexuality. Being a nun meant rejecting all sexual feeling, and she was no longer sure she could do that.

Shortly after Corinne Sullivan's death, Joanna had gone to the maternity floor. The nurse Dr. Murray was seeing worked in the delivery room and Joanna wanted to catch a glimpse of her. She had no intention of introducing herself or making any effort to speak to the other woman. Curiosity had nagged her into taking this action, but in the end Joanna hadn't seen Jenny.

Instead she'd gotten waylaid at the nursery. For reasons she didn't want to examine, she'd stopped in front of the nursery window and stared at the babies. These perfect, beautiful children had caught her attention as soon as she stepped off the elevator.

It had been years since Joanna had held an infant, years

since she'd smelled that special scent. Years since her maternal instincts had struck this hard.

Seeing that she was enraptured by the newborns, the head nurse had invited her inside and urged her into a rocking chair. Then, as if knowing exactly what Joanna wanted, the grandmotherly nurse had placed a newborn in her empty embrace.

The little boy fit perfectly in the cradle of her arms. For a terrifying moment, Joanna had been afraid to breathe, afraid to move. But gradually instinct took over, and she began to rock the baby. Softly, gently. Peace, unlike anything she'd experienced in years, came to her then. A sense of wonderment settled over her, and in that moment she felt completely happy.

Tears had pooled in Joanna's eyes, embarrassing her. Yet no one spoke. Thirty minutes later, when she walked toward the elevator, her original mission forgotten, she was a changed woman.

It was as if she'd seen into her own heart. She was like women all through the ages. She wanted what women had always wanted: to be loved and cherished by a man, and to have that love bring forth children. She wanted a husband and family, and the ache of having neither left a void inside her that couldn't be ignored.

The chapel door opened and Joanna realized she wasn't alone anymore. She made the sign of the cross, sat on the wooden pew and folded back the kneeler. But as she was ready to stand and leave, Dr. Murray moved into the pew beside her.

The shock of seeing him stole her breath. For the longest moment they stared at each other, saying nothing.

Tim spoke first. "I've been worried about you."

Who had told him? How could he possibly have known her doubts and her thoughts when she'd shared them with no one but God?

"Why?"

"I heard about Corinne Sullivan. Did you know her?"

Joanna shook her head. "She was a student at St. Peter's High School but I didn't know her."

"I heard you were with her family when they received the news."

"Yes." It was one of the saddest nights of her life. To the day she died, Joanna would remember the haunting grief of Corinne's parents. To lose a child, especially under such conditions, was a tragedy beyond words. And Jimmy Durango— the poor boy felt guilt as well as grief. None of their lives would ever be the same.

"How are they doing?" Tim asked. He sat only a few inches away, but after their initial greeting he hadn't looked at her again.

How was any family able to cope after the loss of a child? "About as well as can be expected," Joanna said.

He nodded and then, his voice the merest of whispers, he added, "I've missed you. The entire third floor misses you."

"I miss everyone there, too." And she did. Working E.R. wasn't the same. The staff had welcomed her, but Joanna felt like a stranger, trying to find her place and fit in with the others. The suddenness of her transfer had created a certain amount of suspicion and plenty of speculation.

"I know why you asked to be transferred," Tim went on, "and I agree it was for the best, but that doesn't mean you aren't missed."

She bowed her head, not wanting him to read what she could no longer hide. Almost from the beginning Joanna had been physically and emotionally attracted to this man. That attraction had blossomed and taken root in her dreams, those disruptive sexual dreams that continued to obsess her. It was as though the womanly part of her, once repressed, had broken free. Refusing to be ignored, the fantasies had lingered in her mind, in her waking moments, invading even her prayer life.

"But even though I understand why you asked for the transfer, I don't know if it was the right thing for either of us." His words were low and intense. He reached for her hand and held it firmly in his own.

Joanna was astonished by how much his touch affected her. A lump formed in her throat as she splayed her hand and let their fingers intertwine.

"I know I shouldn't touch you, shouldn't even be this close, but Joanna…" He bent his head near hers and his lips brushed her cheek.

Eyes closed, she swayed toward him and their foreheads touched. "So much is happening all at once," she murmured.

"I'm falling in love with you…."

"Don't say it, please." She placed a finger against his lips. "Just let me know where I stand with you. That's all I ask."

"I can't…" Before she could finish, the chapel door opened and Sister Nadine walked inside. She paused when she found Joanna sitting with Dr. Murray and frowned darkly.

Joanna eased her head away from Tim's, but the other nun's gaze lowered to their locked hands. Almost immediately, she turned and walked out of the chapel.

"Does that mean trouble?" Tim asked, exhaling forcefully at the other nun's rapid departure.

Joanna didn't know what it would mean; nevertheless, she tried to reassure him. "It's probably nothing to worry about." He seemed to accept that and she was grateful.

But Joanna was wrong. Sister Superior asked to see her the following afternoon; Joanna didn't need to be told why. It was as if this confrontation was meant to be.

By now, Sister Eloise's office should be a familiar place to her. Joanna recalled the troubles she'd had in the beginning, while she was a postulant and then a novice at the motherhouse in Boston. Battling her stubbornness and her lack of submissiveness had never become any easier.

"Sister Joanna," the head of the convent said, looking up from her desk. She hesitated and seemed to search for the right words. "The last time we spoke, you mentioned your attraction to one of the physicians at St. Elizabeth's."

Joanna merely nodded.

"At that time we both felt it would be best to have you transferred to another area of the hospital."

"Yes, Sister."

"That hasn't helped, has it? You haven't been able to subdue your rebellious nature, have you?"

"No," she admitted, struggling to hold back the guilt. "But

Sister, you reminded me that while we're nuns, we're still women, too. I love this man with all my heart." Never before had Joanna dared to acknowledge her feelings out loud.

"And he returns your love?" she asked.

"Yes… Maybe… I don't know." She prayed he did, but yesterday was the first time they'd spoken honestly, however briefly, about their feelings.

"What do you want to do, Sister?"

Joanna bowed her head, unable to meet her Superior's eyes. "I don't know…I just don't know."

"Would you like to transfer to another convent?"

Joanna looked up and shook her head. The ache inside her intensified. "I want to go home," she whispered.

"You are home, Sister," the other nun said.

"Home to my family," Joanna elaborated. "I need to think about all this. I need time. I'm sorry, Sister Eloise, I'm so sorry. I feel like I've failed you and failed God."

Sister Eloise was quiet for so long that Joanna wondered if she was about to refuse her. "You're sure this is what you want?" she finally asked.

"Yes…I'm not saying I'm leaving the order. What I need is time to sort through these feelings and know my own heart, to consider the future."

"A leave of absence then?"

"Yes," Joanna whispered as the tears burned her eyes. Suddenly the life that had seemed so calm and predictable had become confused. Chaotic. Sister Kathleen was gone. Joanna wasn't quite sure what had happened, but she'd left the day after Corinne Sullivan died. Then there was Sister Angelina, who was devastated by Corinne's death and had been in a state of depression ever since. Now, Joanna, too, was experiencing a crisis of faith.

"Very well," Sister Eloise said reluctantly. "Return to your family."

# chapter 32

## SISTER ANGELINA

Something was wrong with her, Angie decided. She couldn't seem to get enough sleep. That morning, she'd embarrassed herself by falling asleep during lauds. Right in the chapel, she'd nearly keeled over onto Sister Martha. Fortunately the other nun had managed to catch her.

Angie's appetite was nonexistent and the skirt she'd shortened only a couple of months earlier was so loose it hung on her hips.

Only recently she'd tried to talk to her father on the phone and all she'd been able to do was weep. He'd been upset and tried to discover what was wrong, but she couldn't tell him, couldn't bring herself to admit how bad she was. Instead she'd made light of her tears and ended the conversation as quickly as she could.

Sister Superior was worried about her, too. Worried enough to call for a Catholic physician to come and talk to her. Angie didn't need a doctor to tell her she was depressed—or to give her medication.

She knew why she felt the way she did. What she didn't know was how to deal with this never-ceasing mental anguish, this constant sense of guilt and doubt.

Everyone had been so kind and gentle with her. She tried, she really did, to shake off the mantle of grief, but it clung to her. The world seemed dark and ugly, and it seemed that nothing good would ever happen again. All gaiety and laughter had evaporated into the darkness.

As the Christmas holidays approached, there was an air of celebration at the convent, an anticipation of joy. Angie experienced none of this. It was difficult to function, to pretend she was preparing the next day's lessons when she rarely put any thought or effort into her classes anymore. Luckily, with Thanksgiving, there was a four-day break coming this very week.

Staring down at the textbook as the nuns around her worked at the long tables, silence filling the room, Angie tried to force her thoughts onto the next day's lessons, but to no avail.

Instead, her mind continually returned to Corinne's parents. Again and again she was tormented by the question of how Bob and Sharon Sullivan were going to face this holiday season without their beautiful Corinne. How would it be possible for them to put up a Christmas tree and decorate their home when their only daughter had recently been buried? Where was their joy? Where was—

"Sister?"

Angie looked up from her book and realized Sister Martha had been speaking to her.

"I'm sorry," she said. "I didn't hear you."

"There's a man here to see you."

"A man?"

"Yes, Sister. He's quite insistent. He says he's your father."

"My father?" Angie was sure she'd misunderstood. "My father is in Buffalo, New York." The Thanksgiving week was one of the busiest of the year for the restaurant. He would never leave Angelina's to travel at such an important time.

"He would like to see you," Sister Martha said.

Angie got up from the table. Although she knew there must be a mistake, her heart raced. Could her father really be here in Minneapolis?

As she entered the foyer, her steps slowed. It was indeed her father. He stood in the entry, still in his thick overcoat, hat in hand as he waited.

"Daddy," she whispered.

Tony Marcello looked up, his face dark with concern. When he saw her, a smile came to his lips and he held out his arms.

As if she were a little girl again, Angie ran into his embrace. By the time she felt his arms around her, the tears had come, ravaging her with huge, breath-choking sobs.

He cradled her like a child, his hand on her head as he hugged her close. He murmured to her in Italian, in words she hadn't heard for so many years that she barely remembered their meaning. Then they were sitting on the sofa, where he continued to hold her protectively. "Angelina, my poor, sweet Angelina, what has happened to you?" He brushed the hair from her forehead, and in the process dislodged her veil. His eyes searched hers.

Through her tears, his features swam before her. She felt his love, and God help her for being weak and emotional, but Angie needed his strength—just as much as the motherless child she'd once been.

"What has happened to you?" he repeated in a broken whisper as though he too was close to tears.

"She's dead, Daddy. Corinne is dead. I told her it was wrong—I'm the one to blame. I'm the one who urged her to be a good Catholic girl. Then she got pregnant."

"This high school girl?"

Angie nodded. "She panicked—she was so afraid. I knew things weren't right. I sensed it and I did nothing. *Nothing.*" She wailed in grief and guilt and hid her face in his shoulder. "She came to find me instead of going to the hospital…and she bled to death."

"Oh, Angie, sweet, sweet Angie."

"She's dead...gone, and it's my fault."

"No, Angie, no."

Others had attempted to tell her the same thing, but Angie discounted their words and refused to accept her innocence in Corinne's death.

Because Angie believed she *was* responsible. Corinne had come to her time and again and argued against the Church's stand on these important issues. Angie realized now that the girl had come to her seeking answers, searching for a way to rationalize what she and Jimmy were experiencing. Corinne had been seeking a tacit blessing to use birth control.

Angie hadn't given it to her, hadn't agreed with her arguments and as a result, Corinne had chosen to engage in unprotected sex. Then she'd discovered she was pregnant and her world had come crashing down. Angie's world had toppled, too.

As she'd mulled over her conversations with Corinne, Angie reached a conclusion. The girl *was* right. Such intimate decisions as whether or not to use birth control were between a man and a woman, between husband and wife. The Church had no business interfering, no Biblical ground on which to stand. The consequences of this decree were more and more apparent every week at Sunday Mass. Catholics were revolting and walking away from the Church, or at the very least choosing to follow their own consciences in the matter of birth control.

Corinne's words haunted her. If the Church was wrong about birth control, then what else might be a mistake? Angie was afraid to examine that question.

"Angelina, Angelina," her father crooned. "I'm taking you home with me."

She looked up at him, frowning. "I don't think I can leave."

"You aren't in jail. You need to come home."

She didn't argue. She didn't have the strength.

"Go, collect what you need and send Sister Superior to speak to me."

With one exception—her insistence on becoming a nun—

Angie had always followed orders. First from her father and then from the sisters who ran the order and the convents in which she'd lived. She never questioned authority, but accepted whatever she was told, did whatever she was asked. Her thoughts were subordinate to those of others—older, wiser people, whom she'd entrusted with her life.

She stepped away from her father.

"Go," he ordered. "It's time you left, time you realized this place is not for you. It never was, but I couldn't refuse you."

Angie found Sister Eloise in the room where the other nuns sat and quietly worked or studied. "Sister," she said, "my father is here."

"So I understand." Her disapproval was evident.

"He would like to speak to you."

Sister Eloise nodded. "He couldn't have come during the day? It is highly unusual for family members to stop by unannounced this late in the evening."

"No," she said without emotion. "He's here now."

While Sister Superior met with her father, Angie went to her cell, pulled out her overnight case and packed her things. She placed her clothes neatly inside the case; it didn't take long to pack. With her coat over one arm and her suitcase in the other, she returned to the foyer.

Her father stood as she approached.

"I can't allow you to leave," Sister Superior said, her expression severe.

"You can't stop us," her father said, his jaw set. "I've come to take my Angelina home."

"Sister Angelina, I implore you to reconsider."

Without speaking, Angie moved closer to her father's side.

He took the suitcase from her hand and held open the door. The cold night air stung Angie's face as she stepped into the darkness.

"We're going home, Angelina."

"Yes, Daddy. We're going home."

*chapter*

## SISTER KATHLEEN

Kathleen added cream to the large pot of mashed potatoes and turned on the hand mixer. Sean's wife, Loren, was busy preparing the platter of turkey and stuffing for the dining room table.

"Aunt Kathleen, Aunt Kathleen, help me," four-year-old Emma cried as she chased the calico cat around and around Kathleen's legs while two-year-old Paul sat in the middle of the room pounding on an overturned pot with a wooden spoon. The television blared in the background.

"Emma, go see your daddy," Loren said.

"Daddy sent me in here."

The phone rang in the distance. "I'll get it," Sean shouted from the living room, where he was watching a football game. This was like no Thanksgiving Kathleen could remember. In Boston it was a huge family affair, with as many as twenty people, and her mother supervising in the kitchen. At the convent it had been another matter entirely, a formal and subdued celebration but with the same roasted turkey and pumpkin pie. With Sean and his family, it was three adults and the two children in a cramped two-bedroom house.

Her brother, God love him, had taken Kathleen in on a moment's notice. He'd even given her money for the flight to Seattle. She was well aware that she couldn't continue to impose on Sean and his wife. She had to make a decision and move forward.

"Kathleen," her brother called, standing by the telephone.

She turned off the mixer and peered around the corner. "Yes?"

"Do you know a Father Brian Doyle?"

She was so stunned all she could do was nod.

"He'd like to speak to you." Sean held out the receiver, and when she'd accepted it, he returned to his football game, but lowered the volume.

"Father Doyle?" Kathleen asked, pressing the receiver to her ear.

"Sister Kathleen, how are you?"

"I'm well, and you?"

"Good," he said. "Good. It's taken me this long to find you."

"I'm sorry, I should have contacted you."

"No one seemed to want to tell me where I could reach you," he said. "I was finally able to locate your parents in Boston and they gave me this number."

"I'm in Seattle."

"So I understand." He sounded out of breath. "What happened?"

It all seemed too complicated to explain. In the two weeks since she'd left, Kathleen had made an effort to forget.

"Tell me," he urged.

"I told Father Sanders I could no longer keep the books for him," she said, going back to their conversation shortly before his move to Osseo. "Just like you suggested."

"Yes, that's good, but apparently there was some kind of trouble afterward."

"There was," she whispered. All at once she felt too weak to stand and sank down onto the sofa arm. "Father Yates decided to audit the books and almost immediately discovered the discrepancies."

She heard the slow release of Father Doyle's breath. "I was afraid of something like that," he muttered.

"Then Father Yates contacted Sister Eloise."

His silence said everything. He knew without her elaborating how uncomfortable the situation had been.

"I assume you didn't explain that I was the one making up the shortfalls?" he said heavily.

"No."

"Why not?" His voice was incredulous. "I would've stepped forward and told the truth. There was no need for you to go through this alone." She heard him sigh. "In my eagerness to serve the bishop and help Father Sanders, I was more of a hindrance than anything else. Now I see I'm responsible for your troubles as well."

Kathleen disagreed. "I was ultimately the one in charge of the books. Not you. It was only right that I accept responsibility for my role in all this."

"But at what cost?" His words were angry—and regretful. She had no answer to give him.

"Why did you leave the convent?" he asked next. "Or did Sister Eloise send you away?" .

"Sister Superior instructed me to return to Boston," Kathleen said reluctantly. "But I chose to come to Seattle instead."

"But isn't Boston your hometown?"

"Yes, but I was going back in disgrace, an embarrassment to the order and I…I couldn't. I just couldn't look my parents in the eyes and tell them I'd done wrong."

"You didn't," Father Doyle insisted. "I was the one who—"

"We both did," Kathleen whispered.

"Sister Kathleen, I can't tell you how sorry I am."

He had nothing to apologize for. Worse, he blamed himself for not being there to protect her.

"It's my fault," he said. "I'm the one who should've been reprimanded. If I hadn't tried to protect Father Sanders, none of this would have happened."

"I don't think it's necessary to assign blame, Father. What's done is done." Kathleen felt better just hearing his voice. She'd missed him terribly. Other than a few of the nuns she taught with, Father Doyle was her only friend; they'd shared this burden and helped each other and in the process had developed a certain closeness, careful though it was.

"What can I do?" he asked, obviously distressed.

"Do?" she repeated. "Nothing."

"I don't believe that. First thing tomorrow morning, I'm contacting the motherhouse and explaining the circumstances," he said. "I refuse to allow you to be punished."

"Please don't," Kathleen pleaded. "Father, I'm sincere about that. This business with Father Sanders and Father Yates has helped me."

"How?" He didn't sound as though he believed her.

"It's clarified some issues I…hadn't realized I needed to deal with."

"What issues?"

"We don't need to discuss those now." Kathleen preferred not to delve into the whole complicated mess. She felt resentful and angry and misjudged. With Father Doyle gone, she'd been left vulnerable, facing a difficult situation on her own. She'd hoped, had *believed* that her own order would come to her defense; instead her superiors had condemned her without even hearing her version of events.

"If that's what you want." Father Doyle didn't seem happy with her reticence.

"I do." She felt strong, stronger than she had in a long while.

"What about the future?"

"I don't know what to tell you."

"You're leaving the convent, aren't you?"

No one else had asked her that question. Not her brother or her sister-in-law, not her parents. Had they voiced it, Kathleen wasn't sure how she would've responded, but the minute Father Doyle asked, the answer was clear.

"Yes," she whispered, "I've decided to leave."

She heard the priest's harsh intake of breath. "I was afraid you were going to say that."

"I'm positive it's the right decision," she assured him. She stood, easing herself off the sofa arm. She had given nearly ten years of her life to the Church without ever truly questioning her vocation. But in that time, the world had changed—and so had she.

"I called for another reason," Father Doyle said. "I got word this morning that Father Sanders was in a car accident."

"No," she gasped. "Was he drunk?"

"Yes."

"How bad is it?" Her greatest fear was that Father Sanders had injured an innocent party or killed himself in a drunken crash.

"He walked away from the accident and thank God no one else was hurt."

Kathleen murmured her fervent relief.

"God used the accident to get Father the help I couldn't," the priest continued. "He was arrested for drunk driving and the judge placed him in a facility that specializes in the treatment of alcoholics."

She said a silent prayer of thanksgiving.

"Unfortunately—" he sighed "—the press got hold of the story and it's front-page news."

As far as Kathleen was concerned, it was Bishop Schmidt who'd brought the bad publicity down upon the diocese. If he'd listened to Father Doyle and taken steps to help Father Sanders earlier, the outcome might have been very different.

"What about Father Yates?"

The priest laughed softly. "He's been promoted and will be assuming Father Sanders's position as head of St. Peter's."

Kathleen laughed, too.

The line went quiet for a moment, and Kathleen supposed it was the end of their friendship. They had no reason to maintain contact. "Thank you, Father, for calling, and for telling me about Father Sanders."

"I'm the one who should be thanking you."

"Would you mind…I mean, if it would be all right, I'd like to talk to you every now and then." Where she got the courage to ask, she didn't know. But he was a link with her past and she faced so many transitions as she moved toward the future. It would be good to have a special friend she could call when she needed to.

"I'd like that, Sister Kathleen."

"Just Kathleen," she corrected.

"Kathleen," he repeated softly. "Write down my number and phone me anytime you wish."

"Thank you."

After a few words of farewell, she replaced the receiver and looked up to see her brother and Loren and the two youngest O'Shaughnessys waiting by the table. She joined them, their Thanksgiving feast about to begin.

"Are you ready?" Sean asked.

Kathleen nodded. She was ready now for whatever the future held.

# PART 4

# OUT OF THE HABIT

But small is the gate and narrow the road
that leads to life and only a few find it.

*Matthew 7:14*

*chapter*

## KATHLEEN O'SHAUGHNESSY

Sean and Loren insisted Kathleen stay with the family until after the Christmas holidays. By the first week of January, she realized she had to stop relying on her brother. It was time to make her own decisions and to begin relying on herself. Walking away from the convent the way she had, without a word to her superiors, had been an act of defiance and anger. Only recently had she been in touch with the motherhouse. The conversation had been brief; by mutual agreement it was determined that Kathleen would take a one-year leave of absence. She would continue to receive her small salary and she'd start attending classes at Seattle University. St. Bridget's Sisters of the Assumption would pay her tuition fees.

"Are you sure about this?" her brother asked as he loaded her suitcase into the trunk of his car. Retired from the Army, Sean worked at Boeing building airplanes and his wife stayed home with their children.

"Of course, I'm sure," Kathleen told him, although she was

frightened out of her wits. She would be living in a group home called House of Peace, a facility set up by a group of former nuns who had dedicated themselves to helping other women like themselves move from the convent back into the world.

Mother Superior had agreed to give Kathleen this year, with the stipulation that she would accept counseling. It was Sister Agnes's fear that Kathleen's desire to leave was primarily a reaction to the unfortunate circumstances with Father Sanders. Mother was afraid Kathleen would regret her decision later.

"I'll do whatever I can to help you," Sean said, opening the car door.

"You already have," Kathleen said and impulsively hugged him. Nervous as she was, she found it difficult to release him. "I don't know what I would've done without you and Loren these last two months." It was disconcerting to have no home. She'd been under her parents' roof until she'd entered the convent and now, when she was nearing age thirty, she had no place to call her own.

"You'll come see us soon, won't you?" Loren asked, standing on the damp lawn with the two children leaning against her.

"Of course I will," Kathleen promised. "As often as you want." Crouching, she held her arms open to her niece and nephew. Emma threw small arms around her neck, while two-year-old Paul hugged her upper arm. After a few moments, Loren pulled her protesting children free.

Tears filled Kathleen's eyes as her brother backed out of the driveway. "I can't thank you enough," she whispered, not wanting him to hear the emotion in her voice.

"Mom and Dad think you should come home."

"I can't. I don't want to be a burden to them—or to you."

"You're not a burden to me. And Mom and Dad would never think of you as a burden, either."

Perhaps not, but she was a disappointment to her family and she knew it. Kathleen didn't have the emotional strength to answer her parents' questions. Dealing with her new life was complicated enough.

As for seeing a counselor, she welcomed the opportunity to talk about her feelings. Her one wish was that if she had to sort through all the emotions associated with leaving the convent, it be with a counselor she knew and trusted—preferably Father Doyle. The priest, however, was in Osseo, Minnesota, and she was in Seattle.

"You're going to be all right," Sean assured her.

"I know." But she didn't entirely believe it. The world outside the convent was a frightening place. Kathleen didn't know what to expect or how to cope with all the changes that were hurtling toward her.

"You can call Loren or me anytime."

"Thank you." She swallowed hard.

"It can be a cruel, lonely world when you're alone," her brother warned, "but you *aren't* alone. Remember that."

"I will." It was as though Kathleen was in high school all over again and her big brother was giving her advice.

She knew Sean was worried about her, but her brother had his own life and his own problems. Sooner or later, Kathleen needed to start taking care of herself, and there was no better time to learn than right now, at the beginning of a brand-new year. The world of 1973 was a different place than it had been ten years ago.

When Sean pulled up in front of the House of Peace, Kathleen saw that it was a large, two-story white home with one large dormer above a screened-in porch. There was a trimmed laurel hedge on each side of the narrow walkway that led to the front steps. A Christmas wreath still hung on the door inside the porch, and she saw the welcoming glow of lamplight, dispersing a little of the day's gloom.

After a moment, with her brother at her side, Kathleen walked up the steps. She held her breath and rang the doorbell. Someone must've been waiting on the other side, because it opened immediately.

"You must be Kathleen." A woman of about sixty with short white hair and a pleasantly round figure greeted her. "I'm Kay Dickson. We spoke on the phone."

Kathleen felt warmed by Kay's smile.

"Come in, come in." The other woman held open the door for them.

Sean hesitated as he set down Kathleen's suitcase. "I should be getting back home." His eyes questioned her, as if he felt uncertain about leaving her at this stranger's house.

"I'll be fine," she told him, and in that instant she knew it was true.

This was a new beginning for her. She could walk away from her life as Sister Kathleen with her head held high. Yes, there was some bitterness, some anger and hurt feelings, but she would learn to deal with that. Overall she had no regrets. She was ready for this second stage of her adulthood.

"There are five others living here," Kay explained as she led Kathleen up the stairs and showed her the bedroom reserved for her. It had a double bed, a dresser with a mirror and a nightstand that held a small lamp. This would be the first time in her life that she'd slept in a double bed. That room was luxury beyond anything she'd ever known.

"Breakfast is served at six. When's your first class?"

"Eight."

"That's perfect then."

"Am I the only one going to school?" Kathleen hated to ask, but the thought of navigating a college campus on her own felt overwhelming. It wasn't as though she'd been completely sheltered in the convent. For that matter, she'd traveled from one end of Boston to the other on city buses in her teens. But being friendless in a strange town, attending a strange school, was suddenly terrifying.

"Sandy and Pauline are both taking classes at Seattle University. They'll be happy to have you join them."

Kathleen set her bag on the end of the bed. "Thank you." Everyone was being so kind.

"We're having lunch in a few minutes. Please join us. There's a work schedule in the kitchen. We'll ask you to sign up for chores, but it isn't necessary to do anything for the first couple of days. We recognize that this is a major adjustment."

"I want to help," Kathleen said. She needed the comfort of routine and a sense of giving back instead of merely receiving. Although she deeply appreciated everything Sean and Loren had done for her, they'd treated her as though she was recovering from a long debilitating illness. It was only at her insistence that they let her help with even the most mundane household tasks.

After a lunch of pea soup and warm bread—just right for such a cold, gloomy day—Kathleen sat down and wrote her parents a letter, in which she reassured them that she was happy and well. When she'd finished, she tore a second sheet of paper from her notepad and wrote Father Doyle. Her purpose was the same; he'd sounded concerned when they'd spoken on Thanksgiving Day and she wanted to let him know she was fine. She'd mailed him a short letter with a card at Christmas but hadn't heard back.

The phone rang and Kay came into the kitchen, holding open the swinging door. "It's for you, Kathleen," she said.

Surprised, Kathleen walked into the hallway, where the phone rested on a small table by the stairs. "Hello," she said, assuming it was her brother. No one else knew she was at the House of Peace.

"Sister Kathleen—Kathleen—it's Father Doyle. I hope you don't mind that I tracked you down. Your brother told me where I could reach you."

"I was just writing you!"

"I apologize for not answering your Christmas card. How are you?"

She opened her mouth to tell him what she told everyone else—but he was the one person she could trust with her real feelings. "A little shaky, actually."

"I thought so. How can I help?"

He could move to Seattle, become her counselor, hold her hand for the next twelve months and reassure her that she was doing the right thing.

"You could be my friend, Father."

"I already am." He chuckled softly. "We're friends, Kathleen. Good friends."

# 35

*chapter*

## JOANNA BAIRD

"Can I get you anything, honey?" Sandra Baird asked, checking on Joanna one evening early in the new year. Joanna sat in front of the television watching the eleven o'clock news. Five Watergate defendants had pled guilty that day to burglary. The news was dominated by the break-in at the Watergate complex and the possible link to President Nixon.

"I'm fine, Mom," she said, reaching for the remote control. This device was new since she'd entered the convent and she found it both amazing and ridiculous. What was the world coming to when people couldn't be bothered to walk across their living rooms to change channels or turn off the TV?

Dressed in her robe, her mother came into the darkened room and sat on the edge of the sofa. Her father was already asleep. Sandra took Joanna's hand and held it loosely. "It's good to have you home."

It didn't feel good to Joanna. Her mother was suffocating her with attention. And her father, her dear sweet father, was as confused as she was. Half the time he called her Sister and then with a look of pain and regret apologized profusely. He'd loved the fact that she was a nun and had taken such pride in her vocation. Now that she was home, he didn't know how to react to her. All her life, Joanna had been close to her parents. This uneasiness and concern grated until she wanted to scream.

Her father didn't understand why she'd asked for a leave of absence, and she couldn't explain it to him. He wanted her to be happy, but he also wanted her to be a nun.

Her mother, on the other hand, was thrilled to have her home and came up with a hundred reasons each day to entice her back into the world. Since Joanna's return, Sandra had made hair appointments for them both, plus she'd arranged for a manicure and pedicure. She'd taken Joanna clothes-shopping and bought her several new outfits.

As a result, Joanna felt as though she was living with a foot in each world. Part nun, part not—and all of her very confused.

It had seemed so simple when she'd first decided to ask for a leave of absence. All she needed was time away—a few weeks, a couple of months at most. Just enough time to re-view her options.

However, the longer she was away from the convent, the more complex her emotions became. She missed the order and ritual of her life. There was a certain comfort she hadn't ap-preciated in rising and going to bed at the same time each day, in praying and eating according to schedule. It was a life of symmetry. Of harmony. The unfamiliar freedom she experi-enced living with her parents was awkward and confusing.

"You seem so quiet since you've been home," her mother complained.

"Mother, I observed Grand Silence for years. I'm not as talkative as I was when I was a teenager."

Her mother glanced uncomfortably toward the blank tele-vision screen. "Remind me what Grand Silence is again."

"Every night after seven-thirty, we didn't speak."

"Ever?"

"On rare occasions. It was the time we set aside to pray and meditate."

"You were always praying. I never did understand what you had to pray about at all hours of the night and day."

"Mother, I was a nun."

"I know, dear, but…" She gave a wry smile. "Well, that's all behind you now."

"Is it, Mom?" Joanna asked because she wasn't sure.

Her mother patted her hand as though to convince her that soon everything would be as it always had. "By the way, Greg phoned and asked to see you."

Joanna shook her head. "I don't want anything to do with Greg."

"I know. I told him that, but he seems to think—"

"That I left the convent because of him."

"Yes," her mother confirmed.

"I didn't. His visit to Minneapolis had nothing to do with my coming home."

Her mother's fingers tightened around hers. "All your father and I want is for you to be happy."

Joanna gave her mother a reassuring smile and stood. "I'm going to bed now."

"Good idea. You have a big day ahead of you."

Joanna nodded. She was applying for a job at the local hospital. Although her parents wanted her to live with them indefinitely, Joanna couldn't do that. The walls felt like they were closing in on her; she wanted her own place. Thankfully, because of her nursing degree, she could support herself. Joanna was also convinced that through her nursing skills she could find a sense of balance in life.

"Good night, honey," her mother called as Joanna entered her bedroom.

"Good night." Sitting in the dark at the end of her bed, Joanna thought about her interview the next morning. Then, out of habit, she slipped to her knees and reached for her rosary.

When she'd finished the five decades—ten Hail Marys

each—of the Joyful Mysteries, she kissed the crucifix and set the rosary back on her nightstand. As soon as she'd nestled her head on the pillow, Tim Murray's image appeared in her mind. She allowed herself this one extravagance: while in bed, alone, she talked to him. She told him about her day and how confused she felt and she mentioned her regrets. He was involved in several of those. Her feelings for him were tangled up with her dissatisfactions, and she knew she needed a clear head before she spoke to him again.

One regret was that she'd left the convent without telling him goodbye. There hadn't been time. Perhaps he'd assume she'd returned to Providence because of Greg. She hadn't, of course, and she hoped Tim wouldn't think that.

Sometimes, usually at night, she wondered if he still thought about her at all. Did he ask about her? Did he know where she was? Did he care? Or was he relieved that their paths would no longer cross? Joanna could only speculate about the answers. Whenever she did, a sinking sensation settled in the pit of her stomach.

The house was quiet when Joanna woke the following morning. Her father had gone to work, and her mother had a volunteer committee meeting first thing. As though Joanna were a child, her mother had left a note that told her what to eat for breakfast.

Reading the list propped against the sugar canister, she smiled and helped herself to a banana, which wasn't on the suggested menu.

Standing under the hot spray of the shower a few minutes later, Joanna luxuriated in the perfumed soap and creamy shampoo. This was decadence unlike anything she'd known in six years.

While combing her hair, Joanna stared at the fog-covered mirror. As the steam from the shower slowly dissipated, her facial features began to take shape. For a long time she studied her own reflection. It was like watching herself emerge from behind a veil. As good a metaphor as any, she thought wryly. She was becoming reacquainted with Joanna Baird—

but this Joanna was a different person from the one who'd entered the convent six years before.

After dressing for her hospital interview, Joanna poured a cup of coffee and on impulse, picked up the phone. It had been wrong to leave Minneapolis without talking to Tim. He deserved to know what had happened and why she'd left the way she did.

She got his office number from directory assistance and then promptly changed her mind. Wadding up the paper, she threw it in the garbage. Halfway out the door, Joanna changed her mind again and retrieved the phone number. If she called him now, she'd have a legitimate excuse—asking him for a reference.

Her skin went cold and clammy as she dialed the number. The phone rang, jolting her. She closed her eyes, waiting for his receptionist to answer.

"Dr. Murray's office."

"Ah…"

"Would you like to make an appointment?"

Not knowing what else to say, Joanna answered, "Yes."

"Are you already a patient?"

"No, actually—"

"I'm sorry. Dr. Murray isn't taking any new patients without a referral."

"I see." It didn't surprise her to learn that he was a popular surgeon. "In that case, would it be possible to leave a message?"

"Of course."

"Would you please tell him Joanna Baird phoned?"

"B-a-i-r-d?"

"That's correct."

"And your message?"

"Tell him…tell him Sister Joanna phoned to say goodbye."

"Oh. Goodbye," the receptionist said, sounding confused.

"Also, could you please tell him I'd like to use him as a job reference?"

A moment of silence followed and Joanna could hear a pencil scratching. "I'll let him know."

"Thank you," she whispered feeling more foolish than ever. She hung up the phone.

# chapter 36

## ANGELINA MARCELLO

The shades were down and shadows flickered across the bare walls in Angie's childhood bedroom. Her father had left it exactly as it was in 1958, when she'd entered the convent. Judging by outward appearances, not a month had passed. Everything looked exactly the same. Only it wasn't. Angie was vastly different from the eighteen-year-old who'd left home to become a nun.

Her father had stormed into the convent and wrapped her in his protective arms and brought her home. But now that she was back in Buffalo, he didn't know what to do with her. Angie was lost and confused and in such emotional anguish that it took more effort than she could muster to get out of bed in the mornings.

Her father knocked on her bedroom door. "Angelina, are you awake?"

She didn't answer and prayed he'd go away. It wouldn't do any good, but she already knew that.

After a second knock, he opened the door and flipped on the light switch. "It's morning."

She was sitting up in bed, staring at the wall. She squinted at the bright light and wanted to shout at him to turn it off, but that would demand energy and she had none.

"It's a beautiful morning. Look." As if turning on the lights wasn't bad enough, he raised her window blind and sunshine invaded the room.

Angie closed her eyes. She didn't *want* to look at the sunshine. She didn't *want* to speak to her father.

"Angelina!" His voice rose with exasperation. "What's wrong with you?"

Angie said nothing.

"All day you sit here and stare at the wall. You don't talk, you barely eat. Even my zabaglione doesn't tempt you. I heard of a man ready for death who sat up in bed when his wife brought him my zabaglione. Yet my own daughter barely takes a bite."

Angie wanted to reassure her father that it wasn't his cooking. He had surrounded her with his love, spoiled her with gift after gift and tempted her with his desserts, all to no avail. She wanted none of the things he tried to give her. What she wanted, what she *needed,* was forgiveness. But no one could give her that—least of all her father, who couldn't understand her grief.

Angie had failed Corinne and in the process she'd failed herself. The pain of knowing that refused to leave her.

"How can I help you?" he asked, sitting on the corner of her bed.

"You can't, Daddy."

"Talk to me," he pleaded. "Tell me what happened."

Tears moistened her eyelids and she shook her head, unable to get any words past the constriction in her throat.

"A girl in your class died, and you think you killed her?"

Angie nodded. "Yes…in a way, I think I did."

"How?" he asked. "Did you hold a gun to her head? She got pregnant and she tried to get rid of the baby. It's not your fault, Angie. God knows why a beautiful young girl would try to kill her baby, but these things happen." He lowered his voice, frowned and then added a few other comments in Italian, none of which Angie could translate.

"She trusted me."

"She didn't have a mother to talk to?"

"Yes...but I was the one she turned to."

"And you knew this teenager was pregnant and advised her to make an appointment with this abortionist?"

Of course she hadn't! Why did her father insist on asking her these ridiculous questions?

"You won't answer me because you're hauling around this load of guilt you have no business carrying." Impatience sharpened his voice.

"I knew something was wrong," Angie argued, her own voice emotionless. "I knew it but I didn't ask."

"And that's the reason you're nailing yourself on that crucifix up there next to Jesus?" He pointed at the large crucifix on the wall across from her. A palm frond from the Palm Sunday service fifteen years earlier was tucked behind it.

Angie lowered her head and refused to answer.

"What can I do for you?" Her father was shouting now. "Please tell me!"

She shook her head.

Exasperated, he turned and walked out of the room, leaving the door open and the irritating lights on. Angie groaned in frustration. All she wanted was to be left alone and to sleep. She was so tired. But despite her exhaustion, she either tossed and turned the night away or wandered the hall, pacing back and forth. Her eyes burned, and she cursed her inability to escape into sleep. Then just before dawn she'd drift into a fitful slumber, which inevitably ended when her father got up.

She could hear him now, thumping down the stairs. In a few minutes she'd smell the scent of freshly brewed coffee. A little while after that, she'd hear him climbing upstairs again. He would return to her room, carrying a breakfast tray in an effort to persuade her to eat. To satisfy him, she'd nibble one or two bites and leave the rest. She had his routine all worked out.

Sure enough, right on schedule, he trudged up the stairs and brought the tray of breakfast into her bedroom. "I made you coffee," he said as he did every morning. Then he set the tray on her lap. Coffee and a croissant, jelly, butter and a small pitcher of cream.

"Thank you," she whispered, although she wished with all her being that he'd take it away. She wasn't hungry. Sometimes she was afraid she'd be violently ill if she so much as lifted a fork.

Usually her father left then, but he didn't this morning. He walked back and forth at the foot of her bed. Angie watched him, wondering at this sudden break in their routine.

"Angelina," he said, facing her. She suddenly saw how much the years had changed him. Her father was in his early sixties, but he was still robust and she'd never thought of him as growing old. It was a shock to see how lined his face was and how his once-gray hair had gone completely white.

"Yes?" she asked. Trying to please him, she stirred cream into her coffee.

His eyes were sad and empty; his shoulders drooped in defeat. "Do you want to go back to the convent?"

If she had an answer, Angie would have given it to him, but she simply didn't know. For fifteen years she'd dedicated herself to the Church. She'd loved her life, enjoyed teaching and her students, but in her soul Angie knew she'd never stand in front of a classroom again. It just wasn't in her to teach anymore. That wasn't completely Corinne's doing; Angie had burned out. At a loss, she hung her head and didn't answer.

"You can't speak to your own father?" he cried. "If you can't tell me, then who can you tell?"

His pain unsettled her. Angie loved her father more than anyone or anything other than God, and it grieved her to cause him anguish. "I…don't know."

"If you want to go back to Minneapolis, I'll take you." The

fact that he'd made such an offer revealed how truly desperate he was.

"I don't want to go back," she wept, breaking into sobs. "I can't…" If she couldn't teach, she'd be given some other assignment and Angie could think of nothing else that would suit her.

Her father moved closer and set the breakfast tray aside. Then he gently gathered her in his arms. "You cry. Go ahead and cry it out, and then it's over with, okay?"

"I…don't know."

He sighed. "Angelina, I can't stay home any longer."

"Stay home?" She realized it'd been weeks since he'd spent more than an hour or two at the restaurant. In her pain and self-absorption she hadn't recognized the sacrifice he'd made for her.

As if struck by a brilliant notion, he said, "Come to the restaurant with me."

She stared up at him through her tears. He hadn't left her alone in weeks. Weeks! Even when he was away, he made sure someone was in the house with her. All at once it dawned on her why. Her father was afraid she'd commit suicide if he gave her the opportunity.

Angie would never take her own life. That hadn't even entered her mind. Yes, she was depressed and angry with the Church, but taking her own life would condemn her for eternity. And it would destroy her father. She couldn't bear the thought of putting him through such an ordeal. Surely he knew that!

"Angie, come with me," he said, his eyes shining with hope. "It'll be just like when you were a little girl." His large hands gripped her shoulders. "Get dressed now and I'll meet you downstairs."

For the first time since she'd come home, Angie felt the beginnings of a smile. "Okay, Daddy. I'll go to the restaurant with you."

*chapter*

## JOANNA BAIRD
### APRIL 1, 1973

Joanna had forgotten how lovely Providence could be in the springtime. The air was clear and fresh, and she marveled at the newly green trees and budding flowers. She had her own apartment now and was discovering that life as a single woman wasn't nearly as frightening as it had first appeared.

Twice now, Joanna had been asked out on a date. Both invitations had caught her by surprise. She wasn't looking for a relationship, but she'd felt flattered and more than a little flustered. She'd been a teenager the last time she'd gone out with a man—she didn't include that ice cream sundae with Dr. Murray. She'd declined both invitations because technically she was still a nun.

Her job on the surgical floor was fast-paced and interesting, and she loved her work. She was learning to manage her money and remained in close contact with her family. Every Sunday she attended Mass with her parents, keeping her ties to the Church strong. Her parents and the Church were her anchors during this time of adjustment. She'd found that her high school friends were mostly married and their lives were completely unlike her own. She felt uncomfortable with them and she was sure they did with her, too.

Once she had her own apartment and a job, Greg had called her, hoping for a chance to prove himself. Joanna had been kind but firm in her rejection and she hadn't heard from him again, which was a relief.

The phone rang on a beautiful Monday morning as Joanna stepped out of the shower. Her hair was longer now and permed. She liked this new carefree style that was so popular among her peers, although it reminded her a little of a dandelion gone to seed. Wrapping the towel around her, she answered on the third ring.

"Hello," she said breathlessly. Since this was her day off, it was either the hospital calling her in as a substitute or her mother about to suggest they meet for lunch.

"Good morning," her mother said cheerfully. "There's a surprise at the house for you."

"A surprise?"

"A man actually." A male voice could be heard in the background. "Hold on a minute," her mother said.

Joanna strained to identify the voice but it was too faint.

Then her mother was back on the line. "Here, you can talk to him yourself."

"Joanna?"

It was Tim. Dr. Murray! She sank onto the edge of the bed in shock. "Tim?" All these months and she hadn't heard a single word. Not one. Then, out of the blue, he showed up at her parents' home? Her breath went shallow.

"Are you there?" he asked.

"What are you doing at my parents' house?" she demanded.

"I came to see you. Why else do you think I'm here? Would it be all right if I came over?" He sounded impatient and excited at once.

"Yes, please…" Her anger melted away. "It would be very nice to see you. Do you know where I am?"

Her mother had already given him the address, he said, and he was leaving now.

In a record fifteen minutes, Joanna dressed, put on her makeup and dried her hair. Still, her nerves were frayed by the time Tim knocked on the door.

Joanna opened it and stepped back, hands clasped together in front of her, heart pounding hard.

"This, um, is a surprise," she said. She wasn't sure how to act or what to say. He looked wonderful, better than she remembered. It'd been almost six months since she'd seen him, but she hadn't forgotten a thing about him. Not a day had passed in which he hadn't been part of her thoughts.

"May I come in?" he asked.

Joanna wanted to die of mortification when she realized he was still standing in the doorway while she unabashedly stared at him. "Of course! Please." She hurriedly stepped aside.

He walked into the one-bedroom apartment, which was only beginning to reflect her personality. Her mother had helped her add dashes of individuality here and there. For six years Joanna had lived with the barest of necessities. It took her mother's eye to point out small things she could use—a photograph, ivy in a ceramic pot, some colorful tea towels—to turn this apartment into her home.

"You look—" He hesitated. "Different."

Her hand went instinctively to her hair. "Yes, I imagine I do."

He lowered his voice, as if in awe. "You're beautiful—but then you always were."

His compliments embarrassed her and she immediately looked around for a distraction. "Would you like a cup of coffee?" she asked brightly.

"No, thanks."

She poured herself one just to keep her hands occupied and then joined him in the compact living room, where he sat at one end of the sofa and she sat at the other.

"So," she said, holding her mug with both hands. "What brings you to the East Coast?"

"I was in Boston for a symposium. I heard you were in

Providence and decided to take an extra day to look you up."
He made it sound so matter-of-fact.

"How did you know I was here?"

He relaxed against the arm of the sofa and crossed his long
legs, balancing his ankle on the opposite knee. "The hospital
called. You gave them my name as a reference. There were
six Bairds in the phone book, I hit Mark on the third try and
your mother answered."

He'd gone to a lot of trouble, she mused.

"I didn't know what to think when you left without a word,"
he said. "I thought, I hoped—hell, I don't know, but it came
as a shock."

"I'm sorry. I know I should've called."

"Why didn't you?"

"There wasn't time, and I wasn't sure it would be wise...."

"Why not? You had to know how I felt about you. That last
day I saw you, I admitted I was falling in love."

Yes, and his admission had terrified her. "As I recall, you
were dating someone else...and I was, am—" she corrected
"—a nun." She sipped from the mug and noticed her hands
were trembling.

Tim's eyes softened. "You don't look like any nun I've ever
seen," he murmured, and his words reminded her of a similar statement he'd made last fall.

"I've taken a leave of absence."

"For how long?"

"A year," she told him.

"Then what?"

"If I feel the way I do now, and I know I will, I'll write a
letter to Rome and ask to be released from my vows."

"Are you sure you're going to follow through with this?"
He certainly had a lot of questions.

She nodded, set her coffee mug aside and sat up straighter.
She had a few questions of her own. "I phoned and left a message for you," she said, "but you never acknowledged my call."

"Message? What message? You said goodbye. What did you
want me to do? Track you down so I could say goodbye, too?"

"I don't know. It probably wasn't correct protocol to contact you, but…I didn't want it to end the way it did."

"I assumed the only reason for your call was to line me up as a reference."

"No," she said sharply, "that was the excuse I used. I wanted you to know…"

"Know what?"

She shrugged and called herself every kind of coward for being unwilling to confess the truth.

"More importantly, Joanna, tell me why you left."

She raised her eyes to his. "You mean you don't know?"

He reached out and gently grazed her cheek with his knuckles. "Tell me." His eyes pleaded with hers.

Joanna wasn't sure she could.

"I need to know," he continued in a low, seductive voice.

The tenderness in his eyes mesmerized her, and she was unable to look away. "I was falling in love with you, too. I tried so hard not to—but I couldn't discipline myself enough to prevent it."

"That was why you transferred to the Emergency Room?"

She nodded. "I had a talk with Sister Superior, and she advised the move. Later, when we were found together in the hospital chapel, she suggested I needed time away to review my feelings."

"Have those feelings changed?" he asked.

She swallowed tightly. While she was embarrassed about discussing her attraction to him, she was grateful for the freedom to speak honestly. "No."

"After all these months, you're saying you feel the same way about me?"

"Yes," she whispered.

"I'm glad, Joanna."

He lifted her chin until her gaze met his.

"Have I made a complete fool of myself?" she asked.

He shook his head. "I came back from Nam a different man. As far as I was concerned, God was dead. Either that, or he'd never existed. Just when it felt like my life was getting back to normal and I was starting a promising practice, I ran headlong into a beautiful hospital nun. You wouldn't let me forget about God. I remember you once told me that God hadn't given up on me, even if I'd given up on Him."

"I said that?"

"And more. Half the time, I came away from the hospital thinking about you, about arguments I wanted to make and hadn't. You had me muttering to myself. I don't know how you talked me into attending Mass again, but I'm grateful you did. I started sleeping better and my mother noticed a change in my attitude. I told her you were responsible and she assumed you were much older—a nice, friendly nun in her sixties or seventies. I didn't correct that impression."

She'd prayed so hard for Tim Murray and it felt as if God had smiled upon her when she saw him in church that first Sunday.

"I didn't know what to think when I realized I was in love with you," he said.

Joanna's hand went to her heart.

"It troubled me, Joanna. You'd dedicated your life to Christ and I didn't want to feel the things I did. I dated several women and was actually grateful when you got that transfer, but it didn't help. I think you were already a part of me. I've missed you. Not a day goes by when you aren't in my thoughts."

"I miss you, too," Joanna confessed.

"Then you were gone." He shrugged ever so slightly. "I'll admit that at first I was glad. You know what they say—out of sight, out of mind. But it didn't take me long to discover I wasn't going to forget you. Then I was annoyed because you left without a word of farewell. That one phone message only served to infuriate me more."

She smiled.

"I was invited to speak at the symposium and I accepted because it was the perfect excuse to find you. I had to know, Joanna."

"Know what?"

"If you feel about me the same way I feel about you." He stretched out his hand and caressed the side of her face.

"I love you, Timothy Murray. I loved you when I left the convent and I love you even more now." She turned her face into his hand and kissed his open palm.

He pulled her into his arms and brought his lips to hers with a tenderness that made her feel weak. "I just kissed a nun," he whispered.

"And a nun is about to kiss you back." Her lips found his.

Tim held her close, and his breathing was heavy when he lifted his mouth from hers. "Okay, where do we go from here?"

"I still have six months of my leave of absence."

"That long?"

"That long," she repeated. "But the time will fly by. Let's get to know each other as just two people, all right?"

He nuzzled the side of her neck. "That should be interesting with you living in Rhode Island and me in Minneapolis."

"We've both faced challenges before."

"You're going to make me wait, aren't you?"

She sighed as she wrapped her arms more securely around his neck. "You know what they say about good things coming to those who wait. The very best is yet to be, I promise you that." Closing her eyes, she pressed her head to his shoulder. In the depths of her heart she knew Tim Murray would be worth every moment of that wait.

*chapter*

## ANGELINA MARCELLO

The first day Angie visited the restaurant, she sat on a stool and watched her father move between his chefs, tasting the sauces and correcting the herbs and spices. For weeks she simply sat and watched. Then one day, she suddenly realized how much she'd missed the pungent scent of simmering garlic. She closed her eyes and breathed it in the way someone who stands on a beach inhales the scent of salt and sea. At that moment Angie truly felt she'd come home.

Shortly afterward, for reasons she didn't understand, her appetite returned. Every day her father had tried to entice her with his favorite dishes. She refused each one until he offered her spaghetti alla puttanesca, which had been her childhood favorite.

The sauce, made with anchovies, tomatoes and olives, was hot and spicy. Long ago she'd heard that the recipe originated in the red-light district of Rome. Women of the night would

292 *Debbie Macomber*

cook the sauce and set it on their windowsills, hoping to lure patrons to their establishments.

The spaghetti tasted as wonderful as she remembered. *Better* than she remembered. That night she had two huge plates of spaghetti, heaped high with the spicy sauce.

It was as though she'd been awarded an Olympic medal for her appetite. The entire kitchen crew applauded when she finished her second helping. Her father beamed, his eyes brimming with unshed tears. He hurriedly brought her his signature zabaglione, and stood by watching as she ate every last bite.

That was the beginning. The next day it was fettuccine Alfredo. Angie hadn't noticed how thin she'd become—and she'd forgotten how wonderful food tasted—until she started visiting the restaurant. *Everything* smelled so good, and once she'd sampled the familiar dishes, it seemed as if her father's food offered her the comfort she hadn't found anywhere else.

Then one afternoon six months after she'd left the convent, Tony Marcello insisted he had paperwork that needed his attention and asked Angie to do the daily tasting. Reluctantly she'd agreed, seeing through his ploy. He wanted her to assume his role; it had been his plan for her from the time she was a child and she didn't have the heart to refuse him.

Mario Deccio and the other cooks had been with the restaurant for years and knew the recipes as well as—or better than—Angie. Still, they respectfully stepped aside and waited for her approval, the same way they did with her father. The gift she'd once shared with him had never left her, she discovered. Her instincts for the nuances of a dish were as reliable as ever.

In the summer of 1973, Angie began working the restaurant floor, greeting their dinner guests and making recommendations when called upon. It was her job to see that the patrons were satisfied and that their dining experience was everything they had anticipated. People liked her unobtrusive manner and asked after her if she wasn't there. By the end of the season, profits were up twenty percent.

Her father had never been happier, Mario said. That wasn't

all he told her. "Your papa was not the same after you went to the convent," the chef confided. "For a long time we worried. He seemed to lose all interest in life. But you're home now."

It was good to be back. Angie felt guilty for enjoying her role in the restaurant so much. It was almost as though the last fifteen years had somehow disappeared from her memory. From her life…

She might've been able to continue pretending indefinitely if Mario's granddaughter hadn't stopped by early one afternoon. Angie saw the teenager enter the kitchen and nearly collapsed. Gina Deccio was sixteen years old and wore her hair in the same teenage style as Corinne Sullivan. They both had dark, inquisitive eyes. Gina smiled at Angie and it was as if Corinne had stepped into the room.

"Angelina, come and meet my granddaughter," Mario said. His expression revealed his pride as he placed his arm around the girl's shoulders.

"Hello," Angie said, barely able to contain her panic. "If you'll forgive me, I have an errand to run." No one questioned her as she pulled off the apron and hung it on the peg and nearly dashed from the building. It was muggy and warm, late in the summer; Jim Croce's "Bad, Bad Leroy Brown" was playing on a nearby radio as Angie began her walk. She walked and walked for blocks on end.

Her feet hurt but she kept up the punishing pace, her mind racing, driving her further and further from everything that was familiar, everything that had given her solace.

She didn't stop until she found a church. It wasn't a Catholic church, but Angie didn't care. She hurried inside and made her way to the front, then fell onto her knees at the railing. Burying her face in her hands, she silently wept.

She cried until there were no tears left and when she was finished, she sat in a pew and realized those tears hadn't been for Corinne. They'd been for her.

In the months since Angie had set aside the habit of St. Bridget's Sisters of the Assumption, she'd found her place outside the convent. She wasn't going back. This time away wasn't a leave of absence. She wouldn't be returning to the convent in a few weeks or months. She was *never* going back.

Glancing up, she closed her eyes and prayed fervently, begging forgiveness. When she'd joined the convent she had devastated her father. Now she was afraid she'd be disappointing her heavenly Father by leaving it.

She waited for the guilt to come over her like a dark storm. Inwardly she cringed and feared another depression; instead she experienced a new sense of peace. She wondered if it was just wishful thinking; she wasn't convinced God would so easily forgive her for abandoning her vows. There'd be a price to pay. Surely penance would be required before God Almighty would set her free from debilitating guilt and remorse. She'd failed Him, and that couldn't be without consequences. She didn't know how long she sat and waited for some act of penance to reveal itself. It never did.

When she left the church, Angie felt almost giddy. She was free. The emotional shackles were gone. Without guilt, without remorse, she could walk away from her life as a nun.

Her father was white with panic by the time a taxi returned her to the restaurant. "Where did you go?" he demanded, following her inside.

"For a walk."

"You were gone *four* hours!" he shouted.

"It was a long walk."

He put his hands on his hips just as he used to when she was a child who'd disobeyed. "Is that all you have to say for yourself?"

"Yes," she said, and kissed his cheek before reaching for her apron. "On second thought, no."

"No?" His eyebrows shot upward.

"No," she repeated, feeling jubilant. "I've decided to write Rome."

He scowled ferociously. "What are you going to write?"

"I'm going to ask that the Holy Father release me from my vows."

Angie waited, expecting her father to express relief and delight, but he showed no outward sign of happiness.

"Did you hear me, Dad?"

"I heard you." He turned abruptly and went back into his office.

Bewildered, Angie went after him. "Don't you have anything to say?" she asked, standing in the doorway of the small, meticulously organized office.

He looked up, his weathered face lined with worry. "Where are you going next?"

"I'm not going anywhere, Daddy. I'm home to stay."

"You mean it?"

Angie nodded.

Her father took out his handkerchief and dabbed at his eyes. "It was my zabaglione, wasn't it?"

Angie stared at him in disbelief and then realized he was teasing. "Without a doubt," she said.

Her father burst out laughing. He leaped up from his chair, threw his arms around Angie and hugged her. She laughed, too, until the tears ran down her cheeks and the kitchen staff came to investigate.

*chapter*

## KATHLEEN O'SHAUGHNESSY

In August of 1973, shortly after Nixon refused to hand over the secret Watergate tapes as ordered by Judge John Sirica, Kathleen moved out of the House of Peace and into her own apartment. She'd been hired as a lay teacher at St. Joseph's Parochial School, teaching fifth grade, and was jubilant to be self-supporting.

It was the first time in her life that she'd lived on her own. Her parents had visited earlier in the summer; they'd accepted Kathleen's decision and encouraged her to move back east while she reflected on her choices for the future. But Kathleen liked Seattle and this was where she wanted to make a fresh start. Sean was close by and she could visit her parents during the summers. Her mother and father had reluctantly agreed with her plan to live on the West Coast. They parted on warm terms, and Kathleen felt absolved from the lingering worry that she'd disappointed those who loved her most.

More and more, she recognized that she had no desire to

return to the convent. Her counselor, a former nun herself, had helped Kathleen immeasurably. They discussed the complex issues of her role in the Church, past and future, as well as coping with life on the outside. They talked about everything— finding jobs, feeling guilt, the possibility of meeting men…

For part of the summer, Kathleen taught a catechism program. She also led the children's choir, and for pure fun, she was teaching herself how to play the guitar again. That last summer at home, before entering the convent, she'd managed to learn a repertoire of easily played songs.

One afternoon toward the middle of August, Kathleen strolled through Elliott Bay Park after one of her counseling sessions. The blue sky and the warm breeze off Puget Sound enticed her to linger. Someone was playing the guitar and it sounded so much better than her own simple strumming that she paused to listen.

Kathleen found the musician sitting under a tree, dressed in jeans with his long dark hair tied in a ponytail and a kerchief headband. He played a folk song and she sat down on a nearby bench.

"Want to sing along?" he called out.

She shook her head, embarrassed that he'd noticed her.

"I'm Pete," he said.

"Kathleen."

"Good to meet you, Kathleen." He began to play an old song she remembered, "House of the Rising Sun."

"I've been teaching myself the guitar," she said when he'd finished. "I've discovered it isn't as easy as it looks."

"All you have to do is practice."

"I know." She supposed that was something she could be doing right then, but it was such a glorious day, Kathleen didn't want to go home to an empty apartment. So she stayed. Never mind that she owed both Father Doyle and her sister Maureen a letter. Or that she could be getting a head start on her classes for September. This was where she wanted to be.

After another half hour, she finally stood to leave.

"Goodbye, Lady Kathleen. Hope to see you again."

"You too, Pete." He'd begun to play a melody she didn't recognize. So many of the more recent songs were unknown to her.

She waved as she passed him, her mood free, swinging her bag at her side. Another thing she'd had to get used to—carrying a purse.

It soon became a habit to pick up something for dinner from the Pike Place Market and then stop at Elliott Bay Park to listen to Pete. That first time, she hadn't noticed he was a street player, or more accurately a park player. He collected coins in his guitar carrying case; because she considered him a friend, she didn't give him money. However, she often brought him fruit or a drink.

One afternoon she'd bought him a sandwich, and the two of them sat on the lawn and talked. Summer was winding down and Pete was heading south. To school, she assumed, although he'd never actually said.

"You're a teacher," he said, opening a soda can and handing it to her. "You'll be going back to school next week." He sat with one knee raised as he ate his turkey sandwich. She envied the way he seemed to fully enjoy each moment, each sensation.

"I'm starting right after Labor Day." This wasn't a date, she reminded herself. They were just friends, but it felt good to sit with a man and simply talk. This was new to her, this easy camaraderie with the opposite sex. Even as a girl, her exposure to boys had been limited. Sean was almost ten years older and her youngest brother was barely more than a baby while she was living at home. She'd attended an all-girl high school.

Pete lowered his sandwich and studied her with undisguised admiration. "I certainly never had any teacher as beautiful as you."

She must have blushed because he leaned forward and traced the bridge of her freckled nose. Those freckles had been a curse when she was a teenager, but Pete seemed to find them intriguing.

"Don't men say pretty things to you, my lady Kathleen?"

She lowered her eyes, afraid that if she mentioned the fact that she was still technically a nun, he would leap up and race away. That was what the boys in her high school class had done even *before* she'd entered the convent.

Her dates had been few and far between. The minute a boy learned she was interested in the religious life, the relationship, such as it was, would immediately end. Kathleen didn't want that to happen with Pete.

"I'll miss you when you leave," she confessed.

"I won't be gone more than a few months," he said. Then with a small laugh, he leaned forward and kissed her cheek. "Maybe I won't go at all."

Kathleen's spirits lifted. "Really?"

"It's hard to walk away from a red-haired lady."

His compliments flustered her and to distract them both, she asked a practical question. "How will you support yourself?"

He shrugged. "I'm not into material things. My life is simple. Anyway, I could always get a job in a tavern or maybe a coffeehouse. Summer's too beautiful to waste on a real job. That's why I enjoy playing in the park."

Kathleen smiled, loving his free and easy life. She wasn't materialistic herself. When you weren't allowed to own goods of any kind, the hunger for material possessions quickly disappeared. *Things* didn't satisfy. Love was what mattered.

Pete straightened and reached for his guitar, playing a lovely song, one she'd never heard before. People stopped to listen as he strummed.

"That was beautiful," Kathleen said.

"It's a love song. I wrote it for you."

"Me?"

Pete chuckled. "Don't you know how I feel about you, Kathleen O'Shaughnessy?"

Her heart pounded furiously at his words, as though she were running straight into a flaming building.

"You like my music, don't you?"

"Oh, yes—very much."

"Want to listen to a tape of it? We can get a bottle of wine and go to your place."

Kathleen wasn't completely naive. She could listen to Pete and his guitar in person; she didn't need a tape to do so. She suspected the tape was an excuse to come to her apartment so he could kiss her. The silent debate inside her didn't last more than a couple of seconds. "That would be fun."

Pete purchased a bottle of red wine and held her hand in his as she led him into her apartment. She didn't have any wineglasses, so they sipped the merlot out of tumblers. It was mellow, easy to drink, and quickly went to her head.

"This is very good," she said, sitting on the sofa next to him.

His smile was incredible. Pete was incredible. He moved closer and settled his arm around her shoulders. Kathleen rested her head against his neck and when he turned to kiss her, she closed her eyes.

Almost right away, her head started to swim. She'd rarely drunk wine, and it seemed impossible that a single glass could make her tipsy, but it had. Pete kissed her, gently at first and then with deepening passion. His tongue invaded her mouth; Kathleen let it happen. This was foreign to her, but exciting, and she enjoyed their mutual exploration.

"How does that feel, my lady Kathleen?" he whispered.

"Good."

"For me too. How about this?" He rained kisses along the side of her neck and then opened the top two buttons of her blouse. His mouth left a fiery trail down to the edge of her bra, where he let his tongue delve into the valley between her breasts. When he paused, Kathleen held her breath, hardly able to believe what he was doing.

His hands cupped her breasts, taking in their fullness, while he continued to kiss her. She was hardly aware that he'd unfastened her bra, and she groaned aloud as he slipped her blouse over her arms. The bra fell from her shoulders, leaving her breasts exposed.

Kathleen freed her mouth from his. "I don't think—"

"No—don't think, because we're here to feel." Taking her

hand he pressed it against the bulge in his pants. She reacted as if he'd burned her and pulled loose.

Pete laughed and stripped off his shirt. "There," he said, "how's that?" Then he kissed her again with long, slow seductive kisses that dissolved her objections.

Kathleen started to relax and Pete leaned her back until she was flat against the sofa. Then he lay on top of her, pushing her into the cushions. She felt his erection, which seemed to have grown even harder. Pinning her hands above her head, he kissed her lips and worked a line of moist kisses toward her breasts. When his lips took in her nipple and sucked on it, sensation shot through her like an electrical shock. Involuntarily, Kathleen arched upward.

Pete chuckled softly. "That's only the beginning."

"No…"

"Yes, honey." He drugged her with kisses once more, but a moment later, slid off her.

With her eyes closed, Kathleen relaxed again, grateful this had come to an end. They were moving too fast. Then she heard him release his zipper. She tried to sit up, but Pete wouldn't let her. He shoved her against the cushions, and before she had a chance to protest, he was on top of her again. When she attempted to squirm free, he forcefully held her down.

"You don't lead a man this far and then tell him no," he said.

He tried to kiss her, but Kathleen twisted her mouth away from him. The gentle musician she'd met in the park underwent a personality change as he jerked up her skirt and tore off her cotton panties.

"We can make this easy, baby," he murmured.

"No…no! Don't do this. I don't want this."

"Yes, you do," he countered in the same seductive voice he'd used earlier. Even while she tried to push him away, he pried open her legs and rammed his rigid penis deep inside her.

Kathleen gasped at the pain, but if Pete was aware of her discomfort, he gave no indication. Eyes squeezed shut and teeth gritted, he continued to pound her, his body repeatedly slamming against hers. Again and again. Faster and more furious. The pain was dreadful and it didn't ease even when he cried out and then slumped, his deadweight holding her down as he heaved and panted.

"That was fantastic," he whispered.

Kathleen was too shocked to move. Her mouth had gone completely dry and her tongue felt glued to her teeth.

"Oh, honey, you're so tight. So good."

It took her a moment to free her arms enough to push him off her. This horrible man had stolen her virginity. He'd taken advantage of her inexperience. He'd ignored her protests. Standing on wobbly legs, her skirt torn, she grabbed her blouse and held it against her bare breasts. Pointing a shaking finger at him, she cried, "Get out of here!"

Pete sat up, looking stunned. "What's wrong?"

"Get out," she cried, near hysteria now. "Get out." She picked up one of his sandals and threw it at the door.

Pete raised both hands as if to ward off an attack. "I'm going, I'm going. I don't know what you're so upset about. You wanted this as much as I did."

"No! No, I didn't." To be fair, she *had* wanted him to kiss her and had enjoyed their foreplay, but she'd never wanted him to go any further. What he'd done felt like abuse, like an assault. It felt as if he'd crushed her soul. "Now leave." She refused to let him see the tears in her eyes.

"All right, all right." He dressed quickly, then slipped into one sandal and grabbed the second on his way out the door. As soon as it closed, Kathleen picked up his tumbler, still half-full of wine and hurled it at the door. The glass broke and red wine splattered across the carpet and the wall.

Falling onto her knees, she covered her face with her hands and wept. When she rose, the room was completely dark.

Emotionless, she stumbled into the bathroom and turned on the shower. She scrubbed every inch of her skin as she stood under the high-pressure spray, wielding the washcloth with such force she threatened to leave abrasions. The water ran cold before she'd finished.

Dressed in her nightgown, Kathleen sat in the darkened

room and wept again. She needed a friend, someone she could talk to, someone she trusted. Sean would be furious and God only knew what he'd do to Pete if he found him. She didn't want her brother to end up in jail on her account. Her counselor came to mind, but she was afraid of what the woman would say if she admitted her stupidity.

In the end, at two in the morning, when she was sure she'd go crazy unless she heard another human voice, Kathleen phoned Father Doyle in Minneapolis.

He answered the phone himself, sounding groggy. "Father Doyle," he murmured.

"You said I could call you any time of the day or night," she whispered, uncertain he'd recognize her.

"Kathleen?" He seemed instantly alert.

She checked her watch and realized that with the time difference it was 3:00 a.m. "I shouldn't have called."

"What happened?"

Now that she had him on the line, she found it impossible to admit what she'd done. Struggling to keep the panic and the pain out of her voice, she whispered, "I met a man in the park."

"Tell me what happened."

She started to sob. "I can't…"

"All right," he said calmly. "Tell me this. Are you hurt?"

"I…I don't think so."

"Are you in pain?"

"Yes!" she nearly shouted.

"Do you need a doctor?"

"I need a priest," she cried.

There was a short pause and then he said, "I'm here."

They talked nonstop for an hour, and when they'd finished Kathleen felt she had her soul back. The guilt was gone, but her heart ached and so did her body. Father Doyle suggested she swallow a couple of aspirin and try to sleep.

Kathleen took his advice and, to her amazement, fell quickly into a deep, undisturbed slumber. The phone woke her in the morning, and before she had time to consider that it might be Pete, she answered.

"How are you feeling?" It was Father Doyle.

She sat on one end of the sofa and brought her feet up while she tried to find an answer. "I don't know yet. I was in bed...I haven't had a chance to think."

"Ah, so I woke you." Apparently he found that amusing. "Turnabout is fair play."

Kathleen smiled. "Thank you so much for talking to me last night. I didn't know where else to turn."

"I'm glad I'm the one you called."

She swept the long, tangled hair away from her face and sighed. "I did something very foolish. I learned a painful lesson because of it."

"Yes, you did, but I don't want you berating yourself over this. What happened wasn't entirely your fault. In fact, it was more his than yours."

"It doesn't matter whose fault it was." To her, it didn't. What mattered was that she'd lost her virginity to a man who neither valued her nor appreciated what he'd stolen.

"There's something we didn't discuss last night that you need to do," he said.

"What?"

"I want you to see a physician. This is important, Kathleen, so don't ignore me."

He wanted her to tell a doctor what had happened. She *couldn't* do that. "I can't," she whispered, half-tempted to weep. "I can't tell anyone else...."

"Don't worry—I've already made arrangements for you to see a physician friend of a friend. I talked to him and explained the situation. You won't need to say a word. I've taken care of everything."

Kathleen was so grateful she didn't know how to thank him. "What would I do without you?" she asked.

"What are friends for?"

## JOANNA BAIRD

"Nixon's done it now," Joanna said, sitting on the carpet, her back against the sofa and the phone to her ear. It was early November 1973 and she spoke to Tim every night. She could only guess what he was spending on long-distance charges as their conversations sometimes went on for two and three hours. Because of this, he'd had a second phone line installed in his home so they could talk for long periods of time without worrying that he might miss emergency calls.

"Do you seriously think Leon Jaworski is going to grant Nixon any political favors?"

"I don't know," Joanna said, "but as far as I'm concerned that's what you get for voting Republican." She didn't know his political allegiance for a fact, but she had her suspicions.

"You mean to say you voted for McGovern?"

"Darn right I did."

"I don't believe it," Tim cried. "The woman I want to marry is a Democrat."

Joanna's hand tightened around the receiver. "What did you just say?"

"I can't believe you're a Democrat."

"Not that, earlier."

"Are your parents Democrats, too?"

Joanna sighed in frustration. "I don't know how my parents voted in the last election. I want to know what you meant when you said the woman you want to marry."

"*Did* want to marry," he said archly.

"Tim!"

He chuckled. "Okay, okay. You must've guessed by now that I haven't been calling you every night for the last five months because I like the sound of your voice."

"I like the sound of *your* voice." Every night she looked forward to hearing from him. In August, he'd flown out to spend a week with her, but that was all the time he could spare away from his practice. Those seven glorious days had gone by far too quickly.

"Well, okay, I do like the sound of your voice," Tim said in low fervent tones. "But I like a lot more than that." He paused and she held her breath. "You know I love you."

"I love you, too." So much that sometimes she could barely stand being apart from him.

"I've been waiting, Joanna, but I have to tell you I'm getting kind of impatient."

"Waiting for what?"

"That letter from Rome," he said, as if it should be obvious.

"I'm sure it'll be here soon."

He muttered something under his breath.

"You can ask me, though." She didn't need any letter; she knew her heart and had mentally separated herself from the religious life over a year ago. More than anything in the world, she longed to be married to Tim.

"Once you're free, I'll propose."

"Yes."

"Yes, what?"

"That'll be my answer once you get around to proposing.

Listen, perhaps you could talk to my father. He's…a little old-fashioned and it would mean a lot to him if you'd discuss marrying his daughter with him first."

"Are you always this bossy?" he asked.

She was annoyed that he'd called her bossy, because Joanna didn't see herself that way at all. "It was only a suggestion."

"I've already talked to your father and your mother, too."

"You have? When?"

"This summer when I was out there."

"You didn't tell me! What did they say?"

"Oh, they seemed pretty pleased," he said smugly. "But I may have to rethink my plans, since that was before I found out you voted for McGovern."

"A Democrat didn't break into the Republican party headquarters, you know? A Democrat would never do anything as underhanded as that."

His laugh echoed over the line. Joanna was smiling, too. She'd always enjoyed bantering with Tim, and as they'd grown more familiar with each other, their friendship had deepened.

"It's a good thing you live as far away as you do."

"Why?" she teased. "Do you want to throttle me?"

"No, I'm dying to make love to you. I don't know how I'm going to keep my hands off you next week."

Joanna was flying to Minneapolis for Thanksgiving and staying with his mother. "Your mom will make a wonderful chaperon."

He grumbled some remark she couldn't quite catch—and probably wasn't intended to hear. "It's three months since I saw you. I know you were a nun, Joanna, but I was never a priest, and I'm telling you right now, it's damned difficult not to touch you…."

"Good." She loved knowing she tempted him. What Tim probably didn't realize was how tempted she was, too. He knew she wasn't a virgin, but he'd accepted her decision that they should wait until they were married before they made love. With Tim, she didn't want any regrets. When they said their vows, it would be because they were committed to each other for life. With that commitment came the God-given privilege of intimacy. Joanna had cheated herself once and refused to repeat that mistake.

"Good?" he repeated. "Do you *enjoy* torturing a man?"

"Only you." She smiled at the way he grumbled, but she also knew that he respected and loved her enough to honor her wishes. "Before I forget, Mom told me this morning that Greg Markham's remarried."

"So lover-boy is out of the picture."

"He married a woman from the Philippines."

Joanna had been somewhat taken aback. Greg had repeatedly complained about the problems in his marriage due to the differences between Xuan's culture and American attitudes. She'd never learned English properly and seemed to hate Greg for what she perceived as his lack of attention. Naturally, Joanna had only heard Greg's side, although she'd been reluctant to discuss the matter at all.

"I don't care if he married a space alien as long as he accepts that you don't want him in your life."

"He's been out of my life for years. Are you going to be a jealous husband, Timothy Murray?"

"Very."

"Well, I intend to be an extremely jealous wife. I only want you working with male nurses."

"I'd like to work with you," he said. "The hospital still hasn't found a nurse who's even come close to replacing you."

"You certainly know how to flatter a girl."

"I try," he said with mock shyness.

That was the way most of their conversations went.

On Tuesday afternoon the following week, two days before Thanksgiving, Joanna's flight arrived in Minneapolis. It was the first time she'd been back since she'd left the convent.

Tim was waiting for her inside the terminal. She was so eager for the sight of him that she felt she might break into tears when she finally saw him. Wearing a dark overcoat and clutching a bouquet of roses, he made his way through the crowd.

They walked toward each other and when she was close,

Tim took her in his arms, crushing the roses against her. And if she hadn't known it before, she knew it now: He needed her in his life with the same intensity that she needed him.

She'd never approved of public displays of affection but she couldn't wait a second longer for him to kiss her. He half-lifted her and the flowers fell to the floor as his mouth descended on hers.

"Timothy. Timothy."

His name seemed to come from far away. So far that Joanna almost didn't hear it.

"In a moment, Mother," he said.

Tim had brought his mother to the airport? Oh, great! They'd never met, and Joanna was nervous about this first encounter. Tim knew that.

Slowly he released her. With his arm still around her, he turned to the woman in the long wool coat and 1960s-style pillbox hat with matching purse. "Mother, this is Joanna Baird. Joanna, my mother, Alice Murray."

Joanna felt the other woman's perusal of her. "You're the nun."

"Former nun," she said.

Tim's arm tightened around her waist. "The letter arrived?"

She smiled up at him and nodded.

"We're getting married!"

Joanna gave him a puzzled glance. "Yes, I know."

"I mean now. Tomorrow, if it can be arranged."

"Timothy," his mother protested.

"Tim." Joanna had a few objections of her own. "I intend to marry only once and I want a real wedding."

His scowl was fierce. "I hope you can pull it together in a month because that's all the time I'm giving you."

Joanna met his mother's gaze and she noticed her smile. "Can we do it?" she asked Mrs. Murray.

His mother laughed. "I don't think we have any choice. My son took a long time to choose his bride and it wouldn't be a good idea to keep him waiting."

Joanna was in full agreement.

*chapter*

## KATHLEEN O'SHAUGHNESSY

Luckily St. Joseph's Parochial School was within walking distance of Kathleen's tiny apartment. With the gasoline shortage and the long lines at service stations all across America—not to mention the discrepancy between her salary and the cost of living—it would be a lifetime before she could even dream of purchasing her own car.

Walking into the apartment complex, Kathleen stopped to bring Mrs. Mastel her newspaper and mail. "Is there anything else I can do for you?" she asked the eighty-year-old widow.

"Not a thing," the woman told her. "Be sure and pet Seymour on your way out."

"I always do," Kathleen told her. Seymour was the ghost cat who'd died five years earlier and, according to Mrs. Mastel, had joyfully returned to her in spirit form. Kathleen had managed to convince her elderly friend that it wasn't necessary to feed the cat or keep his water dish filled, since he didn't exist as a corporeal entity. Spirits didn't eat or drink, she'd explained gently. The woman's married son had phoned to thank Kathleen. Apparently she was the only person who'd been able to convince his mother that she didn't need to buy cat food anymore—and the smell of rancid tuna no longer pervaded her apartment.

"Oh, dear, it looks like I have one of your letters," Mrs. Mastel said just as Kathleen was heading out the door.

The woman studied the envelope. "It looks important, too." She handed the letter to Kathleen, who thanked her and quietly left.

As she walked upstairs, Kathleen glanced at the return address, and her heart started to pound. Entering her own apartment on the fifth floor, she set her purse and newspaper on the kitchen counter, then examined the envelope a second time. It was the one she'd been waiting for all these months. Her exemption from Rome. A deluge of emotions overwhelmed her and for a moment she could hardly breathe.

After the degrading episode with Pete, she'd felt serious doubts about her decision to leave. Life inside the convent was safe. Protected. It'd taken several long conversations—not with her counselor, but with Father Doyle—before she'd finally made up her mind. In the end, she'd followed through with her original intention and applied to Rome to be released from her vows.

As she sorted through the mail, Kathleen set the bills to one side and found a second, smaller envelope. This one contained a letter, too, and as soon as she saw who it was from, she tore it open. Father Doyle wrote only on rare occasions. Since the incident that summer, he'd made an effort to keep in touch with her as her spiritual advisor. Kathleen was grateful.

He wasn't much of a letter-writer, and she knew that maintaining contact with her must be a chore. Several times she'd been on the verge of telling him it wasn't necessary to write. She couldn't make herself do it; she enjoyed his letters too much. Perhaps it was selfish of her, but in the overall scheme of things, that seemed a comparatively small sin.

She read over the few paragraphs, savoring each word,

and then smiling to herself, refolded the single sheet and returned it to the envelope. The letter from Rome remained unopened. Kathleen knew what it said. Her request had been granted.

The phone rang, startling her. Phone calls were infrequent, since she knew so few people and was only now beginning to make friends, outside of other former nuns. Like her, they tended not to use the phone very often. "Hello?"

"It's Sean," her brother said.

Loren was generally the one who phoned, and it was unusual to hear from him. "What can I do for you, big brother?"

He hesitated. "I'm calling to ask a favor. Loren and I are having a bit of a disagreement, so I'm phoning myself."

"What's the favor?"

"I have this friend. Now listen, it isn't like it sounds."

Kathleen didn't have any idea what it was supposed to sound like.

"I want you to meet him," Sean said. "His name's John. John Lopez. His wife died two years ago, and he's got a couple of kids. I think you'd make him a good wife."

"Wife," Kathleen repeated, laughing. She hadn't even *met* the man and already her brother had the two of them married. He certainly seemed to be leaping ahead. But then, Kathleen knew he was worried about her living alone, even though she'd never told him about Pete. She loved him for his care and concern.

"Well, why not? You want to get married, don't you?"

"Yes, one day. But I'd prefer to choose my own husband and in my own time."

"I'm not saying you have to marry him," Sean insisted, although he clearly had hopes in that direction. "John's a good man and he's had more than his share of bad breaks." He paused and Kathleen heard Loren's raised voice in the background. Obviously her brother and sister-in-law were continuing their argument.

"Will you meet him?" Sean asked. "I'm not asking you to do anything but meet him."

"Okay. I'm willing to do that."

"Just… Kathleen, listen. If you aren't interested in him, don't lead him on, all right?"

"You have my word."

A dinner date was set up for the following night. Kathleen was to walk down to a fish-and-chips place on the Seattle waterfront. John would meet her there. Sean had told her to tie her hair back with a pink ribbon, so John would know it was her. She figured he'd recognize her because she looked like Sean, but she didn't waste time arguing, since her brother already had everything worked out.

The next evening, Kathleen went to a well-known fish-and-chips stand and watched as a solidly built man with blunt features stepped away from the building. "Are you Kathleen?" he asked.

"You must be John."

"I am." As if he wasn't sure what to do, he thrust out his hand.

Kathleen shook it and noticed his handshake was pleasantly firm—neither crushing nor limp. That was a good indication of a man's character, her uncle had always said. "It's nice to meet you," she murmured.

"You, too." He gestured to the inside seating and a large menu posted there. "Would you like to order?"

"Yes, please."

Once they'd decided, John went up to the counter to place their order, then waited to carry it back to the table. While he stood there, Kathleen had an opportunity to study her brother's friend. He seemed nervous and a bit uncomfortable. She understood that; it was how she felt herself. After Pete, she'd socialized some but always in a group. This was the first time she'd been alone with a man since the musician. She trusted her brother, and if he'd set it up, she could be assured of John's decency—and her own safety.

John returned with two cardboard containers of deep-fried fish and salty French fries, plus a small container of coleslaw. They sat across from each other at a red picnic table.

"Sean tells me you're a teacher," he said.

Kathleen licked the salt off her fingers. "Fifth grade. He told me you're a widower."

He nodded. "My wife died in September a couple of years ago. She had breast cancer."

"I'm sorry."

He reached into his wallet and pulled out two pictures. "These are our kids," he said, turning the bent photographs to face her. He pointed at the petite blonde smiling into the camera, holding two small children in her lap. "That's Patty a month before she was diagnosed." Next he pointed at the boy. "That's Steve. He was four then, but he's seven now, and Chelsea. She was two in this photo, but she's just turned five." The second picture was a more recent photograph of the children.

"They're beautiful," Kathleen said.

He stared down at the photographs. "They miss their mother."

"You miss her, too, don't you?"

He looked up as if she'd surprised him with the question. "More than words can say." He replaced the photographs and she noticed that his hand shook slightly.

Kathleen sprinkled vinegar over her fish.

"Patty liked vinegar on her fish, too."

She wasn't sure his comment warranted a response.

"Is there anything you want to know about me?" he asked.

Picking up a French fry, Kathleen paused. "This isn't an interview, John. Why don't we just have dinner and talk?"

"All right," he agreed and seemed to relax. "That would be good, except I have to leave in forty minutes. I don't like to leave the kids at night. Anyway, the neighbor lady said she could only stay until seven-thirty."

"That's not a problem."

"Would you like to meet my kids?"

"Perhaps later," Kathleen said. "I think it would be best if you and I got to know each other first. I wouldn't want the children to get close to me too soon, in case the two of us decided...you know."

"That we aren't compatible."

"Right," she confirmed.

"Good idea. I hadn't thought of that."

"Have you dated often since losing Patty?"

He shook his head. "No. You're the first."

She could've guessed that.

"You like kids, don't you?" he asked.

"Very much."

"Good," he said, sounding relieved. "You're Catholic, right?"

"John, you're interviewing me. I'm not applying for any position here."

"Right, right. Sorry."

"Relax, okay? I'm about the least scary woman you're likely to meet."

He grinned. "I don't know about that." He reached for a piece of fish, took a bite and then glanced up at her. "I like you, Kathleen. Thanks for putting me at ease."

She helped herself to another French fry. "Thank you for inviting me to dinner."

They smiled at each other. John Lopez was a good, decent man, just as her brother had said. And even if it turned out that marriage wasn't a possibility, friendship was.

42

*chapter*

## ANGELINA MARCELLO

Working with her father at Angelina's, Angie discovered a sense of peace she'd thought was lost to her after Corinne's death. She woke each morning and, instead of being overwhelmed by the crushing weight of sadness, she felt purpose and fulfillment.

Until then, she'd never truly understood her father's devotion to his restaurant. It didn't take her long to catch his fervor. In serving good food, Antonio Marcello was opening his home and his culture to the country that had welcomed him and his wife. He was a natural host, and sharing his beloved family recipes was his way of expressing his thanks, as well as providing for his family.

In the mornings, Angie worked with the kitchen crew and the head chef, Mario Deccio. When the restaurant doors opened at 5:30, she played the role of hostess, greeting each guest personally. She remembered people from previous visits and always asked about their health, their families, their businesses. Often she told the story of her parents' flight to America and recounted her earliest memories of the restaurant. With Angie and her father working side-by-side, the restaurant's reputation continued to soar.

In August of 1974, just days after Richard Nixon resigned from the Presidency and Gerald Ford was sworn in as the thirty-eighth president of the United States, Angie found her father sitting in his office intently watching the television news.

"Dad," she said, needing to discuss a pressing problem. The truckers were out on strike and the restaurant's daily deliveries hadn't been made. Unless they had fresh produce, they'd be unable to open their doors that night.

Without moving his eyes from the television screen, her father held up his hand to silence her. "In a moment."

"But Dad…"

"Gerald Ford is the new president."

"I know." Angie had never been interested in politics, but these days it was all her father talked about. Again and again he reminded her how crucial it was to be informed about current affairs. He feared that what had happened in Italy in the 30s and 40s could happen in his new country.

"He is the first president in all of America's history to become president without a national election," he said urgently.

"Yes, Dad, but this is important."

"Very important," he agreed, obviously assuming that she was referring to the political situation. "We must keep a close eye on Gerald Ford."

"I couldn't agree with you more." Knowing she wasn't going to get his full attention, she left the small office, smiling to herself.

"What did your father say we should do?" Mario asked her, nervously fidgeting in the kitchen. "When I spoke to him, he didn't even seem to be aware that there's a truckers' strike going on. The fruit and vegetables are sitting at the warehouse rotting. We have to do something."

Angie didn't have the heart to tell their chef that her father was more concerned about politics than his own restaurant. "He said I should go after the order myself."

"He said that?"

He would have if she'd asked; Angie was convinced of it. "My father has a truck. That's the practical solution, don't you think? I'll drive over and pick up as much as I can haul on my own. If the strike continues, I'll make the run again." She didn't stop to think that she hadn't driven the old truck in years and while she had a driver's license, it wasn't a current one.

"It's a hundred-mile round trip!"

"Yes, I know. I'll be as quick as I can."

The tension eased from Mario's face, and the lines between his eyebrows relaxed. "I don't know what we'd do without you, Angelina."

"Nonsense." But she smiled, aglow at his praise.

Hurrying back into her father's office, Angie said, "Dad, I need the keys to your truck."

"You're driving the truck?" he asked, looking away from the television long enough to regard her with questioning eyes. "Why?"

"Because there's a truck drivers' strike and if we don't get our supplies, we won't be able to open for dinner tonight."

"You're going to drive it all that way by yourself?"

"Yes, I am."

"You can do this?"

She nodded impatiently.

Standing, he slipped his hand into his pocket for the keys. When he placed them in her open palm, his fingers folded around hers and the tears sprang to his eyes. "You came home just in time, Angelina. I always dreamed of this day." Then, as if he'd embarrassed himself, he reached inside his back hip pocket for his handkerchief and loudly blew his nose. Sitting down again, he returned his attention to the TV.

Angelina felt a little misty-eyed herself as she walked out the back door. After all these years, her father's dream of having her work by his side had become a reality. Someday soon—when she'd sufficiently proved her devotion to the restaurant—he would hand over Angelina's to her. In most ways he already had.

It took Angie the better part of three hours to pick up their supplies and drive back. The moment she pulled up to the rear entrance, the entire kitchen crew was there to unload the boxes of fresh produce. Getting everything finished before the doors opened that night would be difficult, but Angie knew that if any staff could manage such a feat it would be hers.

"Where's my father?" she asked.

"I don't know." Mario sounded surprised. "Last time I saw him, he was in his office."

For three hours? While the staff rushed about their duties, Angie searched for her father. He wasn't in the office, which was something of a relief. A lot of people were interested in what was happening politically, but his interest was becoming an obsession.

No one answered the phone at the house.

"Mario," she said, interrupting the chef. "Where could he be?"

"I don't know," Mario said again, growing a little flustered. "Do you want me to cook or do you want me to look for Antonio?"

Angie left him to get on with his work and decided to drive around until she found her father. He sometimes went for a walk or played boccie with friends at a nearby park, but those occasions were increasingly rare. His life was the restaurant and his outside interests were few. She sometimes wondered if he had lady friends. He'd been a relatively young man when her mother died, but if there'd been some romantic interest, Angie had never been aware of it.

When she didn't find him at any of the usual places, she drove home. Although she was outwardly calm, her fears mounted. This wasn't like him. Never, ever, had he disappeared without a word.

Entering the house, she looked around. "Dad!" she called. No answer.

"Dad, where are you?" *Oh, dear God, where is he?* It was

a prayer, as fervent as any she'd ever uttered. She hadn't prayed much since leaving the convent. Some mornings when the alarm rang, she automatically threw back the covers, got out of bed and went to her knees. Reality would assert itself in a moment or two, and she'd remember that this ritual of prayer was no longer part of her life.

On Sundays she'd fallen out of the habit of attending Mass. Then a few weeks ago, she'd gone back to the Protestant church she'd visited during the deepest part of her depression. That was where Angie had found peace, so she'd returned there. Not every week, just once or twice so far, but she liked the sermons and the change from the formal rites she'd always known. For some reason, Angie thought Corinne would approve of her seeking other answers.

Taking the stairs to the second floor, Angie checked in her father's bedroom. To her shock, she found him lying on the bed sound asleep.

"Dad, you've had me worried to death," she cried. Napping in the middle of the day was one thing, but refusing to answer the phone was another.

He didn't respond. Looking more closely, she saw that he was pressing the photo of her mother, which he usually kept on the nightstand, to his heart.

Then she knew. Her beloved father was gone.

Just that morning he'd said Angie had come home just in time. She couldn't possibly have realized how true those words were.

# 43

*chapter*

## KATHLEEN O'SHAUGHNESSY

"Here's your newspaper, Mrs. Mastel," Kathleen said, dropping by the widow's apartment on her way out. It was a bright, sunny August afternoon.

"Oh, thank you, dear." The old woman sat in her overstuffed chair in front of the television, petting her imaginary Seymour. Even after his death the cat gave her comfort. "Are you off to summer school?" she asked.

"Actually I'm meeting a friend for lunch."

"That widower?"

Mrs. Mastel might be eighty years old, but she had the memory of a woman half her age. The moment she'd learned Kathleen was dating John Lopez, she hadn't let up with the questions.

"Not this time. Just a friend."

"Male or female?"

Kathleen laughed. She didn't really mind her neighbor's

interest, but she needed to leave if she was going to be on time. "Male. He's a priest, though."

"Oh, well, God bless you both."

"God already has," Kathleen said and hurried out before the widow could waylay her with more questions.

As she walked out of the apartment building, Kathleen hummed a recent hit "Please, Mr. Postman," which was an appropriate song for seeing Father Doyle. They'd exchanged letters—brief on his part—for the last two years, and talked intermittently over the phone. He was her spiritual advisor and just as importantly, her closest and dearest friend.

His trip to Seattle had come about unexpectedly, and she was delighted. She hadn't seen him face-to-face since before she'd left the convent, back in the days when they'd struggled over Father Sanders's drinking. When Father Doyle had phoned to say he'd be in Seattle for a conference, they made arrangements to meet at a popular coffeehouse near Seattle University.

Kathleen arrived ten minutes early, just to make sure they had a table. To her surprise, Father Doyle was already there. The minute he saw her, he stood. Kathleen maneuvered her way across the crowded space and held out both hands to him. He looked exactly the same—as though time had stood still. She noticed that he wasn't wearing his Roman collar, though, which surprised her; he was dressed casually in jeans and a dark sweater.

The priest's face broke into a wide smile when he recognized her, and while he looked no different, Kathleen knew she did.

"Hello, Father."

"Kathleen," he said, his eyes glowing with warmth as he smiled, studying her after a long hug. "You look wonderful!"

She flushed with his praise. Outwardly she'd changed, and inwardly too. The woman he'd known as a nun had been unsure of herself. But two years out of the convent, Kathleen had learned some valuable lessons. She now moved freely and confidently in the world she'd once feared.

"How are *you?*" she asked, wanting to hear about him for a change. It seemed so many of their conversations centered on what was happening to her.

"I'm doing well," he said. "And you?"

The waitress came just then, before Kathleen could question his answer. She sensed that his conventional response was far from accurate.

"What would you like?" Father Doyle asked.

Kathleen closed her eyes and breathed in the scent of freshly brewed coffee. It was little things like this that she loved about her life now—sitting with friends and spending time with them, eating in front of them and talking openly. "I'll have a cappuccino," she told the waitress.

"I will, too," Father Doyle said.

The woman left, and Kathleen leaned across the table, eager to return to their conversation. She wasn't about to let him sidetrack her, either, as he did all too often. "We've been friends too long for you to fool me, Brian Doyle. What's wrong?"

Her honesty appeared to surprise him. Before her eyes, he closed up, sitting back and crossing his arms. He might as well have raised a sign that said Keep Out. "Nothing. Can't we just have a pleasant conversation after I came all this way?"

"And here you are. So friend to friend, tell me what's wrong."

His refusal to confide in her was upsetting. Hurtful. Particularly because, over the last two years, she'd confided in *him* frequently. He was the only person who knew about Pete. He'd advised her, counseled her and supported her in making her own decisions dozens of times. She loved him for being her priest and her friend.

"You can't tell me?" she asked, frowning.

"No."

"Why not?"

"It's…personal," he murmured an uncomfortable moment later.

"Okay," she said, struggling to disguise her disappointment. "What do you want to talk about?"

"This widower you're dating…"

"Yes. John." They'd discussed the relationship countless times. This was old news.

"How's it going?"

"Fine, I guess." She couldn't understand why he'd asked her about this, of all things. "John's a very nice man."

"You haven't mentioned him in a while. I was just wondering."

Kathleen was doing some wondering of her own. Had she been wrong in her assumptions about Father Doyle? Apparently they *weren't* the kind of friends she'd thought they were. Not if he couldn't share his deepest concerns, yet expected Kathleen to confide hers.

"Are you going to marry him?" Father Doyle asked.

John hadn't asked Kathleen to be his wife but she realized he was thinking along those lines and frankly so was she. "I don't know. Probably." Their relationship seemed to be headed in that direction. It wasn't a passionate romance; mostly they were friends. They were emotionally compatible and the children loved Kathleen. It was more for their sake that John was interested in her, and in all honesty, Kathleen in him.

· "Do I sense hesitation?" Father Doyle murmured.

She watched the waitress set their coffees down before she glanced at Father Doyle. He seemed to be waiting for her answer. But for the first time, she didn't feel comfortable sharing her life with him.

"I don't know," she said again. She got along well with John. At almost thirty, she was eager to start a family. After her one unfortunate experience, dating terrified her, but John was comfortable and safe and he seemed genuinely fond of her. Women had married for less.

"How's Minneapolis?" she asked, thinking that would distract him. It was her way of letting him know that certain parts of her life were closed off to him, too.

"The same as always. Oh, before I forget, I brought you some wild rice," he said. Leaning down, he reached for a small bag on the floor by his chair.

"Thank you." She sipped her cappuccino. Father Doyle had always been thoughtful.

They talked for a little longer. The discussion revolved around her and her teaching position and her family, but there was nothing more about her future. Not once did Father Doyle mention his parish or anything other than the most mundane facts about his life. After twenty minutes, they'd run out of things to say.

"I guess I'd better go," she said. All these years she'd considered Father Doyle someone special in her life, but the relationship obviously hadn't been reciprocal. Disheartened, she stood, collecting her purse and the small bag of wild rice. "It was good to see you," she said formally. "Thank you for keeping in touch. Goodbye, Father Doyle."

He stood, too.

Making her way out of the coffeehouse, Kathleen felt weighed down by disappointment. She wasn't sure what she'd expected from this meeting, what she'd hoped for—but not this awkward, almost painful exchange. She'd made a mistake, assumed things about their relationship that weren't true.

Kathleen was about a block away when she heard Father Doyle call her name. She turned around, thinking she must have left something at the coffeehouse.

He was breathless when he caught up with her. He stood directly in front of her and blurted out, "Don't marry John."

She frowned. "I beg your pardon?"

"Please, Kathleen, don't marry this man."

Had he learned something about John Lopez she didn't know? "Why?"

His face was red but his eyes were clear as they met hers. "I'm leaving the priesthood."

He couldn't have shocked her more. She stared at him, too shaken to respond.

"I've already been released from my duties and have applied to Rome for a dispensation."

Kathleen still didn't know what to say.

"I realize this is a surprise. I wanted to tell you earlier, but I couldn't."

"You don't want to be a priest anymore?" That was hard to accept. Brian Doyle was a wonderful man, the best priest she'd ever known. It would break her heart to see him abandon the Church.

Brian's gaze held hers and she read his sorrow and regret. "I want to serve God. That desire has never left me, but I can no longer remain silent about certain things happening in the Church. The bishop and I cannot agree. This is the only way I have of voicing my dissatisfaction."

All this time he hadn't complained or let her know any of his feelings. He'd helped her through *her* struggles but had never shared his own. She couldn't understand it.

"You never said a word," she whispered.

"I couldn't tell you what was happening. I couldn't tell anyone, not even my family. I decided to leave very recently." He looked around for someplace they could talk.

"There's another café with a patio a couple of blocks over," she suggested.

Within minutes they were seated at the sidewalk restaurant, sipping coffee neither of them wanted.

"I didn't have a conference in Seattle," Brian confessed. "I came because of you."

Kathleen shook her head, hardly able to take in what he was saying.

"When the moment came, when you walked into the coffeehouse, I decided I couldn't tell you. And that wasn't the only thing…. I've been in love with you for years, Kathleen."

Her hand flew to her heart. "I…never knew. Never suspected."

"I made sure you didn't. It wasn't my intention to tell you."

Stunned as she was, Kathleen could barely think. "Is it because of me that you're leaving?"

"No," he said and lowered his head. He reached for her hand and held it tightly in his own. "I released my love for you, Kathleen, when you left the convent. I prayed for you, prayed God would bring a good man into your life, a man worthy of your love. When you mentioned John, I felt He had answered my prayers."

"And now?"

"Now I know God has other plans for us both."

"What happened? Can you tell me that much?"

She could see that whatever it was had broken him in ways she hadn't thought possible. "A new priest joined the parish," he finally said. "He was young and dynamic—and a practicing homosexual."

Before she could stop herself, she gasped.

"He seemed to think I shared his sexual preference and...I went to the bishop."

He didn't need to say more; Kathleen knew what had happened. Bishop Schmidt had reacted in the same manner as he had when Father Doyle had taken Father Sanders's problem to him.

"He transferred you?"

"No, he sent Father Galen to another parish. But Father Galen isn't going to change. I'm not judging his...inclinations, Kathleen. What I object to is his behavior, which is flagrant to say the least—and in a man who took a vow of celibacy. But the bishop and I..." He paused and shook his head. "I love the Church. I have dedicated my life to serving God, but I cannot remain silent and obedient to what I know is wrong."

Her fingers tightened around his.

He raised his probing gaze to her. "Kathleen, if you sincerely love John, then please tell me. I don't want to do anything to hurt you." His voice fell. "I wasn't sure what would happen when we met today."

"I...didn't know what to think when you refused to talk about yourself."

"When you walked into the restaurant, so beautiful and so vibrant, it was all I could do not to blurt out my feelings right then and there. But I realized I'd be doing you a grave disservice. I have nothing to offer you. I'm unemployed and I don't know what the future holds."

"I do," she said, smiling up at him. Turning over his palm, she rubbed it with the edge of her thumb. "Did I ever tell you about this gift I have for seeing the future?"

He smiled back. "I don't think you ever mentioned it before."

"An oversight, I assure you."

"What do you see?" he asked, staring down at his palm.

"I see your life surrounded by love."

"That's encouraging."

"You attract it to yourself by the love you give others." She glanced up and saw he was enjoying her little game.

"Anything about a wife?"

Until that moment, she didn't know how beautiful that word could sound. "Oh, yes, there's lots here about a wife. You'll marry a redhead."

He leaned down and kissed her hand. "I'm partial to redheads."

"My goodness," she said, rubbing her thumb across his palm. "Look at all these children."

"Children?" he repeated, leaning forward for a closer look. "How many?"

She sighed and closed his fingers over hers. "As many as God sees fit to give us."

# PART 5

# THE REUNION

But for me, I know that my Redeemer lives
And that He will stand upon the earth at last.
And I know that after this body has decayed
This body shall see God.

*Job* 19:25-26

Open House for
St. Peter's Convent House
in Minneapolis
August 30th, 2002
From 1-3 PM

All St. Bridget's Sisters of the Assumption
And Former Sisters
Are Cordially Invited
The Convent House has been sold
And has been slated for destruction.

Reconnect with old friends
Let us gather
and
Praise God for our time together

Joanna Murray
1335 Lakeview
Minneapolis, MN 55410
June 12, 2002

Dearest Angelina,

I couldn't mail off this invitation without enclosing a short note. My goodness, where has all the time gone? It's hard to believe it's been thirty years since we were last together. I've thought of you so often and blame myself for not keeping in touch. I think it would've helped us both if we'd made the effort. I deeply regret that we didn't have an opportunity to talk before I made my decision to leave the convent. I tried to contact you shortly after I left, but I learned that you were no longer living there, either.

Those were turbulent times for all of us — personally, professionally and emotionally. I know you blamed yourself for what happened with Corinne, but you shouldn't. You weren't at fault. I sincerely hope the years have been good to you and you've been able to put the pain of those days behind you.

As you can tell from the letterhead, I married Dr. Tim Murray who worked at St. Elizabeth's — this happened in 1974. We have two sons, Michael and Andrew. That's the short version of my news. I hope we'll be able to catch up in August.

It would mean so much to me if you'd attend the Open House. It could be a time of healing for us both. A time for laughter, too, and many, many good memories.

Sincerely,

*Joanna*

(Formerly Sister Joanna)

*Angelina's Restaurant The Finest Italian*
*Food This Side of Sicily*
*2945 31st Avenue SW Buffalo, NY 14220*

June 30, 2002

Dear Joanna,

To say it was a surprise to hear from you after all these years is an understatement. Thank you for thinking of me. I appreciate the personal invitation to the Open House. How sad that the old convent's about to be demolished. But I understand it's been empty for almost ten years and if the order was able to sell it, then all the better. Still...

As for your invitation, I've thought about it constantly since it arrived. I hope I'm not disappointing you, but I've decided against attending. I could give you a list of excuses and all of them would be valid, but the truth of the matter is that I don't have any desire to return to Minneapolis or to the convent. There are too many ghosts I'd need to face, and I'm unwilling to do that.

Don't feel bad about not keeping in touch. I haven't talked or written to anyone since I left. I couldn't. Have you? What about Sister Kathleen? She was always one of my favorites.

You're right — we certainly did have a lot of laughs together. Do you remember those rubber brownies? I still giggle every time I think about the look on Sister Eloise's face.

I'd enjoy hearing from you again, Joanna. Please give me more details about your life, but don't expect me at the Open House.

Sincerely,
*Angelina Marcello*
(Formerly Sister Angelina)

July 1, 2002

Dear Joanna,

Thanks so much for sending the invitation, which came to me through my oldest brother. What a treat to hear from you after all these years! I had no idea the convent in Minneapolis had been sold. How sad. My life is so different than it was when I was a nun. I imagine yours is, too.

Frankly, I'm surprised you stayed in Minneapolis. I couldn't get away from there fast enough. But all's well that ends well, right?

Count me in for the Open House. I can't wait to see you and everyone again.

Yours in Christ,
*Kathleen Doyle (formerly O'Shaughnessy)*

August 1, 2002

Dear Angelina,

I heard from Joanna that you've decided not to attend the Open House at the end of this month. I'm so sorry you won't be there. Is there anything I can say that will change your mind? I'd love to see you.

Dealing with the past is a tricky business, isn't it? Forgive me for being so bold, but I think that unless you face what happened to Corinne — and to you as a result — this tragedy will forever haunt you.

I'm married now, happily so, and have a wonderful family. (I'll tell you more later!) What about you? How have the years treated you? If you can't find it in you to attend the reunion, I'll understand. I'll be terribly disappointed, but I'll understand.

Your friend,
*Kathleen*

*chapter*

## JOANNA MURRAY

### AUGUST 30, 2002

The day of the reunion had finally arrived. An hour before the scheduled event, Joanna, Tim and their two sons opened the doors to what had once been the Minneapolis convent of St. Bridget's Sisters of the Assumption. The convent had closed ten years earlier, and now with the building sold and due to be destroyed, this was possibly the last time she and the others would step inside.

While her men carried in the necessary equipment and supplies, Joanna wandered down the long hallway to what had once been the chapel. Just by the door, she searched the wall for the light switch and flipped it on. Some of the bulbs had burned out, but the room was clearly illuminated.

Looking around the stark chapel with its hard stone floor and rows of wooden pews, Joanna held her breath. Slowly her gaze drifted toward the altar, now stripped bare.

Closing her eyes, she could almost hear the chants of her fellow sisters as their voices rose in worship all those years ago.

Thirty years had passed since she'd walked out of the Minneapolis convent. St. Bridget's Sisters of the Assumption had dwindled down to a few hundred members now. The average age was 69 and there were fewer and fewer women entering the community—and many of them, she'd learned, were in their forties and fifties. Usually widows who'd raised their families and were hoping to serve God in a deeper capacity.

The conservative order had undergone a transformation in the years since Joanna had joined in February of 1967. St. Bridget's Sisters had held out against the changes brought about by the Second Vatican Council much longer than the smaller orders. For one thing, they were one of the last orders to modify the habit. These days, the habit had been discarded entirely. A few still chose to wear a simple black veil and crucifix, but those were mainly the older nuns who, early on, had so rigorously resisted the changes. The Grand Silence was another aspect of convent life that had disappeared.

Women who entered the novitiate were no longer subjected to the Year of Silence, either, the year that had been such a trial for her. How she'd struggled those twelve months, and what valuable lessons she'd learned about herself...

Gone, too, was the Chapter of Faults, public penance and the austere living quarters. While she was organizing the reunion, Joanna had visited a woman who was currently a St. Bridget's sister in Minneapolis. Joanna had a vague recollection of Sister Colleen, who'd been transferred to the convent here shortly before her own departure. This visit had made her aware of the many differences between then and now. In fact, a tour of the apartment the nuns rented had shown her exactly how far the order had come. Sister Colleen had proudly pointed out the cheerful decorations. Even the bedrooms revealed the personality and character of their inhabitants. Joanna recalled her own cell, a bleak room with no hint of either.

The one change that impressed and pleased her most was the openness and friendliness of Sister Colleen and the other two nuns she'd met. They had invited her to lunch and then before the meal, they'd all joined hands for a communal prayer. When she'd expressed her surprise, Joanna learned that the sisters now saw hospitality as akin to godliness. She'd been a nun in the days when eating with anyone other than fellow sisters—or occasionally family—was actively discouraged.

Joanna wondered if these changes, had they come sooner, would have influenced her decision. In retrospect she doubted it. Ritual or lack of it wasn't the issue. Remaining a nun would have deprived her of the children she longed to love.

She walked down the center aisle of the chapel and slipped into a pew. As she sat on the hard wooden bench, emotion swept through her. Her years serving Christ had been good ones. She had no regrets. Not about entering the convent and not about leaving. She'd fulfilled her mission, met Tim and—

"Mom," Michael, her oldest son, grunted as he came into the chapel, carrying a hefty floral basket. "Where do you want me to put this?"

"Over there," she said, pointing to the left of the altar.

"What about this one?" Andrew asked, following his brother.

"On the other side."

As her sons placed the floral displays by the altar, Joanna watched them with a deep sense of pride. They were strong, handsome young men and the joy of her life. She and Tim had decided to wait for two years after their marriage to start their family. She'd wanted to cement their relationship first and Tim had agreed.

"Dad's getting the table set up in the foyer. He'll be along in a minute."

Michael stood with his hands on his hips and glanced around. "You really lived here?"

"I really did."

"It's hard for me to think of my mother as a nun, you know." Like his father, Andrew was six feet tall, but he had the blond hair of the Baird family. Michael possessed his father's interest in medicine and was currently serving his residency in Abbott Northwestern Hospital. Also like his father, Michael wasn't in a hurry to marry and settle down.

Andrew, on the other hand, a recent graduate of the University of Minnesota at Duluth, had majored in chemistry and girls. Odds were her youngest son would be engaged by the end of the summer.

"Do you mind if we take a look around?" Michael asked. "It's not like I'll have the opportunity to explore a convent again anytime soon."

"Feel free," Joanna told them. "But it hasn't been a convent for quite a few years."

"Does that make you sad?" Andrew asked. He was the more sensitive of her sons.

Joanna shook her head. "Not really. It was no longer part of my life by the time it closed."

As soon as the boys had left, Tim walked into the chapel. "I thought I'd find you in here." He slid an arm around her waist and kissed her cheek.

Joanna leaned against her husband of almost thirty years and gave a long, slow sigh. "You wouldn't believe the hours I spent in this chapel." Every morning and evening, she was here for lauds and compline. And if she wasn't at the hospital, working her shift, then she was here at noon for the Angelus, too.

"Praying?"

"Always. We worshiped here as a community. Oh, Tim, I remember how lovely our voices sounded. As a postulant I struggled with the singing, but I came to sincerely love it."

"I came to sincerely love you." He rested his jaw on the crown of her head.

"Most of my prayers here in those final days were for you," she confessed. "Or more accurately, for me and the way I felt about you. Again and again I begged God to keep my heart pure." She turned her head slightly to face him. "You can't imagine what it was like to be a nun and at the same time desperately in love with you."

"Yes, I can," he said, tightening his hold on her waist. "I was a man desperately in love with a nun. How do you think that made *me* feel?"

"Culpable and depraved."

"You know what they say about forbidden fruit," her husband teased, releasing her.

Smiling, Joanna walked to the front of the chapel and straightened the floral displays. After months of careful planning she was suddenly nervous about seeing the other nuns again. This was far different—far more significant—than the high school reunions she'd attended over the years.

"You're anxious," Tim said, sounding surprised.

"A little," she admitted. Naturally, every now and again she'd run into other women like herself who'd once been nuns. Most people, however, were unaware of her previous life, and she was reluctant to mention it. If anyone asked what she'd done before she married Tim, she simply said she was a nurse. She knew from experience that the minute people learned she'd been a nun, there would be an awkward silence or worse, a double-take, and then the inevitable questions. Answering those was the hardest.

Only people who'd lived it themselves could appreciate how important that time had been to her. The woman she was now—the wife, the mother, the nurse, the Catholic—had been created by the years she'd spent as a sister.

It was for this reason that Joanna eagerly anticipated the reunion. Like her, almost all the nuns she'd known had left the order—the statistics were staggering. The last article she'd read reported that between 1969 and 1980, seventy percent of the order had either died or left.

Despite her own decision to leave, it saddened her that so many priests and nuns had forsaken the religious life, and that so many Catholics had abandoned the Church. The scandals that had recently become public were devastating spiritually and emotionally to those who'd remained faithful.

Slowly the Church would recover. Devout Catholics—like her, like Tim—were working hard to rebuild what had been lost.

"I don't regret the time I spent here," she told her husband.

"Neither do I," Tim replied. "We never would've met otherwise."

"Oh, you would've married someone else," she said, confident that one of the lovely nurses who'd pursued him would have captured his attention.

"I don't think so," he said, his eyes serious. "I needed you, Joanna. After Vietnam I came back emotionally empty. I'd turned away from God and anything that had to do with religion. You were the one who showed me the way back."

"And you showed me how to love. You taught me that loving a man, a family, didn't mean loving God any less."

"Thank you, Joanna," he said quietly.

"Mom." Andrew stuck his head in the door. "Someone's here."

"Already?" She glanced at her watch with a sense of panic. She wasn't nearly ready yet! She still had the front table to organize and the food trays to set up and coffee to brew. It would be impossible to do all that and still greet everyone as they arrived.

"I'll start the coffee," Tim said, giving her a chance to greet the first guest.

Kathleen O'Shaughnessy—Joanna recognized her instantly—walked into the chapel.

"Joanna?" she asked.

"Kathleen?"

With small cries of delight, they hurried toward each other and hugged fiercely.

"I thought I'd come a little early and help you get ready."

Joanna relaxed. "I'm so glad you're here."

Kathleen looked around the chapel, and Joanna could see that her friend was experiencing the same emotions she had when she'd first walked inside.

Oh yes, this reunion was going to be good for them all.

# chapter 45

## KATHLEEN DOYLE

### 2002

Kathleen felt such joy to be attending this reunion. "I can't believe we're finally here," she said excitedly.

"When did you arrive?" Joanna asked.

"Just this minute. We drove from Seattle. Brian's parking the car and then walking over to the rectory."

The two hugged again. "I'm just thrilled you could make it."

"I think that means Joanna welcomes the help," a tall man said, entering the chapel. Kathleen assumed he was Joanna's husband. "The coffee's going," he said, smiling at his wife.

"I was hoping I could lend you a hand. It's wonderful that you're doing this." Kathleen had enjoyed her brief correspondence with Joanna and was anxious to catch up with everything that had happened in her friend's life and the lives of the other sisters she'd lived with.

"Wait a minute. Doyle? Brian Doyle?" Joanna said slowly. "Wasn't there a priest at St. Peter's with that name?"

Kathleen nodded.

"You married Brian Doyle, the *priest?*" Joanna asked, not disguising her shock. "I never made the connection."

"Technically Brian is still a priest."

"Whoa!" Joanna's husband held up his hand. "You'd better explain that."

"Tim?" Kathleen suddenly grinned. "I remember now—you're the doctor who came to Mass that one Sunday. Joanna nearly fell out of the choir loft trying to get a better look at you."

Joanna blushed.

"You never told me that," Tim said with a laugh.

Joanna playfully jabbed him in the ribs.

"Explain the comment about Brian still being a priest," Tim said curiously.

"He's a married priest," Kathleen said. "We never intended for this to happen. He made the decision to leave and applied to Rome, but Rome never responded."

"You mean to say it's more than just his letter getting lost in the mail?" Joanna asked, frowning.

Kathleen nodded. "Much more. It's become a political battle of wills. Rome was losing so many American priests that the ecclesiastical authorities decided to ignore requests for the dispensation of vows. Apparently they hoped the priests would ultimately change their minds. In our case, that strategy didn't work."

"I didn't know anything like that was happening."

"Few people do."

"Does he continue to celebrate Mass?" Joanna asked. It was a frequent question.

"Every Sunday. There are so many disenfranchised Catholics in the Seattle area. Over the years we sort of found one another. Brian works a forty-hour week as a loan officer, but on Sunday mornings he's a priest."

"Do you have a meeting place?" Tim asked. "A church?"

Kathleen smiled. "In a manner of speaking. We have everyone over to the house and our living room becomes our place of worship." She marveled at how many people had heard about their Sunday-morning Masses. Former Catholics arrived, needing to talk; Brian offered a willing ear and a way to return to God and the Church, even if the road back was a bit unconventional.

"You actually celebrate Mass in your home?" Joanna repeated.

"We've had as many as fifty people show up, and afterward there's a potluck breakfast. That way, people get to know each other. It's really a wonderful time of fellowship."

"You must have a huge house."

"We have a large family. Once we decided we wouldn't wait for the dispensation from Rome any longer, Brian and I decided to have our family all at once." At Joanna's puzzled look, she explained. "We had a set of triplets and then twins."

"Oh, my."

"A year and a half apart."

Joanna burst out laughing, and Kathleen didn't blame her. There were no multiple births in her family, but Kathleen had broken that statistic—twice. Those early years hadn't been easy, but they'd managed and grown close because of it.

"I don't know whether to give you my condolences or to congratulate you."

"Congratulate us," Kathleen said. "They're all adults, all married and we're already grandparents."

"That's wonderful," Joanna said.

"Now." Kathleen rubbed her hands briskly together. "What can I do to help?"

"Let's get the food set up out front," Joanna suggested.

Kathleen followed her out of the chapel, but just as she was about to leave, she turned to face the altar, now bare and somehow desolate. It'd been years since Kathleen had stepped inside a Catholic church. Years since she'd even thought about this chapel. She smiled at the thought that these days her home was also her church.

Many of the people who came to their house on Sundays knew she was a former nun and Brian a priest. That seemed to comfort those who sought them out. People felt free to express their own differences with the Church, knowing Kathleen and Brian had experienced similar troubles themselves.

Turning resolutely away from her past, Kathleen hurried out to the front foyer, where a wooden table had been set up.

Joanna had everything neatly organized. Under Kathleen's admiring eye, she brought out a lace tablecloth and together they placed that on the table.

"Who all is coming?" Kathleen asked eagerly.

"Sister Martha was the first to respond."

"The choir director?" Kathleen could well remember the woman who'd led them in song, who'd insisted it was their duty to provide music for Sunday Masses.

"That's the one."

"What about Sister Eloise?" She'd had her share of differences with Sister Superior, but she'd always respected the nun who was the head of the Minneapolis convent.

Joanna set a small bouquet of flowers on the table. She straightened and her face became somber. "Unfortunately, Sister Eloise died in the mid-nineties."

"I'm sorry to hear that."

"Julia will be here," Joanna continued. "Judging by what she wrote, she went back to her hometown in Kansas and stayed there. She's still teaching."

"Still?" It had to be in a Catholic school, Kathleen guessed. After leaving, many of them had accepted teaching positions. This time, however, when they stepped into a classroom, they collected a paycheck. Unfortunately many of the parochial schools had closed after the exodus of nuns. It became impossible to keep tuition costs down and still pay teachers a living wage. Until her own children were born, Kathleen had taught first in a Catholic elementary school and when they were older, she'd been a teacher for the Seattle school district. She'd recently retired and now worked for the state in Children's Protective Services.

"What about Sister Angelina?" Kathleen asked.

Joanna shook her head. "I tried to convince her, but she wasn't interested."

"I was afraid of that. I wrote her after hearing from you and I tried to get her to come, too. She never answered my letter. It's a real disappointment not to see her."

"It is," Joanna agreed. "Remember those fabulous Italian dinners she threw together without so much as a recipe? The woman was a marvel in the kitchen," she murmured as she displayed a guest book. "Now I know why. Her father owned a restaurant, which Angelina runs."

"Doesn't surprise me. I never ate better Italian food in my life. Not before and not since."

The front door opened and Kathleen glanced up to see her husband. They'd been looking forward to this trip; it was a vacation and much more for them. A reconciliation with the past, a chance to visit places that had meant so much.

"Was there anyone at the rectory?" she asked.

He nodded. "A young priest from the Philippines."

"The Philippines?"

"Yes, Father Apia is the assistant. And our parish priest is from Nigeria," Joanna said. "He's wonderful. We feel fortunate to have them both."

"Nigeria," Brian said, looking to Kathleen. It didn't surprise her that many of America's parish priests now came from foreign countries. They'd seen this trend developing when priests started leaving the priesthood at a rate that was impossible for the seminary graduates to replace.

"Did you learn anything about Father Sanders?" Kathleen asked.

Regret showed in her husband's eyes. "He died several years back. Father Apia had heard of him, but didn't have a lot of information. Apparently he was killed in an automobile accident."

Kathleen met her husband's eyes. Her question was reflected in his. They both wondered if he'd been drunk at the time.

"It was a sad situation," Joanna said.

"He had a drinking problem," Kathleen ventured, wondering how much, if anything, she should say.

"Yes, that came out afterward."

"Was anyone else killed, do you know?"

"No," Joanna said, "and we're all grateful. Father Sanders was driving the wrong way on the Interstate. Apparently he realized what he'd done and was trying to cross over the embankment. He gathered speed and hit the median at ninety miles an hour."

"Dear God." Kathleen covered her mouth with her hand.

"He flipped the car and was killed instantly." Joanna's mouth trembled. "It was a tragic loss. Father was so well-liked. The entire Minneapolis church grieved for him."

"Do you know anything about Father Yates?" Brian asked, a moment later. "The priest who replaced me?"

"You don't know?" Joanna asked, sounding surprised. "He became Bishop Yates after Bishop Schmidt passed away."

Kathleen couldn't believe it, and from the look on Brian's face, he couldn't, either. On the other hand, Father Yates's ambitions weren't exactly a secret, she thought.

"He wasn't a popular bishop."

"I can imagine," Kathleen murmured.

"He died of cancer a couple of years later."

"I'm sorry to hear that," Brian said, and Kathleen knew her husband well enough to recognize that his sentiments were sincere. This generosity of spirit was one of the many qualities she loved about him. Not a day passed that she didn't thank God for bringing this man into her life.

Without Brian, she might eventually have married John Lopez. She wondered now if it would've been a good marriage. Especially when it was discovered that Kathleen had a reproductive "peculiarity," as her doctor described it. Not until after the twins were born did they learn that her body released more than one egg at a time. All her births were destined to be multiple.

For five years straight, Kathleen didn't sleep through a single night. Neither did Brian. Such demands might have destroyed some marriages, but her husband had been a helpmate in every sense of the word. After giving birth to five children in such a short time, they had no problem resorting to birth control, although Brian had preached against it only a few years earlier.

"Mom." A tall, blond young man came in the door. He stopped when he saw Kathleen and Brian. "Hi," he said, then turned to Joanna. "There's someone outside. I think she might be one of you guys."

"Us guys," Joanna said out of the corner of her mouth.

"She's sitting in her car and I think she's crying. Maybe you should check it out."

Kathleen and Joanna exchanged looks. "Do you think it might be Angelina?" Joanna asked.

"Oh, I hope it is. She *should* be here. This day might wipe out thirty years of pain."

Joanna started for the door and then came back for Kathleen. "Come with me," she urged. "She might be able to refuse me, but she can't say no to both of us."

*chapter*

# ANGELINA MARCELLO

## 2002

Even now, Angie couldn't believe she was in Minneapolis. She knew Joanna was right, that unless she confronted the past, she'd never be able to deal with the future. At the last possible moment, with some encouragement from friends, she'd made plane reservations and arranged for a rental car.

There was a second reason she'd decided to attend the reunion: to visit the Sullivan family. It didn't seem possible that Corinne had been dead thirty years. Thirty years! Countless times Angie had thought about the girl and wished that things had been different—that Corinne had talked to her, that she'd been summoned to the door when Jimmy came looking for her...

Normally Angie would have arranged a meeting with the Sullivans well in advance. Years in the restaurant business had taught her the importance of handling situations in a businesslike manner. Had she thought this through adequately, she'd have phoned ahead.

She hadn't, because she wasn't sure she had the courage to face Corinne's parents. Then she'd awakened less than thirty hours ago and realized she'd been given an opportunity to settle the complex issues of her past. As Joanna had said, she'd regret it if she didn't attend this reunion.

What Angie should have considered was that the Sullivans might no longer live in the area. In fact, a short investigation had revealed that Bob and Sharon Sullivan had moved to Arizona after his retirement in the late eighties.

Almost in afterthought, Angie had sought out Jimmy Durango. She'd looked up his name in the phone book and was amazed to find it. He answered the call himself and the conversation had been one of the most cathartic of her life.

"Sister, I can't believe it's you!" he'd burst out.

She hadn't bothered to correct him about her status. "How are you, Jimmy? Have the years been good to you?"

"They've been very good. I'm married, and Sandy and I have two kids. Matt's twenty and Carol Anne's twenty-two. I ended up doing a stint in the Army a couple of years after Corinne died."

"Did you see the Sullivans often?" she'd asked.

He released a heavy sigh. "No, they didn't want much to do with me, and I can't say I blame them. Having a daughter of my own now, I can understand a lot better what they must've gone through."

Angie felt that was generous of him. She could only imagine the guilt he'd carried with him. He didn't say it, but she suspected that the Sullivans blamed Jimmy for their daughter's death. For most people, it was easier, somehow, to deal with tragedy if they could point a finger at someone else.

"Sister," Jimmy had said. "I don't want you to think I forgot Corinne." His voice wavered slightly. "For almost two years, I went to the cemetery nearly every day. My folks were worried about me. They were right because I felt—I don't know—that life wasn't worth living after she died."

Angie understood that feeling far better than he realized.

"Then one day, it came to me that Corinne had loved me.

She died loving me. The last words I ever heard her speak were to tell me she was sorry and that she loved me. She wouldn't want me killing myself because of what happened to her. That would've made her death even worse.

"Shortly after that, I walked into the Army recruiter's office and enlisted. It was the best decision I could've made at the time."

"I suppose it gave you a new kind of life."

"Yes," Jimmy agreed, "it did. Over the years I kept in contact with Jerry, Corinne's older brother. Her parents went through a rough stretch for a couple of years, too, but like me, they eventually learned to cope with their loss in their own way. Her mother got real active in a pregnancy hotline. Her father retired about fifteen years ago, and they moved almost right after that. Jerry says they seem happy and that they've made a lot of friends in Arizona."

"I'm so glad to hear it."

"Me, too," Jimmy said.

They'd ended the conversation a short while later, and Angie had been fighting back tears ever since. Although it was early, she drove to the convent house and sat in her car, letting the memories wash over her.

A car was parked out front, but she wasn't sure whether it belonged to Joanna or to someone visiting the church. Outwardly, the convent house hadn't changed much. She'd been saddened to learn that it was sold and being torn down. There was no reason for the motherhouse to hold on to the building, which had apparently sat empty for a number of years.

So many memories. Her gaze drifted toward what had once been the high school. That, too, had closed. Years and years of students had walked through those now-vacant halls. Girls like Corinne and Morgan, and boys like Jimmy Durango. Teenagers who were adults now, with grown families of their own.

Angie could only hope that the skills she'd taught there had served her students well throughout the years.

Looking back at the convent, Angie saw two figures step out of the building and walk across the street toward her. She squinted against the bright sun, but instantly recognized Sister Kathleen. How could she miss her with that mass of red hair? And—oh, my goodness—was that Sister Joanna?

Not waiting to find out, Angie climbed out of the car and with outstretched arms, approached the two women.

"Joanna? Kathleen?"

"Angelina?"

Soon she was enveloped in a three-way hug.

"Most people call me Angie now," she said, laughing as they stood apart to study each other and the changes thirty years had brought. She brushed at the fresh tears spilling down her cheeks.

"I'm so *happy* you decided to join us," Joanna said, slipping her arm around Angie's ample waist. She was forty pounds heavier since leaving the convent.

"I'm happy to be here, too." She sincerely meant that.

As soon as she was inside the old convent, Angie was introduced to both their husbands.

"I never got married," Angie told them with a tinge of regret. "I always thought I would. Always wanted to, but it just never happened."

"You have a restaurant?"

She nodded. "The one my father started over fifty years ago." Given the choice, though, Angie would have preferred a husband and children. As she'd told her friends, it just hadn't happened, but not for lack of wishing. Or trying. Twice she'd met and seriously dated men she was interested in; both times the relationships had looked promising. But then, for reasons she'd never really understood, both men had ended the relationships.

As the years passed, she'd come to think the problem might be hers rather than theirs. One of her theories was that having entered the convent at eighteen, her social and emotional development had remained that of an adolescent. She cringed whenever she thought of it, and wondered if it could be true. There was no one she trusted to be honest enough to tell her the truth.

Both men had been married previously; Mark was a widower and Kenneth divorced. Each had been eager to marry again, but after a while, she'd found herself withdrawing. Despite her own desire for a family, she could never make a complete commitment to either man.

However, she'd remained good friends with Mark's two daughters. Angie kept in touch with them and they often turned to her for advice. Although Mark had eventually remarried, neither Janice nor Nikki was close to his second wife.

Their fondness for Angie had been a sweet balm through these last few years. Childless years. When Mark's daughters learned of the reunion, they'd urged Angie to attend. Janice had driven her to the airport and stayed with her until it was time to go to her gate.

Angie liked to think she would've remained friends with Corinne had the teenager lived.

The foyer, with its dark carpet and straight-backed chairs, looked exactly the way Angie remembered, except that the statue of Mary was missing from its alcove.

Joanna and Kathleen stood behind a long table, and while Joanna had Angie sign the guest book, Kathleen sorted through the name tags until she found the one that read Angelina Marcello.

"Sister Martha's coming and Julia, too," Kathleen announced cheerfully. "And Sister Joan, Sister Dorothy, Sister Anne—oh, it'll be so good to see everyone again."

"Would it be all right if I wandered around for a bit before the others arrive?" Angie asked.

"Oh, sure, but there's not much left to see."

"The chapel's still there, but the altar's been stripped," Kathleen told her.

Angie stopped at the chapel first. She stood in the entrance and closed her eyes, listening with her heart as the echoed prayers of the sisters seemed to reverberate around her. So much devotion and love had been sent to God from this room. It was as if Angie could hear those prayers now. She hadn't expected to feel such strong emotion. Perhaps a vague sense of loss and regret, but not these intense feelings that transported her to that most innocent time in her life.

She turned to leave and nearly walked into a young man.

"Oh, hi," he said, balancing a large deli tray. "You wouldn't happen to know where the kitchen is, would you?"

"Right this way."

"Mom thought it'd be a good idea to keep these meat trays refrigerated until we need them."

"Mom is Joanna or Kathleen?"

"Joanna. You were a nun too?" He looked at her in a way that said he found it hard to believe.

"Many years ago," she said smiling to herself.

"Did you know my mom when she was a nun?"

"I did," Angie told him.

"What was she like? I mean, I only see her as my mother."

"I don't imagine she's any different." Angie didn't know the woman Joanna had become, but she could well remember the nun she'd once been. "What did she tell you?"

"Not much, but she's talked about this reunion for months. She's been filling us in—my dad, my brother and me—on where some of the other sisters ended up. I'm sure you'll hear all of that soon enough."

And she did. Angie stayed in the kitchen for much of the reunion. It was where she felt most comfortable. But nuns and former nuns frequently sought her out to exchange stories. It became obvious that the adjustment for her had been relatively easy compared to some of the others.

She carried out deli trays and brewed several pots of coffee. Between trips in and out of the kitchen, she caught snippets of conversation.

"I married the first man I ever kissed. Our marriage didn't last six months. I was devastated," one woman said sadly. "I failed as a nun and then my marriage ended in divorce. I went from being a highly exalted Catholic to an outcast in two fast lessons."

Angie understood. She, too, had fallen from grace.

"I used to drive down to the convent at nights," she heard Sister Martha—now plain Martha Shaw—confess to Joanna. "I missed my life here so much and yet I knew I could never go back. It was months before I stopped doing that. I'm so happy to have this opportunity to say goodbye to our old building."

Angie felt the same way herself. Attending the reunion had been the right decision; she was glad she'd come.

"For me it was a hurting and healing process at the same time," Angie heard Kathleen tell the former Sister Loretta. "I lived in Seattle in the House of Peace and talked about my feelings with a counselor. But just when I was sure everything was going to be all right, something would happen and I'd stumble into a depression. The convent was a safe haven. Here I had community, liturgy, theology and love. The world can be a cruel place when you're alone."

Angie had been saved from that by her father. He'd always been there for her, from the beginning until the end. She felt his love even now, years after his death from a massive stroke.

Once inside the kitchen again, she refilled the coffeepot with water and spooned the grounds in the container before turning it on.

"You should be mingling with the others," Joanna said, stepping into the room.

She smiled. "I will later."

"I never intended for you to take on this task."

"Why not? I saw a need and I filled it. Isn't that what we were taught in the convent?"

Joanna laughed. "You have me there. Kathleen and her husband are coming to my house afterward. Could you join us? I don't feel we've had near enough time to catch up."

"I'd enjoy that very much," Angie said.

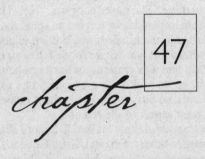

47

chapter

## JOANNA'S HOUSE

Joanna sat on the large sofa in her spacious living room as Tim opened the wine. The reunion had been exhausting but well worth the months of effort that had gone into the planning. Gathering the community of nuns and former nuns one last time had been everything she'd prayed it would be. Now with Kathleen and Angie, Joanna could unwind after a hectic afternoon.

"I can't thank you enough for doing this," Kathleen said, sitting next to her husband. The sky was only beginning to darken, the last rays of the sun casting a warm glow over the lake that was visible from the large living room windows.

Brian Doyle placed his arm around his wife. "It was smart to do this while the convent was still intact. I only wish something like this could be arranged for priests and former priests—the guys I went to seminary with, for instance."

"I didn't know how I'd feel about this weekend," Angie

said, accepting a glass of merlot from Tim Murray. She sat in the recliner and leaned back, her gaze focused on the setting sun. "Even after the plane landed, I wasn't sure coming here was the right thing." She raised her glass. "Now I know it was."

Joanna remembered how Angie had spent much of the reunion secluded in the kitchen. She'd worried about it at first but then realized this was where Angie felt most comfortable. Not only that, she was grateful for the extra help.

"Did you get to visit with everyone?" she asked, fearing Angie had been so busy with details she'd missed out on the most important aspect of the reunion.

"I had a wonderful time. I talked to Sister Julia and Martha and a number of others. Oh, and Sister Colleen."

"I don't remember Sister Colleen," Kathleen said, frowning. She glanced from Angie to Joanna.

"She taught ninth-grade French," Angie explained.

"Oh, yes," Kathleen said. "She must have left the community after we did."

"No," Joanna said. "Sister Colleen's still a member of the order, although she no longer wears a habit."

"Surely she's retired from teaching by now?" Kathleen murmured.

Angie crossed her legs. "I believe so—quite a while ago, I'd say. She didn't mention exactly when, but she did tell me she shares an apartment in the city with two other nuns. All three of them work with the homeless."

"Yes," Joanna said. "I've visited the sisters at their place. And I've seen Sister Colleen at parish events."

"Did she tell you why she stayed?" Kathleen asked Angie. "There must've been tremendous pressure to leave when so many other women did."

Angie shook her head. "We didn't get around to discussing that, but I have the feeling Colleen's been completely content with her life. As I remember it, she always was. She felt then as she does now, that she was doing God's work." Angie paused and sipped her wine. "It did come as a shock to her that I'm no longer a Catholic."

"You mean you don't attend Mass?" Tim asked, moving to the edge of the cushion, openly curious.

Joanna smiled to herself. Her husband was a strong Catholic, and a Eucharistic minister in their church. No one who knew him would believe that at one time he'd rejected God and Church.

"I attend a Protestant church in Buffalo now," Angie explained.

"In our day, that was like joining ranks with the enemy," Joanna said with a laugh. "We didn't dare so much as walk on the same side of the street as one of those *other* churches."

"I talked to two or three women today who've left the Church," Kathleen said. "In fact, not one of them wants anything to do with the Catholic Church. Remember Sister Janet? She's dropped out, and so has Sister Ruth."

Joanna had been so busy acting as hostess that she hadn't had the opportunity for more than brief conversations with any of the visitors. She was hoping her friends would enlighten her.

"I had the most wonderful afternoon," Kathleen murmured. "It was such a validation of the decisions I made, and it was so great to talk to women who understand everything I went through when I first left the convent."

Everyone looked to Kathleen, nodding in sympathy. "That time wasn't easy for me," she said softly. "But I was fortunate in that I had a supportive older brother and a place to go."

"I've heard of nuns who were given little or no support by their communities," Angie added.

"Can you imagine," Kathleen said, "coming out of the convent after twenty or more years with no retirement funds, no savings and sometimes no skills?"

Tim frowned and shook his head. "That didn't happen to any of you, though, did it?"

"No," Kathleen was quick to respond, "but we were relatively young when we left." She gave a slight shrug. "We all went our own ways for different reasons—but there were similarities in each case, too."

Joanna agreed. "I left because I'd grown into a completely

different woman from the nineteen-year-old girl who'd entered the convent with a broken heart. I was so certain I had a vocation. I wasn't prepared six years later to find myself feeling restless and uncertain."

Tim loudly cleared his throat. "You mean to say *I* didn't have anything to do with your decision?"

Everyone laughed, including Joanna. "Yes, dear," she said, playing along. "I was in love and longing for a family, too." But it was more than that. In her pain over the broken engagement, Joanna had turned to God for comfort, convincing herself that He was calling her into His service. Her vocation hadn't been genuine, although no one could have convinced her of that in 1967. If it had been, she'd still be a nun to this day, the same as Sister Colleen.

"I was one of the lucky ones," Angie said. "I had a home and a career waiting for me. Never once did I feel displaced or a burden to my father. According to his friends, the minute I was back, my dad was happier than he'd been since I left."

"A lot of the women I talked to mentioned feeling guilty," Kathleen said.

To Joanna, that made sense. For a time, soon after she'd come home, she too had experienced the burden of guilt.

"I think a lot of us felt lost and displaced," Kathleen said. "For myself, I went from Grand Silence to my brother's house with two preschool children. Emma and Paul had no appreciation for silence."

That comment produced smiles all around.

"I talked with one former nun—I don't think she was part of the community when we were—who spoke of that feeling of displacement," Kathleen continued. "She couldn't go back to live with her parents, nor could she afford to rent a place of her own."

"What about friends?"

Kathleen shook her head. "She didn't say, but I sort of had the feeling that she's been drifting for years, no roots, no real home or family."

"That's sad," Angie murmured.

"I was surprised how many of us have married and divorced," Joanna said. She'd talked to four former nuns who'd married quickly after leaving the convent; after a child or two, their marriages had fallen apart. It made her feel all the more blessed to have Tim in her life.

"A lot of the women I spoke to had problems with relationships," Kathleen added. "Especially relationships with men."

One of the most telling conversations of the afternoon had been with a woman who'd come out of the novitiate at the same time as Joanna. "Sister Joan's been married three times in the last twenty-five years. She said she'd failed God as a nun and then was divorced within a year of her first marriage."

"Talk about going from respected to rejected in two short steps," Tim said, and sipped his wine. He reached for Joanna's hand and they entwined their fingers.

"I want to go back to this issue of relationships with men," Brian said. "Was it a recurring theme?"

"It was," his wife confirmed.

"It must have something to do with how submissive we were taught to be," Angie said thoughtfully. "Remember Custody of the Eyes?" She rolled her own eyes now, mocking the custom of always lowering one's gaze while in the presence of a man.

"I think that submissiveness set many of us up for exploitation by men," Kathleen muttered.

Joanna noted the way Brian's arm tightened around his wife's shoulders, as if offering her love and reassurance. "My biggest problem was money," she said.

"Not enough?" Angie asked.

"No—managing it. Before I entered the convent, as well as when I left, I lived with my parents. As soon as I could, I got my own apartment but I had no idea how to budget my paycheck."

"She still has problems with budgeting." Tim winked, then went around with the wine bottle and refreshed everyone's glass.

"If you had it to do over again, Angie, would you have joined the convent?" Kathleen asked, nodding her thanks at Tim.

Angie hesitated. "Given everything I know now?"

"Yes, everything."

Gnawing on her lower lip, Angie nodded. "I would. I loved being a nun and part of a community. You two," she said, gesturing toward Joanna and Kathleen, "and the others... You were the sisters I never had—the big family I always wanted. It was good for a lot of years, but finally I had to move on. There was the whole mess with Corinne, which was a real catalyst for me. And as it turned out, my father needed me. Just hours before he died, he told me I came back just in time."

A silence fell over them. "I'd do it again, too," Kathleen admitted. "To this day I can't say for sure whether I had a vocation or if I was just living up to my family's expectations. All I know is that I was raised with the knowledge that one day I'd be a nun. That life was everything I'd anticipated and more. After a while, though, I started to wonder about my role in the Church."

Joanna knew that Kathleen might have continued with the community for years if not for Father Sanders, God rest his soul.

"What about you, Joanna?" Kathleen asked. "Would you join the convent if you had a chance to do it all over again?"

Like her friends, Joanna nodded. "I wouldn't be the woman I am today if I hadn't spent those years in the convent. Nor would I have met Tim." She smiled at her husband, this man whom she'd loved for thirty years, and their eyes held for a long moment.

Joining the convent *had* been right for Joanna at that time in her life. She'd found warmth and healing in those years with St. Bridget's Sisters of the Assumption.

"No regrets?" Angie asked, looking around at her friends.

"None," Kathleen said.

"None," Joanna said.

The three raised their wineglasses in a silent toast to the years they'd lived in love and trust and faith. Their lives might have changed in every conceivable way, but those feelings had not—and never would.

# GLOSSARY

**Convent:** The residence of a religious community, especially nuns.

**Mother Superior:** The nun who is the head of a religious community.

**Motherhouse:** The residence of the head of a religious community. Central home for the Order. Nuns are sent from the motherhouse on assignments or missions. Postulants and Novices are trained at the motherhouse. Nuns take their vows there.

**Sister Superior:** The head of a convent or house away from the motherhouse.

**Divine Office:** Compilation of prayers based on scripture, prayed at different hours of the day. The Divine Office consists of Prime, Lauds, Matins, Compline and Vespers, each prayed at different times of the day, also known as Hours.

**Custody of the Eyes:** The habit of keeping the eyes lowered in order to meditate and pray, and away from things that would distract from God.

**Postulant:** The first-year candidate for admission into a religious order.

**Novice:** A second- and third-year candidate for the second stage of becoming a nun. A woman is admitted into a religious order for a period of probation before taking vows.

**Diocese:** The area under the jurisdiction of a bishop. There are 184 dioceses in the United States.

**Chapter of Faults:** A humbling, cleansing way to deeper prayer. A nun kneels before her fellow sisters and her superior once a week to confess the faults of the week and receive a penance from the superior.

**Grand Silence:** The practice of keeping silent from 7:30 p.m. until 7:30 a.m.

**The Year of Silence:** Novitiate candidates are asked to maintain a year of silence while contemplating their vocation in their first year.

Please turn the page to read a preview of

*THE SHOP ON BLOSSOM STREET*
*by*
*Debbie Macomber*

*This deeply emotional story touches on all the themes*
*Debbie's readers love:*

*This deeply emotional story touches on all the themes*
*Debbie's readers love: romance, friendship, the impor-*
*tance of family and community. You'll get to know Lydia*
*Hoffman, who owns the shop on Blossom Street, and the*
*three women who join her beginners' knitting class. These*
*four unlikely friends will involve you in their lives, their tri-*
*umphs and their tragedies, and within a few chapters,*
*they'll become your friends, too.*

*Available in hardcover from MIRA Books*
*May 2004*

## THE SHOP ON BLOSSOM STREET

*The yarn forms the stitches, the knitting forges the
friendships, the craft links the generations.*
　　　　　　　　　　—Karen Alfke, "Unpattern"
　　　　　　　　　　designer and knitting instructor

The first time I saw the empty store on Blossom Street I
thought of my father. It reminded me so much of his bicycle
shop when I was a kid. Even the large display windows,
shaded by a colorful awning, were the same. And there were
flower boxes full of red blossoms—inpatiens—that spilled
over beneath the large windows. That was Mom's contribution: impatiens in the spring and summer, chrysanthemums
in the fall and shiny green mistletoe at Christmas. Dad's
business grew steadily and he moved into increasingly larger
premises, but I always loved his first store best.

I must have astounded the rental agent who was showing me the property. She'd barely unlocked the front door
when I announced, "I'll take it."

She turned to face me, her expression blank as if she

wasn't sure she'd heard me correctly. "Wouldn't you like to see it first? Surely you want to take a look at the apartment above the shop."

"Yes, yes, you mentioned that earlier." The apartment above the shop worked perfectly for me. My cat, Whiskers, and I were in need of a home.

"You *would* like to see the place before you sign the papers, wouldn't you?" she persisted.

I smiled and nodded. But it wasn't really necessary; instinctively I knew this was the ideal location for my yarn shop. And for me.

The one drawback was that this Seattle neighborhood was undergoing extensive renovations and, because of the construction mess, the street was closed off at one end, with only local traffic allowed. The brick building across the street, which had once been a three-story bank, was being transformed into high-end condos. Several other buildings, including an old warehouse, were also in the process of becoming condos. The architect had somehow managed to maintain the traditional feel of the original places, and that delighted me. Construction would continue for weeks, perhaps months, but it did mean that my rent was reasonable, at least for now.

I knew the first six months would be difficult. They are for any small business starting out. The constant construction might create more obstacles than there otherwise would have been; nevertheless, I found the space ideal. It was everything I wanted.

Early Friday morning, a week after viewing the space, I signed my name, Lydia Hoffman, to the two-year lease. I was handed the keys and a copy of the papers. I moved into my new home that very day, as excited as I can remember being about anything. I felt as if I was just starting my life and in more ways than I care to count, I actually was.

I opened A Good Yarn the last Tuesday morning in April. I felt a sense of pride and anticipation as I stood in the middle of my store, surveying the colors that surrounded me. I could only imagine what my sister would say when she learned I'd gone through with this. I hadn't asked her advice because I already knew what Margaret's response would be. To put it mildly, she isn't the encouraging type.

I'd found a carpenter who'd built a series of cubicles for me; three rows of them, painted a pristine white. I'd bought a secondhand cash register, refinished the counter and set up racks of knitting supplies. I was ready for business. The yarn had arrived on Friday and I'd spent the weekend sorting it by weight and color and arranging it neatly in the cubicles.

This should have been a happy moment for me but instead, I found myself struggling to hold back tears. Dad would've been so pleased if he could have seen what I'd done. He'd been my support and my source of strength, my guiding light. I was so shocked when he died.

You see, I'd always assumed I would die before my father.

Most people find talk of death and dying unsettling, but I've lived with the threat of it for so long, it doesn't have that effect on me. The possibility of death has been my reality for the last fourteen years, and I'm as comfortable talking about it as I am the weather.

My first bout with cancer came the summer I turned sixteen. I'd gone to pick up my driver's license that day in August. I'd successfully passed the written and the driving tests. My mother let me drive me from the Washington State Department Licensing office to the optometrist. I was having my eyes examined before the start of my junior year of high school. I had big plans for the day. As soon as I got home from the eye appointment Becky and I were going to drive to the beach. It would be the first time I'd taken the car out by myself, and I was looking forward to driving without my mom or dad or my older sister.

I recall being upset that Mom had scheduled the eye appointment right after my driving test. I'd been having some problems with headaches and dizzy spells, and Dad thought I might need reading glasses. The thought of showing up at

Lincoln High School wearing glasses bothered me. A lot. I was hoping Mom and Dad would agree to let me wear contact lenses. As it turned out, impaired vision was the least of my worries.

The optometrist was a friend of my parents' and he seemed to spend an inordinate amount of time looking into the corner of my eye with this horribly bright light. He asked a lot of questions about my headaches. That was almost fifteen years ago, but I don't think I'll ever forget the look on his face as he talked to my mother. He was so serious, somber…so concerned.

"I want to make Lydia an appointment at the University of Washington. Immediately."

My mother and I were both stunned. "All right," my mother said, glancing from me to Dr. Reid and back again. "Is there a problem?"

He nodded. "I don't like what I'm seeing. I think it would be best if Dr. Wilson had a look."

As it turned out, Dr. Wilson did more than look. He drilled into my skull and removed a malignant brain tumor. I say those words glibly now, but it wasn't a quick or simple thing. It meant weeks in the hospital and blinding, debilitating headaches. After the surgery, I went through chemotherapy, followed by a series of radiation treatments. There were days when even the dimmest of lights caused such pain it was all I could do to not scream in agony. Days when I measured each breath, struggling to hold on to life because, try as I might, I could feel it slipping away. Still, there were many mornings when I woke and wished I would die because I couldn't bear another hour of this agony. Without my father I'm convinced I would have.

My head was completely shaved and then, as it started to grow back, it fell out again. I missed my entire junior year and when I was finally able to return to high school, nothing was the same. Everyone looked at me differently. I didn't attend the Junior-Senior prom because no one asked me. Some girlfriends suggested I tag along with them, but out of false pride, I refused. In retrospect it seems a trivial thing to worry about. I wish I'd gone.

The saddest part of this story is that just when I was beginning to believe I could have a normal life—just when I believed all those drugs, all that suffering had served a useful purpose—the tumor grew back.

It wasn't the expression on the doctor's face that I remember when we learned the cancer had returned. It was the pain in my father's eyes. He, above anyone, understood what I'd endured during the first bout of treatment. My mother doesn't deal well with illness. Dad was the one who'd held me together emotionally. He knew there was nothing he could do, nothing he could say, that would lessen this second ordeal for me. I was twenty-four at the time and still in college, trying to get enough credits to graduate. I never did get that degree.

I've survived both bouts of cancer. I'm not the carefree girl I once was. I appreciate and treasure each day because I know how precious life is. Most people assume I'm older than thirty—whether that's because I look it or they find me more serious than other women my age, I'm not sure. My experience with cancer means I don't take anything, least of all life itself, for granted. I no longer greet each day with careless acceptance. But I've learned there are compensations for my suffering. I know I'd be a completely different person if not for the cancer. My dad claimed I achieved a certain calm wisdom, and I suppose I have. Yet in many ways I'm naive, especially when it comes to men and relationships.

Of all the compensations, the one I'm most grateful for is that while undergoing treatment I learned to knit.

While I survived cancer twice, unfortunately my father didn't. My second tumor killed him. That's what my sister Margaret believes. She's never come right out and said it, but I know that's what she thinks. The truth of it is, I suspect she's probably right. It was a heart attack, but he aged so much after that second diagnosis I'm sure it affected his health. I knew that if he could've switched places with me, he would have done it gladly.

He was at my bedside as much as possible. That's what Margaret can't seem to forgive or forget—the time and devotion Dad gave me throughout this ordeal. Mom, too, as much as she was emotionally able.

Margaret was married and a mother or two before the second tumor was even discovered. Nevertheless, she seems to assume that she's somehow been cheated because of my cancer. To this day, she acts as if being sick was my *choice*, an option I preferred over a normal life.

Needless to say, my sister and I have a strained relationship. For Mom's sake, especially now that Dad's gone, I try my best with Margaret. She doesn't make it easy. She can't hide her resentment, no matter how many years it's been.

Margaret was against my opening a yarn shop, but I sincerely doubt she would have encouraged me in any undertaking. Her eyes seemed to brighten with glee at the prospect of seeing me fail. According to the statistics, most new businesses do go under—usually within a year—but still, I felt I had to give the yarn shop a chance.

I had the funds. The money is actually an inheritance I received from my maternal grandmother who died when I was twelve. Dad invested it wisely and I had a small nest egg. I could and probably should save it for what Mom calls a "rainy day," but it's been raining every day since I turned sixteen and I'm tired of holding on to it. Deep down, I know Dad would approve.

As I said, I learned to knit while undergoing chemotherapy. Over the years I've become an accomplished knitter. Dad always joked that I had enough yarn to open my own store. Recently I decided he was right.

I love to knit. There's a comfort to it that I can't explain. The repetition of weaving the yarn around the needle and then forming a stitch creates a sense of purpose, of achievement, of progress. When your entire world is unraveled, you tend to crave order, and I found it in knitting. In fact, I've read that knitting can lower stress even more effectively than meditation. And I guess for me it was a better approach, maybe because there was something tangible to show for it. Maybe because it gave me a sense of action, of *doing* something. I didn't know what tomorrow held, but with a pair of needles in my hands and a ball of yarn in my lap, I was confident I could handle whatever lay ahead. Each stitch was an accomplishment. Some days all I could manage was a single row, but I had the satisfaction of that one small achievement. It made a difference to me. A very big difference.

Over the years I've taught a number of people how to knit. My first students were other cancer patients undergoing chemotherapy. We met at the Seattle Oncology Center. Before long, I had everyone in the clinic, men included, knitting cotton washcloths. Soon every doctor and nurse had enough knit washcloths to last a lifetime. After washcloths I had my band of beginning knitters progress to a small afghan. Certainly I've had some failures but far more successes. My patience was rewarded when others found the same serenity I did in knitting.

Now I have my own shop and I think the best way to get customers in the door is to offer knitting classes. It would take a lot of people to sell enough yarn to stay in business if I offered a class in washcloths, so I've chosen a simple baby blanket to start with. The pattern's by one of my favorite designers, Ann Norling, and uses the basic knit and purl stitches.

I don't know what to expect, but I'm hopeful. Hope to a person with cancer—or to a person who's had cancer—is more potent than any drug. We live on it, live for it. It's addictive to those of us who've learned to take one day at a time.

I was making a sign advertising my beginners' class when the bell above the door chimed. My first customer had just walked in and I looked up with a smile on my face. The pounding excitement in my heart quickly died when I realized it was Margaret.

"Hi," I said, doing my best to sound happy to see her. I didn't want my sister showing up on my first morning and attacking my confidence.

"Mom told me you'd decided to go ahead with this idea of yours."

I didn't respond.

Frowning, Margaret continued. "I was in the neighborhood and thought I'd stop by and see the shop."

I gestured with one arm and hated myself for asking. "What do you think?" I didn't bother to mention that Blossom Street was decidedly out of her way.

"Why'd you name it A Good Yarn?"

I'd gone over dozens of shop names, some too cute by half, some plain and ordinary. I loved the idea that "spinning a yarn" means telling a story, and sharing stories with people, their experiences, is important to me. Another legacy of the clinic, I suppose. A Good Yarn seems like a warm and welcoming name to me. But I didn't explain all that to Margaret. "I wanted my customers to know what to expect when they walk in the door. I sell quality yarn."

Margaret shrugged as if she'd seen a dozen knitting shops with more impressive names than mine.

"Well," I said, despite my determination not to ask again. "What do you think?"

Margaret glanced around a second time, although nothing had changed after her first inspection. "It's better than I thought it would be."

I considered this high praise. "I don't have a large inventory yet, but I'm hoping to build up the shop over the next year or so. Of course, not all the yarn I've ordered has arrived. And there's more I'm planning to get, some wonderful imports form Ireland and Australia. Everything takes time and money." In my enthusiasm I'd said more than I intended.

"Are you expecting Mom to help you?" The question was blunt.

I shook my head. "You don't need to worry. I'm doing this entirely on my own." So that was the reason for her unexpected visit. Margaret thought I was going to take advantage of our mother. I wouldn't and the question offended me, but I bit back an angry retort.

Margaret glared at me as if she wasn't sure she should believe me.

"I cashed in my Microsoft stock," I confessed.

Margaret's deep brown eyes, so much like my own, nearly doubled in horror at what I'd done. "You didn't."

What did my sister think? I had the cash required for such a venture lying around in my bottom drawer? "I had to." Given my medical history, no bank would consider granting me a loan. Although I've been cancer-free for four years now, I'm considered a risk in just about every area.

"It's your money, I guess." That way Margaret said it implied I'd made a terrible decision. "I don't think Dad would have approved."

"He would've been the first one to encourage me." I probably should have kept my mouth shut, but I couldn't help myself.

"You're probably right," Margaret said with the caustic edge that never failed to appear in our conversations. "Dad could deny you nothing."

"The money was my inheritance," I pointed out. I suppose her share is still accumulating profit.

My sister walked around the shop, eyeing it critically. Considering Margaret's apparent dislike of me, I don't know why my relationship with her is so important, but it is. Mom's health is fragile and she hasn't adjusted to life without Dad. Soon, I'm afraid, it'll be only be Margaret and me. The thought of not having any family at all terrifies me.

I'm so grateful not to know what the future holds. I once asked my father why God wouldn't just let us know what tomorrow would bring, and he said that not knowing the future is actually a gift because if we knew, we wouldn't take responsibility for our own lives, our own happiness. As with so much else in life, my dad was right.

"What's your business plan?" Margaret asked.

"I— I'm starting small."

"What about customers?"

"I've paid for an ad in the Yellow Pages." I didn't mention that the new phone directory didn't come our for another two months. I'd distributed flyers in the neighborhood too, but I didn't know how effective that would be. No need to hand Margaret ammunition.

My older sister snickered. I've always hated that scoffing sound and had to grit my teeth in order to hide my reaction.

"I'm just getting ready to post a sign in the window for my first knitting class."

"Do you seriously think a handmade sign taped in the window is going to draw people into your store?" Margaret demanded. "Parking is a nightmare out there and even when the street's open again, you can't expect much traffic through this construction mess."

"No, but—"

"I wish you well, but—"

"Do you?" I asked, cutting her off. My hands shook as I walked over to the display window and secured my notice for knitting classes.

"What's that supposed to mean?"

I turned to face my sister who, at five foot six, stood a good three inches taller than me. She outweighed me by about twenty pounds, too. Looking at us now, I wonder if anyone would guess we were related and yet when we were small we looked quite a bit alike.

"I think you want me to fail," I said honestly.

"That isn't true! I came this morning because…because I'm interested in what you're doing." Her chin went up a notch as if she were daring me to challenge her again. "How old are you? Twenty-nine, thirty?"

"Thirty."

"Don't you think it's time you cut the apron strings?"

That was blatantly unfair by I let it pass. "I'm trying to do exactly that. I left Mom's house and I moved into the apartment upstairs. I've started my own business, too, and I'd appreciate your support."

She turned her hands over to display her palms. "Do you want me to buy yarn from you? Is that what you want? You know I don't knit and have no desire to learn. I much prefer to crochet. And—"

"For once," I said, cutting her off a second time, "couldn't you think of at least *one* nice thing to say?" I waited, silently pleading with her to dig inside her heart for token words of encouragement.

My request seemed to be an overwhelming task for Margaret. She faltered for several seconds. "You have a good eye for color," she finally said. She gestured toward the display of yarn I'd arranged on the table by the door.

"Thank you," I said, hoping to sound gracious. "That wasn't so hard, now was it?" I didn't mention that I'd used a color wheel to help create the display. Hard as it was for Margaret to offer me praise, I certainly wasn't going to give her an opportunity to withdraw it.

Had we been closer, I would've told her the real reason I decided to open a yarn store. This shop was my affirmation of life. I was willing to invest everything I had to make it a success. Like the Viking conqueror who came ashore and burned his ships behind him, I had set my course. Succeed or go under.

As my father would say, I was taking responsibility for a future I couldn't predict.

The bell above the door chimed again. I had a customer! My first *real* customer.